# TRADING DAY BY DAY
## WINNING THE ZERO-SUM GAME OF FUTURES

F.H. "CHICK" GOSLIN

TRADING DAY BY DAY © 2003 by Finley H. Goslin, Jr.


Published by California Publishing
7412 High Ave.
La Jolla, CA 92037


EDITING AND COVER DESIGN by Priscilla Ann Goslin, S2M2 Design (www.S2M2.com)

INTERNAL DESIGN & COMPOSITION by Diane Papadakis, Pakaáge Designs (www.pakaage.com)

SMR CHARTS provided by Brad Crotzer (www.smr.com)

Printed in the United States of America

ISBN 0-9740921-1-8

**DISCLAIMER** — Futures (and stock) trading involves substantial risk. Do not trade with money you cannot afford to lose. While the approach and method presented in this book are sound and based on years of study and experience, in the end it will be the specific application of these techniques that will determine an individual trader's success or failure. Trading offers substantial potential rewards, but not even the best of methods can provide any guarantee of ultimate monetary success.

# CONTENTS

# TRADING

*Approach it as a challenge.*

*Confront it as a puzzle.*

*Play it like a game.*

*Treat it like a business.*

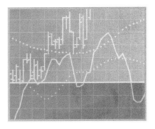

# INTRODUCTION

WHY TRADE? To make money, of course. However, for most successful traders there is something about trading that goes far beyond making money—something intensely personal.

Trading the markets is essentially a competition, an intellectual competition. If you were to ask successful professional athletes why they play their sports, very few (if any) would say solely for the money. If you were to ask what motivates them, they would say personal pride, the challenge and, above all, playing well and winning. I believe the majority of consistently successful futures traders would say the same about trading.

It is the pursuit of excellence, not money, that motivates the exceptional individual. Only the mediocre are driven purely by a desire for money. It is an individual's passion, not lust for money, that produces excellence. Nevertheless, trading is fundamentally a business, and the basic purpose of a business is to make money.

Trading the futures markets is similar in many ways to professional poker. In both trading and poker, money moves back and forth between the players while the "house" takes a small cut of each transaction. Both are zero-sum games (minus costs, of course). Both require a combination of science and art, a mixture of knowledge and intelligence. Both are highly competitive big-money games where a large amount can totally disappear and a small "stake" multiply many times over. Moreover, no true "player" of either game would bother playing for long if there were no money involved.

................

Trading is a combination of challenge, puzzle, game, and business. Therefore, a trader needs to be somewhat multidimensional—philosopher, scientist, game player, and businessperson— to be successful. A fund or corporation trading the futures markets can hire several people to perform these multiple functions, but you and I are "individual" traders and so must fulfill all of them ourselves. Consequently, accomplishing this complex task requires understanding, discipline, constant awareness, and the ability to act decisively when necessary.

So we are confronted with a tremendous challenge here: to become consistently successful futures traders. The first step in surmounting this challenge is solving an extremely difficult puzzle: the puzzle of price movement. However, only solving the price puzzle will not be enough; we will also need to "play" the game of trading correctly. Unfortunately, even this will not be enough because to survive and prosper in this extremely competitive business called *trading*, we will also need to be sound businesspeople. Obviously, being and doing all of this well at the same time is not easy, but if and when finally achieved, the rewards, both personal and financial, can be extraordinary.

# AUTHORITY

ANYONE CAN PROCLAIM; WORDS ARE CHEAP AND EASY. However, while most words are trivial, some have the weight of truth. So, what are the words in this book? Noise or substance? And if substantive, under what "authority" have they been written?

In J. D. Salinger's *"Raise High the Roof Beam, Carpenters,"* (Little, Brown and Company, 1963), one of the characters reads his baby sister a Taoist tale. The story goes something like this.

A Chinese nobleman, Duke Mo, needed a new horse; but, he did not want merely a good horse, he wanted an absolutely superlative horse. Unfortunately, his resident horse expert, Po Lo, had grown old and was no longer capable of undertaking the type of rigorous search required to find such a horse. The Duke asked Po Lo if he could recommend someone else for this important job. "Well," said Po Lo, "there are many well-known horse experts perfectly capable of finding you a good horse. However, if you want the truly exceptional horse, we must look beyond reputation and monetary success and find someone whose focus is seeing the inner truth of horses. Fortunately, I do know an individual whom I believe could find you the superlative horse; his name is Chiu-fang Kao. However, be aware that Kao's eye for horses has brought him neither fame nor riches."

This absence of fame and wealth caused the Duke some skepticism and concern, but since he respected Po Lo, he ultimately accepted his recommendation and sent this man named Chiu-fang Kao out in search of a truly superlative horse.

Three months later Kao returned with news he had found a horse and that it would arrive shortly. The Duke excitedly asked for details. What color was it? Was it a stallion or a mare? Surprisingly, Kao did not seem to know. "Uh," he slowly and somewhat absentmindedly replied, "it's…a, a dun colored mare."

Strangely, though, when the horse arrived it turned out not to be a brown mare at all, but was instead a coal black stallion. Perplexed and disturbed by this the Duke summoned the old Po Lo and loudly complained that this man he had recommended, this Chiu-fang Kao, must be either a fool or a fraud. "How," he demanded, "could Kao know anything at all about horses if he could not distinguish between a mare and a stallion, nor even see the obvious difference between brown and black."

Surprisingly, Po Lo showed no sign of concern. Instead he calmly responded: "Fear not, sir. Hearing this I am actually greatly relieved. Over the many years I have known Kao I have learned that what he looks for in a horse is its significant essence, its inner truth. By focusing so intently on the substance, he occasionally misses the superficial. Kao's seeming confusion about the horse's color and sex indicates to me that this horse's inner truth, its essential being, must shine through so brightly that its color and gender did not even register with him. Kao's overlooking such ultimately nonessential details as color and sex indicates to me that he has almost certainly fully succeeded in his mission and brought you exactly what you requested, an exceptional horse."

Subsequently, just as Po Lo predicted, the horse did indeed turn out to be a truly superlative animal.

................

What counts in any endeavor is the significant essence, the fundamental truths. Who directs you to this essence, who points out these truths, is of no real consequence. It is the truth that matters, not the wealth, reputation or fame of the one directing you towards it. Focus on whether what you read and see herein is true or false; waste no time or energy on the writer of the words. Pay no attention to his personal history or his "authority," or lack of it. Let truth be your only authority.

Only a fool unquestioningly accepts the words or ideas of another solely because of a big reputation and/or substantial monetary success. The wise look and listen to any and all with an open mind, and once they have seen and heard, they then challenge and test with a skeptical mind. Be open to what you read and find here, but treat all of it with some healthy skepticism. Then, after you have looked and listened, accept and use solely that which you yourself find to be true and effective.

Whether I am rich, famous, or an established authority on trading is of no real importance. It is the truth that is important, not the one pointing out this truth. Is it true and effective? That is all that counts.

................

Trading is a very competitive business. For an individual to succeed in this simple—but oh so diabolically difficult—game, he or she must be an independent thinker. You cannot be a weak-minded conformist choosing whom to pay attention to solely on the basis of record and reputation. Ultimately you must see the truths of trading for yourself. Over the following pages I will suggest and point out a great deal about trading. It will be up to you to find out whether any or all of it is true and effective. In other words, you will need to find out for yourself whether or not it works for you.

However, do not be concerned: You are not wasting your time reading this book. You will not be misled by anything you read here. In fact, you will find much of value. I know nothing about horses, but I do know a great deal about futures trading and the futures markets. Over the past thirty-some years I have learned the essence, the very truth, of trading. Over these thirty frequently intense years of—sometimes quite literally—blood, sweat, tears, and cheers, I have discovered what is significant in trading and what is not. So know this: I understand both trading and the futures markets. The time you spend with this book will prove not only intellectually worthwhile, but also just may help you make a little—or maybe even significantly more than a little—money.

# TRADING VS. INVESTING

TRADING AND INVESTING ARE VERY DIFFERENT ACTIVITIES. It is important to be clear about the differences between the two.

"Trading" is simply the exchange of money for an asset, an exchange made with the clear and definite intent or hope of later trading that asset back for more money. Since these assets are bought to be sold rather than bought to be owned, what they happen to be is essentially immaterial.

"Investing," on the other hand, is the purchase of an asset without any pre-intent to sell. Family businesses, cabins at a lake or in the mountains, cottages at the seashore, fine art and jewelry, collections of any kind (stamps, coins, etc.)—assets such as these tend to be investments. They are not bought with the sole intent of selling or trading them later. They are bought to be used and possessed. Consequently, what they are is all important.

Traders are not confused about what they do; they *trade*. They trade money for positions (in a market), and then later trade those positions back for more or less money. However, some self-described investors tend to mistakenly believe they are making investments, when in reality they are simply making long-term trades. The truth is that many self-described "investors" are actually just long-term traders. Assets bought to be sold are trades, not investments.

An individual truly *investing* in the stock market should, regardless of the size of the investment (one share or a hundred million shares), act as if he or she were buying the entire company as a family business. This approach to buying stocks might be called the Warren Buffet style of investing. When Mr. Buffet buys shares in a company, he always acts as if he were buying the entire company and planning on it becoming the family business for generations to come, although he might sell these shares at any time.

Conversely, some *traders* mistakenly act as if they are investors, when in reality they are merely intermediate-term or long-term traders, meaning they waste time and energy worrying about the supposed underlying *value* of the asset they are trading. As a result they focus too much on whether the price is "high" or "low." This is a waste of time and energy, because from a trader's perspective the whole concept of "value" is essentially meaningless. In free markets, prices can always go higher or lower than current levels, regardless of any perceived or supposed "value." The concept of high and low (i.e., value) essentially does not exist in *trading*.

Traders need to focus on price movement and should not get distracted by "value." Investors, on the other hand, should focus on value and not be too distracted by short-term price movement. For traders it is price *movement* that counts, not price location ("high" or "low"). When trading, regardless of the time frame, it is higher and lower that are significant, not high or low.

So, be clear about what you are doing—trading or investing—and act accordingly.

Be advised, this book is solely about trading.

.................

# CLEAR YOUR MIND

As long as you are spending precious time and energy reading this book, before you go any further I suggest you temporarily erase everything you know about trading from your brain, including (especially!) your trading history. From this point forward proceed with only the rudimentary knowledge of how futures trading works. Temporarily "store" all accumulated knowledge and experience about trading and the futures markets elsewhere.

Do not worry though: Neither your current knowledge of trading nor your past trading experiences will disappear from your brain. Unfortunately, they will quickly return to distort your vision and hinder your actions. Regardless, do yourself a favor and at least temporarily put away your past and take a completely fresh look at trading. For a brief period let us try to find some clarity and truth about this oh-so simple, yet oh-so-difficult, activity called futures trading.

Surely, success and failure at trading are not random. It just cannot be that the relatively few consistently successful traders were simply born skillful or lucky, or both. There simply must exist at least some fundamental truths and natural laws that directly and profoundly affect trading results. Empty your mind of its past successes and failures, and then together let us see if we can discover something true, usable and worthwhile—some fundamental *natural laws*—about trading and markets.

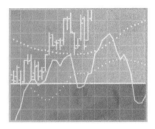

# APPROACH

*Trading is easy.*
*Trading successfully is difficult, very difficult.*

*Anyone can trade.*
*But only a few trade successfully, very few.*

TOUGH GAME, TRADING. It is a sad fact but studies have shown that the overwhelming majority of traders, whether in futures or stocks, end up losing. Few in the trading industry admit this, but everyone in the business knows it is true. Our mission as individual traders is to beat these long odds. While this may not be "mission impossible," it is definitely "mission not easy."

Futures trading is a zero-sum game. Whenever we go long or short a futures contract, there is another trader taking the other side. For every "long" in the futures markets, there is a corresponding "short." When we are betting the price will go up, someone else is betting it will go down, and vice versa. Trading is a competition, an intellectual competition.

Whether it is stocks or futures, trading is simply a huge, ultra-competitive money game. In fact, trading is the biggest money game in the world. However, unlike big-money sports games, such as professional golf, tennis, baseball, and football, virtually anyone can play in the "major leagues" of trading. This is one of the unique aspects of trading. You do not have to work your way up through some trading minor league before being allowed to trade. You do not have to go through any kind of qualifying process to play in the trading big leagues. *Anyone* who can come up with the minimum margin can instantly become a full member of the biggest money "trading league" in the world—the stock and futures markets. There are absolutely no minimum levels of experience, knowledge or ability required before being allowed to compete against the absolute best in the trading world. All you need is a little money.

Now think about this: Would you bet thousands of dollars a day you could beat the absolute best in the world in golf, tennis, boxing, chess, bridge, or poker? Would you try to make a living by going head-to-head against the best baseball, basketball, or football players in the world? Obviously you would not. Yet the truth is every time we make a trade in a futures market, or buy a share of stock, that is exactly what we are doing. Every time we make a trade, be it stocks or futures, we are competing against (among others) the very best traders in the world.

For example, when I go long or short the Yen, I am trading (i.e., competing) against (among others) the most informed, knowledgeable, experienced, and talented traders of the Yen in the world.

The same is true about any other market you or I might trade. In each of these markets we are always trading (competing) against large corporations and giant financial institutions (including governments), as well as many successful professional traders. This is extremely tough competition for any individual to succeed against on even one trade, much less on any kind of consistent basis.

In addition, every single one of us individual "amateur" traders considers himself or herself to be at least above average in intelligence, otherwise we would not even think about trading. Consequently, since all individual traders are above average and all the other players are pros, then each of us starts out average, at best. In other words, no matter how bright we might be, we cannot count on any natural edge in brain power to see us through to eventual success. The point is no matter how smart and clever we may think we are, virtually all of our competition consider themselves at least as smart and clever, and indeed may even be smarter and more clever.

The brutal truth is every market is full of extremely well-informed, very knowledgeable and exceptionally talented traders. Therefore, no matter how well-informed, knowledgeable or talented a trader you or I might consider ourselves to be, a great deal (if not most) of our competition will always be better informed, more knowledgeable and experienced, as well as more talented.

The bottom line is there is simply no way any individual, no matter how well informed or knowledgeable, can successfully compete in the business of trading (be it futures or stocks) *if* —and this is the big if—he relies solely on his natural talents, and his decisions are based primarily on information and/or knowledge of the asset being traded.

For example, you or I can never know more about the supply of cocoa than the Ghana Marketing Board, nor can we ever know more about the demand for cocoa than companies like Hershey and Mars. In other words, knowledge of supply and demand for cocoa is a "field" upon which we simply cannot compete. The same applies to any other market we might trade, be it stocks or commodities. You and I simply cannot compete if the competition is one of "figuring out," based on information and knowledge of supply/demand, what a market's price "should" be tomorrow, or at any other time in the future.

In addition, the unpleasant fact is no matter how big and fast our computers may be and how clever our trading software, a good deal of our competition is going to have bigger and faster computers powered by software at least as clever as ours. I recently read in *Futures Magazine* about a futures fund manager who utilizes seventy-five computers and a staff of twelve specialists to help him administer his trading programs. Face it, there is absolutely no way you or I, as individuals, can compete with that level of technological power and expertise.

**BE ABSOLUTELY CLEAR ON THIS POINT:** As an individual you simply cannot compete in the futures (or stock) trading "game" on the basis of natural talent or information and knowledge of the asset being traded. Nor can you compete in computing power and technical expertise. In fact, it is an enormously delusional conceit to think otherwise. To do so is as great a conceit as thinking you or I could successfully compete against the world's best golfers, tennis players, football players, basketball players, and so on. Therefore, every time you decide to make a trade based on information or knowledge of the asset being traded, be aware that what you are doing is no different than stepping into the ring with the heavyweight champion of the world. So, be intelligent; do not approach trading by relying on natural talent, technological expertise, or information and knowledge of the asset.

Looking at trading in this way, meaning looking at the level of competition realistically, it is not surprising most individual traders end up losing. Considering the high level of competition, it is actually more surprising *any* individual traders ever succeed. And of course some very definitely do.

Now, seeing all of this—that you and I cannot compete in terms of natural talent, information, knowledge, and computer expertise—should not be discouraging; actually, it is liberating. The endless effort to acquire information and knowledge about multiple different markets, as well as the never-ending accumulation of ever more intricate and elaborate trading systems, is not only very time consuming but also labor intensive and costly. Seeing very clearly that the pursuit of information, knowledge, and technical expertise is both futile and pointless frees time and energy for far more productive use.

The question then becomes, is there *any* way an ordinary individual (like you and me) can successfully compete in the stock and futures trading business? Is there any means of leveling the playing field in trading? Fortunately, the answer to both questions is yes.

We cannot compete at the competition's level in terms of information, knowledge (of supply/demand), and technological expertise; therefore, what we need to do is change the nature of the trading game to one where we can compete. We need to change the basic nature of the game in such a way that we will be competing on essentially equal terms with our expert competition. Since we cannot climb up to the competition's level, we need to bring the competition down to ours. The way to do this is to break the game/business of trading down to its simplest, most fundamental level.

At its absolute, most basic, lowest level, trading is nothing more or less than a simple up or down numbers game. It is a numbers game with a clear, simple, and never-changing objective: sell higher than you buy; buy lower than you sell. Do this correctly and more profitably more often than not and you will win the game. Do not and you will lose. It is that simple and basic. Trading is just an up or down numbers game. That is all: nothing more, nothing less.

In a simple up or down numbers game, *all* players, regardless of who they might be—individuals, professionals, corporations, governments—operate on the exact same level. What this means is that a number moving up and down is no different to you and me than it is to a corporation loaded with information, knowledge, and experts. No matter who is looking at it, a number is just a number. Consequently, approaching trading as a basic up/down numbers game instantly changes the game's emphasis from one of *knowing* information, knowledge, and technology to one of *observing* price movement, and then acting on those observations.

Making this fundamental conceptual shift in the way we approach trading immediately changes it from an endeavor where the primary question is "why" to one where the sole question is "what." Instead of endless, and inevitably fruitless, attempts to decipher *why* a price has moved a certain direction in the past and why it should now move a particular direction in the future, the primary (only?) focus becomes *what* the price (i.e., the number) has done in the past and *what* it is doing now. The question is not why, it is what!

The simple fact is that we individuals will rarely, if ever, be able to compete in trading when the primary question is *why*. However, if we change the essential question to *what* (a price has done in the past and is doing now), then we can compete.

"Why" is concerned with knowledge; "what" is concerned with observation. You and I can never compete in knowing (the field is simply too vast), but we can very definitely compete in observing. Therefore, the correct approach for the individual trader is to trade based on what you *see*, not on what you *think*.

Never forget, in the business of trading we are rewarded or penalized solely on whether we are right or wrong about *what* the price does. In trading we are not rewarded, in any way whatsoever, for being correct about *why* a price moves (assuming there even is a correct "why"). We are rewarded only for getting the "what" of price movement correct. It is what the price does that counts, not why.

## THE BOTTOM LINE ON "APPROACH"

We only trade price. We do not trade information. We do not trade knowledge (of the asset being traded). Nor do we trade computing power and expertise. We do not trade anything at all other than price, i.e., the number. Therefore, since the only factor that counts in this game is the price, it is only smart to focus all, or almost all, our attention on this number—on the price and its movement; in other words, what the price has done in the past and is doing in the present.

Approach the game/business of trading in this manner—an up or down numbers game where the focus is on *what* the price does, not *why*—and you will be on the right path to success as a trader.

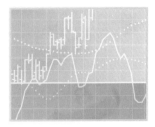

# METHOD

APPROACHING TRADING AS AN UP OR DOWN NUMBERS GAME unquestionably levels the playing field; unfortunately, it does not "tilt" it in our favor. It does not give us an "edge," and without an edge we will still be at a disadvantage. The transaction costs of trading—commissions, exchange fees, charts and/or charting software, plus the fact we must buy the offer and sell the bid—act to turn even a simple fifty-fifty up or down numbers game into a game where we start with the odds clearly against us. The problem is, to succeed over an extended period of time, we must be able to shift the odds in our favor; we must have a consistent "edge."

So, the question is whether there is any way to gain a competitive advantage when playing the trading game as a simple, straight up or down numbers game. Fortunately, there is, and it involves seeing, understanding, and then utilizing the fundamental truths and natural laws of trading.

If the challenge confronting you was to build an airplane, bridge or rocket, what would be the most intelligent way to start? It would be by learning the laws of aerodynamics or the fundamentals of structural engineering or the basic truths of rocket science. In other words, before commencing any difficult challenge, the intelligent first step is to start with the fundamentals, the basics, the underlying truths, the natural laws.

To qualify as a "natural law," a proposition must have an inherent, structural truth to it. A natural law must be, by definition, a constant or essentially eternal truth. Therefore, by necessity, a fundamental truth or natural law of trading needs to be fairly general, not overly specific. So, does a simple up or down numbers game like trading have any fundamental truths or natural laws? And, if so, what are they?

**THERE ARE THREE NATURAL LAWS OF TRADING—NO MORE, NO LESS—AND THEY ARE:**

    1 ~ THE FUTURE IS UNKNOWN;

    2 ~ CONTINUATION IS MORE LIKELY THAN CHANGE;

    3 ~ PRICES FLUCTUATE.

Each of these "natural laws of trading" is a fundamental, structural, and eternal truth of trading (and, incidentally, of pricing). While these laws may be superficially self-evident and obvious, as we proceed you will see how a clear understanding of these three natural laws, and how to apply them, can "tilt" the field of trading in your favor, thereby giving you a clear, definite, and consistent "edge" when trading.

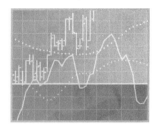

# THE FIRST LAW OF TRADING
## (The Philosophical Law)

THE FIRST LAW OF TRADING IS "THE FUTURE IS UNKNOWN." This clear, concise, self-evident statement is the first fundamental truth, or natural law, of trading. This law may be simple and obvious, but I cannot overemphasize its importance.

I consider this law the "bad news" law of trading. The objective of trading is to "bet" correctly on the future; therefore, discovering that this future cannot be known is bad news indeed.

One problem with acting in accordance with the first law of trading is we do not like the insecurity of an unknown future. No one likes to feel insecure. We prefer to think we have a good idea of what is coming next, even if these ideas are usually mere wishful thinking. When the choice is between warm but false illusion and cold but true reality, warm illusion usually wins. In many activities this preference for delusion over reality is not necessarily much of a liability; unfortunately, in trading, it tends to be fatal. There is no place for delusions in trading. To survive and prosper in the trading business, the future must always be seen as it is: truly unknown.

...................

*Trading is like a voyage down an unexplored river.*

*We can know where the river has been and see where it is headed,*
*but we can never know what lies around the next bend.*

*We can know what a price has done in the past and see what it is doing now,*
*but we can never know what it will do tomorrow.*

...................

The first law of trading, the future is unknown, is the "philosophy" law of futures (and stock) trading. The basic meaning of the word "philosophy" is love of wisdom. Wisdom comes from truth, not falseness. So, be philosophical about this truth that the future is unknown. See the reality of it and then live completely with this reality; accept its constant unpleasantness every trading day, day in and day out. Just resign yourself to the ever present feeling of uneasiness this truth brings. However, make sure you do not do this only intellectually; insist on doing it in actuality, meaning make sure your actions are in accordance with this truth.

Seeing the future as truly unknown should make a trader feel uncomfortable. This first law of trading really is an unsettling and unpleasant truth. However, it is better to feel uncomfortable yet be on solid ground than feel comfortable and be on shifting, unstable ground. As individual traders, our best and possibly only chance to compete successfully against the powerful competition we face every day is to rely on a solid foundation of truths and natural laws.

Operating under this first law of trading means that when we try to look forward into the future we see nothing. In other words, as a trader we see that the future is nothing but a black, impenetrable void. The point is that the future is always in a "not-yet-made" state, which is why it is unknown.

Now, since the future is unknown this means we cannot do anything about it. Therefore, what the first law of trading forces us to do is essentially ignore the future. This is an interesting concept. The correct way to trade the futures markets is to waste no time and energy trying to see into the future. If we should ignore the future when trading futures, where then should our focus be? On what is left: the past and present.

The best way to prepare to confront the unknowable future is by careful study of the past and clear observation of the present. In other words, focus attention and expend energy on that which you can do something about, not on what you cannot.

....................

At the San Diego airport there is a full-size replica of the "Spirit of St. Louis," the plane Charles Lindbergh flew when he became the first man to fly across the Atlantic. Other than its small size and somewhat fragile appearance, what is most striking about it is that it has no front windshield. Its only windows are on the sides. Lindbergh could not see what lay ahead, he could only see what was below him and to his sides. This meant he could only know where he had been (the past) and where he was at the moment (the present); however, he could not know or see where he was going (the future).

Lindbergh started his long flight having not slept for over twenty hours (he was surprised by sudden good weather and decided to take advantage of it despite his lack of sleep). Yet in spite of this he was able to stay awake and alert for the thirty-plus hours it took to reach Paris. I believe one of the main reasons he was able to do this was because he could not see forward and thus was never lulled into a false sense of security by clear sky ahead. The constant feeling of insecurity this arrangement produced helped keep him awake. (Having no automatic pilot, if he had fallen asleep he would have crashed.) Plus, since he could not see ahead, he was forced by the design of the plane to not waste any time or energy in trying to do so. Instead, he focused all his attention on where he had been and where he was at the moment, and then simply extrapolated forward where he would "most likely" go next.

As traders, we would be wise to do the same. We need to operate as if there is no forward window into the future of price movement. Study and know the past, carefully observe and pay attention to the present, but see as absolute fact that the future is unknown, so just ignore it. The future will unfold as it will; we cannot control it. However, we can control how we enter this unknown future.

*The past is already made and thus is dead and unchanging;*
*therefore, the past can be studied and known.*
*The present is always being made and thus is alive and moving;*
*therefore, the present can be seen and observed.*
*However, the future is not yet made and thus is neither dead nor alive;*
*therefore, the future cannot be known or seen.*

# THE SECOND LAW OF TRADING
## (The Art and Science Law)

THE SECOND LAW OF TRADING IS **"CONTINUATION IS MORE LIKELY THAN CHANGE."** This clear and simple statement is an underlying structural truth of trading—and price movement. This law is the "art and science" law of trading. It is also the core of virtually every successful trading methodology. It is truly the "good news" law of trading because it is a truth upon which a sound trading method can be built.

The second law of trading simply applies the natural laws of physics to the movement of prices. It is the equivalent of saying a physical body clearly moving in one direction is more likely to continue moving in that direction than change. Therefore, since "price" is and acts in many ways similar to a "physical body" in motion, this means the "price" also is more likely to continue moving in its current direction rather than change.

....................

Trading is a numbers game and these numbers we trade are "prices." The question is, what exactly is this "price?"

In a free market, "price" is simply the precise point where a service or an asset is willingly exchanged (i.e., traded) for a like quantity of currency. In trading, "price" is the specific "number" where these exchanges take place. However, from a trading perspective, price is much more than this basic definition.

Trading is a constant contest between buyers and sellers, longs and shorts, bulls and bears (i.e., between those betting up and those betting down). One side is always trying (hoping) to push the price up, the other side is always trying (hoping) to push it down. In effect a market is a never ending "push"-of-war between two sides, buyers and sellers. The "price" is the score of each one of these individual contests (i.e., trades) and price charts are running score cards that reflect the recent results of these contests/trades.

Charts present in visual form the record of each market's recent price battles. They provide a history of price movement. In horse racing, players look to the racing form to see past records. In sports betting, bettors look at the won/lost record of each team or individual. In trading, we look at the price charts; we look at the charts to see if they might reveal any tendencies and/or trends of recent price movement.

For example, if a chart showed one side (up or down) clearly dominating (i.e., consistently winning) over an extended period, and your challenge were to pick the winner of the next "contest" (i.e., guess the next price move), would you bet on the recent consistent winner or loser? In other words, would you anticipate a continuation of the established pattern or a change?

Trading on an expectation of continuity rather than change is merely betting the side (up or down, long or short) that has been consistently winning will continue to do so. The fact is, history clearly shows that the side with the better recent record is more likely to win the next contest. In markets, as in life, continuation is more likely than change. Winners tend to keep winning, losers tend to keep losing. Markets that have been going up tend to keep going up, markets that have been going down tend to keep going down.

However, there is one major difference between ordinary life and the markets. In sports gambling, for example, if you want to bet on the favorite (the one with the better recent record), you have to do so at unfavorable odds or give up points. No casino or bookie will accept an even-money bet that the champ will beat the chump. Casinos and bookies will not accept even-money bets champs will beat chumps for the simple and obvious reason that they are in the business of making money and therefore do not bet against the odds. In other words, in order to maintain an edge, casinos and bookies require an advantage in odds or points when accepting bets on favorites.

The markets are different though. The futures (and stock) markets do allow even-money "continuation" bets. This means the markets constantly provide a trader with a potential built-in advantage or edge. Any time you place a trade that is based on a continuation of existing momentum and trend, what you are doing is betting the recent consistent winner will continue to win, a bet that is *more likely* to be right than wrong. The good news about trading stocks and futures is that in the markets you can bet high probability propositions and be paid as if they were only fifty-fifty, or even-money, bets.

The point is that in futures trading, payoffs on winners and losers are not based on actual probabilities or true odds. For payoff purposes, every trade is treated as a fifty-fifty proposition, regardless of its true probabilities. In trading you do not get a bigger payoff for correctly picking long shots, nor a lesser payoff for being right on high probability propositions. Unlike diving and gymnastics, there are no "degree of difficulty" bonus points in trading. A $1000 a contract profit earned by buying the exact low is not worth a penny more than a $1000 profit earned by buying in the middle of an established uptrend, even though the former is much more difficult than the latter.

Since a price with clearly established momentum and trend (i.e., a pattern of continuity) is more likely to continue in its current direction rather than change (and natural law dictates that it is), and if the payoff is the same whether you trade with this higher probability or against it, then obviously the intelligent action is to trade on the expectation of continuation rather than change.

Trading with clearly established momentum and trend is twice smart; first, the probability of success is greater—better odds, and second, the payoff is better than the actual probability— better risk/reward.

Seeing the truth of all this means the logical next step is to find or develop some "reasonably reliable"—obviously perfection is impossible when the future is unknown—indicators of past and current price energy flow. We need to know past to current price energy flow (i.e., trend/momentum) in order to see what continuation would be.

(**NOTE:** *Whenever I use "trend" I mean long term. When I use "momentum" I mean intermediate term and short term. For trading purposes I consider long term to mean months, intermediate term to mean weeks, and short term to mean days.*)

.....................

I started out in this business knowing virtually nothing about trading or the markets. My first trade, a (pork) belly spread, was done solely on a tip/recommendation from a floor broker. I put up $400 in margin (this was in 1968), and within two weeks closed out the trade with a little over $400 profit. Making a 100 percent profit in two weeks definitely caught my attention. Unfortunately, several years later when I became a broker/account executive with a small Chicago "Merc" firm (in May 1970), my results were quite different. My first two years of trading with both my and other people's money ("OPM" as it was called) was almost a 100 percent failure.

While I did not have specific legal authorization to trade for my clients, I did have verbal permission to act if and when "necessary." In practice this meant I made essentially all the trading decisions. This was the way virtually all the brokers and clients at the firm operated. Each broker essentially made all the trading decisions for his clients.

As far as I could tell, total failure was the sad but inevitable result for every client, although no one ever told them this ugly fact. However, this universal failure was not through any lack of effort. Every broker at that firm tried his absolute best to trade profitably. The problem was it just did not happen. Oh, we would all have our winning trades and some of us would have good winning streaks from time to time, but the equity in the customers' accounts inevitably shrunk. Eventually every account would be closed out with losses (and most often this meant virtually all of the account's equity had been lost).

I found this persistent failure extremely frustrating and as a result was constantly looking for a better way to trade. Being a slow (but eventual) learner, after a couple of years I finally realized what I, and everyone else, was doing simply did not work. The basic approach most everyone seemed to use was to look for a market we thought was going to make a "move" (for whatever reason), and then trade for that move. Everyone was essentially a position trader and would be long the bellies, or short the cattle, or long the beans, or short the sugar, and so on. We would trade in and out of these positions, but the basic idea was to position for a "move." Every trade had a theoretically sound logic and reasoning behind it. Some trades would work, more would not, but the sad fact was inevitably every account's equity somehow simply disappeared. The money just vanished into thin air, all gone.

Then one day a fellow broker heard me complaining that there had to be a better way. He showed me the SMR charts (SMR Charts, PO Box 7476, Boulder, CO, 80306-7476 - www.smr.com). I had seen charts before, of course, but SMR's were different; they had these three lines on them. At a glance I could see that these lines and the price seemed somehow to be connected. When the price went up, the lines also worked their way higher, and when the price moved lower, the lines worked their way lower also. Right away I knew this had potential, at least much more potential than what I had been doing (although that was not a very high "bar" to clear). The question was how to put these lines, which were somehow connected to the price, to practical use.

I have been working on the best answer to this deceptively simple question for many years. Unfortunately, there is no absolute, definitive, "correct" answer. The reason for this is that SMR's lines are trend/momentum lines, and trading by trend and momentum is both a science and an art; and by definition, art can never be absolute and definitive.

.................

OK, as we say in bridge, let's review the bidding. We have seen that we, as individual traders, cannot compete in terms of information, knowledge, or computer expertise. We have seen that the only way for us to have a chance in this very difficult endeavor called trading is to change the nature of the trading game from a "why," or information and knowledge game, to a "what," or observational game. Furthermore, we have seen that the best way to approach a numbers game is to base our method on natural laws.

I have stated there are three natural laws of trading, no more no less. The first law, the future is unknown, simply states an obvious truth. However, in doing so it eliminates wasting energy on attempting to predict an unknowable future and instead focuses energy on studying the past and observing the present. The second law, continuation is more likely than change, is essentially the natural law of motion applied to prices. Out of this law comes the logical conclusion that an emphasis on identifying patterns of past to present continuation requires some reasonably reliable indicators of past and current price energy flow (i.e., some indicators of trend and momentum).

This is where we are now: In order to bet on continuation we need to be able to identify what continuation would be. We need to be able to identify past and current price energy flows. We need some reasonably reliable indicators of trend and momentum.

There are, no doubt, many reasonably reliable indicators of price trend and momentum. The ones I have used for over a quarter of a century, during which time I have found them to fully qualify as reasonably reliable, are the three trend/momentum indicators provided by SMR charting service of Boulder, Colorado (www.smr.com). The method I will present here utilizes these three indicators of trend and momentum (i.e., past and current price energy flows). However, the basic principles of the trading method I will present here apply to, and can be used with, any trend/momentum indicators—as long as they are reasonably reliable. It is important to state again that indicators of trend/momentum can only be "reasonably reliable." Perfection in trend/momentum indicators is impossible because the future is unknown; however, fortunately, perfection is not necessary for success. "Reasonably reliable" tends to work just fine.

# THE SMR TREND/MOMENTUM INDICATORS
## (The "SMR Lines")

WE HAVE ACCEPTED THAT WE, AS INDIVIDUAL TRADERS, cannot compete in terms of complexity; therefore, we need to keep everything as simple as possible. A simple way to measure trend and momentum is to use three time periods: short term, intermediate term, and long term (short term meaning days, intermediate term meaning weeks, long term meaning months.)

## THE LONG-TERM TREND INDICATOR

A long-term trend indicator needs to be able to measure, with reasonable reliability, the price energy flow of the past few months. For a long-term trend indicator, SMR and I use a simple ten-week or 50-day moving average (i.e., about two and a half months). Actually, SMR uses a 49-day moving average. SMR attaches some mystical significance to the number 49. It may or may not be there; I do not know and do not believe it makes any difference—49 day, 50 day, same for me. Regardless, the 50-day moving average is probably the most commonly used time period to measure trend; and, most importantly, I have found it to be more than adequate at doing so.

Actually, I believe it is better to refer to the long-term trend as the ten-*week* moving average rather than a 49- or 50-*day* moving average. Since I consider long term to mean months, it is only logical to measure long term in terms of weeks rather than days. Additionally, reading trend/momentum indicators is somewhat of an art, and any art requires a degree of freedom. Thinking and referring to trend in terms of weeks rather than days tends to produce a more general, and thus freer, way to look at trend.

There are two basic ways to measure trend and momentum. One is through the use of simple arithmetic moving averages, like the 50-day moving average. While I believe a straight mathematical moving average is the best way to measure long-term trend, I prefer a different approach when measuring shorter term price energy flows.

The basic idea in using simple moving averages to measure trend is that if the price is higher now than it was a few months ago, then the trend is up (and vice versa). However, for shorter time periods (i.e., weeks and days), I believe a more accurate way to measure price energy flow is through momentum oscillators.

## MOMENTUM OSCILLATORS

An oscillator is a measurement of price energy flow that moves above and below a neutral point or line. In other words, this momentum indicator *oscillates* above and below a zero line. To construct a price oscillator, all you do is calculate both a short-term moving average of the price (say the closing prices of the past few days) and a slightly longer term moving average of the price (say the closing prices of the past couple weeks), and then simply subtract the second number from the first. Doing this will result in either a plus or minus number. Next, plot the daily number this produces onto a graph and then connect the daily "dots" to make a line. Net result will be a momentum line that oscillates above and below zero.

The basic idea of an oscillator like this one is, if the price has been moving up faster over the past few days than it has over the past couple weeks, then the line produced by this type of oscillator will point up. An upward pointing line indicates the momentum of the price is upward. (And, of course, the reverse is true for the downside). An oscillator provides a good picture of the direction, and to a lesser extent speed, of short-term price momentum. Over the years I have found oscillators, specifically SMR's, tend to be reasonably reliable indicators of short-term (i.e., days) and intermediate-term (i.e., weeks) price momentum. I believe oscillators are better indicators of short-term and intermediate-term momentum than simple moving averages.

Charting software can construct a wide variety of price momentum oscillators. There are probably many different specific oscillator formulas that could work well in trading. The specific formula a trader uses to construct short-term and intermediate-term oscillators is not as important as developing a familiarity with the oscillator's tendencies and characteristics—just so long as the indicators are "reasonably reliable" (as SMR's are).

I have been working with SMR's momentum oscillators for over a quarter of a century and have found they easily qualify as "reasonably reliable" indicators of short-term and intermediate-term price momentum. In addition, I am very familiar and comfortable with their tendencies. If you feel the same about similar oscillators you may have been working with for a long time, then stick with them. Remember, moving averages and oscillators are simply reasonably reliable indicators of price trend and momentum; none are absolute or perfect.

(**NOTE:** *For obvious reasons SMR does not want me to divulge the specific oscillator formulas for their two proprietary momentum lines. However, they have given me permission to give the following general descriptions. In addition, on their Web site (www.smr.com) SMR provides the daily oscillator numbers for every market they chart. This data is provided for subscribers to enable daily updating of the SMR charts. These charts are also available for downloading (updated daily).*

## THE SHORT-TERM MOMENTUM INDICATOR

A short-term momentum indicator needs to be a reasonably accurate measurement of the price energy flow of the past few days. I use what SMR refers to as its "solid line" for a short-term indicator of price momentum. I prefer to call this indicator the "short line" or "SL." (Note: In my first book, *Intelligent Futures Trading*, I called this line the "Timing Line" since it is used primarily for shorter term timing; however, "short line" or "SL" is simpler.)

SMR's short-term momentum oscillator is constructed by taking about a two-, three-, or four-day moving average of the closing price and subtracting around a nine-, ten-, or eleven-day moving average of the closing price. Subtracting one number from the other will produce either a positive or negative number (and occasionally zero). Then, as mentioned above, simply connecting the "dots" (i.e., each day's oscillator number) on a chart will produce a line that oscillates above and below zero.

The shorter the two time periods used to construct this type of oscillating moving average, the more directly connected the line will be to the movement of the daily price. Therefore, a "2/9" line—using a two-day moving average of the closing price minus a nine-day moving average— will be more sensitive, move up and down more quickly, than a "4/11" line. A 2/9 line will be more sensitive to price moves but more erratic in its movement. A 4/11 line will be less sensitive but less erratic (i.e., change directions less often). And naturally, a 3/10 line would fall somewhere in between.

## THE INTERMEDIATE-TERM MOMENTUM INDICATOR

An intermediate-term momentum indicator needs to be a reasonably reliable measurement of the price energy flow of the past few weeks. I use SMR's other proprietary line for an intermediate-term momentum indicator. SMR calls this line their "dotted line," or DL; I refer to it as simply the "middle line," or "ML." (Note: In my first book I called this line the "Confirming Line" since it's used to confirm signals, but "middle line," or "ML," is simpler.)

SMR's intermediate-term momentum line (ML) is simply a smoothed out (around three weeks, i.e., 15-, 16- or 17-day) moving average of their short-term oscillator (the SL). Since this middle line, or ML, is a moving average of the short-term oscillator, it too will oscillate above and below zero.

As stated earlier, the specific formulas and techniques used to create trend/momentum indicators are not overly important, as long as the resulting lines are reasonably reliable. Any number of different trend/momentum indicators could be created using the above formulas as starting points, and almost any of them would be effective enough for successful trading—as long as they were reasonably reliable (like SMR's are) and you became familiar with their tendencies.

For example, for those who like to work with stochastics, renowned trader Linda Rashcke, a long-time subscriber to SMR charts, describes in her book *Street Smarts* (co-authored with Laurence Connors and published by M. Gordon Publishing Group) a stochastic formula she states produces momentum lines whose movements are very similar to SMR's momentum oscillators. The stochastic formula she gives is "7%K and 10%D." (I assume anyone who is familiar with stochastics will understand this formula and know how to construct it on charting software.) However, I am not a fan of stochastics as find it has some serious limitations (mainly its upper and lower limits, which tend to keep traders out of sustained moves). I find SMR's momentum indicators to be far superior to stochastics as well as other momentum formulas I have encountered, and so naturally I prefer to stick with their indicators.

Of course, if a trader so desired, he or she could use any trading software program and construct trend/momentum lines covering many more time frames. Momentum indicators can be constructed covering anywhere from minutes to years. My preference, and recommendation, is to keep it simple: Subscribe to the SMR Charts and then update them daily from their Web site. Over many years of trading I have learned that for the individual trader, clear, simple, and direct invariably works best. Getting the charts and daily data from SMR is the clearest, simplest and most direct way to obtain reasonably reliable trend/momentum indicators, as well as quality charts.

(**NOTE:** *I have no financial interest in SMR Charts and, other than a complimentary subscription, receive no compensation from them. I recommend SMR and their chart service solely on merit, a quality I have found SMR to possess in abundance for over a quarter of a century.*)

# THE TREND LINE

THE "TREND" LINE'S FUNCTION is to indicate the existing long-term directional price energy flow. The trend line is simply a ten-week (or 49-day as SMR prefers) moving average of the closing price.

The basic idea of the trend line is, if the current price is higher than it was a couple of months ago (i.e., ten weeks ago), then the trend of the price is presumed to be up. It is simple: If I am heavier now than I was a couple of months ago, the *trend* of my weight would be up. Or, if the equity in my trading account is higher now than it was a couple of months ago, then I can correctly conclude I have been making money trading, i.e., the trend would be up. Therefore, if the price is higher now than it was a few months ago, we can assume the current trend of prices is up, and vice versa for the downside.

There is no magical, mystical, absolute significance of a 50-day, or ten-week, moving average. However, history has shown a 50-day or ten-week moving average is a reasonably accurate measurement of trend over a broad spectrum of markets. Ten weeks is long enough to filter out any short-term aberrations of price movement, yet short enough to react to fundamental changes in price direction. Obviously, there will be times when a 40-day (or eight-week) moving average will be a more accurate reflection of current trend, and other times when a 60-day (or 12-week) will be more accurate. However, I have found the ten-week (50-day) moving average works just fine. In other words, it fully meets the criteria of being a "reasonably reliable" indicator of price trend.

A good way to visualize price movement is to see it as a "river" of energy, flowing first in one direction and then the other. When looking at price energy flows in this way, the trend is seen as the underlying "current." In a real river the surface water may surge back and forth depending on the wind and/or tide, but the underlying current will keep pushing relentlessly downstream. In markets the same is true; the underlying current of price energy flow (i.e., the trend) also will tend to assert itself over time.

You are probably aware of the saying "the trend is your friend." This saying is derived from the second law of trading. Just as a body in motion is more likely to continue moving in its current direction rather than change, so too the movement of a price is more likely to continue its current trend rather than change. Therefore, since a clearly identifiable trend in price is more likely to continue than change, if you trade in the direction of the trend, it will tend to be your friend.

Look at the charts on the following two pages (March Unleaded Gas and March Silver). Notice how in each of these cases the trend maintained its direction for many months, even while the daily and weekly movement of the price chopped up and down somewhat erratically. Moreover, notice how when their trends did change direction, they then proceeded to follow the new trends as reliably as the old. Naturally, I have chosen two good trending markets for examples; however, you could look through the SMR chart book at virtually any time and you would find many, if not most, of the markets in trends that had been maintained in one direction for many months. It is simply the nature of prices (and physics); once a trend has been clearly established, it tends to continue.

Some market theorists argue that the longer a trend has been in effect the closer it will be to changing direction. I believe the facts show the exact opposite to be true. The truth is the longer a trend has been in effect the greater the probability of that trend continuing. Many traders avoid markets that have been trending for a long time due to a fear these trends just cannot go on much longer. This is a mistake. Remember, continuation is more likely than change.

Some traders also tend to make the mistake of primarily looking for trades in markets where the trend shows signs it may be almost ready to turn. This also is a mistake; continuation is even more likely when the trend is well established. In other words, do not spend too much of your time and energy trying to get in at the "beginning" of price moves. Instead focus your attention and energy on trading those markets already in clearly established trends. Of course, any time a trend shows solid signs of being on the verge of changing direction, there is nothing wrong with trading for this possibility. However, the bulk of your trades should be in markets where a solid trend is a clear reality, not merely a fuzzy potential.

Over any meaningful period of time, the best (i.e., highest probability) trades will be in those markets with well-established trends. Therefore, it is only intelligent for a trader to focus energy and attention first on the markets with the strongest trends, and then only secondly look to those markets where the trends may be about to become clear.

Unfortunately, primarily trading markets already in well-established trends seems to go against our natural instincts. Maybe it is too boring, too easy. Many traders spend too much time looking for the next major trend change, the next big bull or bear market. This probably comes from a natural desire to get in at the beginning of moves—buying near *the* low and selling near *the* high. Attempting to do this must appeal to many "amateur" traders since most advertisements for charting software and trading systems seem to highlight their supposed ability to pick bottoms and tops. Evidently, this must be what sells best, and if so, then it is just one more reason why most individual traders end up losing. They focus on trying to pick the soon-to-be clear trends, rather than trading with already well established trends.

......................

Unfortunately, our natural, or human, instincts are one of the many obstacles to successful trading. Very often in trading the correct action is not the instinctive action. Therefore, most successful traders find it necessary to make a conscious effort to act correctly, such as forcing themselves to focus on trading markets already in well established trends. The unpleasant fact is that in trading we frequently need to force ourselves to act intelligently, meaning act in accordance with natural laws and truths. Sadly, we simply do not tend to act intelligently naturally. In fact, since the overwhelming majority of individual traders lose, what feels most natural must, by definition, usually be wrong. Obviously, if the easiest, most natural actions in trading consistently proved profitable, then most individuals would win rather than lose; the facts show the opposite to be true.

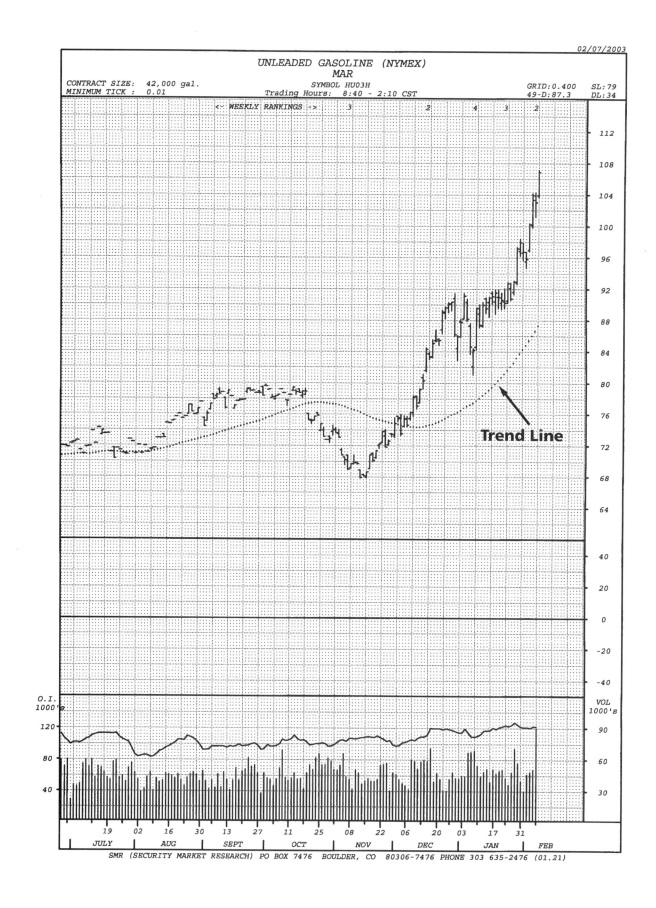

02/07/2003

UNLEADED GASOLINE (NYMEX)
MAR

CONTRACT SIZE:   42,000 gal.                     SYMBOL HU03H                              GRID:0.400   SL:79
MINIMUM TICK :   0.01                    Trading Hours:   8:40 - 2:10 CST                  49-D:87.3    DL:34

<- WEEKLY RANKINGS ->          3              2         4      3      2

**Trend Line**

O.I.
1000's                                                                                               VOL
                                                                                                    1000's

SMR (SECURITY MARKET RESEARCH) PO BOX 7476  BOULDER, CO  80306-7476 PHONE 303 635-2476  (01.21)

02/07/2003

SILVER (COMEX)
MAR

CONTRACT SIZE:   5000 TROY OZ.
MINIMUM TICK :   0.001

SYMBOL SI03H
Trading Hours:  7:25 - 1:25 CST

GRID:1.000    SL:-34
49-D:473.9    DL:-2

SMR (SECURITY MARKET RESEARCH) PO BOX 7476  BOULDER, CO  80306-7476 PHONE 303 635-2476 (01.21)

Markets do not trend with equal consistency. Some markets tend to trend more reliably than others. The basic rule for reliability of trending is the bigger the market—"bigger" meaning the more underlying "units" there are of the item being traded—the more consistently the market will trend. In simple physics terms, the bigger the mass the more likely it will continue moving in its current direction.

The biggest markets are the currencies. There are immeasurably more dollars/yen/euros/pounds, etc. floating around than there are live cattle in feedlots, beans in silos, silver in storage, and so on. Therefore, it is not surprising currencies tend to be among the best trending markets — "best" meaning highest reliability of a trend continuing once it is clearly established. Consequently, a clearly established trend in a currency market is very likely to continue. Therefore, as a rule, a trader should almost always trade with the trend in the currencies (only going against the trend when and if an excellent case can be made it is on the verge of turning).

Right behind currencies in terms of trending reliability are the interest rate markets, with the shorter the term the greater the reliability of trend (e.g., 90-day Eurodollars) and the longer the term the lesser the reliability (e.g., 30-year bonds). At the other end of the trend reliability spectrum, not surprisingly, are the live meat markets (live cattle, live hogs, and feeder cattle). These markets involve millions of units, while the currencies number in the multitrillions. This "bigger-the-mass-the-more-reliable-the-trend" rule is also why stock indexes tend to trend more reliably than individual stocks.

A secondary rule on trend reliability is the more storable a commodity (i.e., the longer it can be held in storage without deteriorating), the better the reliability of its trend. Therefore, metals markets tend to trend more reliably than more perishable commodities, like corn and soybeans. Then the grain markets (as well as markets like sugar, cocoa, coffee, cotton) tend to trend more consistently than the meat markets.

Of course these are generalizations and there will always be exceptions. Sometimes meats will trend well and currencies will not, but over time the truth of this basic trending rule will prevail.

The more long term oriented you are the more you should emphasize and rely on the trend. Furthermore, as a general rule, long-term traders should focus on the currencies and interest rate markets (the best trending markets). However, any market in a solid trend is always a viable candidate for trading, regardless of a trader's trading time preferences: short term, intermediate term, or long term.

## MARGIN-OF-ERROR

Any time-measurement of trend will always be somewhat approximate. Obviously, in a free market prices simply do not move according to some strict, absolute mathematical formula. Neither life nor markets are reducible to strict mathematical formulas. Any trend indicator, no matter how reliable, will always be merely an approximate "indication" of current price trend, and anything approximate needs some margin-of-error.

I have found using plus or minus two weeks (ten days) to be a good margin-of-error for a ten-week (50-day) moving average. For example, if the eight-week moving average has changed direction but the ten-week has not, yet <u>ALL</u> other indicators are pointing in the same direction as the eight-week line, then for trading purposes it is acceptable to consider the trend to have changed, i.e., consider it within the margin-of-error. However, it is important to be cautious in applying this margin-of-error and not overdo it (especially in the more reliable trending markets like currencies and the interest rate markets).

.....................

Trading rules should never be thought of as absolutes. In trading we are dealing with an unknown future constantly unfolding in front of us; therefore, we always need to maintain a certain amount of flexibility in our day-by-day actions. So, be willing to give the trend line a margin-of-error of plus or minus two weeks (ten days), but only apply this margin-of-error when the rest of the picture clearly supports doing so. In other words, anticipating trend changes is permissible when within the margin-of-error, but even then it is best to do so cautiously. Keep in mind that most of us tend to over anticipate trend changes (we look for trends to change more often than they do). My experience has been that when it comes to trend changes, in the long run you will be better off being a little late rather than a little early. The extra profit made by correctly being early on some trend changes will tend to be more than wiped out by what is lost when early and wrong.

## ANTICIPATING THE TREND LINE

A "moving" average is simply an average that is continuously recalculated. A 50-day moving average of a price is an average of the past fifty days of closing prices that is recalculated daily. To roughly recalculate this moving average, simply compare the price you are adding to the moving average (i.e., today's closing price) to the price you are taking off (i.e., the price ten weeks ago). If the new day is higher than the old one, the moving average will move up (i.e., uptrend), if lower it will go down (i.e., downtrend).

Therefore, to anticipate the direction the moving average will head next, simply compare the price area of the past few weeks with the prices around ten weeks ago. In other words, if current prices are clearly higher than they were ten weeks ago, we can anticipate the ten-week moving average will continue to move up; if lower, we can anticipate it will continue to move down.

For example, if eight, nine and ten weeks ago the S&P was trading in the low 1100's and it is trading in the mid 1300's now, we can safely assume that the moving average will continue to move up over the next few weeks. Numbers around 1100 are going to be dropped off the moving average and numbers in the mid 1300's will probably be added; therefore, since the numbers to be added are higher than those that are going to be dropped off, the average will move higher. However, we are simply *anticipating* the most *likely* future direction of the moving average, not its guaranteed direction. Keep in mind, should the current numbers (prices) suddenly change significantly, then our anticipation of the future direction of the moving average must also change.

This "anticipation" concept is one you absolutely *must* fully understand in order to be able to anticipate the movement of trend/momentum indicators (i.e., the lines). Therefore, to repeat, in order to anticipate the most likely immediate future movement of any moving average, simply compare the numbers you will most likely be adding to the moving average to the numbers you will be dropping off. If you expect to be adding higher numbers than the numbers to be dropped off, then anticipate that the moving average will move up; if the numbers most likely to be added are lower than the numbers to be dropped off, then anticipate that the moving average will go down.

To help me anticipate the future movement of the trend line, the first action I take when looking at a chart is to count back ten weeks and circle the prices from the middle of that week. This way I am able, at a glance, to anticipate how likely or unlikely it will be for the trend to change in the immediate future. I do this by visually comparing current prices to prices ten weeks earlier, i.e., those in the circle. If they are roughly the same, then the line could turn easily; if they are far apart, then the line is unlikely to change direction anytime soon.

Look at the charts of the March Unleaded Gas and March Silver on the preceding pages and compare the current prices to the prices ten weeks earlier. Do this and you will see at a glance how difficult or easy it would have been to turn the existing trends. Suggest you also take a period a month or two earlier and count back ten weeks from there and make the same comparison; then see for yourself what the trend did in the ensuing weeks.

When trading futures we want to be positioned not only with today's trend/momentum, but even more so we want to be positioned with tomorrow's trend and momentum. However, be clear about what we are doing here; we are **not** trying to predict tomorrow's prices. What we are trying to do is "anticipate" what our reasonably reliable trend/momentum indicator *lines* will look like tomorrow, and the few days after.

The basic idea is that it is easier and more effective to anticipate or predict the future movement of trend/momentum lines than it is to anticipate or predict *price*. Therefore, what we do is look at the current price trend/momentum indicators, anticipate what these indicators most likely will look like over the next few days, and then position accordingly. We are trading price, but we make our trading decisions primarily by anticipating the most likely future direction and location of our reasonably reliable trend/momentum indicators. If these indicators are pointing up, we trade from the long side; if they are pointing down, we trade from the short side.

So, when using moving averages as indicators of trend/momentum, it is imperative that you constantly look back at the numbers you will be dropping off the various moving averages and compare these numbers to the ones most likely to be added. Whenever I look at an SMR chart my eyes immediately check the numbers coming "off" of each of the three lines and compare these with the numbers most likely to be "added." I do this starting with the trend, then going to the inter-mediate-term line, and finally to the short-term line. I do this every time, without fail, always! I do this because it is the best way to anticipate where the lines most likely will be tomorrow and the few days after that. You would be wise to train yourself to do the same.

We trade futures, not presents or pasts; therefore, anticipating the near term (i.e., next few days) future location and direction of the trend/momentum lines is of utmost importance. While the future price is unknown, it is possible to make an educated "guesstimate" of the future direction and location of our reasonably reliable trend/momentum indicators (i.e., the lines). Since these indicators are directly related to the price movement, if we are consistently positioned with them, then we should be consistently on the right side of price movement.

## TRADING AGAINST THE TREND

I am aware there is an inherent appeal among many traders to at least occasionally trade against the trend. I believe the primary reason for this is the illusion of an "attractive" price. A market that has been going down for ten weeks or more, or a market that is below its price of ten weeks ago, by definition is going to have a relatively "low" price. This "low" price will frequently look attractive to buy (and, of course, when the trend is up and the price is "high" it will look attractive to sell). Prices that have been in long lasting downtrends will always appear cheap or low; and prices that have been going up for a long time will always look expensive or high. The danger of these seemingly attractive prices is the second law of trading: Continuation is more likely than change. In this game, "high" tends to indicate even higher and "low" usually means even lower—regardless of past history.

Unfortunately for my net worth, over many of my early years of trading I made far too many against-the-trend trades. While I have not kept records, I have absolutely no doubt I lost far more on these against-the-trend trades than I made (even though I have made some great against-trend trades). I believe the same is probably true for most traders. However, even more damaging than the amount lost on against-the-trend trades were the profits not realized due to missing good with-the-trend trades. Far too often, trading against the trend misdirected my focus, and as a result I missed numerous excellent entry points for very profitable with-the-trend trades.

I believe one of the worst things that can happen to a trader, especially a beginning trader, is to make a profitable against-the-trend trade. This good result will make him or her want to do trade-against-the-trend again. It is the equivalent of hitting a hundred-to-one shot your first trip to the race track. This would tend to make you think betting long shots is a good way to win, when in reality it is a path to almost certain failure.

Against-the-trend trading has a tendency to be addictive; the more you do it the more you want to do it. One reason for this is that when an against-the-trend trade starts out a loser, a trader's initial reaction is that he was just a little "early" on his timing. Therefore, there is a strong temptation to try again and buy or sell more at what now has become an even "more attractive" price.

One of the few "never, never" rules of trading is to never, never add to a loser if it is against the trend. Adding to an against-the-trend loser is just stubborn fighting the market, i.e., the prevailing price energy flow. It is trying to impose your will on the market. Furthermore, it is acting in direct opposition to natural law. Adding to an against-the-trend loser is simply allowing self-righteous stubbornness to rule rather than humble intelligence. Better to surrender and win than fight and lose.

Since many very bad things can happen to you when you trade against the trend, it is better to just not do so. Act intelligently (meaning act in accordance with the natural laws of trading) and do not trade against the trend (with the exception of those rare times the margin-of-error permits, and even then only if other indicators strongly support doing so). It has taken me a long time to fully accept this truth, even though I "knew" it to be true early in my trading career. Even now, knowing what I know, occasionally I am tempted to make against-the-trend trades. "Knowing" truth is not enough; you must also consistently act in accordance with this truth.

Now, having said all this—in other words, argued as strongly as possible against trading against the trend—I am a realist, and thus aware you may choose to disregard this advice from time to time. Therefore, if you insist on trading against the trend, here are some basic rules for doing so.

## AGAINST-THE-TREND TRADING RULES

First, be much more selective getting in. Second, be *much, much* less selective getting out. Third, trade smaller quantities. And fourth, never, never add to a loser. However, the fundamental problem with these against-the-trend trading rules, as sound as they are, is that in real life they are extremely difficult to follow. When you trade against the trend you will always be getting in at an attractive price (based on recent history); therefore, if the price does move in your favor, you will begin to wonder if maybe the major trend might be in the process of turning. Next you will start to think you just might have caught "the" top or bottom and as a result may have a really great trade underway. Once this possibility enters your mind you will find it extremely difficult to get out with a moderate profit. Inevitably, you will start to believe a huge profit may be available if the trend really does turn, and thus will tend to overstay your welcome. The fact is, the very nature of against-the-trend trades tends to make it almost impossible to follow good counter-trend trading rules.

Back in my days in the brokerage business, another broker in our office had a client who lost substantial amounts (high six figures and more) every year, year in and year out. This trader was very successful with all his other business ventures, but in futures trading he lost consistently. Since consistency of any kind is valuable information in this game, occasionally I would ask his broker about his positions. Without exception, every time I checked, virtually every position would be against a strong trend, and usually these were "old" positions with big losses. My guess is he was merely applying to futures trading what had worked well in his businesses. He was buying "cheap" and selling "expensive," and then waiting for normal business cycles to correct these "temporary" extremes. Unfortunately for him they rarely did.

To me this trader was a minor trading "tragedy." Here was an individual who would have made a really great long-term trader. He had the funds to absorb short-term moves against him and the psychological patience (stubbornness?) and toughness to hold on to trades for a long time; this is the perfect combination for a long-term trader. Unfortunately, he had the fatal flaw of insisting on trading against the trend. He had to buy "cheap" and sell "expensive."

A stubborn trader with deep pockets (meaning lots of margin) can, and almost certainly will, do very well if he consistently positions with the trend in any/all strong trending markets (regardless of current relative historical price levels). Time will always be on his side. Since he has the patience and margin to wait for time (i.e., the trend) to work, he will invariably do very well over any meaningful period of time. However, that same combination of stubbornness, lots of margin, and consistently positioning against solid trends is a recipe for certain failure. This approach is virtually guaranteed to produce an almost constant stream of big losses.

In trading it is important to know yourself. You need to know what sort of "time span" you will most often act upon. What I mean is that if you are a "jumpy" or short-term trader—find it difficult or impossible to hold positions for long periods and instead get in and out frequently—then you have to adjust your trading style accordingly. Conversely, if you are a patient or long-term trader—hold for long periods regardless of short-term price movement—then you need to use a trading or time style to capitalize on these tendencies. Know yourself, then use that knowledge to adjust your trading style accordingly.

For a trader who insists on consistently trading against strong trends, the only possible way to succeed is to be an extremely short-term trader (holding positions no longer than two or three days), as well as be very selective (by only positioning when momentum is clearly in your favor or you can make an excellent case it is about to turn in your favor). One of the worst trading styles is to be a long-term trader who consistently trades against strong trends. This combination will inevitably result in consistent, big losses. Quite logically, this means the opposite combination would have an excellent chance for success.

Time always favors the trend, meaning over time the odds favor the price eventually moving in the direction of the existing trend—i.e., continuation is more likely than change. The stronger and more established the trend, the more likely this will turn out to be true. Therefore, as long as the individual mentioned above continues to use the approach of holding long-term positions against strong trends, he is virtually guaranteed to keep losing substantial amounts.

On the other hand, some of the biggest trading profits I have personally witnessed were produced by a client of mine (in the late 1970s when I was a broker with E. F. Hutton). This trader used virtually the exact opposite approach to the one mentioned above. He too was a buy- (and occasionally sell-) and-hold trader. He looked for markets that were clearly trending, preferably up, and then positioned with this trend. While he did not actually look at a chart to find strong trending markets (he was not a chart person), by personal preference he sought to be positioned in good uptrending markets. After he took his initial position, he would then lightly (usually only one or two contracts at a time, sometimes up to five) add to this position every few days. Therefore, the longer the trend lasted the bigger his position would become. Naturally, when he caught a good trending market and kept slowly adding contracts, the profits would frequently become substantial.

Unfortunately, he too had a fatal trading flaw. Whenever he caught a very good trending market and built up some big profits, he would tend to become permanently attached to the trade and simply would not get out even when the trend finally did change direction. The only time he would liquidate contracts on his good trades was either to meet margin calls or to roll over to a later month (when faced with delivery). Over several years I watched his account repeatedly go from the fifty thousand dollar area up to the six hundred thousand dollar area, and then back down again. He must have made this round trip at least five or six times in the mid to late 1970s. Then in 1979 he really caught some good trending markets and in less than seven months ran his equity from near zero up to over three and a half million. (He was in on the great bull runs gold and silver had in late 1979, early 1980.) Sadly though, once again he proved incapable of getting out once the trends finally turned, and in the two months after the highs were made in the precious metals (January 1980) his equity dropped all the way back to almost zero (although he did withdraw a couple hundred thousand on the way up). He never recovered from the loss of these giant profits; it was just too big a psychological blow. To my knowledge he has never been able to get a good run going again, and rarely, if ever, trades anymore.

My experience has been that most long-term traders have this same flaw; the longer they hold a position the more difficult it becomes for them to exit the trade. It is as if the same law of continuation applies to their holding on to trades; the longer they are in a position the more likely they will be to continue to hold on, regardless of price movement. Once firmly established in a trade, many long-term traders seem to become almost incapable of getting out, regardless of what the price does.

Once the trends on my client's positions finally turned against him he just could not accept liquidating his positions at significantly worse prices than only a few weeks earlier. The quick drop in his equity from three and a half million down to two-plus million was too much for him to accept. In other words, he could not get out after that big and quick a "loss" (even though he was still hugely profitable). Instead he chose to assume, more likely he blindly hoped, that this particular price reversal was simply a temporary interruption in the uptrend he had ridden so profitably for the preceding many months. Sadly, he believed and relied on the trend as long as it was going in the direction he thought it "should"; however, once the trend fully reversed, he could not accept this new direction because it did not fit his desires. Therefore, he just held on stubbornly until his equity finally returned to essentially zero and the final margin call forced the liquidation of his last positions. The trend he had ridden for so long changed from being his friend to becoming his mortal enemy simply because he did not—indeed appeared to be unable to—change with it.

...................

This is a very tough game, trading. To walk away a winner you not only need to know how to trade, you also need to know yourself. We all seem to have potentially fatal trading flaws within us. For most it is simply a lack of understanding of the natural laws of trading/pricing. For these traders there is essentially no hope, no chance. However, simply knowing the correct approach and methodology is not enough. We also need to know ourselves and then be able to adjust our methodology to fit.

This is a difficult combination not only to put together but also to maintain through all the inevitable emotional ups and downs of trading. For each of us, successful trading requires clear personal knowledge and then maintaining a delicate balance between our strengths and weaknesses. If ever lost, this balance can be very difficult to regain (a fact I know all too well).

...................

A trader once asked me to recommend a good "fundamental news" market letter. He said he was a fairly good short-term trader as long as he knew which basic, general direction to focus on—up or down. He thought if someone could just tell him the general direction of price movement based on the current fundamental supply/demand situation, then he could take care of the rest. I told him there was an excellent "market letter" that was very good for exactly that purpose; it was called the "trend." All he had to do was look back ten weeks. If the price was higher now than it was then, he should consider the fundamental supply/demand situation to be bullish; if lower, he should consider the fundamentals bearish.

It is simple: If the price has been going up for the past few months, then demand has been over-powering supply; if the price has been going down persistently for the past few months, then supply has been overpowering demand. The trend of the price gives you all the fundamentals of supply/demand you will ever need to know in order to trade successfully. Not only does the trend tell you what the fundamentals are, and have been, but at a glance you can see, and therefore know, what this trend is at any moment in time. Just use the trend to tell you what the market supply/demand fundamentals are at the moment; there is no need to waste time and energy on detailed supply/demand research. The trend will do your fundamental supply/demand research for you, and do it quicker, clearer and better than you, or any group of "yous," can.

There is one final reason to limit your trading to with-the-trend trades. Every day, in every market, you are faced with three choices: long, sidelines, or short. Limiting your trading to with-the-trend trades eliminates one of these choices, thereby leaving you with "only" having to decide whether to be in with the trend or on the sidelines. Choosing correctly between two options is much easier than choosing among three. Over time this simple statistical advantage alone can prove to be the difference between success and failure.

## BOTTOM LINE ON TREND

Accept the truth. Adhere to the natural laws of trading and just do not trade against the trend (unless the margin-of-error allows, and even then, only if and when the rest of the technical picture is clearly very promising for a new trend direction). As an individual trader you do not have many friends in this tough and sometimes brutal business. However, the trend is always sitting there ready and willing to be your friend. All you need to do is accept this friendship by allowing the trend to dictate the direction you trade each market. Over any meaningful period of time the existing trend will be a far, far better indicator of future price movement than you, me, or anyone else. Therefore, you would be extremely wise if you keep the trend as your very best and most reliable trading friend.

# THE INTERMEDIATE-TERM MOMENTUM LINE

THE FUNCTION OF THE INTERMEDIATE-TERM MOMENTUM LINE (the ML or middle line) is to indicate, with reasonable reliability, the price energy flow of the past few weeks. The SMR intermediate-term momentum line does this well. The effectiveness of SMR's intermediate-term momentum line is in some ways surprising because, of the three trend/momentum lines, the intermediate-term momentum line is the most removed from actual price movement.

The trend line is a straight moving average and so is directly reflective of actual price movement. However, the middle line (ML) is once removed from price movement because it is a moving average of the differential between two other moving averages. Yet, in spite of this indirect connection to the daily movement of the price, the ML does its job very well.

Remember, what counts here is the truth. I have learned over the years not to be too concerned about how or why an indicator might work. One basic rule of technical trading is, if an indicator does its job reasonably well, then do not worry too much about the how and why of it. Even though the ML is not constructed directly from price movement but is instead a moving average of the difference between two other moving averages, its speed and direction are still solely a result of the speed and direction of price movement. Since we are trading price and price alone, it is important our primary indicators be based on price movement.

As mentioned earlier, the trend can be accurately visualized as the current of a river (a river of price energy). In the same way, the intermediate-term momentum line can be accurately equated to the "tide" (of price energy). The trend tends to push relentlessly onward like the current of a river, while the intermediate-term momentum line (the ML) tends to cycle up and down like the phases of the tide.

If you look at the charts on the next two pages you will see how the ML does a very good job of moving in fairly even and rhythmic cycles with the comparable intermediate-term cycles in the price movement. Notice that while the price is constantly jumping up and down on a daily basis, the ML tends to move in one direction for several days, even several weeks, at a time without changing direction. This sustained intermediate-term cycling-type movement gives a trader a reasonably reliable indicator of intermediate-term price energy flows, which is of substantial value when trading.

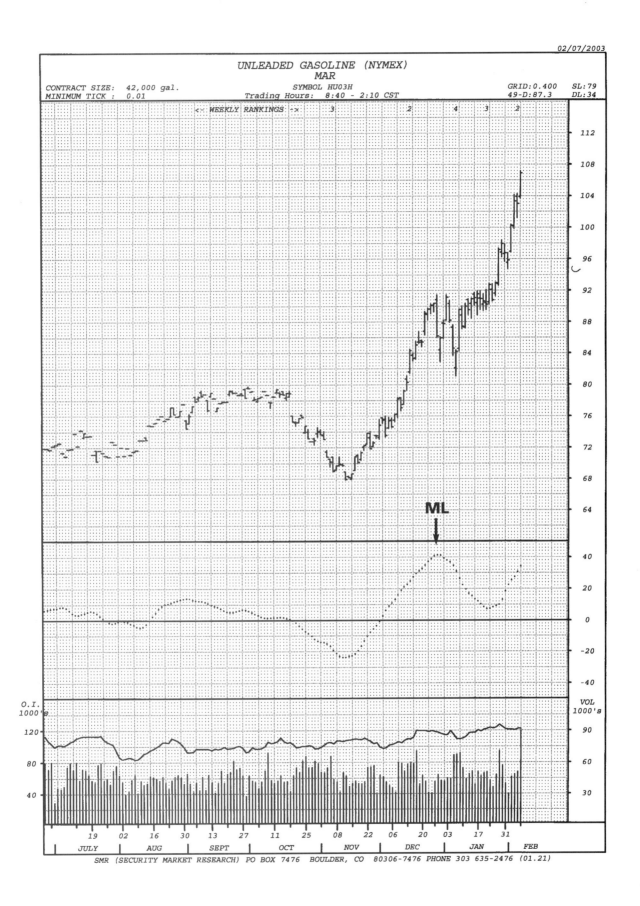

02/07/2003

UNLEADED GASOLINE (NYMEX)
MAR

CONTRACT SIZE:   42,000 gal.                              SYMBOL HU03H                              GRID:0.400    SL:79
MINIMUM TICK :   0.01                          Trading Hours:  8:40 - 2:10 CST                      49-D:87.3     DL:34

<- WEEKLY RANKINGS ->        3           2        4      3      2

ML

SMR (SECURITY MARKET RESEARCH) PO BOX 7476  BOULDER, CO  80306-7476 PHONE 303 635-2476 (01.21)

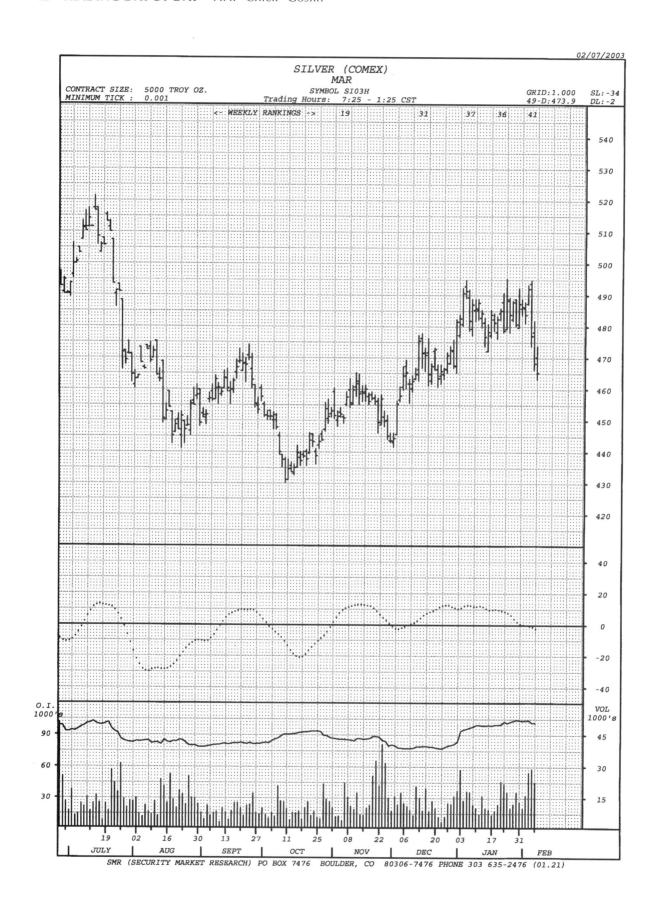

## MARGIN-OF-ERROR

Because reading the charts is partially an art, as with the trend, there must be some looseness to the intermediate-term momentum line. Therefore, for a margin-of-error on the ML, I use up to five days. Remember, the ML is an approximately three-week moving average of the SL; therefore, if I can make a reasonable case the ML will turn within five days, I can consider it to be within the margin-of-error to turn.

The momentum lines are derived from the price; therefore, they are, by necessity, following or lagging indicators (meaning they tend to follow price movement rather than lead it). To compensate for this natural lag between price and line, it is frequently necessary, or at least helpful, to act before the lines actually turn. Giving each line a margin-of-error in their turning time makes it easier to act in advance of them actually turning. In other words, giving each line some margin-of-error creates a bigger time "window" for action.

If you can make a sound case the ML will turn within at least the next five days, then it is acceptable to act as if it were going to do so, i.e., you can consider it to be within the margin-of-error of turning. Therefore, you can consider a few days one way or the other to be "close enough" when considering direction of the ML. (Note: Once you see some specific examples on the charts, all this will become clear.)

## LOCATION OF THE INTERMEDIATE-TERM MOMENTUM LINE

For the trend line, location has no bearing; only its direction (up or down) and the sharpness or shallowness of its current up or down move matter. However, for the intermediate-term momentum line (the ML), both direction and location are significant. By location I mean whether it is above or below zero, whether it is positive or negative. The direction of the ML is somewhat more important than its location, especially if the directional move is sharp; however, location does count, and the farther above or below zero the more meaningful the location of the ML tends to be.

## ANTICIPATING THE INTERMEDIATE-TERM MOMENTUM LINE

The ML (middle line) is anticipated in the same way as the trend. Remember, the ML is a moving average of the SL. Therefore, simply look back to see what numbers (of the SL) are going to be dropped off (from ten to sixteen days ago), and then compare these numbers with where the SL is now, as well as where it will most likely be over the next few days. If the numbers to be dropped off are lower than the numbers that will most likely be added, then you can anticipate that the ML will be moving up near term (and vice versa).

It is simple. If higher numbers are going to be added to the moving average than are to be dropped off, then the moving average will move up; if lower numbers are to be added to the moving average than are to be dropped off, then the moving average will move down.

While it is important to be positioned with the *current* direction and location of the ML (long if it is up, short if down; long if it is above zero, short if below zero); it is even more important to be positioned with the immediate *future* direction and location of the ML (i.e., where it will be over the next few days). Therefore (repeating this for emphasis), to anticipate the most likely location and direction of the ML over the next few days, compare current location of the <u>SL</u> (remember the ML is a moving average of the SL, not the price) to the location of the SL two to three weeks ago.

One of the first things to look at on a price chart is where the price was eight, nine and ten weeks ago compared to where it is now (for trend anticipation purposes). Then next look at where the SL was between two and three weeks ago compared to where it is now (and where it most likely will be over the next few days). Looking at both these situations will tell you at a glance how likely or unlikely it is for these two lines (trend and ML) either to keep moving in their current directions or change direction.

## TRADING AGAINST THE INTERMEDIATE-TERM MOMENTUM LINE

With only a few special exceptions (primarily when the "margin-of-error" permits) I feel it is better not to trade against the trend line. However, trading against both the direction and location of the ML is fully acceptable in many instances; however, the same basic rules that apply to trading against the trend apply to trading against the ML (especially when the ML is moving sharply). In other words, if your trade is against the directional movement of the ML, then that (against ML) trade should be treated as a short-term trade (generally two to five days in duration), and position size (i.e., number of contracts) should be smaller than if trading with the trend, and so on.

## BOTTOM LINE ON THE INTERMEDIATE-TERM MOMENTUM LINE

Think of the ML as the "tide" of price energy flows. By this I mean look at the ML as a good indicator of intermediate-term price "cycles," cycles that tend to last for weeks, not days or months. Consider both the direction and the location of the ML to be significant, but give the direction somewhat more weight. The sharper the angle of ascent or descent of the ML the more significant it is and, to a lesser extent, the farther above or below zero the more meaningful.

# CONCURRENT MODE VS. CROSSCURRENT MODE

OK, HERE IS WHERE WE ARE. We acknowledge we cannot compete if the competition is based on information and knowledge of supply/demand; therefore, we will waste no time or effort trying to do so. We see that one truth (the first natural law) of trading says the future is unknown; therefore, we will not waste time and energy trying to see into this unknown future. In other words, we will not try to predict or guess where prices are going. We also see that another truth (the second natural law of trading) stipulates that continuation (of price movement) is more likely than change. Therefore, we needed, and found, some reasonably reliable indicators of price trend and momentum—SMR's three trend/momentum lines.

To keep it simple we have limited our measurements of trend/momentum to long, intermediate, and short term (long meaning months, intermediate meaning weeks, and short meaning days). We then determined that a 50-day or ten-week moving average of the price is a reasonably reliable indicator of long-term trend. Next we accepted (and as we go along you will see for yourself how effectively) that SMR's intermediate-term momentum indicator (the ML) is a reasonably reliable indicator of intermediate-term momentum (and trend).

What we are trying to do here is observe the price movement of a market, from past to present, and in so doing attempt to discover some clearly identifiable price energy flows. Now, how do we start putting all of this to some practical use?

....................

As mentioned earlier I believe it is helpful to visualize the movement of market prices as if they were rivers of energy—unexplored rivers whose future paths are unknown. Picture the trend (the ten-week moving average) as the prevailing "current" of these rivers of price energy and look at the intermediate-term momentum line (the ML) as the "tide" (cycling in and out).

Now, when a river has both a strong current and a powerful tide moving in the same direction (i.e., moving concurrently), it will be very difficult for the surface water to move against this underlying concurrent flow for very far or for very long. Market prices are no different. When both the trend and intermediate-term momentum of a market's price are moving in the same direction (concurrently), then the daily price movement will tend also to be persistently in that same direction. Conversely, if the underlying current and the tide of a river are moving opposite one another (i.e., are at crosscurrents), then the result on the surface is usually choppiness. Once again, market prices act no differently. When trend and intermediate-term momentum are at crosscurrents, the price will tend to move in a choppy, more sideways manner.

**CONCURRENT MODE** is when trend and intermediate-term momentum (ML) of a market are both pointing in the same direction (i.e., concurrently). This market "mode" will tend to produce sustained, with-the-trend market moves; or, at the least, it will not produce much in the way of counter-trend moves.

**CROSSCURRENT MODE** is when trend and intermediate-term momentum (ML) of a market are pointing in opposite directions (i.e., at crosscurrents). This market "mode" will tend to produce choppy, more sideways-type market moves; or at the least, with-the-trend movements will be more limited in time and distance.

If you look at the charts on the following two pages you will see that both markets tended to make their best, most sustained, with-the-trend moves when they were in concurrent mode. In addition, when they were in concurrent modes any counter-trend moves were limited in time and distance. Furthermore, you will see that when either market was in crosscurrent mode their prices tended to move in a choppy, more sideways manner.

As we go through the charts later in the book you shall see that these tendencies (of concurrent and crosscurrent modes) tend to be remarkably consistent. Naturally, it is not perfect; nothing is in trading. However, having and knowing the tendencies of these two technical background "modes" can be extremely helpful to your trading. Being aware of these tendencies enables a trader to know when to look for sustained moves versus when to focus on shorter-term trades, as well as when to hold big positions versus small ones.

It is very important to be always aware of whether a market is in concurrent or crosscurrent mode, and then act accordingly. It is also important to be aware of whether the particular "mode" is solid or tenuous. By this I mean how easy or difficult would it be for the mode to switch to its opposite condition over the next few days (again, this is done by "anticipating" the most likely near term movement of both trend and intermediate-term momentum lines).

## BOTTOM LINE ON CONCURRENT VS. CROSSCURRENT MODES

Once trend and intermediate-term momentum of a market are determined, the next step is to see whether they are moving concurrently or are at crosscurrents. This is **VERY IMPORTANT** because it tells you how long you should plan to hold on to the trade as well as how aggressive to be in your positioning. In other words, whether a market is in concurrent or crosscurrent mode is a good indication of both odds and risk/reward. Therefore, always be fully aware of whether a market is in concurrent or crosscurrent mode, as well as how solid this mode is. ***The odds of success are best and the risk/reward most favorable when positioned with a solid concurrent mode.***

02/07/2003

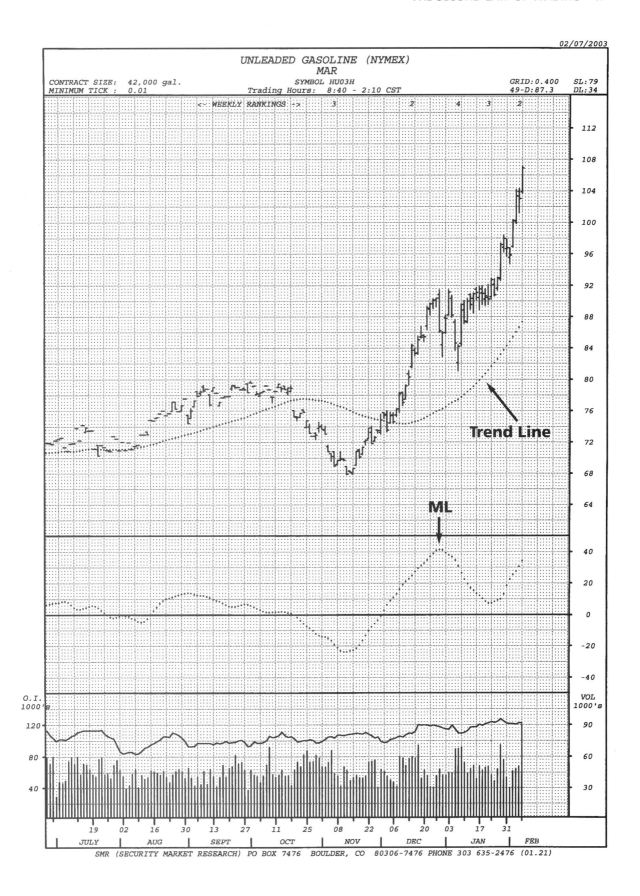

UNLEADED GASOLINE (NYMEX)
MAR

CONTRACT SIZE:   42,000 gal.          SYMBOL HU03H                    GRID:0.400    SL:79
MINIMUM TICK  :   0.01          Trading Hours:   8:40 - 2:10 CST      49-D:87.3    DL:34

<- WEEKLY RANKINGS ->

Trend Line

ML

O.I.
1000's

VOL
1000's

19    02    16    30    13    27    11    25    08    22    06    20    03    17    31
JULY        AUG         SEPT        OCT         NOV         DEC         JAN        FEB

SMR (SECURITY MARKET RESEARCH) PO BOX 7476  BOULDER, CO  80306-7476  PHONE 303 635-2476 (01.21)

# THE SHORT-TERM MOMENTUM LINE

THE TREND LINE SHOWS US THE *DIRECTION* TO TRADE A MARKET; it is the *direction* line. The intermediate-term momentum line (ML) indicates approximately when it is best (in terms of probabilities and risk/reward) to be positioned with the trend; the ML *confirms* the trend. And finally, the short-term momentum line (the Short Line or SL) helps us time entry and exits of trades; it is the *timing* line.

The basic function of the short-term momentum line (SL) is to indicate, with reasonable reliability, the price energy flow of the past few days. The SMR short-term momentum line does this as well as can be expected, considering how erratic short-term price movements in the futures markets tend to be.

Of the three SMR trend/momentum lines, the SL moves the most erratically and irregularly, meaning it shifts direction much more frequently than the other two. Despite this relative inconsistency of movement, the SL's primary use is to help determine specific *timing* of trades. (This emphasis on short-term timing is why in my first book I referred to this line as the "Timing Line.")

I have compared the movement of price to a river flowing into an unknown future. When looking at this "river" of price energy, I visualize the trend as the "current" of the river and the intermediate-term momentum (ML) as the "tide." In the same vein I visualize the short-term momentum line (SL) as the "wind." However, not an ordinary natural wind but more like a wind from a mythical "wind god" who needs to take a breath periodically. What I mean by this is that surges in the SL are invariably interrupted by periodic pauses or countermoves. Prices act similarly. Even the strongest price surges have brief pauses and minor countermoves.

Another way to look at the SL is to think of it as a boxer throwing a punch. The SL indicates potential short-term surging (or punching) power. For example, if the trend is solidly up but the SL is on a several day dip and around recent lows ("recent" compared to lows of the past few months), then this indicates any minor counter-trend move should close to ending. This combination (trend up, SL near recent lows) indicates the market has some potential buying power. It is similar to a boxer who has cocked his arm back and thus has substantial punching power ready to be unleashed.

On the other hand, consider a situation with the trend still solidly up, but this time the SL is on a multi-day up move and is around recent highs. This combination indicates potential short-term energy may be somewhat spent and thus the price may be temporarily overextended to the upside. It is the equivalent of a boxer who has extended his arm (i.e., thrown his punch) and thus does not have much short-term punching energy left. In boxing terms, the boxer's arm is extended and so he will have to pull it back at least a little in order to build up some punching power again.

Whether visualizing the SL as wind from a mythical "short-term, price energy flow god"or as the arm of a boxer, the basic point is the same:The SL is closely connected to short-term (few-day) price moves. Prices do not move in a straight line; they surge and pull back. Therefore, recent patterns of the SL give a fairly good read on how much potential short-term energy a price move possesses at any specific time.

A strong uptrend but low SL means plenty of short-term upside potential. A strong uptrend but high SL means short-term upside energy may be running out of steam. (And, of course, the reverse is true on the downside.) What this means is it rarely pays to buy when the SL is around recent highs or sell when it is around recent lows, simply because short-term price energy flow at these times will be, by definition, somewhat extended.

However, there is a major exception to this basic SL rule. When a market is in a solid concurrent mode (both trend and ML pointing in the same direction), then the price can keep pushing in the direction of trend and ML for an extended period (even weeks), regardless of how overextended the SL might become. In fact, an extremely high SL within a solidly concurrent mode to the upside tends to indicate significantly higher prices to come. In other words, an extreme move in the SL in the same direction and within a solid concurrent mode is a sign of an unusually powerful move, and thus is not an indication of short-term exhaustion.

The point is that any and all patterns of the SL need to be looked at through the lens of the market's background technical condition—meaning whether the market is concurrent or crosscurrent, and how solidly. For example, if both trend and ML are solidly up, then a turn down in the SL tends to be fairly insignificant; however, if both trend and ML are solidly down, then a turn down in SL tends to be quite significant. The first example is a case of minor surface backwash in a river where the current and tide are surging in the other direction—meaning it is probably an insignificant event. In the second example you have short-term momentum turning in the same direction the trend and intermediate-term momentum are already moving—this is much more significant since it is like giving a good push to an object already moving.

Trend and ML establish the technical background of a market; they set up the "prism" for looking at the SL. Therefore, look first at the technical background (trend and ML), then factor in the recent pattern and the current location/direction of the SL.

....................

The short-term momentum line (SL) acts as both a short-term price speedometer and compass. It tells us the direction and speed of current short-term price momentum. The SL measures the *past* to *present* direction and speed—but not future. The future is yet to be made and thus is unknown. However, while the future is unknown it is more likely to be a continuation of the current situation rather than a change.

....................

The SMR trend/momentum lines (SL, ML and trend) provide us with probabilities, that is all. In this difficult game all we can realistically expect to receive from indicators are reasonably reliable probabilities; we can never expect any degree of certainty.

If you require certainty in order to function, then trading is not for you. If certainty is a requirement, then I suggest you become a journalist, an actor or something along those lines. Go into a "word" profession. In word and image professions, such as journalism and acting, being right or wrong is unimportant; what counts are the "correct" words and images. Self-righteous "certainty," regardless of how consistently wrong it may be, is no real hindrance to success as a journalist or an actor. However, trading is different; trading is a total reality profession.

Trading is a numbers business. No amount of words or images, no matter how clever they may be, can ever change the numbers (i.e., prices). That is the difference between words and numbers, as well as the difference between word and image professions and numbers professions. Words are infinitely malleable, the truth of their meaning totally dependent on the honesty of the speaker or writer. Numbers, on the other hand, are completely inflexible, even if the speaker or writer is totally dishonest. Numbers/prices do not lie; they are what they are regardless of who speaks or writes them. Being clever with words and images does not help a trader. In fact, cleverness with words is a hindrance in trading because it diverts attention from truth—from the reality of the numbers.

The self-righteous die young in trading. It is the humble, cold-eyed realist, with enough arrogance to act decisively, who survives and prospers in the trading game.

.....................

Of the three SMR trend/momentum indicators (lines), the short-term momentum indicator (SL) requires the most interpretation or art. Fortunately, most of this interpretation is basic common sense—such as up is positive and down is negative. Both the direction and location of the SL are important; however, unless the SL is at recent highs or lows, the direction is more significant than the location.

Following are some tendencies of the short-term momentum line. Naturally, since the SL is just a short-term indicator, all these tendencies apply for only a couple of days, at most. Furthermore, these tendencies are only tendencies. They are not reliable enough to override clear and solid overall line patterns (of the trend/ML, and of all three lines together). Therefore, apply and use any of the following tendencies lightly.

## TENDENCIES OF THE SHORT-TERM MOMENTUM LINE

1 ~ In terms of direction: The sharper (i.e., faster) the SL is moving up or down, the more weight its current directional move should be given (for the next couple days). Conversely, the shallower (i.e., slower) the SL is moving up or down, the less weight its directional movement should be given.

2 ~ In terms of location: The SL's position relative to its recent (i.e., past few months) highs and lows is meaningful. The closer to these recent highs/lows the SL gets, the more likely the current short-term directional move is about to end, or at least pause.

3 ~ Higher highs and higher lows is a sign of strength, and vice versa.

4 ~ An SL pattern something like this "__I" (sideways followed by turning up sharply) is more positive than a pattern like this "I__" (sharply down followed by moving sideways) and, of course, the same is true if you turn these patterns upside down.

5 ~ A sudden (one or two day) increase in the speed of ascent or descent of the SL is meaningful since it indicates an increase in short-term price momentum.

6 ~ Divergences between price and SL are meaningful. A price/SL divergence occurs when one of the two (price or SL) makes a new recent high (measuring over the past couple weeks) and the other does not. A divergence where the price reaches essentially the same recent high, but the SL misses making a new high by a substantial amount is more reliable than the reverse. In other words, when price and SL diverge (in making or not making new highs/lows) you should treat the SL as a more reliable indicator of the future than the price. (Note: Following is an in-depth explanation of price/SL divergences, along with a chart full of examples that will make all this much clearer.)

## MARGIN-OF-ERROR

For the trend line, a margin-of-error of up to ten days is acceptable. For the intermediate-term momentum line, a margin-of-error of up to five days is permissible. For the short-term momentum line, I use a margin-of-error of up to two days. What this "margin-of-error" means is, if the only technical indicator stopping you from making a trade is the SL pointing in the wrong direction but you can make a sound case the SL will probably turn within two days, then it is OK to override the current direction of the SL (i.e., it is close enough to be within the "margin-of-error").

## ANTICIPATING THE SHORT-TERM MOMENTUM LINE

Anticipating the trend (ten-week moving average) is done by comparing where prices were ten, nine and eight weeks ago to where they are now. Anticipating the intermediate-term momentum line (ML) is done by comparing where the <u>SL</u> was ten to sixteen days ago to where it is now (and will most likely be the next few days). Anticipating the short-term momentum line is done by comparing where the price was two and three days ago to where it is now.

## TRADING AGAINST THE SHORT-TERM MOMENTUM LINE

It is more acceptable to trade against the SL than it is to trade against the trend or the ML, particularly when a market is in a solid concurrent mode. However, in spite of this, over any extended period of time you will tend to make most of your money when positioned with the SL and lose most of your money when positioned against the SL.

So, why not just position with the SL? There are several reasons. The main reason is, if the SL tends to be a day or two late on short-term moves, simply following the SL would produce too many "whiplash"-type trades. Another problem is that the initial thrust of many/most market moves will come with the SL pointed in the opposite direction. This means it is usually more necessary to anticipate changes in the SL than in the other two lines. Unfortunately, it is also more difficult to anticipate changes in the SL than in the other two lines.

## BOTTOM LINE ON THE SHORT-TERM MOMENTUM LINE

The SL is, in a very real sense, the most complex and complicated line of the three SMR trend/momentum lines, and as such it requires the most interpretation or "art" to use well. As in any art, using the SL well requires some practice. However, in spite of its complexity and relative inconsistency, the SL can be very helpful in providing revealing clues about most likely near-term price movement. Therefore, it pays to work at learning the tendencies of this line, as well as developing an "art" to reading it. (*The next two pages show the charts with all three lines.*)

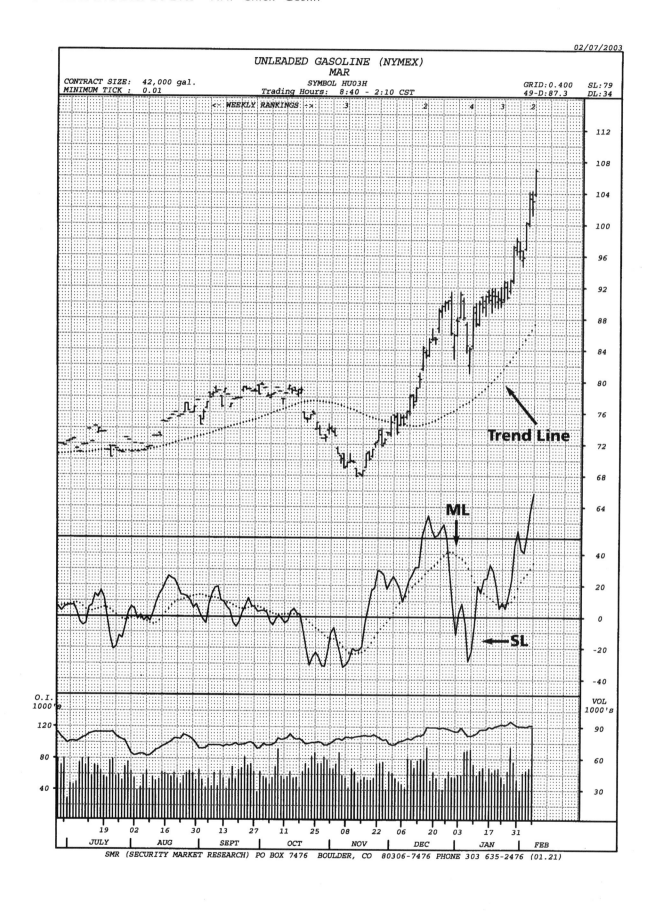

02/07/2003

SILVER (COMEX)
MAR

CONTRACT SIZE:  5000 TROY OZ.                    SYMBOL SI03H                    GRID:1.000      SL:-34
MINIMUM TICK  :  0.001                   Trading Hours:  7:25 - 1:25 CST                49-D:473.9      DL:-2

SMR (SECURITY MARKET RESEARCH) PO BOX 7476  BOULDER, CO  80306-7476 PHONE 303 635-2476 (01.21)

# DIVERGENCES BETWEEN PRICE AND SL

A PRICE/MOMENTUM DIVERGENCE OCCURS WHEN the paths of the price and a momentum oscillator *diverge*, i.e., move differently from one another. Both price and momentum oscillators move up and down. In this up-and-down movement periodic highs and lows are made. Naturally, these periodic highs and lows are only clear afterward;however, once clear they can then be compared to a previous high or low as to whether they are higher or lower. A price/momentum divergence occurs when either the price or oscillator makes a higher high or lower low, and the other does not.

The idea behind price/momentum divergences is that the momentum oscillators tend to be a "truer" reflection of internal price strength or weakness than the price itself. The theory is that if and when the oscillator is *diverging* from the price in terms of its current versus previous high or low, then treat the oscillator as the better (than price) indicator of most likely future price action. For example, if the price makes a higher high but the oscillator makes a lower high, this indicates a lessening of upside price energy and the likelihood of some near-term price weakness.

The chart on the facing page (June 2002, Canadian Dollar) contains multiple price/momentum divergences. Keep in mind that divergences are always very clear after the fact, but not so clear as they are happening. Generally, divergences have to be anticipated; however, doing so is not that difficult once you know how to anticipate the movement of the oscillators.

Compare points 1A and 2A (of the SL) to points 1 and 2 (on the price chart). Point 2A is clearly higher than point 1A, yet the price at the comparable point 2 is clearly lower than point 1. Therefore, the oscillator was showing a definite decrease of downside price momentum despite the fact that the price had pushed to clear new lows. This was a sign of probable near-term price strength and that is exactly what happened. Next compare points 3A and 4A of the SL to the comparable price points 3 and 4. Note how the price made a slightly higher high, while the SL made a slightly lower high;this indicated a decrease in upside momentum and was a sign of some probable near-term price weakness. Again, that is exactly what happened.

Price/momentum divergences are a useful tool in trading; however, they are far from perfect and therefore should only be used as an additional indicator. Divergences should not be allowed to override otherwise solid price energy flows of trend, ML and SL.

**A few basic rules on divergences:**

1 ~ Divergences where the difference in highs/lows in the SL are great but those of the price less so tend to be more reliable than vice versa;
2 ~ Multiple divergences (such as those at points 5A, 6A, and 7A) tend to be more reliable and result in longer lasting moves than single divergences (such as the one at 1A/2A);
3 ~ Divergences occurring with the trend tend to be much more reliable and lasting than those that occur against a trend, especially when the trend is strong.

## BOTTOM LINE ON DIVERGENCES

Pay attention to potential and actual divergences, and act on them when they are with the prevailing price energy flows (trend/ML); however, be careful not to overweight them (especially when they come against a clear trend).

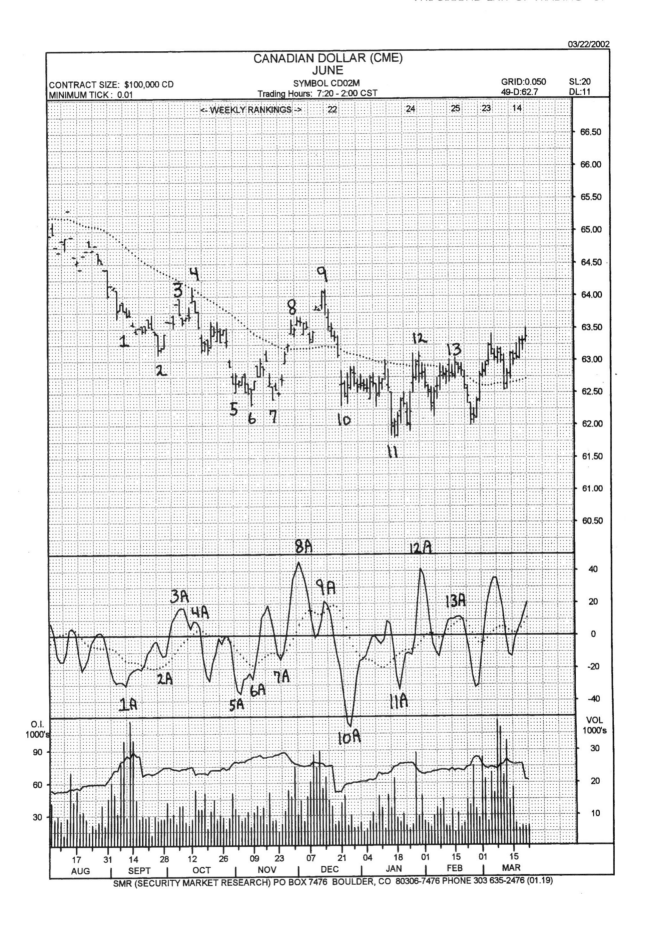

# THE PRICE

THE TREND LINE TELLS US THE DIRECTION TO TRADE. The ML indicates when and how aggressively to trade with the trend. The SL helps with specific timing of trades. These three trend/momentum lines fully qualify as being reasonably reliable indicators of price energy flow. The problem is we are not paid on the direction or location of trend/momentum indicators, no matter how reliable or accurate they may be. In trading we are paid solely on "price." In the end we are always trading price. Therefore, it is the price chart that helps us decide exactly where to get in and out. The price chart helps answer the specific "where" and "when" questions.

Never forget this: We are not trading trend/momentum lines, supply/demand, sentiment indicators or any kind of "logic"—we are trading price! The function of the trend/momentum indicators (the lines) is to help us trade the price. The reason we rely on the lines to help us trade the price is because the lines tend to reflect price energy flows more clearly than simple price movement alone. Therefore, the lines can be "read" well on a more consistent basis than looking at the price alone.

Throughout the examples later in this book I will point out some fairly reliable price chart patterns. Unfortunately, some of the most popular price chart patterns—such as double bottoms, head and shoulder patterns, and trend lines—I do not find reliable enough to pay much attention to or use. These types of chart patterns are artificial and arbitrary, and as such simply do not comply with the natural laws of trading/pricing. However, among the chart patterns I have found to be reliable enough to use are bull/bear flags, breakouts, false breakouts, island reversals, and dips/rallies. Additionally, these chart patterns do comply and adhere to the natural laws of trading.

**1 ~ BULL AND BEAR FLAGS:**  A bull flag is formed when a market moves up sharply and then moves sideways for anywhere from a few days to a week or so. This creates an image of a flagpole (the sharp up move), with a flag waving to its right (the period of sideways action). A bear flag is just the opposite, a several day sharp down move, followed by a week or so of sideways price movement (i.e., an upside down flag pole with the flag waving out to the right). This chart pattern simply reflects a price surge followed by a pause. The normal expectation for bull/bear flags is an eventual *continuation* of the initial price surge (i.e., a move in the direction of the "flagpole").

**2 ~ BREAKOUTS:**  A breakout occurs when the price finally and decisively moves beyond a clear chart resistance (on upside) or support (on downside). Support/resistance levels on a chart are simply places on the price chart where up or down moves have stopped "several" times in the recent past. Again, this is simply the "law of continuation" in action. Any with-the-trend breakouts should be expected to continue, while against-the-trend breakouts are less likely to continue.

**3 ~ FALSE BREAKOUTS:**  A false breakout (or, more accurately, a "short-lived" breakout) is when a price clearly moves beyond (breaks through) a well established resistance level, but then fairly soon afterward moves right back below this resistance level. (The same is true on the downside with support levels.) The amount of time this "false" breakout holds before failing can be any-where from a day or two to a couple of weeks.

A false breakout is a clear case of a failure to continue, and as such is a strong sign of price energy "exhaustion." I have found false breakouts to be among the most reliable chart patterns. I have found they frequently signal at least an intermediate-term (i.e., in terms of weeks) ending of the preexisting price energy flow and often even can mark major tops or bottoms. It seems that what happens on false breakouts is that an existing price energy flow uses its last burst of directional energy to push through a stubborn support or resistance level, only then to find this effort has exhausted all remaining energy for that direction, thus the price then has nowhere to go but head back in the opposite direction.

**4 ~ ISLAND REVERSALS:** An island reversal is a "cluster" of days (or, occasionally, a single day) on the price charts that (due to a sudden and big reversal in price direction) is left standing distinctly alone and apart from the rest of the prices on the chart (i.e., it looks like an island). An island reversal "cluster" can be anywhere from one day up to several months, but the key point is that this price cluster stands clearly alone and apart on the chart.

A classic "island" will stand truly apart from the rest of the chart; however, this is not a requirement. Any cluster of price "bars" on the chart that are left standing apart from the rest of the daily price bars is an island. As with false breakouts, islands are also a good indication the previously existing price energy flow has been exhausted and a new directional flow is now in effect.

I have found island reversals to be quite reliable in indicating an end to the existing price energy flow and the beginning of at least an intermediate-term (i.e., weeks) new one. In other words, island reversals are like false breakouts in that they are very good indicators of at least intermediate-term tops and bottoms.

**5 ~ DIPS/RALLIES:** When I started out as a broker, one of the veteran traders used to tell me to "buy the dips." Great, I would say to myself, what's a dip?

When a market is in a clear uptrend, a "dip" is defined as two days down or the low of the past three days. Conversely, when a market is in a clear downtrend, a "rally" is defined as two days up or the highs of the past three days.

When the trend is solidly up, a couple of days of downside action will usually bring in new buyers as well as start to reduce selling. The bulls will use the dip to initiate positions, and those who have been short (with losses) will use it to get out, or at least lighten up.

Trading is a competition. When I buy the lows of the past several days in an uptrending market, I may not be buying at the best price of the next few days, but I will be buying at a better price than every buyer of the previous few days, and that is a start.

## BOTTOM LINE ON PRICE AND PRICE CHARTS

The correct procedure when reading a chart is to look at the indicators (the lines) first, and then the price chart. However remember, in the end, price is the only "indicator" that counts. Price is more important than any and all technical indicators, regardless of how reliable these may be. Indicators are there to indicate probabilities of price movement, but in the end, price movement itself rules.

# THE THREE-POINT SYSTEM
## (The mathematics, or science, of the "lines")

(**NOTE**: *The first time through, this point system may seem a little complicated, but once we go through a few charts it will become clear and easy to calculate.*)

While there are only three trend/momentum lines on the SMR charts, sometimes they can look like they are going in ten different directions at once. In other words, at times the line patterns can be very confusing. Therefore, in order to clarify and quantify them I developed a mathematical point system.

The beauty of numbers and lines is their objectivity. A line that is moving up is moving up, regardless of how much you or I would like it to be moving down. Lines will always have an absolute objectivity to them. They will be pointing up, down or sideways, and no amount of rationalization or interpretation can ever change this.

The three SMR lines have repeatedly (for over a quarter of a century) proven themselves to be "reasonably reliable" indicators of a market's existing long-, intermediate-, and short-term trend and momentum. Therefore, it stands to reason that whenever the "majority" of these three reasonably reliable indicators of trend and momentum are pointing in the same direction, then the "odds" will tend to favor the price moving in that direction for the immediate future. This is the second law of trading at work: Continuation is more likely than change.

The "three-point system" is designed to mathematically *quantify* what these three lines are showing at any one moment in time. This is done by assigning each line a point value of plus one (+1), zero (0), or minus one (-1), depending on location and direction.

1 ~ The "trend line" is awarded points based solely on its current direction: plus one (+1) point if trend is up, zero (0) points if trend is sideways, and minus one (-1) point if trend is down.

2 ~ The intermediate-term momentum line (the ML) is awarded points based on both its direction and location (meaning whether it is up or down and whether it is above or below zero); plus one half (+1/2) point if pointing up or minus one half (-1/2) point if pointing down; and, plus one half (+1/2) if it is above zero, or minus one half (-1/2) if below zero.

3 ~ The short-term momentum line (the SL), like the trend, is awarded points based solely on direction: plus one (+1) point if pointing up, zero (0) if sideways, and minus one (-1) if down.

The basic theory of the three-point system is that whenever a significant majority of three reasonably reliable trend/momentum indicators are pointing in the same direction, then the odds should favor the price moving in that direction for at least the next day (or few days).

As a rule you should only trade with the trend; therefore, it is only logical to count only the with-the-trend points. Therefore, when the trend is up, only count the pluses, and when the trend is down, only count the minuses. (In other words, do **NOT** "net out" the total points by subtracting "minuses" from "pluses.")

## REVIEW OF THE LINES AND THE POINT SYSTEM

1 ~ The trend line is a ten-week, or 50-day, moving average of the price. It tells you the direction to trade the market. Only pay attention to this line's direction. There is no "high" or "low" for this line, only a direction. Award one (+1) point if the line is currently pointing up, zero (0) points if sideways, and minus one (-1) point if down. Give this line a "margin-of-error" of up to two weeks or ten days (i.e., meaning you may adjust the point value up or down if you see a "realistic" probability the trend line will change direction within the margin-of-error's time frame of ten days).

2 ~ The intermediate-term momentum line (ML) is an approximately three-week moving average of the short-term momentum line (SL). Since it is a moving average of an oscillator (the SL), the ML will also oscillate. These oscillations or cycles tend to reflect intermediate-term cycles of price movement. Both the direction and location of the ML are significant and should be measured. Award one half point based on direction (+1/2 if up, -1/2 if down). Award the other half point based on whether it is above or below the zero line (+1/2 if above zero, -1/2 if below). The margin-of-error for this line is anywhere from three to five days. (Note: If this line is at zero, then you can either assign zero points or assign points based on where it will most likely be the next trading day.)

3 ~ The short-term momentum line (SL) is an oscillator constructed by subtracting a roughly two-week moving average of the closing price from about a half-week moving average of the closing price. Only the direction of this line is counted for point system purposes (+1 if up, -1 if down, 0 if sideways). However, since this line is in some ways a short-term timing tool, it is also important to pay attention to its current relative position versus its highs and lows of the past few weeks. As a general "rule," it does not pay to buy when the SL is in the area of its recent highs or sell when it's in the area of recent lows. Conversely, if positioning with the trend, it will often pay to sell when SL is in area of recent highs (when trend down) and buy when in area of recent lows (when trend up). The exception to this rule is when a market is *solidly concurrent*. In these situations, where the SL is and what it is doing are relatively unimportant.

In essence what this point system does is tell you at a glance what the current trend/momentum "status" of any market is at the moment. This "Status" is a snapshot picture of the cumulative price energy flow of a market at a specific moment in time. Knowing the Status of a market helps us take advantage of the second law of trading—continuation is more likely than change— because it gives a good indication of what current price energy flow is and thus what continuation should be.

The point system mathematically establishes the current trend/momentum "Status" of a market. The Status is, in effect, a "position indicator" since it represents what the trend/momentum lines indicate the position should be in any market at any one moment in time.

## BASIC TRADING RULE OF THE "THREE-POINT SYSTEM"

1 ~ If the trend is up and the point total is plus two (+2) or more, then the trend/momentum "Status" is "Bullish." A Bullish Status means that a clear majority of our reasonably reliable trend/momentum indicators are pointing up and so the odds for the immediate future favor the price moving up. Therefore, when the Status of a market is Bullish, long positions are justified.

2 ~ If the trend is up and the point total is plus one and a half points or less, or if the trend is down and the point total is minus one and a half points or less (i.e., anytime the points total is between plus one and a half and minus one and a half points), then the "Status" of the market is "Neutral." What this means is that the trend/momentum lines do not indicate a clear price energy flow at the moment. Therefore, when Status is Neutral, then "sidelines" is the indicated position.

3 ~ If the trend is down and the point total is minus two (-2) points or more (down to minus three), then the "Status" of the market is "Bearish" and short positions are justified.

## "CONFIRMING" RULE

As a *confirmation* of current intermediate-term momentum, you should have at least one half (1/2) point from the intermediate-term momentum line (ML) in the direction you wish to trade. To "confirm" or "qualify" a trade, at least a half point needs to come from the ML. However, it is permissible to override this "confirming" rule if the trend is particularly "solid"—meaning it will be virtually impossible to change the trend's direction for the next few weeks.

**TO SUMMARIZE:** Two or more with-the-trend points and Status is Bullish if trend up or Bearish if trend down. Anywhere in between, from plus one and a half to minus one and a half, and Status is Neutral. For a fully legitimate Bullish or Bearish Status, at least one half point needs to come from the ML.

Basically the "Status" (or position indicator, if you prefer) indicates the most favorable position at any specific moment based on *current* trend/moment. However, we trade "futures," not "pasts." Therefore, it is vitally important to always look ahead and anticipate what the Status will most likely be tomorrow and the few days after tomorrow (by comparing the most likely numbers to be added on to the moving averages to the numbers that will most likely be dropped off). By looking ahead and anticipating, we are attempting to be positioned in line with what the Status will be tomorrow and the next day or so. Therefore, we need to always look at both current Status *and* at what the Status will most likely be over the next few days.

## BOTTOM LINE ON THE THREE-POINT SYSTEM

The "Status" (or position indicator) is a mathematical formula designed to clearly and objectively measure the prevailing trend/momentum situation at any one moment in time. The SMR trend/momentum lines and the three-point system of using them are the "science" of trading. The daily interpretation of these three trend/momentum lines and their patterns is the "art" of "reading" the lines. Unfortunately, I do not believe it is possible to use the Status as a straight, mechanical trading system. The lines are trailing or lagging indicators which means that waiting for them to be positioned clearly in one direction too often ends up being a little too late to produce consistent profits. Therefore, we have to apply a little bit of art to interpreting the line patterns. We have to learn to anticipate them; we have to learn to "read" them.

The following example is a "classic" case of trend/momentum trading. Naturally, for my first example I have chosen a price move that "worked" according to plan. In the learning of any art it is best to start with simple, clear cases, and then from these move on to the more complex. Later I will present a wide variety of examples. Some will follow the rules/laws well, others will be more complex. However, let us start with a classic case.

While writing this book I was also putting out a daily market letter covering about twenty futures markets. All of the daily market commentaries accompanying the examples in this book are reprinted verbatim from that daily market letter. They are as I wrote them at the time. In other words, they are "real time" observations and trading suggestions. In a very few instances I have made some very minor editing corrections to make them read better; however, I have not gone back and changed anything in them in an attempt to make me look better.

What I will do on this, and the other chart examples, is give you my commentary as it was written at the time and then add some after-the-fact critique of this real-time daily commentary. I will point out what I did right, as well as what I overlooked. The point here is not to show my particular ability or inability to "read" markets. The objective is to show how the natural laws of trading apply in real life examples, as well as reveal how easy it is to make trading mistakes when in the "heat of battle." There is a big difference between looking at charts after the fact, with no money riding on the outcome, and using them to trade in real time when meaningful money is at stake.

(**NOTE:** *When I wrote the following market commentaries, December Cocoa was the front/active month, and so naturally I was covering it. However, within a couple of weeks the most active month became March and my coverage in the letter also switched. Therefore, to keep it simple I have used the March charts right from the start, rather than switching from December to March half way through the example. The two months, December and March Cocoa, moved in tandem during this period with the only difference being that March was priced about ten points higher. Therefore, I have made the appropriate point adjustments in my commentaries. Again, the point of this and the other examples is not whether I was right or wrong at the time but how they illustrate the approach and method laid out in this book.*)

Once again, the commentary at the top of each page is what I wrote in "real time." The commentary below these "real time" comments is an "after-action" critique of both what I originally wrote as well as the basic approach/method laid out in the book and how it worked in this case.

I will take up the third law of trading, prices fluctuate, later. This is the business law and is very important to the bottom line. However, first let us work on the art and science of reading the lines and prices.

# March 2002 Cocoa (Nov 5)

The following is my assessment of the situation in Cocoa, written after the close of the market on November 5, 2001:

## REAL-TIME COMMENTARY

**11/5 (Monday):** Mar Cocoa - Status - Neutral. Trend sideways, ML neutral, SL neutral to marginally negative, line pattern neutral and indicates sidelines. Price action slightly negative on fairly minor down day but price held at recent support levels. Trend indecisive but if can mount any kind of rally over next week or two then trend will turn clearly up again. ML on good up cycle and, like trend, also in position for sustained up cycle if can get any strength from here over next week or so. SL on pattern of slightly higher highs/lows and in position for decent bullish divergence (since price close to recent lows but SL still a ways away). Line pattern remains too neutral to make good case for position (in either direction), but is now set up nicely for a good bullish pattern if can rally from this area over next few days. So can once again begin to go long in this area on an "anticipation" basis. Bottom line: Lines says sidelines but prefer light "anticipation" buys in 990 to 1000 area tomorrow with idea of adding if price can hold, or rally, from here over the next few days (a close under 980 would make short-term momentum too negative to stick with longs, so would use that level for stops for time being).

...................

## AFTER-ACTION CRITIQUE

Status is Neutral. Trend is indecisive, so zero points there. ML is below zero, which equals minus half (-1/2) point, but is on an up cycle, which means plus half (+1/2) point. SL is pointing down, so that means minus half (-1) point. Since trend neutral, status is neutral. On the chart I have circled the price from ten weeks earlier. Note how current price is marginally higher than ten weeks earlier, but is clearly higher than prices eight and nine weeks earlier. This meant trend would turn clearly up even if price stayed the same, and any decent up move in price would turn trend decisively up. Note also that ML is on an up cycle, and since SL is well above where it was three weeks earlier (currently +6, three weeks ago -22), could anticipate ML continuing to move up. Also note how SL is on a series of higher lows/highs (a bullish pattern). In addition, have already put in one bullish divergence between price and SL and are on the verge of a second. So, what I saw when looking at this chart was a neutral situation at the moment, but also one that had some very positive potential. What I was looking for here was some price strength over the next few days, which would turn SL up for third higher low, because if this happened, then would have a solidly bullish pattern. Situation here was potentially very positive, meaning could make case to start buying "in anticipation." I chose a close below 980 for a stop since such a close would greatly accelerate the down move in SL, thus make any quick turn back up (in SL) highly unlikely, and would therefore negate all of the above anticipations. It is frequently necessary to anticipate line movements and overall patterns, but when/if what is anticipated does not come about, you then must adjust to the new reality. In this situation a good case could be made for these anticipations, plus the risk was low since stop point was only a couple hundred dollars per contract away (fifteen to twenty points).

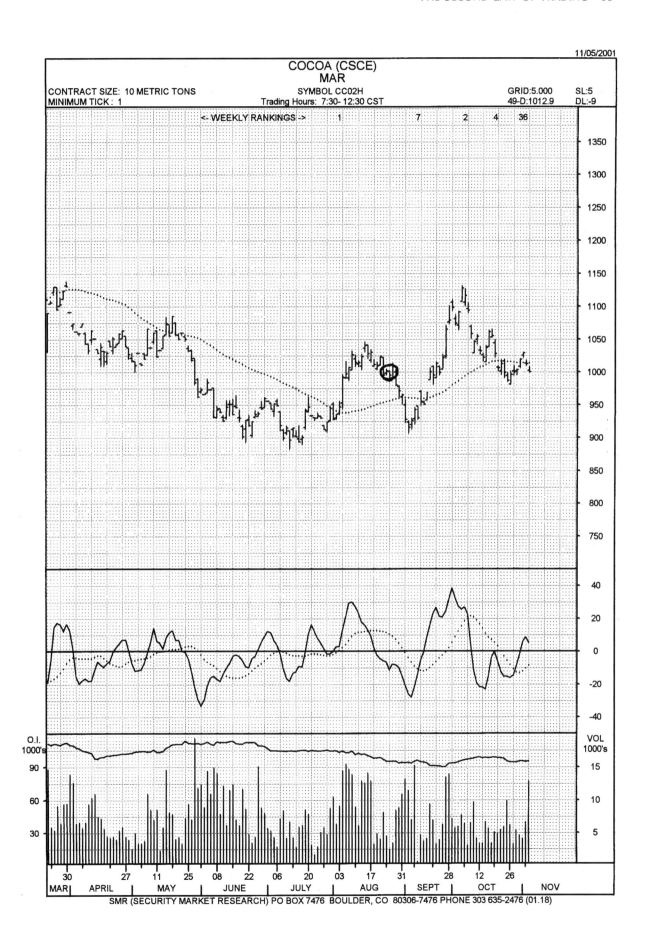

# March 2002 Cocoa (Nov 6)

## REAL-TIME COMMENTARY

**11/6 (Tuesday):** Mar Cocoa - Status - Neutral (to Bullish). Trend sideways, ML neutral, SL neutral to slightly negative, line pattern neutral and indicates sidelines. Price action neutral on quiet sideways day, but at moment see sideways here as more of a positive than a negative. So have a potentially decently positive situation now since trend will steadily strengthen to upside next couple weeks (as long as hold here or higher). ML in slight up cycle and in position for a sustained up cycle if can get any strength, and SL making some slightly higher highs/lows (as well as being in position for moderate bullish divergence, again if can get any strength). Not the most positive of pictures, and this market difficult to trade due to shortened hours (especially out here on West Coast since trading takes place very early in morning), but still can make decent case for light "anticipation" longs. Bottom line: Lines say sidelines, but continue to prefer light anticipation longs with stops at 984.

.....................

## AFTER-ACTION CRITIQUE

Status still neutral since trend remains indecisive. Points for Status are unchanged from day earlier. Overall situation basically unchanged from previous day, but in this type of situation I saw a quiet, sideways day as a positive since did not increase the current downward short-term price energy flow. Pattern was now set up well to turn solidly positive, so light anticipation longs were fully justified here, especially since stop point remained very close. On other hand, close stops were merited because even a moderate down day from here would turn the line pattern too negative to stick with longs. A close under 984 area would put price too far under the 50-day moving average line for comfort (if long) and tilt the trend clearly to downside. In addition, such a close would have accelerated the down move in SL, thus making it unlikely it would turn up for a third higher low. So, market appeared right on the "fence" here with upside having better odds (or at least much better potential).

At this point the market was on a two and a half day dip. When I started out in this business (at the Chicago Merc), the more experienced traders would always say "buy the dips, sell the rallies." This always sounded like a good idea, but none of them ever told me how to define dips and rallies. Naturally everyone wants to buy dips rather than rallies, and sell rallies rather than dips. After all, the objective is to sell higher than buy, and buy lower than sell.

Over the years I have found that when a market is in a solid trend, then most of its short-term counter-trend moves will tend to be limited to two or three days. Remember, on a short-term basis I define a "dip" in an uptrending market as either two days down or the low of the past three days of trading (and vice versa in a downtrending market—two days up or the highs of past three days). So, even though this market was not in a clear trend at moment, it was on a normal sized dip. In other words, chart showed a potentially quite positive situation, price was "attractive" (best price of past several days) and stop point was close—meaning worth putting on some anticipation longs.

11/06/2001

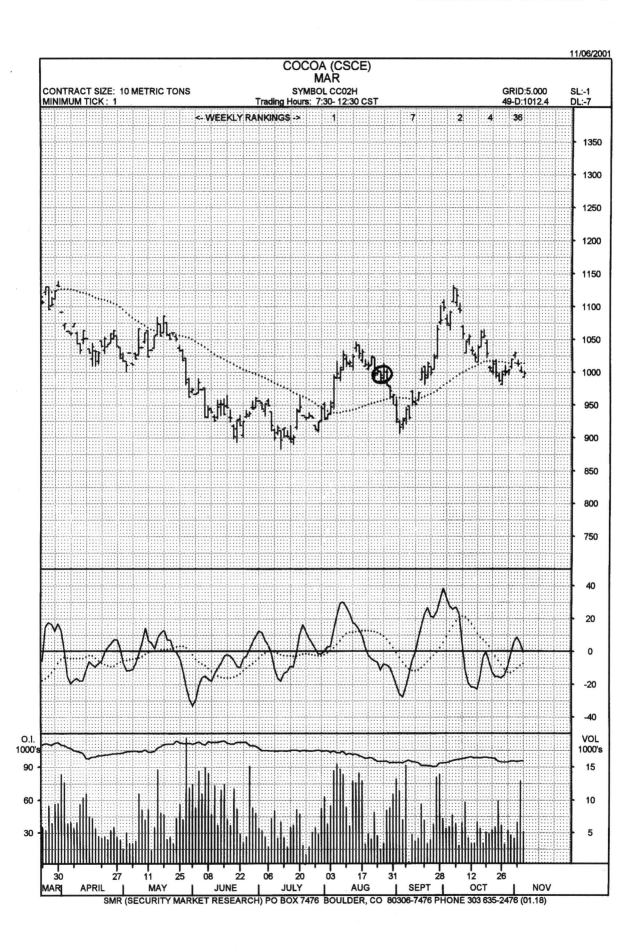

COCOA (CSCE)
MAR

CONTRACT SIZE: 10 METRIC TONS          SYMBOL CC02H                        GRID:5.000     SL:-1
MINIMUM TICK : 1               Trading Hours: 7:30- 12:30 CST              49-D:1012.4     DL:-7

SMR (SECURITY MARKET RESEARCH) PO BOX 7476  BOULDER, CO  80306-7476  PHONE 303 635-2476 (01.18)

# March 2002 Cocoa (Nov 7)

**REAL-TIME COMMENTARY**

**11/7 (Wednesday):** Mar Cocoa - Status - Bullish. Trend up, ML positive, SL positive, line pattern positive and indicates long. Price action very positive on up spike type day and clear breakout to upside. Market now in fairly solid concurrent mode to upside and odds always favor upside when this the case. SL has now made three higher lows and on verge of making third higher high and this also quite positive. Can make good case today a with-trend, non-news-related spike to upside and these quite reliably indicate more to go on upside. So, all signs positive here at moment, meaning odds clearly favor higher and possibly sharply higher. Bottom line: Can be (and still go) long with stops 1015 on close basis for now.

.....................

**AFTER-ACTION CRITIQUE**

Status has turned solidly Bullish. The trend is up so have +1 point there. The ML is on an up cycle so have +1/2 point there; however, it is still below zero, although this -1/2 point is not counted since trend is up. (Remember, we only count points that are in the direction of trend.) SL has turned up so can count +1 point there as well. Therefore, point total at moment here is +2 1/2 points and so Status has now switched from Neutral to Bullish. What this means is that a clear majority of normally reliable indicators of trend and momentum are now pointing up and so the odds favor the price *continuing* to move up.

A series of higher lows and highs on the SL is a clear indication that short-term momentum is gathering strength (and vice versa for the downside). In addition, have put in a classic double divergence here. I have always found this type of double divergence to be among the most reliable.

In price/momentum divergences the basic rule is the momentum line carries more weight than the price. In this particular case, the first divergence (between the lows of price and SL on about 18 October compared to those on about 30 October) was a somewhat less reliable type—i.e., the price made a significantly lower low, but the SL just barely made a higher low. Whereas the second price/SL divergence here is a more reliable type. Comparing the lows of price and SL from about 30 October to those of 5 November shows that the SL missed making a new low by substantial amount, while the price just barely missed making new low. Divergences where price just barely makes a new low (or does not quite make a new low as in this case) but the SL misses making a new low by a substantial amount tend to be more reliable than the reverse. (And, of course, vice versa when going the other direction.)

I selected the new stop point to be slightly above the previous day's close since viewed a close back at this level (or lower) as clear sign this up move simply a one day aberration and thus best to get out. (The reference to "non-news-related, with-trend spike" is a rule that will be covered later.) Once it was obvious this market was going to close above 1025, then could have justified taking a full long position. At moment here have all signs clearly positive, so longs were fully justified. If not already in, then would try to buy unchanged or better on open, and if unable after first 15 to 30 minutes, then would buy at market.

11/07/2001

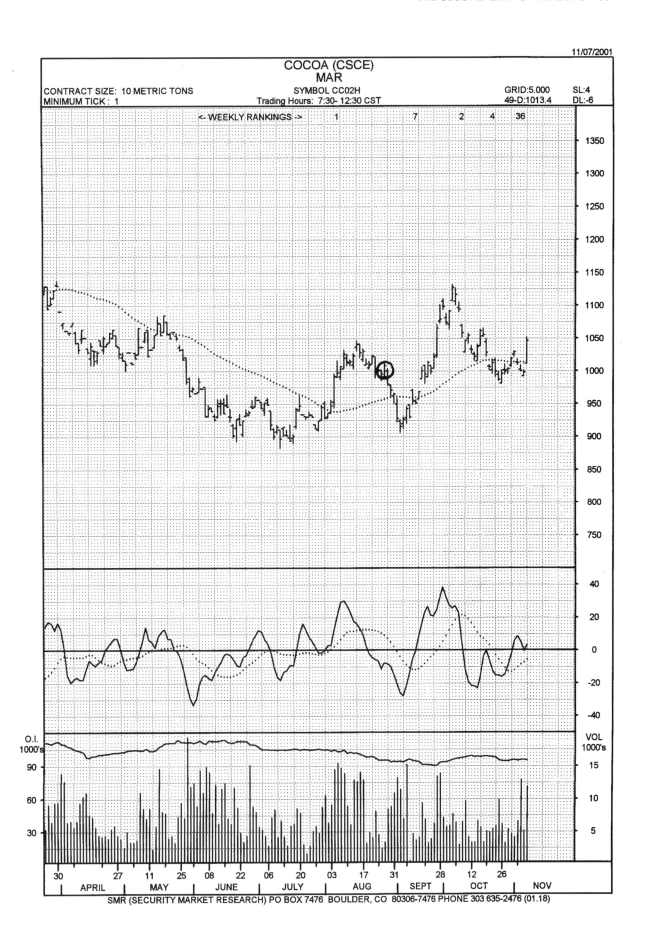

COCOA (CSCE)
MAR

CONTRACT SIZE:  10 METRIC TONS
MINIMUM TICK : 1

SYMBOL CC02H
Trading Hours: 7:30- 12:30 CST

GRID:5.000
49-D:1013.4

SL:4
DL:-6

<- WEEKLY RANKINGS ->      1        7      2      4    36

SMR (SECURITY MARKET RESEARCH) PO BOX 7476  BOULDER, CO  80306-7476 PHONE 303 635-2476 (01.18)

# March 2002 Cocoa (Nov 8)

## REAL-TIME COMMENTARY

**11/8 (Thursday):** Mar Cocoa - Status - Bullish. Trend up, ML positive, SL positive, line pattern positive and indicates long. Price action quite positive on second big up day in a row. Market now in solid concurrent mode to upside and so odds favor even higher prices ahead. Yesterday (and today as well) clearly qualify as with-the-trend, non-news-related up spikes and spike rule is that this type of up spike much more likely to continue than be short-lived. This market one of strongest commodities at moment (if not strongest) and so on relative strength basis one of best to be long (always want to work at being long the strongest markets and short the weakest). Big rally off the lows couple months ago ran up 250 points in three weeks and would not be surprised to see similar or bigger move this time. If figure "official" line entry point on this trade was 1040 in Dec and 1050 in March, and use rough margin level of $1000 (this a little above exchange minimum but a realistic margin level), then have already reached 50 percent of margin profit. However, acceptable to override this profit taking level when/if market is in solid concurrent mode and since this case here prefer waiting to take any profits. Bottom line: Can be long with stops essentially out of range (can go without stops for now).

....................

## AFTER-ACTION CRITIQUE

Status remains bullish because point totals are the same: uptrend equals +1 point, ML in up cycle equals +1/2 point (do not count -1/2 point for ML below zero since trend is up and only count with trend points), and SL up equals +1 point; therefore, have 2 1/2 points with trend meaning Status is Bullish. Market has been in concurrent mode to upside for a week and is now in very solid concurrent mode because both trend and ML have virtually zero chance of turning down anytime soon. Price would have to drop below prices of nine, ten weeks ago to turn trend down—price now 1100, and nine, ten weeks ago was in 950 area, so this highly unlikely. For ML to turn down, SL would have to drop well below zero, and since it is currently at almost +20 and moving up sharply, this also highly unlikely.

On the price chart have a clear upside breakout with both of past two days gapping higher. Therefore, all signs about as positive as can get at moment.

The first law of trading states that the future is unknown. This is the bad news law of trading. The second law of trading is the good news law since it states that while the future may be unknown, it is also more likely to be a continuation of current trend/momentum than a change; and the stronger and more solid current trend/momentum, the more likely it is to continue.

Many (amateur) traders will look at a situation like this one and will be anxious to take profits if long; and if not already long, will not get in here due to feeling it is too late. This is the wrong approach, wrong in the sense that it is against natural laws. Even if this market has reached a high area, it is extremely unlikely it will reverse either quickly or meaningfully. Therefore, if long here should stay long with no stops necessary; and if not long, could (and should) still go long. Bet continuation, not change.

11/08/2001

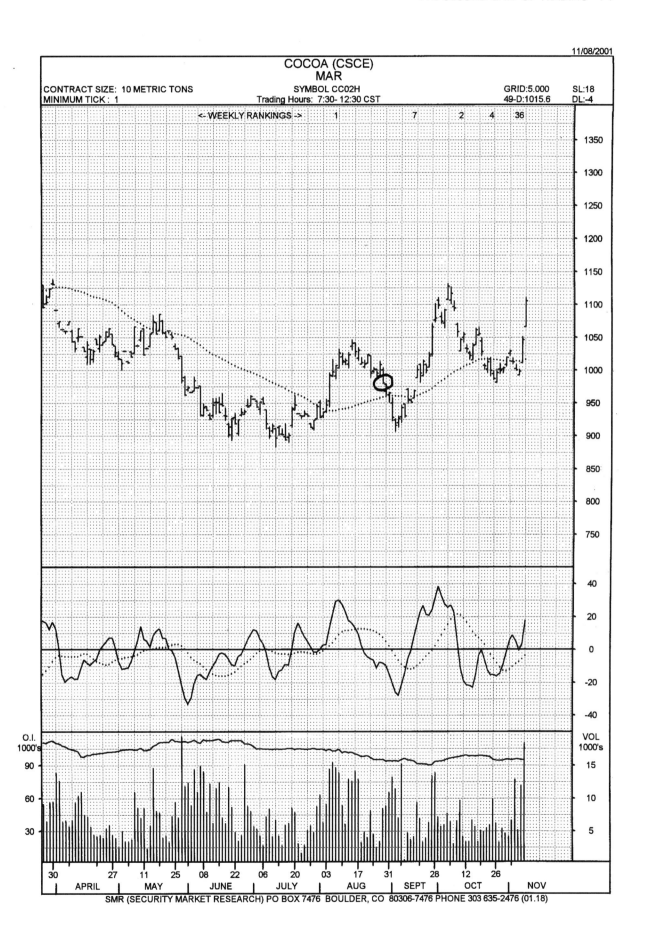

COCOA (CSCE)
MAR

CONTRACT SIZE: 10 METRIC TONS
MINIMUM TICK : 1

SYMBOL CC02H
Trading Hours: 7:30- 12:30 CST

GRID:5.000
49-D:1015.6

SL:18
DL:-4

<- WEEKLY RANKINGS ->     1        7      2      4     36

SMR (SECURITY MARKET RESEARCH) PO BOX 7476  BOULDER, CO  80306-7476  PHONE 303 635-2476 (01.18)

# March 2002 Cocoa (Nov 9)

**REAL-TIME COMMENTARY**

**11/9 (Friday):** Mar Cocoa - Status - Bullish. Trend up, ML positive, SL positive, line pattern positive and indicates long. Price action very positive on third big up day in a row (and each has come with opening gap and close on day's highs). Market remains in very solid concurrent mode to upside and so odds favor even higher prices ahead. Have now made 100 percent of margin profit from "official" line entry levels two days ago and slightly more than 150 percent of margin profit from "anticipation" entry points of three days ago. Can always make decent case to take at least some profits when reach these profit levels, especially when do so in two, three days; however, see little likelihood have seen any kind of highs yet (although could always back off briefly). This market currently strongest market on board and basic rule is to be long strongest markets. All signs remain solidly positive here and so see no reason to take any profits yet, but getting due for some kind of dip. Usually when have this big a move in such a short period of time leave a lot of traders behind, as well as get a lot of shorts "stuck" very badly. Therefore, first dip (day or two down) will be invariably brief and quickly there-after will make new highs. COT remains neutral and so not a factor at moment. Bottom line: Can be long with stops out of range (do not need stops on longs here, regardless of where bought them—even if at today's or Monday's highs—since any dip from here will almost certainly be shallow and short-lived).

....................

**AFTER-ACTION CRITIQUE**

Status remains solidly Bullish with point total still +2 1/2 and on verge of going to +3 (since ML will move above zero tomorrow). All trend/momentum and price chart indicators are solidly positive; therefore, since "continuation is more likely than change," should continue to move higher, or at least will take quite a bit of choppy, sideways action to fully stop upside momentum.

Again, many traders who may have bought few days earlier will feel a great urge to take profits here; however, if going by natural laws and probabilities, the best approach is to stay long. In addition, many traders who may have missed the move will not be able to buy at these "high" levels, yet natural laws say odds still clearly favor more to upside. Therefore, both odds and risk/reward remain good for upside.

"COT" mentioned above stands for Commitment of Traders report and will cover that later. Will also cover the references to percentage of margin profit later. What I am trying to do at the moment is simply show you a classic example of how natural laws of trading apply to price movement.

If you compare the current three day up surge to the up surges this market made in early August (from 925 area up to 1050) and in early September (again from 925 up to 1125), you will see that the trend/momentum line patterns were not nearly as powerful then as they are at the moment. While in both those cases the moves were eventually given back, it took a period of time of choppy, sideways type price movement before the upside price energy had dissipated enough to let prices turn down. The point is, powerful upside energy usually needs to stop first before it can turn down.

11/09/2001

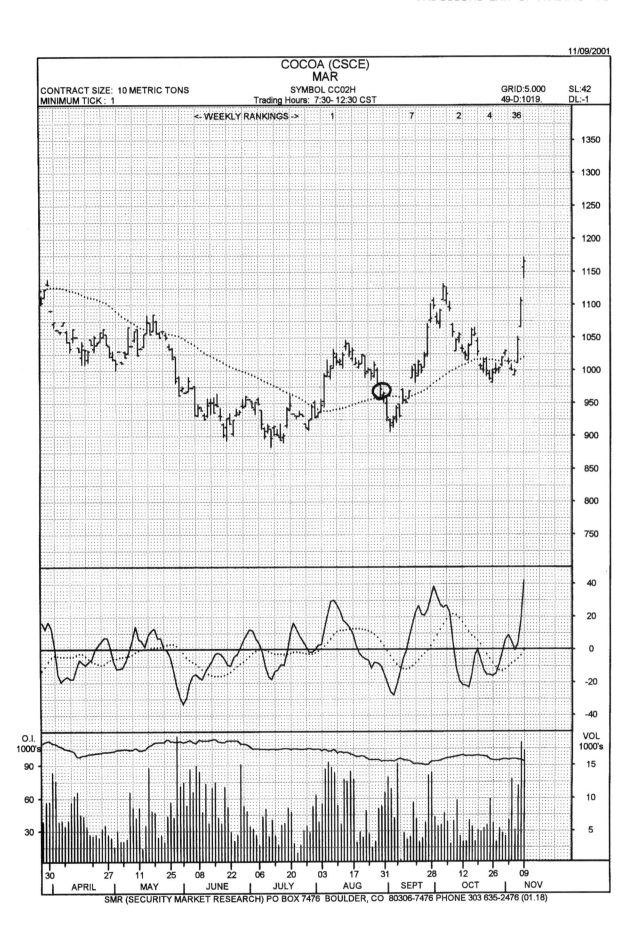

COCOA (CSCE)
MAR

CONTRACT SIZE: 10 METRIC TONS
MINIMUM TICK : 1

SYMBOL CC02H
Trading Hours: 7:30- 12:30 CST

GRID:5.000
49-D:1019.

SL:42
DL:-1

SMR (SECURITY MARKET RESEARCH) PO BOX 7476  BOULDER, CO  80306-7476 PHONE 303 635-2476 (01.18)

# March 2002 Cocoa (Nov 12)

## REAL-TIME COMMENTARY

**11/12 (Monday):** Dec Cocoa - Status - Bullish. Trend up, ML positive, SL positive, line pattern positive and indicates long. Price action neutral to slightly positive as closed unchanged, but came back well from a minor early dip. Market remains in very solid concurrent mode to upside and so odds favor higher prices ahead. This market currently just about strongest of commodities and basic rule of trading is should always look for any legitimate technical reasons to be/go long the strongest markets, and have plenty of legitimate reasons to be/go long this one here. When have both trend and momentum this strong, and are so "early" in a good move, will rarely get much, if any, counter-trend movement for at least a couple weeks, and will usually get more to upside. Therefore, odds continue to favor upside here and can continue to make good case to be (and still go) long. Bottom line: Can be (and still go) long here with stops out of range (do not see any need for stops for now as would take a close at least under 1095 before start to get concerned about being long).

. . . . . . . . . . . . . . . . . . .

## AFTER-ACTION CRITIQUE

Status remains solidly Bullish with plus three points. Uptrend equals +1, ML both above zero and on up cycle equals +1 (+1/2 for each) and up SL equals +1. In addition, market remains in extremely solid concurrent mode since neither trend nor ML have any realistic chance of turning down any time soon. For trend to turn down, price would have to drop below 950; and for ML to turn down, SL would have to drop below zero—and neither of these even remotely likely.

Note in daily letter how I kept saying it was not too late to buy, and if long already, there was absolutely no need to consider taking profits in spite of profits being substantial. Also, I continued to see no need for stops of any kind here since would have taken a one day collapse in price to turn picture anywhere near negative enough to indicate should get out.

Therefore, at moment all signs remained very positive with odds for upside still high. Furthermore, even at these levels, risk/reward on longs was still very favorable. Also might note how couple days earlier I had mentioned how the previous up surge had moved price 250 (to 300) points up from low to high, and since current up surge is much more powerful, could reasonably expect to see at least similar amount up, and probably more. At this point, the up move had picked up 175 points, which meant it was reasonable to expect considerably more upside potential.

Of course, no market goes straight up forever. No matter how positive the price energy flow, there will always be brief pauses and minor dips of some kind. The point is that in this type of powerful situation you should be mentally prepared for minor dip/brief pause and not let them bother you. In fact, a trader could be prepared to initiate new longs if/when did get such a dip.

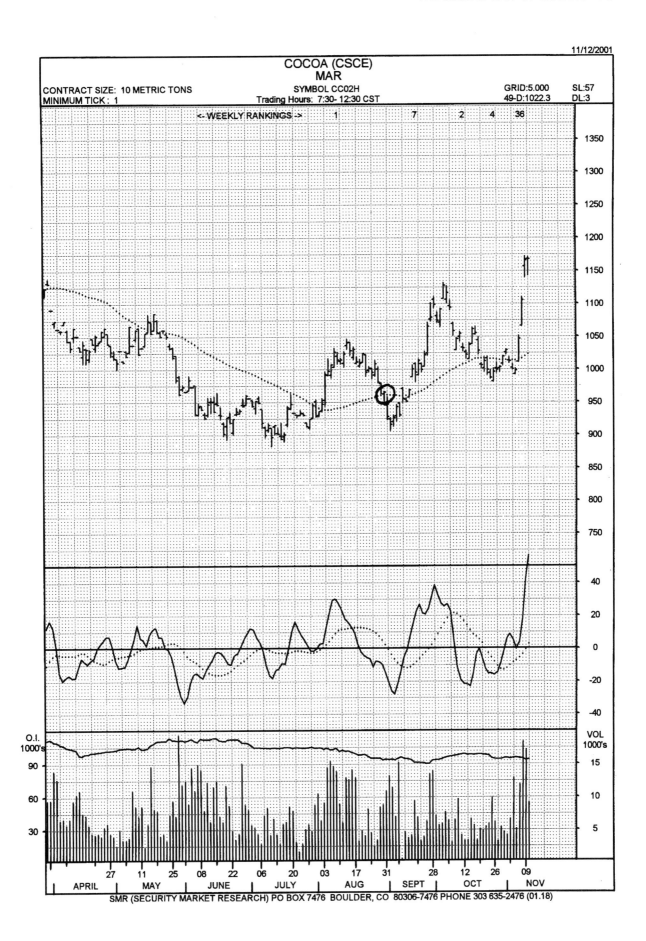

SMR (SECURITY MARKET RESEARCH) PO BOX 7476  BOULDER, CO 80306-7476 PHONE 303 635-2476 (01.18)

11/12/2001

COCOA (CSCE)
MAR

CONTRACT SIZE:  10 METRIC TONS
MINIMUM TICK : 1

SYMBOL CC02H
Trading Hours: 7:30- 12:30 CST

GRID:5.000
49-D:1022.3

SL:57
DL:3

<- WEEKLY RANKINGS ->     1        7        2     4     36

# March 2002 Cocoa (Nov 13)

## REAL-TIME COMMENTARY

**11/13 (Tuesday):** Dec Cocoa - Status - Bullish. Trend up, ML positive, SL positive, line pattern positive and indicates long. Price action quite positive as recent up surge resumed today after just one day pause. Market remains in extremely solid concurrent mode to upside and so odds indicate even higher prices ahead. When get a head of steam up as strong as this one can feel quite sure that when do finally get anything can call a dip (couple days down), it will turn out to be short-lived as there are many still left on sidelines wanting to go long as well as many shorts "stuck" and wanting to get out, or at least reduce amount short. "Should" not be any serious downside risk for at least another week and a half or so. When this up move started five days ago I believe I mentioned that last up surge went 250 points and should expect this one to have a good chance to equal that move. Are now closing in on those levels; however, trend/momentum so strong to upside see no reason to take profits yet (although have learned never to argue with trader who wants to take good profits when have them, am just giving the odds here). If using $1000 as margin (a little high but reasonable level) now have over 150 percent of profit from "official" line entry level of 1040 on Dec and 1050 on March, and 200 percent profit on margin from "anticipation" entry levels (990 on Dec and 1000 on Mar). Historical pattern is 250 percent of margin profit about "max" ever get before a market turns back at least enough to turn pattern to neutral, but pattern here remains very positive. Bottom line: Can be long with stops out of range (do not need stops at this time).

..................

## AFTER-ACTION CRITIQUE

Status remains solidly Bullish with all three lines clearly up and ML above zero (therefore, have +3 points). Market also still in very solid concurrent mode to upside since virtually zero chance of either trend and ML turning down anytime soon.

As a general rule, when both price and SL reach recent extremes (highs in this case), a market has at least some very short-term downside vulnerability. If look at chart will see that SL is at a recent extreme high. "Normal" high for SL cycles has been in plus or minus thirty area, and at moment SL is at plus sixty-six. By recent extreme high (low) in price I mean simply that price is higher (lower) now than has been in past month or so.

My general rule is always can make some case to take at least partial (if holding multiple positions) profits when both price and SL reach recent extreme levels. However, this general rule can, and usually should, be overridden when a market is in a solidly concurrent mode. At the moment, this market remains in an extremely solid concurrent mode.

Therefore, due for some kind of pause/dip here but markets march to their own tunes, and right now this one showing no signs of slowing its up surge. When have a move as powerful as this one, can be almost certain that first downside action that comes even close to being called a "dip" will be a good buying opportunity for at least a short-term (several day) trade. Therefore, saw no need to take profits yet, nor any need for stops.

11/13/2001

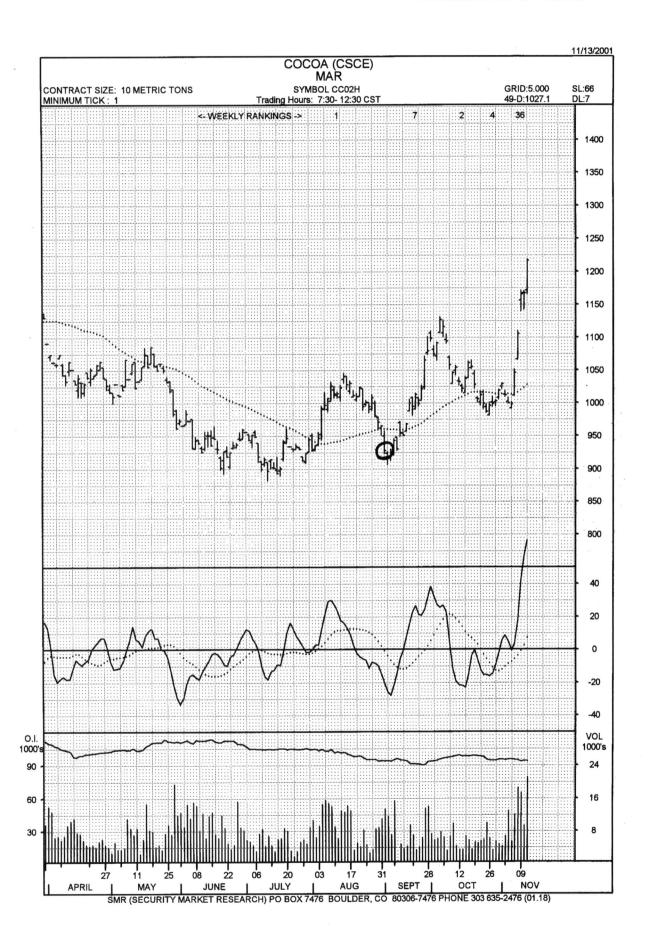

COCOA (CSCE)
MAR

CONTRACT SIZE:  10 METRIC TONS
MINIMUM TICK : 1

SYMBOL CC02H
Trading Hours:  7:30- 12:30 CST

GRID:5.000
49-D:1027.1

SL:66
DL:7

<- WEEKLY RANKINGS ->        1        7        2        4        36

SMR (SECURITY MARKET RESEARCH) PO BOX 7476  BOULDER, CO  80306-7476 PHONE 303 635-2476 (01.18)

# March 2002 Cocoa (Nov 14)

## REAL-TIME COMMENTARY

**11/14 (Wednesday):** Mar Cocoa - Status - Bullish. Trend up, ML positive, SL positive, line pattern positive and indicates long. Price action slightly negative on decent downside reversal. Market remains in very solid concurrent mode to upside so odds favor higher prices ahead. At today's highs hit 200 percent of margin profit from "official" line signal and 250 percent of margin profit from "anticipation" buy point. SL turned down slightly from an extreme high, but with market in such solid concurrent mode this not significant. In today's *The Wall Street Journal* Cocoa was feature commodity story and old saying is this usually marks at least a temporary pause in up move. Reason for this is by time news media hears about and writes about a big move, this means not many left to buy. Journalists have very long history of being the last to catch on to anything, and they are no different when writing about markets. Today also had small "feel" of temporary blow-off to upside. Therefore, could be due for minor, brief dip here; however, any dip should be a buying opportunity. Would never argue with taking some profits when they are this big and have come in such a short period of time, but highly unlikely have seen any kind of meaningful high yet, and highly likely any dip from here will be short-lived and shallow. Bottom line: Can be long with stops still out of range (still no need for stops here),and would view any price under 1170 as good enough dip to either go long or add to longs.

....................

## AFTER-ACTION CRITIQUE

Status remains Bullish. Trend up so this +1 point, ML up and above zero so this +1 point (+1/2 for being up, +1/2 for being above zero), and SL now down so this -1 point. Since only count the with-trend points, this means still have +2 points, so Status is still Bullish. Market also continues in very solid concurrent mode to upside since both trend and ML powerfully up with virtually zero chance of either turning down any time soon. Price would have to drop below 950 to turn trend down and SL would have to go below zero to turn ML down and neither even remotely close to those levels.

Have finally had a down day; therefore, could start looking for something that would qualify as a "dip" to initiate any new longs if wanted to. Naturally, if were already long, absolutely would not have to add. While adding to long positions here would be perfectly acceptable trading, doing so should be done only by very aggressive traders since as soon as added to longs, nervousness about position would increase significantly.

I mentioned 1170 as potential buy point because if that price were hit tomorrow it would be second day down and low of past three days within an overall very solidly bullish pattern, and thus would qualify as a dip. I continued to see no reason for stops since almost regardless of what price did next day the overall pattern would remain solidly positive. The basic idea for stops is to put them at levels where the basic technical picture would change. Since the only price that would turn this solidly positive picture even to neutral would have been a close at least below 1100 (which was over a hundred points down), I saw no reason for stops.

Therefore, in a situation like this would just sit tight with longs (or look to add) and let market take its course.

11/14/2001

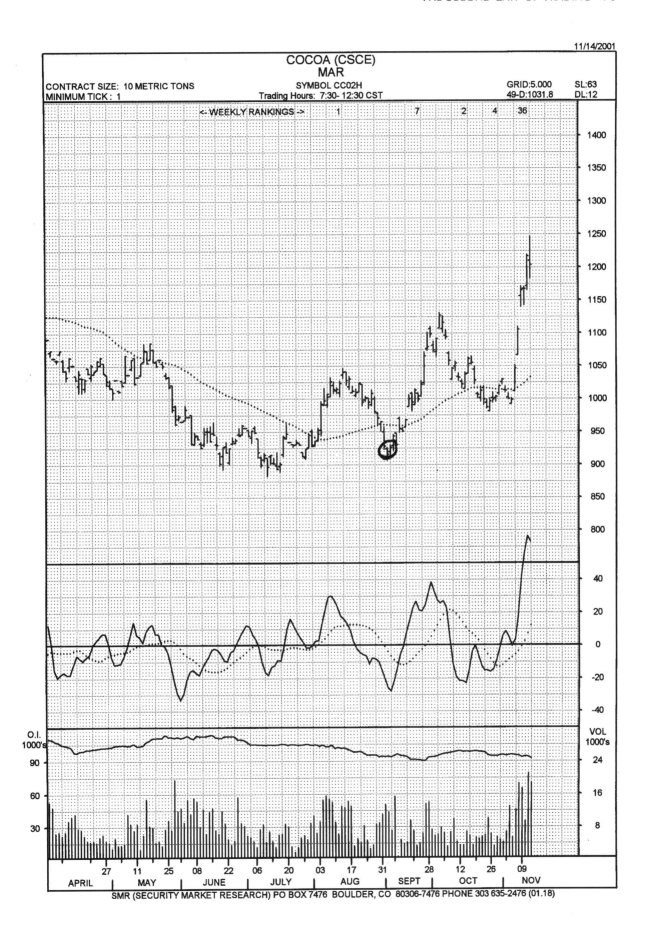

SMR (SECURITY MARKET RESEARCH) PO BOX 7476 BOULDER, CO 80306-7476 PHONE 303 635-2476 (01.18)

# March 2002 Cocoa (Nov 15)

**REAL-TIME COMMENTARY**

**11/15 (Thursday):** Dec Cocoa - Status - Bullish. Trend up, ML positive, SL positive, line pattern positive and indicates long. Price action positive on moderate up day as market showing no interest in dipping more than very briefly. Market remains in solid concurrent mode to upside and so odds continue to favor even higher prices ahead. When get a powerful pattern like this one, usually do not get anything meaningful on downside until have at least ten days of SL up around highs, and still have week and a half before that happens. What this means is little significant downside risk here, other than brief dips, which are always possible of course; however, how much upside will get is always unknown. As individual trader first emphasis always has to be on risk, and so when have a situation where odds are so high that have little in way of risk (on downside here) then want to be in trade. Several days ago (on third day of current sharp rally) I said could buy even at those "highs" with little risk, and so far that has proven true. This was not a "guess"; this was based on natural laws of trading (and pricing). This doesn't mean it will happen every time get this type of pattern, only the overwhelming majority of time, and this is all can ever expect when trading. Bottom line: Can be long with no stops.

....................

**AFTER-ACTION CRITIQUE**

Status remained solidly Bullish with all three lines up; therefore, point total was back to +3 (SL turned back up slightly). Market also was still in very solid concurrent mode to upside. This meant all trend/momentum indicators were still very positive indicating that odds favored higher prices ahead, in spite of being on major up.

While it may look clear and obvious that a trader should be long here and calmly holding without any thought of taking profits, trading in real time is not so easy. Even if were long from the 1000 level, every trader was going to be thinking about taking profits when price has made this big an up move. During the day the price bounces around; it is always easy to get "scared" on a momentary dip and suddenly get urge to take the big profit. In situations like this one, what I find works best is to be absolutely clear the night before that the next day will be a "no action" day on any existing positions in this market. Get that thought solidly set in your mind the night before and then just be an interested observer of the next day's price action, otherwise you may succumb to the inevitable momentary urge to cash in these big profits. And since overall pattern was still so solidly positive, there was no real reason to do so.

Therefore, would just stubbornly stick with any/all longs at this point and if market sold off and ended up giving some back, then so be it—that would just be the "breaks" of trading. The point is that when trading and find a situation where the odds clearly favor a move in your direction, just stick with the odds and hold on.

I still did not see any reason for stops in this situation since would have taken a complete collapse (and this was highly unlikely with price energy flows so strongly up at moment) to run price down to level where overall positive pattern would have turned back to neutral.

11/15/2001

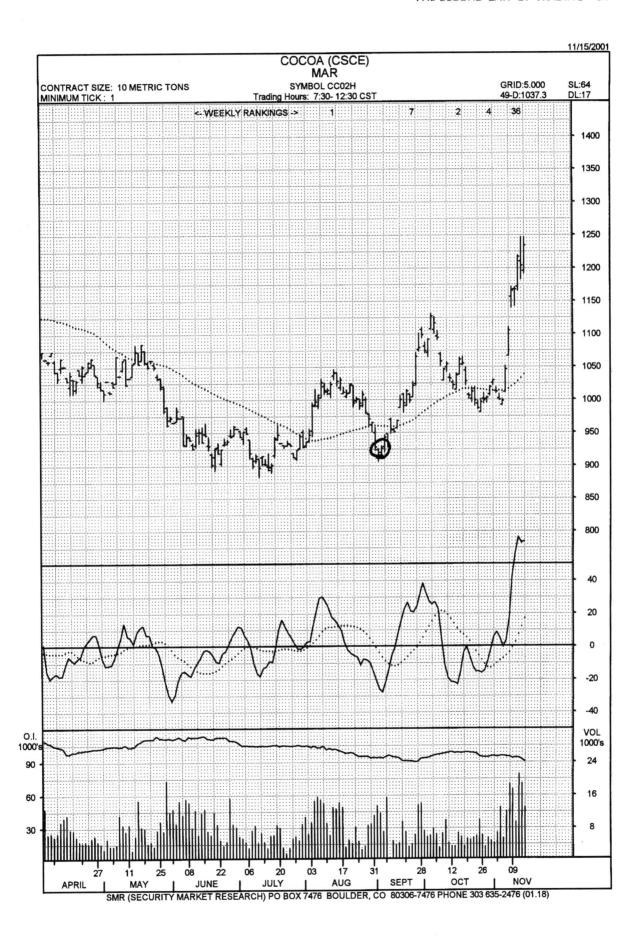

COCOA (CSCE)
MAR

CONTRACT SIZE: 10 METRIC TONS
MINIMUM TICK : 1

SYMBOL CC02H
Trading Hours: 7:30- 12:30 CST

GRID:5.000
49-D:1037.3

SL:64
DL:17

<- WEEKLY RANKINGS ->     1        7      2    4    36

SMR (SECURITY MARKET RESEARCH) PO BOX 7476  BOULDER, CO 80306-7476 PHONE 303 635-2476 (01.18)

# March 2002 Cocoa (Nov 16)

### REAL-TIME COMMENTARY

**11/16 (Friday):** Mar Cocoa - Status - Bullish. Trend up, ML positive, SL positive, line pattern positive and indicates long. Price action positive on another good up day, but did fade some late although closed mid-range, not near lows, and so action still positive. Market remains in very solid concurrent mode to upside and so odds continue to favor higher. However, at today's high's came very close to 250 percent of margin profit from "official" line signal (and 300 percent of margin profit from "anticipation" buy point) and over past couple years can only remember one signal that produced more than this, so clearly now pushing it a little on short-term basis. However, when have type of chart and line pattern have here, hardly ever get anything significant on downside until get at least a couple of dips and then quick rallies back to area of recent highs—meaning even if do dip from here will almost certainly move back up quickly. Therefore, continue to see little in way of meaningful downside risk here. Can never argue with taking at least some partial profits when reach these levels, but doubt there is any big rush to get out of longs here since at worst only will have to ride through a couple day dip before price returns to recent highs. COT now bearish as commercials now moderately net short, but this to be expected on such a big rally and should not have any immediate negative impact (although, this now a background negative). Bottom line: Can be long with no stops.

......................

### AFTER-ACTION CRITIQUE

Status still Bullish since have +1 point for uptrend and +1 point due to ML being both above zero and on up cycle. SL turned down again slightly, but this does not change Bullish Status. Concurrent mode continues very solid and still virtually zero chance of this changing any time soon since both trend and ML remain solidly up.

In situation like this one there is really not much to say or much to comment on since should be long from much lower levels and should just be holding here waiting for market to show some early signs may be running into resistance, and so far none.

Again, will cover the percentage of profits rules later in money management (third law) section. Main objective here is simply to show classic example of how natural laws of trading and point system based on SMR's trend/momentum indicators work; and so far it is working quite well here. However, keep in mind that what takes only a few minutes to review here covers full twenty-four-hour days, in reality. There is a lot of time during the day, both when markets are open and when closed, for a trader's mind to start conjuring up all sorts of strange scenarios about what might happen that could take away these big profits. Just have to override these stray thoughts and stick with the natural laws of trading, and at the moment all laws and rules indicate odds still strongly favor more to upside.

Therefore, in this situation should just stick with any longs and still have no need for any stops.

11/16/2001

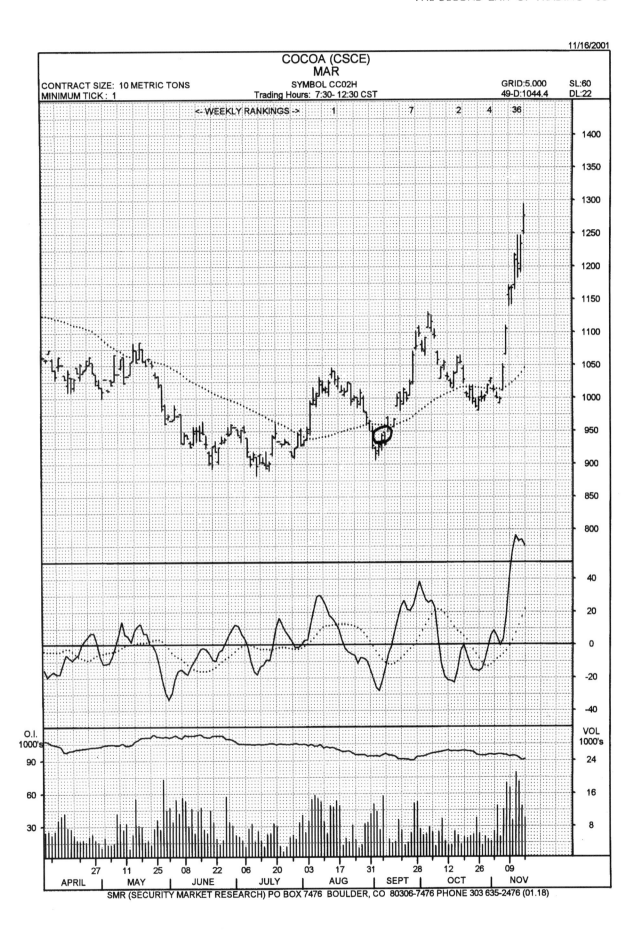

COCOA (CSCE)
MAR

CONTRACT SIZE: 10 METRIC TONS
MINIMUM TICK : 1

SYMBOL CC02H
Trading Hours: 7:30- 12:30 CST

GRID:5.000
49-D:1044.4

SL:60
DL:22

<- WEEKLY RANKINGS ->     1          7        2      4    36

SMR (SECURITY MARKET RESEARCH) PO BOX 7476 BOULDER, CO 80306-7476 PHONE 303 635-2476 (01.18)

# March 2002 Cocoa (Nov 19)

## REAL-TIME COMMENTARY

**11/19 (Monday):** Mar Cocoa - Status - Bullish. Trend up, ML positive, SL positive, line pattern positive and indicates long. Price action neutral on basically unchanged day, but with SL at such an extreme high and coming down slowly and price also on big rally see sideways here as more positive than negative. Overdue for some kind of dip, but underlying technical picture still solidly positive and so doubt any dip will go far or last long. Market remains in very solid concurrent mode to upside and this means odds favor even higher prices ahead. Cocoa feature story in *The Wall Street Journal* again today and this can be sign due for short-term dip, but had similar bullish story several days ago and did not stop the up move. Therefore, other than taking good profits, which can never argue against, odds clearly favor higher and so no reason to sell yet. Bottom line: Can be long with no stops for now.

......................

## AFTER-ACTION CRITIQUE

Status remains solidly Bullish since both trend (+1 point) and ML (+1 point with +1/2 for above zero and +1/2 for up cycle) still have essentially zero chance of turning down any time soon. This also means concurrent mode to upside remains very solid.

Again, not much to say about this situation as all signs remain positive, and even if do get dip near term, the pattern is so positive any dip almost certain to be shallow and short-lived.

Therefore, point here would be just to relax and make sure have no thought in mind at all of selling, no matter what market might do on intra-day basis. I still saw no need for stops. When the time comes for stops, "market" (i.e., trend/momentum indicators, price chart, and action) will start to give some negative signs, and so far none of those. For example, if look back at previous up move during end of September/early October, you will notice that SL and price had minor bearish divergence at the highs (price made slightly higher high, but SL made slightly lower high). You will also see how at that time had ten full days of SL being at recent highs, which meant ML (which is moving average of SL) was beginning to become vulnerable to a down cycle. At the moment here have nothing at all in way of negative warning signs in this market; therefore, saw no need for any cautionary steps (such as stops or looking to take profits).

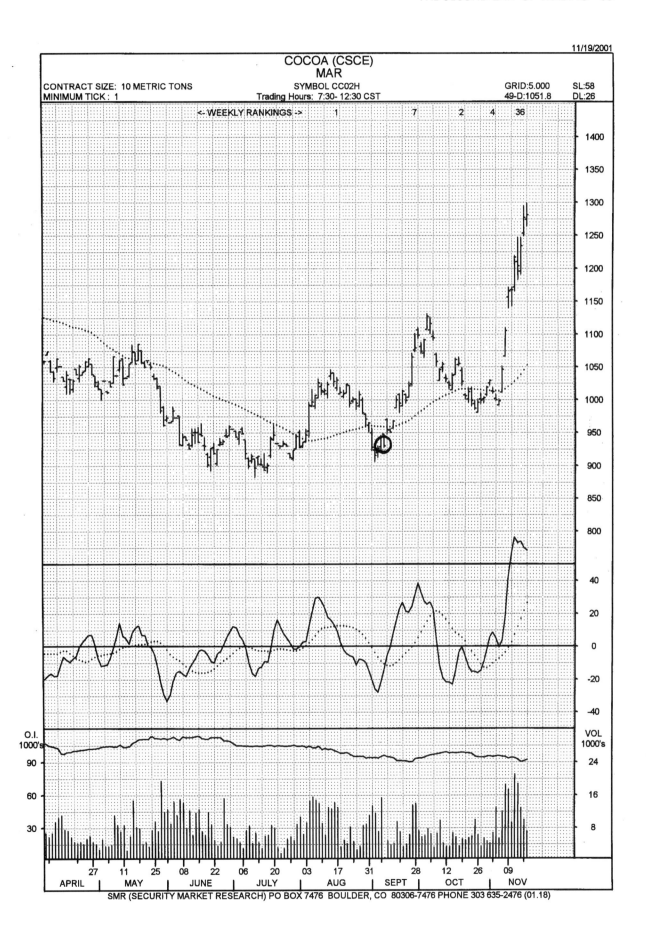

11/19/2001

COCOA (CSCE)
MAR

CONTRACT SIZE:  10 METRIC TONS
MINIMUM TICK : 1

SYMBOL CC02H
Trading Hours: 7:30- 12:30 CST

GRID:5.000
49-D:1051.8

SL:58
DL:26

<- WEEKLY RANKINGS ->     1          7       2     4    36

SMR (SECURITY MARKET RESEARCH) PO BOX 7476  BOULDER, CO  80306-7476  PHONE 303 635-2476 (01.18)

# March 2002 Cocoa (Nov 20)

## REAL-TIME COMMENTARY

**11/20 (Tuesday):** Mar Cocoa - Status - Bullish. Trend up, ML positive, SL slightly positive, line pattern positive and so indicates long. Price action neutral on small down day, but came back well from some early weakness. Market remains in very solid concurrent mode to upside and so odds continue to favor higher. Now on minor day and a half dip with the past three days' lows of 1245 now qualifying as a "good" entry level for new longs. Are seeing some resistance here in high 1200's, but both price chart and line pattern indicate odds favor even higher prices ahead and little likelihood of meaningful down from here. Can never argue with taking profits when have had this big a move, but "should" see higher near term. Bottom line: Can be long with no stops necessary.

....................

## AFTER-ACTION CRITIQUE

Status remains clearly positive since both trend and ML still solidly up. Uptrend equals +1 point, ML above zero which counts for +1/2 point and on up cycle which counts for another +1/2 point, therefore have total of +2 points with an uptrend. Market remains in solid concurrent mode to upside since neither trend nor ML have any chance of turning down soon (i.e., over next week or so).

Upward price momentum is slowing some though, and this is reflected by the more decisive down move in SL. However, I continued to see nothing in way of negative warning signs here since a couple day pause at high price levels is nothing to be concerned about after such a big up move. Markets rarely turn around quickly from a pattern this powerful. Normally, will almost always (nothing ever 100 percent in this game, which is what makes it so difficult) get some kind of technical warning signs before significant price reversals, and nothing here at moment.

Have another potential buy point now since any move down to 1245 would qualify as a buying opportunity since it would be lowest price of past three days and second day down within an overall solidly positive pattern.

Therefore, this was still a situation where would just have to steel the nerves and stick with longs, regardless of next day's action. Believe in this type of situation the best approach for a short-term trader is to just set mind the night before that next day would be a "no action" day for any longs in Cocoa, and then just watch what happens with interest.

Once again, I saw no need for stops since any legitimate stop points would have been out of realistic range.

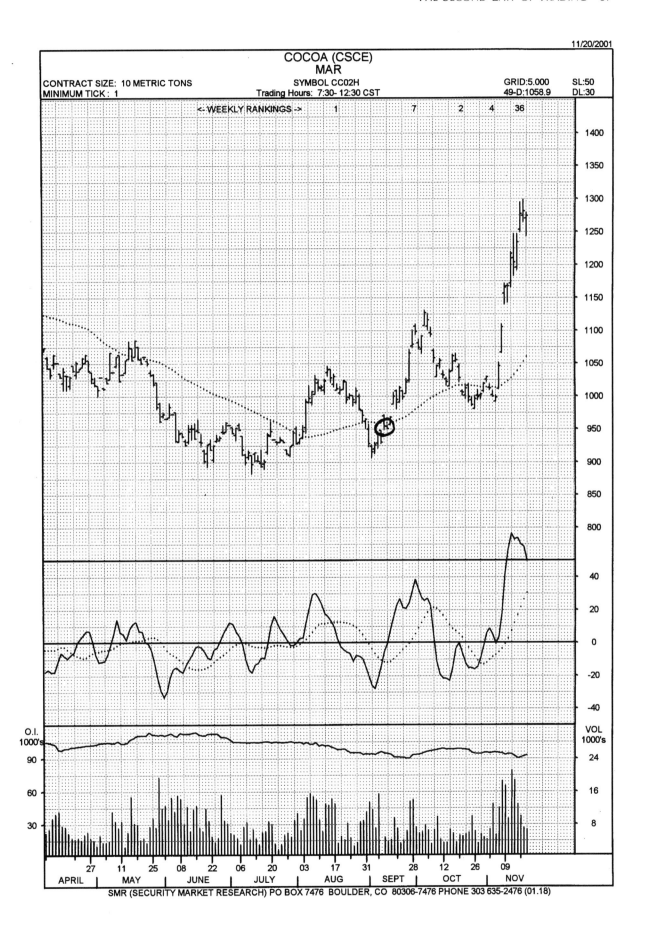

11/20/2001

COCOA (CSCE)
MAR

CONTRACT SIZE: 10 METRIC TONS
MINIMUM TICK : 1

SYMBOL CC02H
Trading Hours: 7:30- 12:30 CST

GRID:5.000      SL:50
49-D:1058.9    DL:30

<- WEEKLY RANKINGS ->       1        7      2      4    36

SMR (SECURITY MARKET RESEARCH) PO BOX 7476  BOULDER, CO  80306-7476 PHONE 303 635-2476 (01.18)

# March 2002 Cocoa (Nov 21)

## REAL-TIME COMMENTARY

**11/21 (Wednesday before the Thanksgiving four-day break):**  Mar Cocoa - Status - Bullish. Trend up, ML positive, SL neutral, line pattern positive and indicates long. Price action slightly negative on minor down day, but going down very begrudgingly. Market remains in solid concurrent mode to upside and as a rule when concurrent mode this powerful, do not get meaningful dip until can make case on verge of switching to crosscurrent, and this still four to seven days (or so) ahead. Frequently, when a line pattern is this powerful, do not get significant break until after ML turns down and also have at least a couple bearish divergences between price and SL, and both of these long way away. One basic rule for profitable trading is to look for excuses to be long the strongest markets and vice versa (short the weakest). Cocoa is strongest market on board at moment with no meaningful technical negatives in sight. In addition, the price is on first "official" dip after major up surge, which means can make good case to buy here. Another old trading "rule" says to always buy the first dip in a new bull market, and this clearly qualifies in both respects (first break and new bull market). Bottom line: Can be long, can go long, stops still unnecessary (according to the "rules," if it dips from here you should buy more, not sell).

....................

## AFTER-ACTION CRITIQUE

Status remains Bullish with same point total (+2) as past few days. Market also remains in fairly solid concurrent mode to upside.

Only potential warning sign here at moment was SL moving down and picking up a little speed. Looking at situation now, can see where if next day or two had been moderately down, the SL would have moved down to zero within few (two, three) days, and this would have turned pattern back to Neutral as well as switched concurrent mode to crosscurrent. However, meaningful dip so soon after such a big and sustained up move is always highly unlikely (although always have some exceptions to every rule in this game).

The main point in this situation is if upside still "good," then should not see much, if any, to downside from here since have already had a three day pause/dip, and this usually all "good" markets need before ready to head up with trend again.

Might note that have now built a small bull flag over past three days and these are usually resolved to upside.

Therefore, picture here not as solidly positive as it had been, but it was still plenty positive and continued to fully justify being long.

11/21/2001

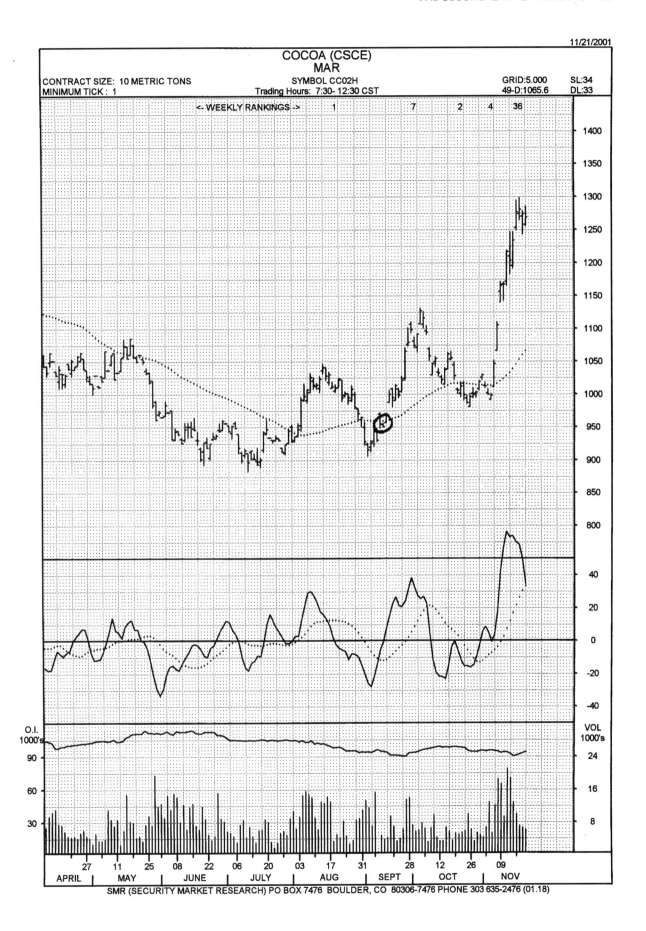

COCOA (CSCE)
MAR

CONTRACT SIZE:  10 METRIC TONS
MINIMUM TICK :  1

SYMBOL CC02H
Trading Hours:  7:30- 12:30 CST

GRID:5.000        SL:34
49-D:1065.6       DL:33

<- WEEKLY RANKINGS ->        1            7        2      4    36

# March 2002 Cocoa (Nov 26)

## REAL-TIME COMMENTARY

**11/26 (the Monday after Thanksgiving):** Mar Cocoa - Status - Bullish. Trend up, ML positive, SL slightly positive, line pattern positive and indicates long. Price action positive on decent up day and close at new highs. Market remains in solid concurrent mode to upside and so odds continue to favor higher. Still nothing in way of meaningful negatives in technical picture here, but have now had nine days of high "SL" numbers; therefore, in another day or so will have first potential for negatives. Normally in this type of pattern would not expect to see anything meaningful on downside until had at least chance for a single bearish divergence (between price and SL). Would need a close above 1325 tomorrow to turn SL back up and thus give potential for a subsequent bearish divergence. Therefore, all signs remain positive here. Commercials continuing to slightly shift to short side, but rule is as long as this continues odds actually favor higher prices ahead. Bottom line: Can be long without stops for now.

....................

## AFTER-ACTION CRITIQUE

Status still solidly positive with same point totals (+2 as a result of trend being up and ML being both above zero and on up cycle). Concurrent mode to upside remains quite solid also since would need SL below zero to change it to crosscurrent (turn ML down), and with today's up day the SL down move slowed significantly.

To repeat: Concurrent mode means when have both trend and ML pointing in same direction. Think of the trend as the current (as in current of a river) of the price energy flow and think of the ML as the tide (as in ocean tide) of the price energy flow. If both current and tide solid in one direction, then any surface moves back against this direction are almost sure to be limited in distance and short-lived in time. So far this has been exactly what has happened here. Ever since very first day this market moved up sharply it has been in very solid concurrent mode, and any price moves down have been very limited in distance and in terms of time.

If look back over past eight months of price movement on this chart, you will see that while the market has on occasion briefly penetrated the ten-week moving average line, this trend line has actually done a good job of delineating the prevailing trend. Also, if look at the ML cycles for the past six months or so on this chart, you will see that the ML has done a very good job of signaling intermediate-term price energy flows. Therefore, the combination of these two lines has given an excellent indication of the background technical situation at all times. When both trend and ML have been pointing in same direction (up or down), the price has generally moved in that direction; and when these two lines have been moving opposite each other (i.e., were at crosscurrents) the price movement has been choppier and has not adhered to the trend as well. I have always found that concurrent mode situations (and the more solid the better) invariably present the best odds and risk/reward times to be positioned. Therefore, a trader should always focus on these concurrent situations.

The situation here remained one where should just stick with longs.

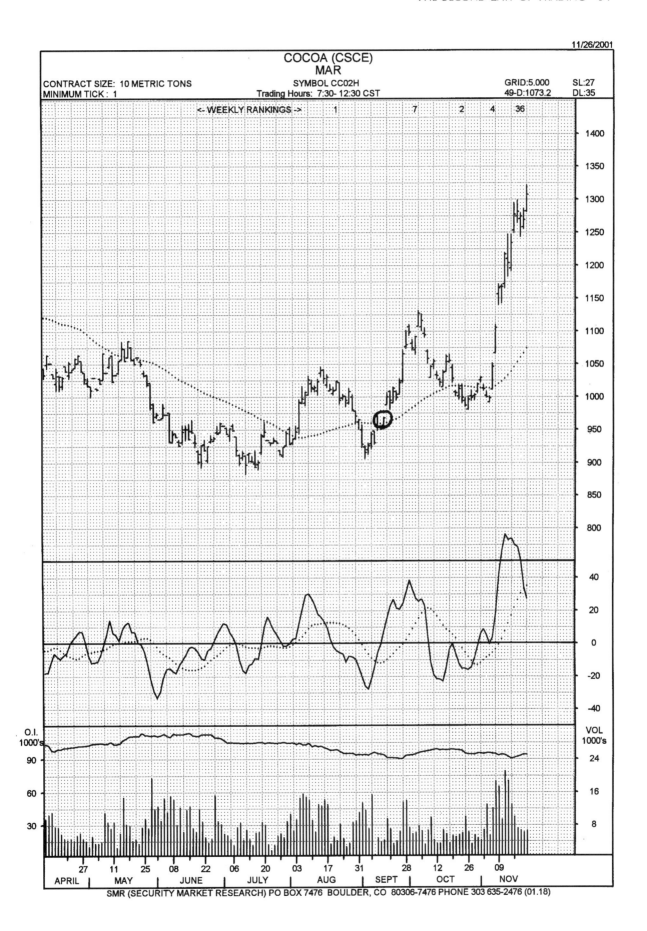

11/26/2001

COCOA (CSCE)
MAR

CONTRACT SIZE: 10 METRIC TONS
MINIMUM TICK : 1

SYMBOL CC02H
Trading Hours: 7:30- 12:30 CST

GRID:5.000
49-D:1073.2

SL:27
DL:35

<- WEEKLY RANKINGS ->   1   7   2   4   36

SMR (SECURITY MARKET RESEARCH) PO BOX 7476  BOULDER, CO  80306-7476 PHONE 303 635-2476 (01.18)

# Mar 2002 Cocoa (Nov 27)

## REAL-TIME COMMENTARY

**11/27 (Tuesday):** Mar Cocoa - Status - Bullish. Trend up, ML positive, SL neutral, line pattern positive and indicates long. Price action slightly negative on moderate down day. Market remains in solid concurrent mode to upside and so odds continue to favor higher. Up move getting a little ragged now since have run into some upside resistance in 1300 area, but still nothing in way of negative technicals so see no reason to liquidate longs yet (other than having 250 percent of margin profits and can never argue too hard against taking profits when this the case). SL has now been moving down slowly for a little over a week and so no longer overbought on short-term basis. Bottom line: Can be long with stops still out of range (continue to see no need for stops here at moment).

...................

## AFTER-ACTION CRITIQUE

Status remains Bullish since both trend (+1) and ML (+1 on +1/2 for up and +1/2 for above zero) continue positive; and, for same reason, this market remains in concurrent mode to upside.

What have seen here past week has been a case where market was somewhat short-term overbought since both price and SL were at recent extreme highs; however, what is interesting to note here is that this overbought condition had been worked off (by SL moving down) even though the price continued to move up. SL has come down from its extreme high, yet price has pushed higher. This type of pattern is usually a sign of solid internal price strength in a market, since have been in period when could/should have seen some price weakness, yet market so strong it kept pushing higher.

While have had a couple of brief pauses/minor dips over past week or so here, none of them "officially" qualified as dips where could have initiated new longs. However, whenever a market is in a pattern as solidly positive as this one has been in, a trader can always make some case to simply buy at the previous day's close. However, this is only for very aggressive traders. The point is that if on its close you can make a solid technical case (based on trend/momentum, etc.) that a position (long or short), if fully justified (meaning odds clearly favor additional continuation move), then there is nothing wrong with simply trying to position at unchanged or better on open. Exceptionally good markets (those in very solid trend/momentum moves) frequently will not give much in way of dips/rallies to position on; however, they will invariably give plenty of chances to position at unchanged—and this point frequently will look like good entry point a few days later.

Therefore, situation here weakening slightly (SL still down and ML slowing up move), but it remains positive enough to stick with longs with no stops. I can understand why some (many?) would prefer to have some kind of stops in here (say just under 1250), and would not argue too much against doing so. However, at the time just did not see or feel anything negative enough here to see any necessity for any kind of stops.

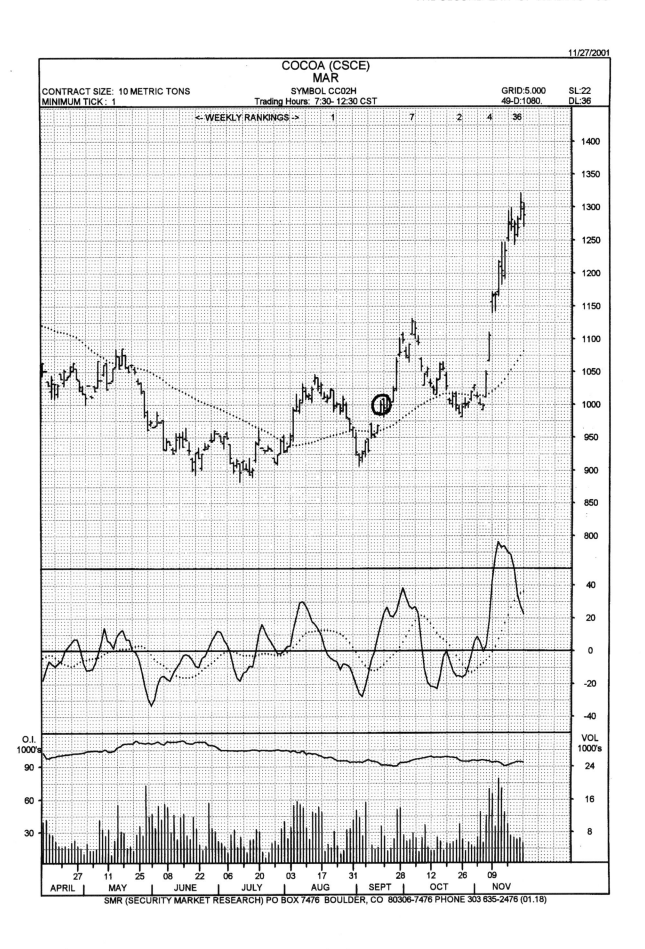

11/27/2001

COCOA (CSCE)
MAR

CONTRACT SIZE: 10 METRIC TONS
MINIMUM TICK : 1

SYMBOL CC02H
Trading Hours: 7:30- 12:30 CST

GRID:5.000
49-D:1080.

SL:22
DL:36

<- WEEKLY RANKINGS ->    1    7    2   4   36

O.I.
1000's

90

60

30

VOL
1000's

24

16

8

27
APRIL

11
MAY

25

08
JUNE

22

06
JULY

20

03
AUG

17

31

28
SEPT

12
OCT

26

09
NOV

SMR (SECURITY MARKET RESEARCH) PO BOX 7476 BOULDER, CO 80306-7476 PHONE 303 635-2476 (01.18)

# March 2002 Cocoa (Nov 28)

## REAL-TIME COMMENTARY

**11/28 (Wednesday):** Mar Cocoa - Status - Bullish. Trend up, ML positive, SL neutral, line pattern positive and indicates long. Price action neutral on fairly quiet, sideways-type day. Overall pattern still positive enough to stick with longs, but now getting some potential negatives so can start to make legitimate case to get out of most (or all, if prefer) of longs. ML now within margin-of-error to turn down and close to getting another in series of very minor lower highs in SL and both of these are short-term warning signs. So, would put any remaining longs here on fairly strict probation or start using a reasonably close stop now. However, even if do get a meaningful sell off here doubt would last for very long. Bottom line: Can be long but would now use stops in 1264 to 1275 area, in addition would liquidate all but token longs (or even all longs) if market unchanged or lower anytime after first few minutes (in other words, now would treat all longs on an "up or out" basis for tomorrow).

....................

## AFTER-ACTION CRITIQUE

Status is still fairly solidly bullish here, but ML is now slowing its up move and so if were to get any sharp down tomorrow the SL would move below zero quickly (within couple days). Therefore, beginning to see some warning signs for longs. Have the same situation with the concurrent mode to upside, since any sharp weakness for day or two and this would end. However, overall pattern remains clearly positive enough to be long here, so no need to run straight for exits.

Obviously I began to get a little uncomfortable with longs here and so for first time since second big up day have suggested stops. Furthermore, these are reasonably close ones since they are within thirty points and that is not much after three hundred point up move.

I mentioned putting longs on "fairly strict probation." What I meant by this was to put the burden of proof (on sticking with longs) on the market right from opening (meaning either price performs by moving up quickly or just get out). If, and as long as, market trading higher on day, then would stick with longs; however, any signs of negative intra-day action to downside, then idea would be to get out. There are many times when I feel this technique (putting a trade on "probation" for the day) works quite well and this looked like one of them.

Therefore, up until this point (from first breakout day to upside) I have been nonchalant about any meaningful downside risk (actually just sounded like it in writing; in reality, am always nervous to at least some degree when in a position). The point is that up until now there has been no reason to even think about taking profits (other than profits being very big, which is always "some" reason); however, now this market was starting to give some warning signs so needed to change approach—needed to be ready to sell if action was negative in any way. On other hand, since odds still favored the upside, wanted to let the market "talk" first—meaning take a look at early action. As a back up to protect against any sudden down move, it is not a bad idea to put stops in while watching to see early action, and if decide to sell before stops hit, then just cancel them. Having stops already in allows for some time to decide whether to get out earlier on any negative intra-day action.

11/28/2001

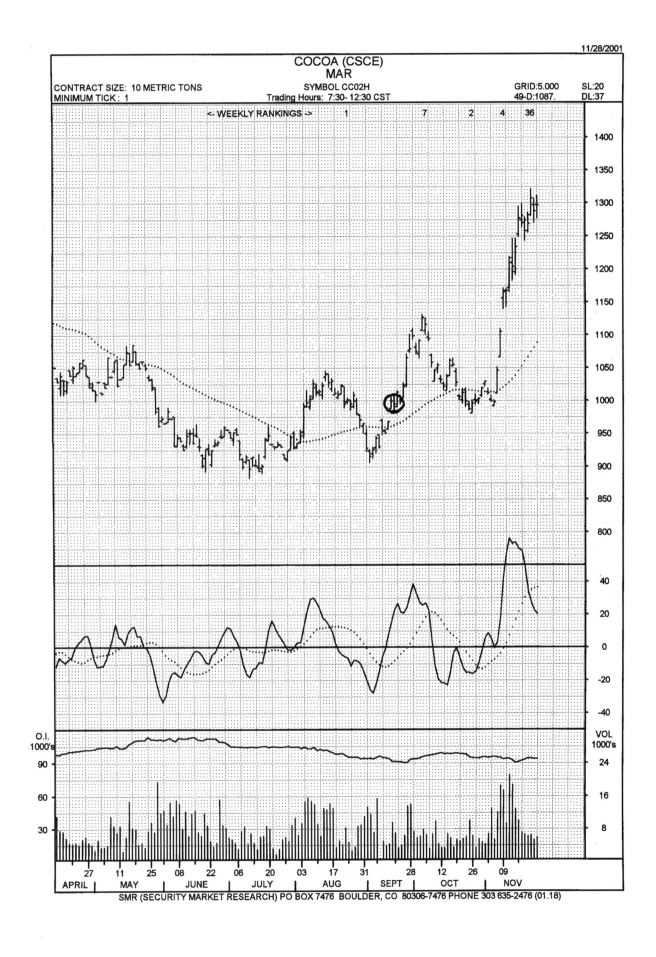

COCOA (CSCE)
MAR

CONTRACT SIZE:  10 METRIC TONS
MINIMUM TICK :  1

SYMBOL CC02H
Trading Hours:  7:30- 12:30 CST

GRID:5.000
49-D:1087.

SL:20
DL:37

<- WEEKLY RANKINGS ->        1          7        2      4    36

SMR (SECURITY MARKET RESEARCH) PO BOX 7476  BOULDER, CO  80306-7476 PHONE 303 635-2476 (01.18)

# March 2002 Cocoa (Nov 29)

## REAL-TIME COMMENTARY

**11/29 (Thursday):** Mar Cocoa - Status - Bullish. Trend up, ML positive, SL positive, line pattern positive and indicates long. Price action quite positive as gapped higher and closed at new high's with zero downside pressure. Market remains in good concurrent mode to upside. Yesterday suggested putting longs on "probation," but since opened higher and pushed higher all day, no need to sell. However, due to turn up in SL, now have potential for a bearish divergence between price and SL, and will unless price keeps surging to upside next few days. Although even if do get a decent dip, near-term overall pattern remains so positive, highly unlikely dip would go more than two, three days. Therefore, it is simply a question of whether willing to ride through next dip or try to anticipate it and then buy back on dip. So far no technical signs indicating dip imminent, but dips can come without much warning. Therefore, would keep longs on some form of probation and move stops up a little tighter if want to play it tight, or can just go without stops and be prepared to ride through first real dip in this solid bull market. Bottom line: Can be long with stops now in 1299 to 1309 area on regular (as versus close only) basis.

..................

## AFTER-ACTION CRITIQUE

Status remains Bullish. Trend is up, so this +1 point. ML is both up and above zero, so this is +1 point (+1/2 for being in up cycle, +1/2 for being above zero). SL is now up again, so this is +1 point. Therefore, now the point system is showing +3 points, which means Status is Bullish. Since both trend and ML remain up, the market continues to be in concurrent mode to upside.

This is a good time to point out that having more points is not necessarily better. In other words, +3 points is not necessarily more positive than +2 points; in fact, in this particular case I see it as less positive. Up until now had felt that would need to see at least some bearish divergences before market was in any serious danger for downside, and with previous day's upturn in the SL, now were in position for a potential bearish divergence (since price at clear new highs, but SL still a long way from making new highs). Plus, the ML was now well within margin-of-error (up to five days) of turning down since have had about thirteen days of a very high SL. Therefore, any meaningful downside action and the SL would turn down sharply, and this in turn would inevitably have turned the ML down in day or two.

Therefore, in spite of a solid up day and a close at sharp new contract highs, I saw the technical situation as having some potential to turn negative fairly quickly. Remember I commented early in this move that usually do not have any serious downside risk in a powerful up move like this until get to point where ML has chance to turn to a down cycle, as well as have chance for some bearish divergences between price and SL—and had reached that point.

What happens to me (and am sure most other traders) is that we tend to be very nervous and skittish early in a move like this one; however, as it continues on for several weeks the persistent upside action slowly works its way on our trading psyche and we become more and more bullish. Unfortunately, our feelings tend to be wrong most of the time. Trade on what you see, not what you feel.

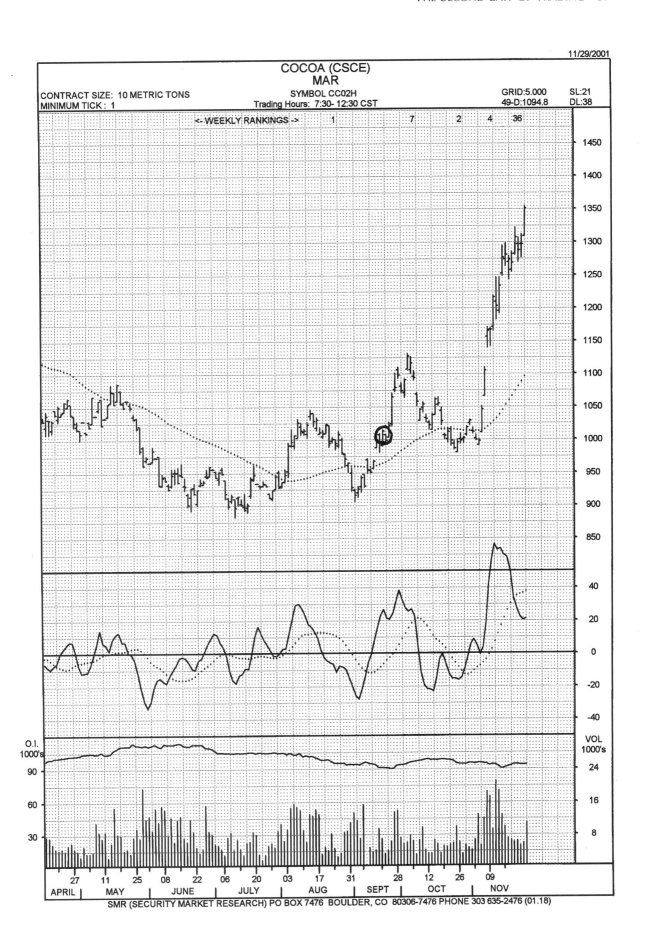

# March 2002 Cocoa (Nov 30)

## REAL-TIME COMMENTARY

**11/30 (Friday):** Mar Cocoa - Status - Bullish. Trend up, ML positive, SL positive, line pattern positive and indicates long. Price action neutral to slightly negative on minor downside reversal. Market still in concurrent mode to upside, but this now within a few days of switching back to crosscurrent (and will unless price pushes up sharply). Current longs now have reached 300 percent of margin profit level and this at extreme end of historical patterns, as well as about all ever get. So can still be long but would not argue against taking profits here with idea of buying back when finally do get a "legitimate" dip (couple good days down). Have minor warning sign from COT as commercials now slightly negative. Bottom line: Can be long with stops now just under 1320 (preferably entered anytime after first thirty minutes or so).

...................

## AFTER-ACTION CRITIQUE

Status still Bullish since all three lines up and ML above zero (meaning still have +3 points). Market is still in concurrent mode; however, as mentioned above, this now getting fairly shaky since now have close to three weeks of very high SL numbers. (Remember, ML is about a three-week moving average of SL.) Therefore, even a couple of moderate down days would send SL below +20 and thus turn ML to a down cycle. If this were to happen, then the down cycle of ML would most likely be sustained for some time since would then be "taking off" almost three weeks of very high SL numbers. In addition, now had clear potential for a bearish divergence between price and SL since price is at clear new highs, but the SL is still a long way from making new highs.

Notice that the past two days I made sure had stops in, as well as had them fairly close, whereas up until few days earlier had not seen any reason to even have distant stops in place. Markets change their nature, and when they do, a trader has to change tactics.

You should be able to see why over previous few days I became increasingly concerned about being long this market. This was not just guessing; it was based on the natural laws of trading, as well as reliance on reasonably reliable indicators of trend and momentum. There would have been nothing wrong with continuing to be long here since pattern was still bullish; however, had enough warning signs that would normally take at least partial profits so would have had only a token number of longs remaining, and would have had stops in at fairly close levels. However, also important to note that stop point of 1320 I was now using was a higher price than all but the prior two days. Therefore, jumping out before getting some clear warning signs was not necessary in this case.

Upside was still favored here, but the situation was getting shakier by the day and thus needed to have "finger on trigger" to liquidate positions, either through stops or at the market on any clearly negative action.

11/30/2001

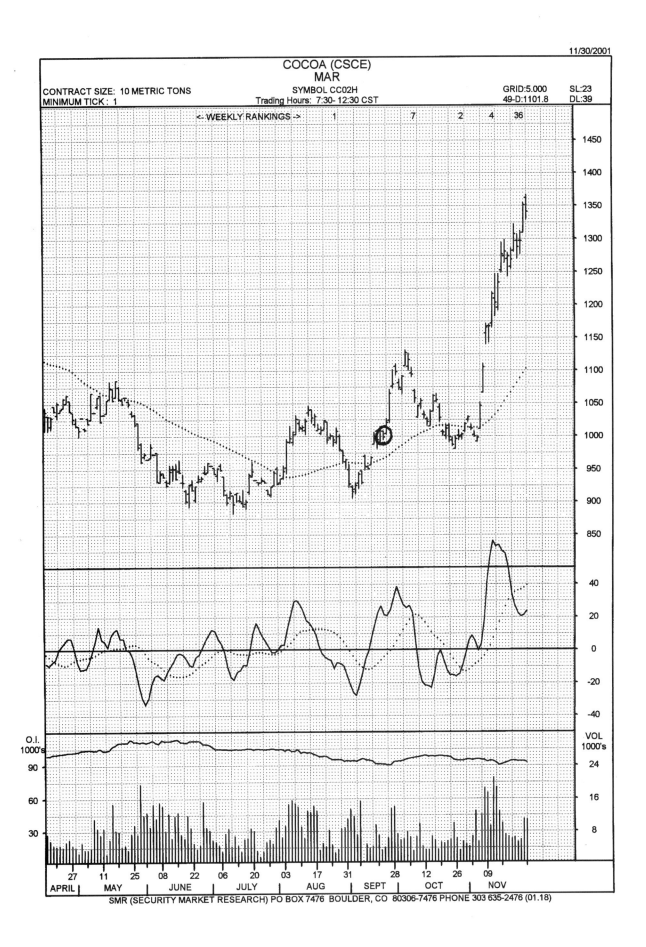

COCOA (CSCE)
MAR

CONTRACT SIZE: 10 METRIC TONS
MINIMUM TICK : 1

SYMBOL CC02H
Trading Hours: 7:30- 12:30 CST

GRID:5.000
49-D:1101.8

SL:23
DL:39

# March 2002 Cocoa (Dec 3)

## REAL-TIME COMMENTARY

**12/3 (Monday):** Mar Cocoa - Status - Bullish (to Neutral). Trend up, ML positive, SL neutral, line pattern positive and indicates long. Price action slightly negative on second minor down day in a row. Market still in concurrent mode to upside but this will almost certainly change tomorrow or next day. Slight turn down in SL gives a minor bearish divergence between price and SL; however, this type of divergence rarely produces a significant dip, and any dip it does produce is usually a buying opportunity. Two days down makes this an "official" dip now, but market "feels" like has at least a little more to go on downside. Stop point hit on open today; therefore, now prefer being on sidelines temporarily. Line pattern almost certainly will turn to Neutral after tomorrow. Having both lines shaky and stop being hit indicates sidelines best for now, but if get much more of a dip should just be a buying opportunity. If long-term trading, see major sell off here as highly unlikely so could just stick with longs. If out, would wait for more of a dip before going long again. This type of situation could make decent case to start going long again on scale down basis over next few days with any price under 1270 tomorrow a good place to start buying (but would save some ammunition for next few days as well). Bottom line: Lines say can still be long, but now prefer sidelines temporarily as stops hit and lines should go to neutral after tomorrow.

...................

## AFTER-ACTION CRITIQUE

Status was still Bullish since both trend (+1) and ML (+1) still up; however, the ML was now on verge of turning to down cycle and so would probably lose that half point next day, and unless the SL turned up (and would only do so if price up very sharply) pattern would go to Neutral. Furthermore, since ML was on verge of turning to what looked like could/should go into a sustained down cycle, this meant were about to go from concurrent mode to crosscurrent mode.

If look back through past eight months of this chart, will see that it had not paid to be long while ML was on solid counter-trend move (i.e., market was in crosscurrent mode) and all signs pointed to this being imminent.

However, can note by my tone that the sustained up move had turned me, psychologically, very bullish. I obviously wanted to be long since had become convinced by the persistent upside action that this market could not go down much, or for long. This is natural tendency after sustained moves. We tend to be very skeptical in beginning, only to have steady with-trend pressure gradually turn this early skepticism into solid bullishness. Invariably, this bullishness usually gets strongest just before a significant counter-trend move. With this market now moving into what looked like could/would be a sustained period of crosscurrent mode, this was a time for some good restraint. If a trader followed the "rules" on this market over the previous three weeks, then could have produced substantial profits without ever being under any real price pressure. Naturally, a trader will always feel some pressure/fear when positioned in a trade; however, the price never put any serious downside pressure on anyone long here (at least until past two days).

(**NOTE:** *Will now skip forward one month so you can see what happened.*)

12/03/2001

COCOA (CSCE)
MAR

CONTRACT SIZE: 10 METRIC TONS
MINIMUM TICK : 1

SYMBOL CC02H
Trading Hours: 7:30- 12:30 CST

GRID:5.000      SL:21
49-D:1108.2    DL:40

<- WEEKLY RANKINGS ->     1        7      2    4    36

SMR (SECURITY MARKET RESEARCH) PO BOX 7476 BOULDER, CO 80306-7476 PHONE 303 635-2476 (01.18)

# March 2002 Cocoa

If you look at the chart you will see that had a third decent down day (after contract high day), and then a two day sideways-type pause, which was followed by a couple more decent down days.

On the fourth of December I made the following comment in the market letter:"Question is, what now? Market now in solid crosscurrent mode and 'rule' is this usually means will see more choppy-type action rather than trending action. However, when get such a big, sustained up move like have had here, normally do not see much in way of meaningful downside for some time, so it 'should' be good idea to be buyer on dips with idea of selling on what 'should' be inevitable, multiple swings back up to area of recent highs. In fact, it would be extremely unusual if even short-term highs have been made here (based on line and chart patterns). Only problem is have to buy when both price and lines pointing down and go with no stops for time being; so will be buying on 'faith' that past patterns will repeat."

The so-called market wisdom of "*never* adding to a loser" is one that I believe is false. While somewhat rare, there are definitely some situations where it is not only not wrong to add to a loser, but it is the intelligent action to take. However, need to be careful doing this and should only do so in special situations, meaning only in situations where trend is very strong (and trading with trend, of course), and you have to be willing to give up at some point if the line patterns turn solidly against you. In this particular case, scale down buys (with an average price around 1250) produced profits of approximately $700 per contract (or about 75 percent of margin), and only had to suffer through one bad day (the day market traded under 1225). After a sustained move in one direction, especially if it is a new bull/bear market, the first dip/rally is almost always quickly reversed. An old trading saying: "Always buy the first dip in a new bull market and sell the first rally in a new bear market." There is a lot of truth to this. However, when and if you do this you must be prepared to go without stops and have to be willing to keep buying/selling as price moves against trend. The best way to do this is to spread your positioning out over both time and price. Only add once every day or two, and only if can do so at meaningfully better prices. Then be ready to take profits very quickly on first sharp move back with trend. Again, this is only recommended for experienced traders.

This chart example (March 2002 Cocoa) shows very clearly that an individual does not need to "know" anything at all about the commodity being traded to make good profits. It is far more important for the individual trader to know and understand the natural laws of trading and how to apply them than it is to know anything at all about the fundamental supply and demand for a market. In this case, knowing and understanding the "rules" as I have outlined them in this book would have enabled you to produce big profits in Cocoa in a very short period of time, with only minor risk. It was not necessary to know a cocoa bean from a jellybean; however, it was absolutely necessary to know the "rules" and laws of trading. I did not guess at anything during this time period, nor did I predict the future. I just followed the rules. Since these rules are based on natural laws, I had an "edge" that enabled me to succeed without knowing anything at all about the supply/demand situation in cocoa.

Note also how reliably this market has followed the concurrent/crosscurrent rules. Crosscurrent mode periods have seen no trending action, but concurrent has.

01/02/2002

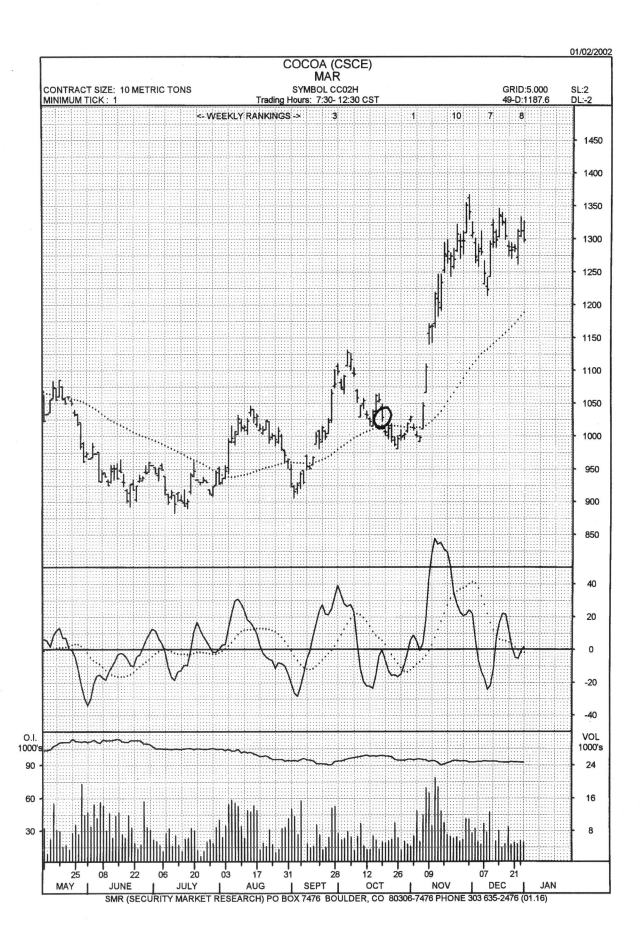

COCOA (CSCE)
MAR

CONTRACT SIZE: 10 METRIC TONS
MINIMUM TICK : 1

SYMBOL CC02H
Trading Hours: 7:30- 12:30 CST

GRID:5.000          SL:2
49-D:1187.6         DL:-2

<- WEEKLY RANKINGS ->          3          1          10          7          8

# THE THIRD LAW OF TRADING
## (The "business" law)

THE THIRD LAW OF TRADING IS **"PRICES FLUCTUATE."** This is also a clear, concise, simple statement that is a fundamental, structural, eternal truth of trading. It is the "practical" law of trading. It is the "business" law.

*Of course* the future is unknown; this philosophical law of trading is the correct way to "approach" trading. *Obviously* continuation is more likely than change; this theoretical law of trading is the "game," or science part, of trading. However, trading is a business, and what counts in the end are the real dollar results. Therefore, when it comes to money in a trader's pocket, the most important truth, or law, of all is "prices fluctuate."

What this means is that while continuation is more likely than change, this continuation is not a straight line; continuation invariably occurs in a somewhat jagged manner. Therefore, since continuation contains a meaningful degree of intermittent fluctuation, it is important to have a business plan for dealing with this fact.

To have a successful trading *business*, a trader must, with some consistency, sell higher than he buys and buy lower than he sells. The ultimate bottom line in trading is that to make money we have to take profits; to survive we have to control losses. To be successful at the end of the day, month, and year, a trader has to make more than he loses.

What then is the most businesslike way to go about doing this? By simply treating your trading "business" like you would any other business, which means working at achieving consistent day-to-day, week-to-week, month-to-month profitability rather than trying to strike it rich on the occasional great trade.

Neither Microsoft, GE, nor IBM relies solely on one product or one big sale. They do not bet everything on one deal, and neither should you in your trading business. Successful businesses establish desired (acceptable) profit objectives for each product, as well as limits on how much risk to accept on any one project. As a trader it is important you do the same.

In other words, it is important you *manage your money* properly by taking profits when they are "good," by taking losses before they become too "bad," and by diversifying risk over several markets at a time.

## MONEY MANAGEMENT

The whole idea of trend/momentum trading, or natural law trading, is to identify moments in time when markets have, or appear about to have, a clearly established directional trend and momentum, and then position with this trend/momentum.

The Status, as defined above, is a reasonably accurate representation of a market's current trend/momentum condition. As a general rule, any time the Status is Bullish or Bearish the odds will favor the market moving in that direction for the next day or so. This is simply the law of continuation in action. Therefore, whenever this is the case (i.e., the Status is Bullish or Bearish), those markets will be offering you an "edge," a statistical advantage. The question is how to take advantage of this "edge" in a businesslike manner.

If given ten potential trades whose probabilities of success ranged from 55 percent up to 80 percent, what should you do? If you were a large corporation, the answer would be to make every trade, while committing more capital to the trades with the highest probabilities. However, for an individual trader, I believe the correct answer is to focus all, or virtually all, your attention and energy on the highest probability propositions, and pass on the more marginally favorable ones.

Futures markets can be very volatile. Trading takes a lot of psychic energy, and the more different trades held at one time the more attention and energy required. Therefore, trading more than two or three markets at a time can be very consuming. Trading multiple markets at one time is a little like juggling; it is much easier to juggle two or three balls than six or eight. Furthermore, no one can learn to juggle six balls by starting with all six balls. The only way to learn to juggle multiple balls at one time is to start with two balls, and once this is learned go to three, and so on. Holding and managing futures positions in multiple markets at the same time is no different. Therefore, it is best to start by only trading one or two (or three at most) different markets at a time. Then, once some consistent success has served to build a foundation of confidence, gradually try trading more markets.

Naturally, all "Status" conditions do not present equal probabilities. A Bullish or Bearish Status in solid concurrent mode will have better odds than a Bullish or Bearish Status in strong cross-current mode. Concurrent mode trades (where trend and ML are both pointing in the same direction) are the trades that, by natural law, will have the best probability of success. Therefore, it makes *business* sense to focus energy and capital on those markets that are either in, or appear about to be in, a concurrent mode.

## CONTROLLING RISK (LOSSES)

An individual trader, regardless of how small a percentage of net worth is committed to trading, has to operate on the basis that his or her trading capital is limited. When capital is limited, the first focus has to be on risk, with the first objective survival.

The first step to ensure survival is to not allocate too much trading capital to any one trade. A good way to do this is to establish "personal position limits" for each market (meaning maximum number of contracts allowed per market). The size of these personal position limits is dictated both by the size of the account and the volatility of a market.

Naturally, every trader has different acceptable risk levels. A multimillionaire with a $50,000 trading account will have much different acceptable risk levels on any one trade than someone whose $50,000 account represents his entire net worth. Therefore, the following numbers can be adjusted upward, somewhat, if you can afford the additional risk. Following is how I would suggest structuring a $25,000 (or multiples thereof) trading account.

The markets used in this example are markets I currently follow and trade. Each trader needs to set up his or her own account structure based on his or her market preferences.

The first suggestion is to break your trading account into groups of "similar" markets (meaning markets that tend to be affected by the same economic factors and so tend to move together). The point is to prevent concentrating too much risk in any one group of similar markets.

### First divide the account into four separate groups of similar markets.
*For example:*

1 ~ The Stock Index group (allocate approximately 30 percent of your account's equity to this group): Dow, S&P, and/or NSDQ;

2 ~ The Anti-Dollar group (allocate about 25 percent of equity): Swiss (and/or Euro), Yen, Gold, and Silver;

3 ~ The Industrial & Interest Rate group (about 25 percent of equity): Bonds (and/or Notes, Eurodollars), Petro complex (Crude, Heating Oil, Unleaded), Cotton, and Copper;

4 ~ The Food group (about 20 percent of equity): Corn, Wheat, Bean complex (Beans, Meal and Bean Oil), Sugar, and Cocoa.

These subgroup allocations are approximate. Obviously, if you are faced with excellent continuation patterns in the food group and the stock group is very mixed at the moment, then it is perfectly acceptable to "borrow" some margin equity from stocks and allocate it to foods. However, only go over these suggested allocation numbers when the technical argument to do so is very good. Furthermore, when and if you do temporarily over position in one group, as soon as the trend/momentum indicators cease to be exceptionally favorable, go back to your normal trading levels.

As far as number of contracts to do in each market, as a basic rule, do not risk more than about $1000 a day in any one market (per $25,000 in the account). For example, since the S&P (at this moment) can easily move twenty points in a day, you would not want to hold more than one e-mini S&P for each $25,000 in your account. However, at the moment, a reasonable one day move/risk in the Beans is about ten cents (or $500 a contract), so you could hold up to two contracts of Beans per $25,000 of trading capital. Then, when and if normal daily price movement of a market changes (i.e., a market becomes more or less volatile), simply change your personal position limits accordingly.

(**NOTE:** *The larger an account, the lower these allocations should be—meaning while three contracts of wheat might be my limit on a $25,000 account, with a $100,000 account I would consider ten contracts, rather than twelve, to be more appropriate.*)

The essential point is to keep your positions "small" enough to avoid any panic-type actions caused by unexpected adverse short-term price action. For long-term success it is invariably better to be positioned "too small" than "too big." Markets can be volatile and frequently make many short-lived, "false" moves. When positioned "small," the cost of waiting for reasonable clarity is acceptable. When positioned "too big," the risk of being a little late in acting is so great it tends to induce actions based on guesses rather than reality.

As an example, I would consider the following personal position limits (per market and group) to be *businesslike* for a $25,000 account (based on current, i.e., 2002, volatility).

> 1 ~ Stock Index group: One contract of either the "$5 Dow," e-mini S&P, or e-mini NSDQ per $25,000 (the $5 Dow is the half-size Dow contract);

> 2 ~ Anti-dollar group: One Swiss, one Yen, and up to three contracts of precious metals (any combination of Gold and Silver adding up to three);

> 3 ~ Industrial & Interest Rate group: One contract of either Bonds or 10-year Notes (two contracts of Notes acceptable if pattern solid), up to two Eurodollar contracts, one contract of the "Petro" complex (either Crude, Heating Oil, or Unleaded), and up to two contracts of Copper;

> 4 ~ Food group: Up to three Corn contracts, up to three Wheat, up to two Beans or any combination of Meal or Bean Oil up to three contracts, up to three Sugar, and up to two Cocoa.

Now let me be clear. I am not implying that you should hold all of these contracts at the same time. The point is simply that, from a risk standpoint, these quantities of contracts per market are reasonable personal position limits for a $25,000 speculative trading account. Of course, if the pattern in the Yen happens to be very strong and the pattern in Swiss mixed, then you could justify doing up to two Yen per $25K as long as you did no Swiss. (In other words, it is acceptable to "borrow" some Swiss risk and assign it to the Yen when the situation clearly dictates doing so.) The basic idea is not to commit more than about a quarter of your account's equity (and presumably its risk) to any one group of similar markets (meaning markets that will tend to move somewhat together).

The numbers mentioned above should be adjusted when changes in market volatility occur and/or trend/momentum patterns are unusually strong. If a market becomes more volatile, then you should reduce your personal position limits, and conversely, increase them on decreases in volatility. Utilizing a general approach like this will keep your risk exposure in any one market or group of similar markets under control. In addition, adhering to these personal position limits will allow you to use generous stops on your positions, thus giving every trade the maximum opportunity to work (i.e., time to respond to the underlying trend/momentum price energy flows).

## GETTING IN (AND OUT)

The first step in the business of trading is the actual initiating of positions. First we have to get into trades. We have to put trades on. We have to pull the trigger. Most traders have little problem getting into trades; putting them on is usually fairly easy to do. (The bigger problem most traders have is getting out, but more on that later.) The real problem most people have is getting in at the right time. This is really what a trader means when he or she says, "I can't pull the trigger." If the trader is making trades, then he or she is pulling the trigger. Thus, the real problem is that the trader is not "pulling" at the right times.

First accept the fact—the absolute fact—that you cannot get in (or out) at the exact, precise perfect time and price. Being exactly right is not possible in trading; however, being "about" or "approximately" right is definitely possible. Therefore, start by working at trying to do the possible, not the impossible. Perfection is impossible. Approximation is very possible. Strive for approximation rather than perfection. Not only is it easier, it is ultimately more effective.

Therefore, when and if a price is in the general area where you want to buy or sell (basis the lines and price chart), just do it. Pick up the phone and place the order, at the market. If and when the technicals become clear, do not waste your time and energy "chasing" the price by moving limit orders around in an attempt to get in or out at the absolute best possible price. Instead, have a general price area and/or general time where and when you wish to buy or sell (based on the technicals, of course). Then, as soon as the price approaches and/or reaches that area and time, just act. Close enough is good enough when you have a good method, and the trend/momentum method laid out here is good (because it is based on natural laws and truths).

## HERE ARE SOME GENERAL RULES FOR INITIATING POSITIONS

If after the market has closed you decide that a position is fully justified, first try to position in the evening market (if the market has one) with a limit order at unchanged or better. If you do not get positioned in the overnight market, then try to position with a limit order at unchanged or better for about the first fifteen to thirty minutes of the day trading session. If still unable, then just cancel the limit and go at the market. The point is, if the previous day's close is a "good enough" price to initiate a position according to the current technicals, then try to get in at that price for a "while." However, if unable to position with limit orders, then just get in at the market. In other words, when trend/momentum become clear, it is OK to try to position at unchanged or better for a while; but just make sure to get positioned fairly quickly.

As a general rule, I believe it is best to limit your intra-day trading decisions as much as possible. I believe most traders make better decisions when the market is closed. It is always easier to see a stationary target more clearly than a moving one. However, if and when a market makes a big enough intra-day move to suddenly fully justify initiating a position, then use the same approach listed above. When and if the odds are in your favor you can briefly try to get in at current prices or slightly better; but if unable, just make sure you get in. When the odds clearly favor a certain directional move, the longer you wait to get in the more likely the price will move "away" from you. Time always favors the current trend/momentum; therefore, when price energy flow is clear, the quicker you get positioned with this flow the better.

## LIMITS VERSUS MARKET ORDERS

Prices go through cycles and phases. They ebb and flow. They fluctuate and surge. Sometimes a limit order is the better tactic; other times a market order is a better tactic.

## THE BASIC RULES ON LIMIT VERSUS MARKET ORDERS

1 ~ Use market orders to position when the current trend/momentum situation is already clearly pointing in one direction;

2 ~ Use limit orders when short-term momentum is currently moving against the direction you plan to trade but you can anticipate an imminent change in the trend/momentum situation (such as Status shifting from Neutral to Bullish or Bearish, or vice versa).

Think of the price as a train you are trying to jump aboard. If the train is pulling in to (i.e., approaching) the station, you can afford to take some time and try to judge the best place and time to jump on board. However, when the train is clearly leaving the station, then the best action is to just hop aboard as best you can—and usually the sooner the better. When the price and short-term momentum are moving counter trend and so coming back toward you—meaning down if you want to buy and up if you want to sell—then use a limit order to try to get in at a "good" price. However, when short-term momentum and price have clearly turned back with the trend, do not waste time and energy on trying to get the "perfect" price; just position at the market.

Of course, buying a dip is always better than buying a rally (and vice versa); however, depending on the situation, sometimes the exact opposite may be the "correct" action. The stronger the trend/momentum, the better the odds the price will continue its current move, therefore the quicker you should get in and the slower you should get out—regardless of whether the price is on a dip or rally. The more mixed the trend/momentum, the lesser the odds the price will move with the trend, therefore, in these cases, the more selective you can be about getting a "good" price.

In addition, the earlier in a strong price surge you position, the less the monetary risk will be (because the stop level will be closer) and the greater the potential profit will be (because the move is just starting). Therefore, always make a point of getting in very quickly whenever trend/momentum turns suddenly, and obviously, powerful. The point is, these are the situations where the odds will be the most favorable, the risk will be smallest, and the potential reward will be greatest. In others words, having both odds and risk/reward in your favor is a good combination. Therefore, when it exists, *act!* by getting in quickly.

Every market situation is somewhat unique, so you have to adapt your entry procedure to the current trend/momentum conditions. Your job as manager of your account is to look at reality as reflected in the lines and current price action, and then act as best you can in each case. This means working at consistently acting according to natural laws and proven methodology, and not on emotional, fleeting hunches.

## BOTTOM LINE ON LIMIT VERSUS MARKET ORDERS

1 ~ Get in quickly and sloppily (at market) when trend/momentum clear;

2 ~ Get in slowly and selectively (use limits) when anticipating a change from "iffy" to very clear in trend/momentum;

3 ~ Get out slowly and selectively (use limits) when trend/momentum still fairly strong, but starting to show signs of weakening;

4 ~ Get out rapidly and sloppily (at market) when trend/momentum have clearly turned.

## TAKING PROFITS

There are two ways to decide when and where to take profits: (1) by the size of the profit and (2) by the trend/momentum line pattern and the price chart picture. Generally, I believe you should take most of your profits following the "size-of-profit" rule. (By "size" I mean according to the percentage of initial margin requirement.)

Margin is simply good faith money deposited by you to cover any potential losses on your futures contracts. Margins are set by the various exchanges and are essentially determined by recent price volatility. The exchanges want to make sure your margin is sufficient to cover at least the current day or two standard deviation of price movement. The exchanges (and your broker) want to make sure you have enough margin deposited to cover any reasonable price moves over at least the next couple days (for the simple reason that they are responsible for any losses you do not cover). The bigger the recent price moves, the higher the margins will be, and vice versa.

Margin requirements are a reasonably good reflection of the existing potential price movement for the next couple of days. In effect, margins automatically tell you what a "good" short-term move would be for any market at any time. Therefore, it is only logical to use margins to determine basic "size-of-profit" rules for taking profits.

### THE TWO GENERAL TAKING-PROFIT-BY-"PERCENT-OF-MARGIN" RULES ARE AS FOLLOWS:

1 ~ When the profit on a trade reaches 50 percent of margin, begin to look for a good reason to take profits;

2 ~ When the profit on a trade reaches 100 percent of margin (or more), you need a legitimate reason NOT to take profits.

The primary "reason" NOT to take profits when they reach or exceed 100 percent of margin is the market is in a solid concurrent mode. (By "solid" I mean neither trend nor ML have any chance of changing direction over at least the next few days or week, i.e., the concurrent mode is truly solid.) When this is the case, then it is perfectly acceptable—and frequently better—to give the trade some more time to work (i.e., allow the profit time to get bigger).

Most, if not all, of the trades that produce more than 100 percent of margin profit will be those in solid concurrent modes. However, it has been my experience that even in cases where the profit on a trade manages to reach levels of 250 percent or more of margin (and this level of profit is somewhat rare), a good portion (a third or so) of the profit often will be lost in the few days before the lines finally switch back from Bullish or Bearish to Neutral. Trades that achieve really big profits tend, for some reason, to give back a good chunk of their profits in a very short time when the with-trend price move ends and turns back against the trend. What this means is that getting out "too soon" when in good trades tends to end up producing an equal, or frequently better, profit than waiting for the lines to finally switch back to indicating sidelines best (i.e., when a Bullish or Bearish Status switches back to Neutral).

If your trading account is large enough to hold multiple contracts on a trade, then I suggest you consider the following approach: Take partial profits around the 50 percent margin level, additional partial profits at 100 percent of margin, additional profits at 150 percent, and then let the rest ride until you can make a good case the Status is on verge of switching back to Neutral. This approach is true pyramiding. Visualize a position starting with four contracts, then going to three, then two, and finally one and you have a pyramid. Of course, a trader would need to start with at least four contracts to do the above. Again, these position levels could be, and usually should be, overridden when/if the market is in a solid concurrent mode.

This "percent-of-margin" method is an arbitrary, mathematical approach to taking profits; however, it is one I have found to work quite well. Naturally, this is just one general approach. Every trader has to adjust the taking of profits, like all other aspects of trading, to his or her personality and account size, as well as to the current technical patterns.

The other way to determine when and if to take profits is to use the trend/momentum line patterns.

## THE BASIC RULES FOR USING TREND/MOMENTUM LINES TO DECIDE WHEN AND WHERE TO TAKE PROFITS ARE AS FOLLOWS:

> 1 ~ Anytime the SL (the short-term momentum line) nears or reaches a recent "extreme" (i.e., is in area of the past few months' highs if long and/or in area of past few months' lows if short), then you can make a case to take some profits;

> 2 ~ The exception to this is when the market is in a solid concurrent mode, and the more solidly concurrent the better the case to override a recent high/low in the SL (and not take profits).

I mentioned earlier that a good way to look at the SL is to think of it as a boxer throwing a punch. When trend is up and SL is at recent lows, then the "arm" is cocked back and there is plenty of potential upside energy ready to be unleashed. When trend is up and SL is at recent highs, then the "arm" is fully extended. However, when the market is in a solid concurrent mode, this means the "boxer" throwing the punch is a powerful heavyweight and still has plenty of energy left in his arm, even though it is extended. Conversely, when the market is in a strong crosscurrent mode, or the underlying trend/ML pattern is essentially sideways, then consider an extended SL to be the "arm" of a weak lightweight who is unlikely to have any punching power left. In other words, the underlying pattern of the trend and ML tell you how worried to be about a fully extended SL and how urgent the need to take profits might be.

## BASIC RULE ON USING LINE PATTERN VERSUS SIZE OF PROFIT

The more clear and solid the line pattern, the more you should rely on the lines; the more "iffy" or shaky the line pattern, the more you should rely on the arbitrary mathematical (percent-of-margin) size-of-profit method.

(*Note: The size-of-profit and the line-pattern methods are both sound, general approaches to profit taking if you are short- and intermediate-term trading. However, if you are a dyed-in-the-wool long-term trader, like the two long-term traders I referred to earlier, then the approach should be different. I will provide some suggestions for long-term traders later.*)

Conventional market wisdom says to "let your profits run." However, unless you are a true long-term trader (meaning in reality, not merely in intent), I believe this widely accepted and repeated truism is actually a "false-ism." Let your profits run to where? Until they disappear and turn into losses? No. As a trader, to make money you must take profits.

## TO MAKE MONEY YOU HAVE TO TAKE PROFITS

There is simply no other way. In trading you are going to take losses: impossible to avoid this. Sometimes events will blind side you; other times you will simply be wrong. The only way to overcome these inevitable losses is to make sure you take some profits when they happen to be "good."

Successful trading is, to a large degree, dependent on mental attitude. After all, it is a mental game. Having a positive attitude and being confident are extremely important for success. The only event more psychologically debilitating to a trader than giving back a good profit on a trade is taking a big loss. And sometimes it is actually more psychologically harmful to give back a big profit than take a big loss. Therefore, it is essential to try to consistently "feed" and bolster your mental attitude and confidence by taking at least some profits when they are "good." Having some good profits in the "bank" makes future confident action much easier, and therefore more likely to be successful.

In a decision-making game like trading, where every decision involves a meaningful amount of doubt, confidence will play a tremendous role in the outcome. Consistent moderate success builds confidence much better than rare exceptional success. I believe that for the overwhelming majority of traders, persistent consistent moderate success will produce a better financial bottom line than rare exceptional success. Therefore, for both business and psychological reasons, the intelligent approach is to start taking profits when they reach reasonably acceptable and desirable levels, and the area of 50 to 100 percent of margin in profits is "good" by any definition. In other words, the businesslike approach is to be more afraid of giving back *good* profits rather than being fearful of missing out on *giant* profits.

I believe that in the long run the overwhelming majority of individual traders would come out better if they followed something like these general percent-of-margin profit-taking rules instead of vainly trying to catch the really "big moves." In my experience, looking for the big move is not too harmful to results if trading is being played as simply a game, meaning the monetary results are unimportant. However, if trading is in any way a business—meaning if the net monetary results are important in any way whatsoever—then always looking for big moves can be very detrimental to success. In the *business* of trading, the pursuit of the rare giant profit is the enemy of taking good profits.

There is a story attributed to the legendary, early twentieth-century trader Bernard Baruch. Supposedly, one day a young man approached him in the park and asked him what was the key to his success. Mr. Baruch responded by simply saying: "I always make a point of getting out 'too soon.'" Meaning, he did not try to squeeze every possible cent of profit from every trade by letting his fear of leaving some profits on the table be more powerful than his fear of giving back good profits. In other words, he maintained a basic business sense about his trading. He started taking profits when they were "good" and did not worry about missing the occasional giant profit. He treated his trading as a *business*, not as a lottery-type affair with a slim potential for giant jackpots.

## TAKING LOSSES

Unfortunately, it is not possible to trade without having to take losses from time to time. There are three methods for determining when it is necessary to take a loss: by the line pattern, by the price chart, and by the size of the loss.

**1 ~ THE LINE-PATTERN METHOD OF DETERMINING WHEN TO TAKE A LOSS:** This method is simply to act after a clear shift, or in anticipation of a probable imminent shift, in the Status from Bullish or Bearish back to Neutral. In other words, if you are long or short with the Status and it changes (or you anticipate it is on the verge of changing) from Bullish or Bearish back to Neutral, then, even if you have a loss, simply get out of the trade at the market. Again, it is OK to try to get out at unchanged for a few minutes; however, usually in this type of situation it is best to just get out. Since you have a loss on the trade, by definition it has not gone according to plan. When a plan goes bad, most of the time the sooner you abandon it the better.

As far as stops go, using the line pattern and the anticipated line pattern as the determinant of where to place stops is somewhat of an art. Throughout the many chart examples later in the book I will show how I practice this art, and hopefully this will help in your practice of it.

**2 ~ THE PRICE-CHART METHOD OF DETERMINING WHEN AND WHERE TO TAKE LOSSES:** This method is simply looking at the chart and choosing an appropriate point to place your stop loss order. However, finding the "best" chart points to place stops is, to a large degree, more of an art than a science. The basic rule is, you want to place your stops at the point where the line pattern will materially change for the worse (meaning switch back to Neutral from Bullish or Bearish). You want to place your stop at the point where the price "should" not go if the trade is a "good" one (meaning goes according to natural laws). There is no point in taking a loss as long as the underlying line pattern remains clearly in your favor (still in the direction of your trade) and the price has not moved to a level that would change this pattern. Furthermore, because the line pattern is determined based on closing price, generally I prefer (whenever risk is acceptable) to use close-only stops.

**CLOSE-ONLY STOPS VERSUS REGULAR STOPS:** A "close-only stop" simply means the stop is not activated until the closing range for that day. If the price is at, or beyond, the stop price on the close (below on a sell stop, above on a buy stop), then the position is liquidated at the market during the closing period. The benefit of using close-only stops is your position will not be liquidated on a brief, potentially aberrant, intra-day move. The risk in using close-only stops is your stop may be executed at a meaningfully worse price, so the loss will be bigger than planned. To limit this additional risk I recommend using what I call "late-in-the-day/close-only stops." What I mean by this is if the price is at, or clearly beyond, the stop level "late" in the day (meaning in the final 30 to 60 minutes of trading), then go ahead and liquidate the trade at the market rather than running the risk of taking a much bigger loss by waiting for the close.

While sometimes using close-only stops will produce significantly bigger losses than by using regular stops, I believe the times you will avoid getting "incorrectly" stopped out (meaning stopped out on an intra-day move only to then have the market reverse sharply later in the day and the trade ends up "working") will more than make up for the occasional bigger loss. In the long run I believe selective use of close-only stops will produce a better bottom line for your trading business. However, since risk is increased with close-only stops, you need to manage each situation to ensure none get out of control, meaning if volatility is too great it may not be feasible (i.e., it will be too risky) to use close-only stops.

**3 ~ THE SIZE-OF-LOSS METHOD OF DETERMINING WHEN AND WHERE TO TAKE LOSSES:** This method is fairly simple. Just determine how much you are willing to risk on a trade and then put a regular stop at that price level. As far as percent of margin, in very general terms, using the same basic percent of margin for taking profits is reasonable. In other words, if the loss reaches 50 percent of margin, look at the line pattern to see if there is a legitimate reason to close out the trade and take the loss (meaning has the pattern materially changed for the worse). If the loss reaches 100 percent of margin, then you must have a very good reason to hold onto the position rather than just giving up and taking the loss.

## BOTTOM LINE ON TAKING LOSSES

While I prefer emphasizing the size-of-profit (percent-of-margin) method to determine when and where to take a profit (except on solid concurrent mode trades), when it comes to taking losses, I believe this method (loss as percent of margin) is the least effective and should only be used as a last resort. I believe a combination of line pattern and price chart levels tends to work best in the long run when determining where and when to take losses. The key is to look for the price level where the line pattern will materially change, as well as the point on the price chart a price "should" not reach if the market is still "good" for the direction you are trading. Then, if the price moves beyond this "should-not-go" level for any significant time (15 to 30 minutes or so) intra-day, or does so late in the day or on the close, then simply close out the trade, take the loss, and move on to the next trade.

## BOTTOM LINE ON THE THIRD LAW OF TRADING

Trading according to the three natural laws of trading and relying on reasonably reliable trend/momentum indicators (such as SMR's) should put you in position to profit from any/all decent moves in several markets at the same time. In addition, you will be able to do this without ever being exposed to excessive risk. If you follow this general approach and method, develop a certain talent at reading your charts, and then act on what you see, you should find your account producing consistent profits without too much stress or strain. However, you have to work at it every day. To be successful you have to "manage" your account (i.e., be a good manager of your trading business), just like the manager of any other business.

What this means is you have to keep constant track of what is happening with both the price and the trend/momentum lines in each market you are trading. You have to make sure that you are positioned with the trend/momentum indicators in each market, or what you anticipate the lines will soon be, as well as ensure you are holding an appropriate number of contracts. Sometimes you will make the wrong decision; other times you will be right. As a business-person you just have to accept that perfection in this business of trading is impossible. All you can do is focus energy on making the best, most intelligent decisions you can in each case.

If the result (i.e., MONEY!) is important in even the slightest way, then you have an obligation to operate and manage your trading account as a business. If you are a multimillionaire and put on a one-contract S&P position, the monetary impact is trivial. On the other hand, if you have only five thousand dollars to speculate with and put on a one-contract position in the e-mini S&P, then the results of that trade are of critical importance. In the former you can afford the luxury of having your vision distorted and your actions affected by desire and bias. However, in the latter case you must, by necessity, act in as "pure" a manner possible, meaning in compliance with probabilities and realities, in line with natural laws, and in accordance with sound businesslike practices.

This is the third law of trading: prices fluctuate. It is the practical law, the business law. Prices fluctuate; they do not go up or down in straight lines. So, to operate your trading account as a business, it is necessary to take profits when they are good, control losses before they become too large, and diversify your risks over several markets at once.

Run your trading program as a business. In other words, operate your trading business like a mini version of IBM, GE, or Microsoft. Always strive for consistency of profits while avoiding taking major risk exposure on any one trade. Constantly work at trading intelligently on a trade-by-trade basis, day in, day out. Trading intelligently day by day means following and adhering to the natural laws of trading while consistently acting in a businesslike manner.

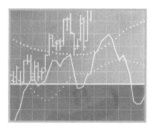

# RELATIVE STRENGTH

THE LAW OF CONTINUATION applies not only to directional price movement but also to the relative or comparative strength and weakness between different markets. What this means is that the markets currently strongest will tend to continue being the strongest and the markets currently weakest will tend to remain the weakest.

A couple of years ago (in the late 1990s) I held a few seminars on futures trading. The night before the first of these I used a simple method to measure which markets were the strongest and which the weakest. My objective was to provide a real-time example of the tendency for relative strength and weakness to continue.

I made a copy of the chart of each futures market and circled the price from ten weeks earlier on each one. Then, by simply "eye-balling" each chart, I separated them into three groups: the markets in clear uptrends (meaning the price at the moment was clearly higher than it had been ten weeks earlier); the markets in sideways trends; and those in clear downtrends. Then, I arranged each group in descending order from strongest to weakest. The net result turned out to be three groups of about eight to ten markets each, with each group arranged in descending order from strongest to weakest. I printed these results and handed them out the next day.

During the seminar I presented the basic rule of relative strength, which is: Once clearly established, comparative or relative strength and weakness between different futures markets is more likely to continue than change. Therefore, a trader should always look for reasons to go long the strongest markets and short the weakest.

Unfortunately, going long the strongest and short the weakest markets tends to be "unnatural" for many traders. Instead, what seems to be natural for many traders is believing that markets that have been going up (and down) for a long time simply will not—indeed cannot—continue to do so much longer. As a result, most traders tend to be much more interested in buying when prices are "low" (i.e., have been going down for a long time) and selling when "high," rather than vice versa. This is the old buy-low, sell-high theory of trading. Unfortunately for those using this approach, in futures trading low usually means even lower and high tends to mean even higher.

Six months after this seminar I happened to come across my copy of this relative strength data. Naturally I was curious to see how it had worked out. So I methodically went through the current chart book and produced another list of the strongest and weakest markets. When I compared the two lists I was pleased—but not overly surprised—to see that only one or two markets in each group had migrated to another group. The overwhelming majority of the strongest markets six months earlier were still the strongest, and the same was the case with the weakest, as well as those that had been in sideways trends. Virtually all the markets had continued to move in the clear direction they had been moving six months earlier; the existing patterns of relative strength had continued, not changed.

Interestingly, I had conducted the identical experiment with the SMR stock book (SMR also publishes charts on about fifty individual stocks). However, at least for that particular time period, I was surprised to discover that essentially every stock had switched groups. My experience with individual stocks is very limited, so I do not know if this was an aberration or if stocks are just not as reliable as futures markets in terms of consistency of relative strength/weakness. I have not repeated this experiment, but I know from thirty years of watching the futures markets that once relative strength/weakness is clearly established between individual futures markets, it is much more likely to continue than change.

There are two basic means of measuring relative strength between markets. The first is through a simple comparison of the past several months' worth of price movement (i.e., relative strength or weakness of trends). This is the basic, straightforward approach I used in the experiment mentioned above. I believe this is the best (meaning most reliable) method to use for long-term trading. The second method of measuring relative strength is through a comparison of the past week or so of both price movement *and* momentum line patterns. I find this approach tends to work better for very short-term trading (i.e., the next few days to a week or so).

In addition to the consistency of relative strength among all futures markets, there is also a marked consistency of relative strength within some groups of "similar" markets. Over the years I have found the groups of similar markets that are the most reliable in terms of internal relative strength are the Grain group (Corn, the Bean complex, Wheat, and Oats), the Currency markets, and the Precious Metals (Platinum, Gold, and Silver). Once relative strength/weakness is clearly established within any of these groups, it tends to continue for some time. Therefore, for example, once one market within the Grain group is clearly stronger than the others, it will have a strong tendency to continue being stronger for an extended period of time (meaning as long as many months), and vice versa for a market that is clearly the weakest.

Next in terms of reliability of internal relative strength are the Stock Index group (Dow, S&P, NSDQ, and Russell 2000) and the Crude complex (Crude Oil, Heating Oil, and Unleaded Gasoline). While fairly reliable in terms of internal relative strength/weakness, these two groups can reverse existing relative strength suddenly and fairly dramatically for short periods of time. Therefore, a trader has to be more careful when relying on this indicator in these markets. Among other markets, the Natural Gas market tends to move independently of the Crude complex. I find the Meat group (Live and Feeder Cattle, Live Hogs and Pork Bellies) to be fairly unreliable in terms of consistency of internal relative strength. Finally, unique markets, such as Cotton, Orange Juice, Cocoa, Coffee, and Sugar tend to move independently.

## BOTTOM LINE ON RELATIVE STRENGTH

In terms of relative or comparative strengths and weakness between *all* futures markets, the second law of trading clearly prevails: Continuation is more likely than change. The strongest futures markets tend to remain the strongest, the weakest markets tend to remain the weakest, and those moving sideways tend to continue to do so. Secondarily, within certain groups of "similar" markets, relative strength also tends to be very reliable; unfortunately, in other groups there is little reliability. Therefore, it is important to know which is which. Grains, Currencies, and Precious Metals are the most reliable groups in terms of internal relative strength, with Stock Indexes and the Crude complex coming next. However, the remaining market groups and the individual unique markets are generally unreliable in terms of any "internal" (group) relative strength.

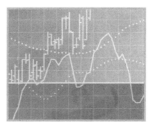

# KNOW YOURSELF

THERE IS NO "ONE SIZE FITS ALL" best way to trade the markets. Some of us are better suited for short-term trading; others better for long-term trading.

One of the first and most important steps you, as a trader, *must* take in order to be successful is to know yourself. You must be realistic about what you can and cannot do. You must be aware of your ingrained conditioning as well as any strong personality traits. You must accept your tolerable risk levels as well as your profit desires. In other words, you must know yourself.

If your objective were to become a professional athlete, the first step would be a realistic assessment of physical traits and athletic abilities. If you are on the short and slow side, basketball would be out of the question, regardless of personal desires. If you are on the frail and passive side, then linebacker in the NFL would be unattainable, regardless of wishes. If you are on the large and muscle-bound side, becoming a successful marathon runner would probably be out of the question. The point is that regardless of what your or my personal desires might be, for us to be successful we need to put realistic self-knowledge above personal desires.

The same is true when determining what type of trader you are best suited to be. Do a realistic assessment of yourself; know yourself. Some of us are best suited for long-term trading, others for short-term trading. For example, long-term trading requires great patience and "deeper pockets" (meaning having significantly more margin per contract since trades need to be given plenty of room to work). While on the other hand, short-term trading does not require much in the way of patience and can be done on a tighter "budget" (since stops can—and should—be fairly close).

Short-term trading involves significantly more decision making than long-term trading; therefore, to do it well an individual must have a much greater tolerance for mistakes. Conversely, you cannot expect to be a successful long-term trader if you are inclined to be quick to get out whenever a trade moves somewhat against you. Additionally, you should not try to be a short-term trader if you have difficulty pulling the trigger on trades. The point is that different "time styles" of trading require different personality traits and characteristics. Therefore, it is essential to know yourself and then choose the time style of trading that best suits you, regardless of which type of trader—short term or long term—you would like to be.

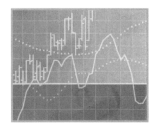

# LONG-TERM TRADING METHOD

THE INDIVIDUAL BEST SUITED FOR LONG-TERM FUTURES TRADING is usually someone who has been conditioned through stock market "trading": in other words, someone who is accustomed to buying a stock and then holding it for extended periods of time. Normally, a long-term futures trader should be an individual who approaches futures trading with the same basic outlook he or she would have when trading/investing in the stock market. This type of individual is preconditioned to allocate substantial margin for each contract and hold through any short- to intermediate-term periods of adverse price movement. Both traits are necessary for successful long-term trading.

Unfortunately, the typical stock market trader/investor also comes to futures trading with some decidedly negative conditioning. The primary negative is that he or she invariably wants—even appears to require—a "story" to support every trade. By this I mean he or she needs to have a definite "opinion" (based on fundamental supply/demand factors) on which direction a market should move and why it should do so. This type of individual tends to be way too focused on the "why" of price movement, and this can be a deadly trait for a futures trader. Remember, we simply cannot compete in this game when the question is "why" a price has moved, or should move, in a particular direction. Therefore, if this description applies to you, the first step is to drop any and all opinions about "why" a market will move in a particular direction. Instead focus on "what" a market's price has been doing, and especially on "what" it has been doing *relative* to other markets.

The key to being a successful long-term futures trader is to be consistently long the strongest (uptrending) markets and short the weakest (downtrending) markets. The simplest, most direct, and best way to determine which markets are which is by simply comparing, on a frequent (at least weekly) basis, the relative strengths or weakness of the different markets' trends (i.e., their ten-week moving averages). Simply go through the process I did while preparing for my seminar (as discussed earlier).

Now, of course, it is necessary to apply some common sense to these comparisons, and by this I mean looking back not only at where the price of each market was ten weeks earlier but also to where it was eight and nine weeks earlier as well. Naturally, if the price ten weeks ago was way out of line with the surrounding time period (because it was on a short-lived spike in price, up or down), then you have to make adjustments. All trading and chart reading requires some common sense interpretation and adjustments; it cannot be totally rigid and mechanical. The point here is that the best approach/method for long-term trading is to allow maximum opportunity for the law of continuation and the rule of relative strength to work for you.

Of course, trends and relative strength patterns do not last forever. Periodically they change. The trick in long-term trading is to be reasonably adept at recognizing when these changes have occurred (or, preferably, when they are about to occur). Among the "tools" to use in attempting to recognize imminent changes in trend and relative strength are the methods discussed earlier for "anticipating" changes in the "direction line" (i.e., anticipating changes in the trend or ten-week moving average), as well as watching for momentum line and price-chart patterns that tend to precede major directional changes of price. Examples of these would be line patterns with multiple bullish (if trend down) or bearish (if trend up) divergences between price and short-term momentum (SL), plus false breakouts and island reversals on the price charts.

Some basic money management tools should also be applied to this type of trading. The percent of margin for taking profits rules should be discarded as these apply more for short-term trading and are not particularly applicable or beneficial for long-term trading. Instead, as long as the market remains one of the strongest or weakest, an effort should be made to slowly, but steadily, add contracts to each position.

One way to do this is to add contracts to your initial position whenever the SL moves back close to the zero line (i.e., use short-term counter-trend moves to add additional contracts). In addition, you should be more heavily positioned when in concurrent mode and lighter when in crosscurrent mode. Naturally, all of this requires judgment. And when judgment is used, sometimes you will be wrong. The important thing is to just keep adjusting, and if you make a mistake (such as getting out in anticipation of a trend change but then the trend does not change), then simply correct this mistake by quickly repositioning. Remember, the basic objective is to be consistently positioned in a way so as to give the law of continuation and the rule of relative strength every opportunity to work for you. The way to do this is to keep adjusting your positions so that you are consistently long the strongest markets and short the weakest.

## BOTTOM LINE ON LONG-TERM TRADING

Rely primarily on strength of trend and relative strength when deciding which markets to be positioned in; however, always keep an eye on momentum line and price-chart patterns for signs of potential changes in trend and relative strength. Be positioned heavier when the market is in concurrent mode and lighter when in crosscurrent mode. Rely on what you "see" on the charts (the "what" of trading) and put little, if any, weight on opinions you may hold (the "why" of investing). Allow plenty of margin for each position, then just be patient and give the natural laws and rules of trading plenty of time to work for you. However, never forget that eventually you will have to take profits and stop trading that particular market in that direction. Therefore, try not to become too attached to any one position, no matter how much you may believe it is headed ever higher or lower. In other words, do not be like my former client who ran a few thousand up to several million in seven months but then could not stand to get out of his positions even after the trends clearly had turned against him, so that in less than three months he allowed that several million to dwindle back to zero.

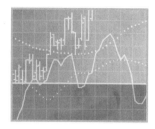

# THE "SPIKE" RULE

YOU ARE A TRADER. You are sitting there watching your normally reliable technical indicators. Suddenly the market surges dramatically. A giant move happens in minutes. Or, you wake up one morning, check the markets, and one of them is sharply higher or lower. In either case, the move is so big and fast it sends your indicators (and thoughts) spinning out of control. If the surge is against you, your heart drops to the pit of your stomach; you feel somewhat nauseous and frightened. It is as if you are in an airplane that has suddenly dropped several thousand feet. If the surge is in your favor, you sit up abruptly, energized by a burst of adrenaline. You feel like you have just won a minor lottery. What happened? What's the news? What's going on? You turn up the volume on CNBC with one hand as you speed dial your broker with the other.

You are in the middle of a surprise "price spike," probably the most difficult situation a trader ever experiences. Thrown completely off balance by the speed and magnitude of the move, you are confused and very unsure of what to do (partly because one-day price spikes tend to throw otherwise normally reliable trend/momentum indicators temporarily "off"). You ask yourself, is this the start of a sustainable price surge or is it only an unusually bright flash in the pan? In other words, is the move a "continuation spike" or an "aberration spike." What you do next is critically important. Do you go with the spike or do you fade it? Get it right you win big; get it wrong and you can take a serious hit.

A "price spike" is defined as a sudden, surprisingly large, one-day price surge big enough to make you spontaneously exclaim: "Wow! What the #*@! is going on in the———market?" To qualify as a "price spike," a one-day move has to clearly stand out on the charts as "extraordinary." It is not simply a good-sized, one-day move. To be a "spike," a one-day move should be the biggest recent one-day move on its chart, as well as be at least somewhat "technically" unexpected.

Here is how to handle this most difficult of trading situations. As soon as you recognize a one-day move as being a "spike," ask yourself two questions:

    1 ~ Is the spike with or against the trend?
    2 ~ Is the spike due to a specific news event or is it essentially unexplainable?

Use a standard 50-day moving average to determine the trend and use the intra-day spike price as the "last" or most recent price on the average. "Specific news event" means something new for that day and includes such events as surprise interest rate cuts, unexpected comments from the Fed Chairman, government interventions in a currency market, surprise world political developments, surprisingly strong or weak economic reports, exceptionally surprising earnings reports or warnings, and so on.

To determine whether the big one-day move is a "continuation spike" or an "aberration spike," simply follow these two "rules":

## THE TREND RULE ON SPIKES

1 ~Against-the-trend spikes should be considered most likely "aberrations";
2 ~With-the-trend spikes should be considered most likely "continuations."

## THE NEWS RULE ON SPIKES

1 ~ Be skeptical of spikes with an obvious, news-related cause (i.e., these are more likely "aberration" spikes);
2 ~ Respect all spikes with no specific cause (i.e., these are more likely "continuation"spikes).

## THERE ARE FOUR POSSIBILITIES WITH THESE RULES

1 ~ An against-the-trend, news-related spike—this is the combination most likely to be an aberration spike;
2 ~ A with-the-trend, unexplainable spike—this one is most likely to be a continuation spike;
3 ~ An against-the-trend spike with no specific cause—this one should be treated as a "wild card" spike since it is sometimes capable of overcoming all but the strongest trends;
4 ~ A with-the-trend, news-caused spike—this is the least reliable in terms of the spike rule.

(**NOTE:** *As a general rule you should give the "Trend Rule" more weight than the "News Rule"—with the stronger the trend, the heavier the weight.*)

Market history shows that spikes occurring against a solid trend have a strong tendency to return quickly, usually within a few days, to their pre-spike price levels. The trend is like the undercurrent of a river; unless an against the current surface surge is powerful enough to completely turn around the fundamental direction of the river, the preexisting longer term underlying current will fairly quickly overpower the countercurrent surface surge. Markets are no different. Counter-trend price spikes are usually quickly reversed.

Conversely, it is only natural that spikes occurring with the trend would have a strong tendency to continue. Pushing a price suddenly and sharply in the direction it is already moving tends to have the effect of giving the existing trend and momentum a sudden big surge of new energy. Therefore, with-the-trend spikes tend to have at least brief (several day to a week or two) continuation surges; however, the length of these surges are usually dependent on whether they are news related (i.e., news caused) or not.

News-related, with-the-trend spikes do tend to continue for a while (a week or two); however, after that relatively brief surge this type of spike is frequently reversed. For example, when a market that has been in a long uptrend is suddenly hit with some very bullish news, this seems to prompt most of those on the sidelines waiting or thinking about buying to go ahead and do so, while at the same time this news event serves as a catalyst to make most of the weak shorts in the market cover. This combination borrows ahead on buying power (both from new longs getting in as well as shorts covering). Then, once this spurt of buying is exhausted, the up surge tends to run out of energy. (The same is true of a long-lasting downtrending market hit by surprise negative news.) Therefore, with-the-trend, news-related spikes tend to be tricky since they usually have a big with-the-trend surge, but it tends to not last very long. The trick is to recognize when it has exhausted itself, and this is difficult to do because emotions tend to take over when price is surging so strongly and the news is with the surge.

Surprise news events tend to have only a transitory effect on prices because their impact is almost always primarily psychological. Most news events simply do not materially affect the underlying fundamental supply/demand situation of a market, and even when they do, it takes time to change existing reality. The psychological shock of a surprise "news event" will almost always dissipate within a day or two when it comes against the trend, and within a week or two when it comes with the trend.

On the other hand, markets rarely make big one-day moves for no reason whatsoever; therefore, unexplainable price spikes usually have unseen, but valid, causes. When there is no obvious explanation for a one day price spike, the true reason for the move is frequently an underlying shift in the basic supply/demand equation (at least for the near term). And as such, this type of spike will tend to signal the beginning of a sustainable move regardless of existing trend.

How long to stay with a trade based on a "continuation spike" or an "aberration spike" depends on the underlying trend (the more solid the trend, the longer a trader should give the trade). As a rule, once the price of an "aberration spike" (e.g., a down spike in an uptrending market) has returned to its pre-spike level, then the "spike rule" is no longer in effect and you should resume relying on your regular trend/momentum indicators. Once a "continuation spike" has continued to push with the trend for anywhere from a few days to a week or two, then a trader should go back to his or her regular technical trading process.

On the following pages are three examples of spikes. On the left page is the chart as of the day of the spike and on the right page is the chart of several days later.

The first example is of the surprise interest rate cut in January 2001. This was a good example of a "news-related, against-the-trend spike" (i.e., meaning it was most likely an "aberration spike"). This interest rate cut came as a big surprise to the markets and prompted a very sharp one-day rally in a clear downtrending stock market. Yet, the price quickly returned to the approximate price levels existing just prior to the rate cut announcement.

After the early January surprise rate cut, the price of the S&P futures took only two and a half days to return to its pre-announcement levels. However, since the existing downtrend was not solid, the price just barely made it back to pre-spike levels. Regardless, the price did retrace its spike.

The second example is of a one and a half point down move in June Bond futures on April 10, 2001. This was a good example of an "unexplainable, with-the-trend spike" (i.e., most likely to be a "continuation spike"). This one-day move was sudden, and surprisingly, big, yet it occurred on no specific news. After holding in the area of the spike day's close for three days, the price dropped another two-and-a half points over the next week. Since the underlying downtrend was strong in this case, the continued downside pressure was to be expected.

The third example is a three-dollar upside "pop" in July Meal on April 30, 2001 (which clearly stood out on the chart). This was a good example of an "unexplainable, against-the-trend spike." The weakness of the prevailing downtrend meant this "non-news-related, against-the-trend spike" was likely to continue. As the chart shows, the price of July Meal moved more than ten dollars higher in next three weeks, and in the process actually turned the trend up.

These are just three examples of the effectiveness of this "spike rule." Do a little research as well as watch what happens in the future and you will see for yourself just how effective these guide-lines tend to be.

Therefore, to sum up: If a spike is with the trend, go with it, at least for a few days or a week; if it is against the trend, tend to fade it. If the spike has an obvious cause, be skeptical of it lasting; if it has no specific explanation, respect it. Use the strength or weakness of the trend to fine tune the application of these rules.

Of course, no trading rule works all the time, so every trading rule should have an escape plan in case of failure. Most of the time the extreme price of an against-the-trend spike is hit on the spike day (usually near the close); however, on an occasional against-the-trend spike the price will push a little farther the day or two after the spike day. Therefore, the rule for trading "against-trend" spikes is to give up when and if the price exceeds the extreme price of the spike day plus the next two days. The rule for giving up on trades made due to "with-trend" spikes is if the price retraces (i.e., gives back) the entire spike, then you should get out. When a with-the-trend spike quickly (i.e., several days or a week or so) returns to its pre-spike price level, this is a sign the spike was an aberration.

Naturally, there is a certain amount of subjectivity to applying these rules; however, I have found them to be unusually reliable in all futures markets (although somewhat less so with individual stocks). Bottom line: These rules are a very good way to intelligently deal with the shock of surprise one-day price spikes.

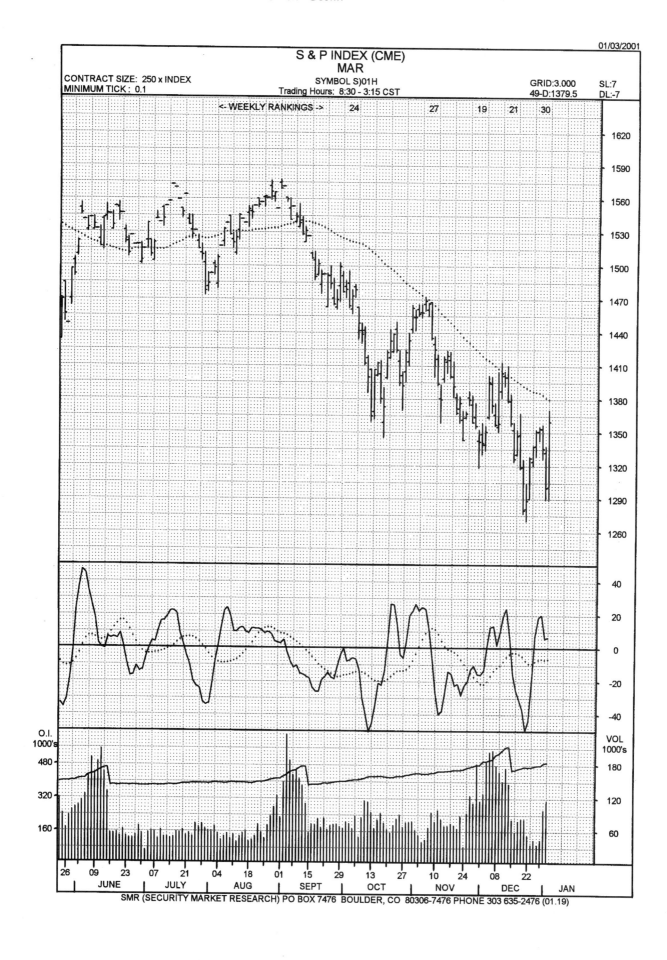

S & P INDEX (CME)
MARCH 2001

CONTRACT SIZE: 250 x INDEX
MINIMUM TICK : .10

SYMBOL S)01H
Trading Hours: 8:30 - 3:15 CST

GRID: 3.000 SL: -13
49-D:1374.4 DL: -10

<- WEEKLY RANKINGS ->

SMR (SECURITY MARKET RESEARCH)   PO BOX 7476   BOULDER, CO 80306-7476   PHONE 303-635-2476

04/30/2001

**SOYBEAN MEAL (CBOT)**
**JUL**

CONTRACT SIZE: 100 tons
MINIMUM TICK : 0.1

SYMBOL SM01N
Trading Hours: 9:30 - 1:15 CST

GRID:0.500
49-D:152.2

SL:10
DL:2

<- WEEKLY RANKINGS -> 10 10 7 10 13

200
196
192
188
184
180
176
172
168
164
160
156
152
148
144
140
136

40
20
0
-20
-40

O.I.
1000's

VOL
1000's

120

80

40

60

40

20

29 13 27 10 24 08 22 05 19 02 16 02 16 30 27
SEPT | OCT | NOV | DEC | JAN | FEB | MAR | APRIL

SMR (SECURITY MARKET RESEARCH) PO BOX 7476 BOULDER, CO 80306-7476 PHONE 303 635-2476 (01.19)

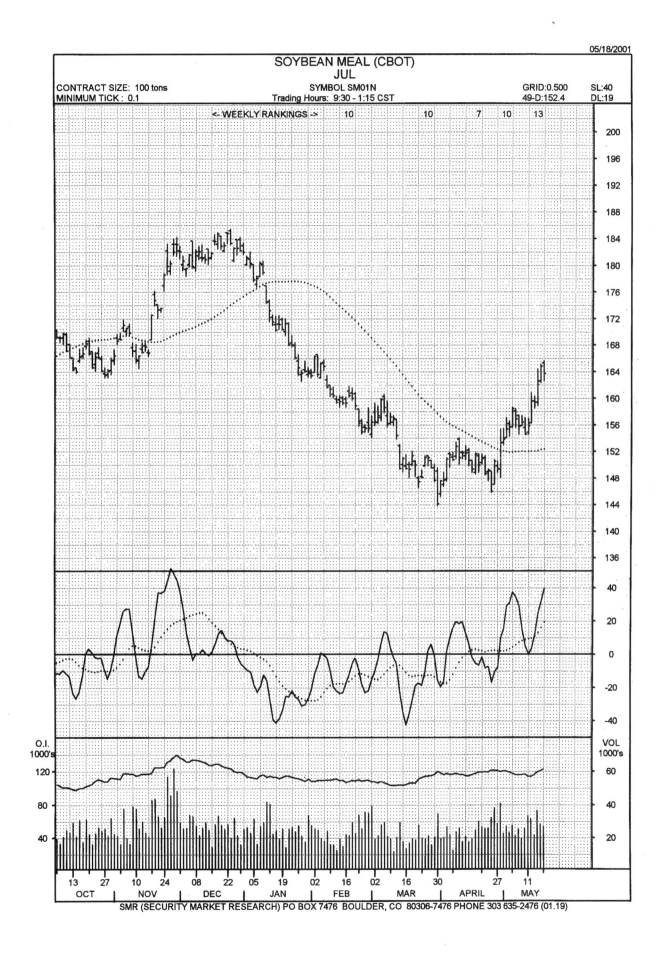

05/18/2001

SOYBEAN MEAL (CBOT)
JUL

CONTRACT SIZE:  100 tons
MINIMUM TICK : 0.1

SYMBOL SM01N
Trading Hours: 9:30 - 1:15 CST

GRID:0.500
49-D:152.4

SL:40
DL:19

<- WEEKLY RANKINGS ->          10                    10              7      10      13

O.I.
1000's

VOL
1000's

SMR (SECURITY MARKET RESEARCH) PO BOX 7476  BOULDER, CO  80306-7476 PHONE 303 635-2476 (01.19)

# THE "MISTAKE" RULE

BY "MISTAKE" I DO NOT MEAN POSITIONING when your reasonably reliable indicators are clear, yet in spite of this the trade is just not working. This is not a "mistake"; rather, it is merely the law of probabilities demonstrating that probability is not certainty. No trading system or method works one hundred percent of the time; therefore, when an intelligently motivated trade clearly is not working, simply take the loss and move on to the next trade.

There are several types of true "mistakes" traders make. The primary mistake most traders make is the "impulse" trade. Unless you are superhuman or a robot, occasionally your emotions will get the best of you and you will make an "impulse" trade. Impulse trade decisions are usually made intra-day and tend to occur when a market makes a sudden price surge and the trader buys the rally or sells the dip out of a fear of "missing the move." Or conversely, a trader may liquidate a position prematurely (meaning before the indicators, i.e., the lines and price say it *should* be exited) out of a sudden fear it is not going to work. Or, a market may be in a good trend and an intra-day surge in the direction of the trend prompts a trader to impulsively add an excessive extra number of contracts at what turns out to be a "bad" price (i.e., recent high if buying, low if selling).

Trading can be an extremely emotional activity. Markets get very volatile from time to time, and since futures trading involves a high degree of leverage, this means major changes in your financial well-being can occur in very short periods of time. In an active market, intense and competing feelings of fear or greed can wash over you several times a day. It can be very difficult to resist the urge to act when these feelings of fear or greed become intense. It is only natural to feel intense pressure to act even though there ms really no reason, according to the price and lines, to do so. As a result of these pressures, inevitably you will make some decisions you would not have made in a more sober, calmer emotional state.

In other words, from time to time you will impulsively make a trade that a short time later, once you have calmed down, you will realize you should not have made. You will know you should not have made the trade because you will look at the charts and ask yourself, "Why in the world did I do that?" The net result: You are suddenly in a trade that is against all—or virtually all—you know to be intelligent trading practices. It may even be against the preponderance of trend and momentum indicators and there are no realistic signs these reasonably reliable indicators will change soon. In other words, you are suddenly relying exclusively on "hope."

Now, please believe me on this: "hope" trades have an extremely low probability of success. You would think that "hope" trades should have at least a random fifty-fifty probability of working in your favor; unfortunately, this is not the case. In fact it has been my experience that the greater my reliance on hope, the lesser the chance for success. There have been times in my trading life when, for whatever reason, I lost all connection to intelligent trading practices and somehow found myself just flailing away at the markets, buying every rally and selling every dip in a desperate attempt to get something right. I have been through times of such desperation that I have looked skyward and pleaded, "Please turn this #@*%!!!! market around. I really need this market to go up (or down) right now!"

Unfortunately, the "trading gods" have never responded to my pleas, and for good reason. At those times of great desperation, I was, by definition, positioned against the prevailing price energy flow and thus was going against the natural laws of trading (and pricing). In other words, I was pleading for the river to suddenly turn and start running upstream.

In a contest between hope and natural laws, natural laws will inevitably prevail. If (when?) you are reduced to relying on hope, most likely it will be because you have abandoned natural laws. The truth is, when all you have going for you on a trade is hope, then you have little or no hope.

Never trade on "hope" alone. Never stick with a mistake in the "hope" it might work. Do not make the mistake of thinking "anything is possible, markets have moved against strong trend and momentum before." Of course they have. The low probability event does occur every once in a while. However, that is not the point.

Even if your long-shot "hope" trade works—it will still only pay you one-to-one odds—remember there is no bonus for hitting the long shot in trading. On the other hand, there will always—in every trading day—be multiple markets where the odds will be clearly in favor of one direction or the other, markets where current price energy flow is clearly established and the law of continuation will have a high probability of working. Therefore, if you ever discover you have made a "mistake," if you find you have impulsively and emotionally positioned against natural laws, against all that you know to be sound and intelligent trading practices, then just swallow hard, take a deep breath, let your shoulders slump in resignation and defeat, and simply surrender to reality by correcting the mistake IMMEDIATELY!

Mistakes of this type (against trend/momentum) not only have a low chance of working out well, they also tend to poison the rest of your trading. What I mean by this is that sticking with what you know is a mistake in one market can, and usually will, cause you to start messing up any and all well conceived trades in other markets. The unpleasant truth is that foolish, poorly conceived trades tend to contaminate well conceived, wise trades. Therefore, treat "mistake" trades like some contagious virus; get rid of them immediately and then do not look back. Once corrected, forget them.

## BOTTOM LINE ON MISTAKES

Do not trade on "hope!" Do not trade against the odds! As soon as you realize you have made a mistake—and all traders do from time to time—just correct it immediately! Your job as the manager of your trading business is to ensure you consistently trade intelligently, as well as persistently act in a businesslike manner. Your job as manager is to insist your trading business does not "flout" natural trading and pricing laws solely out of some personal desire, bias or impulse. Your job as manager of your account is to make sure any and all "emotional mistake" trades are corrected quickly. Regardless of what direction you may think, believe, or wish a market's price should move, it is your duty, your obligation, your job as the manager of your trading business to follow the odds by adhering to the natural laws of trading. Therefore, when and if you recognize you have made an obvious mistake, simply correct it immediately, at the market, and then go on with your trading life.

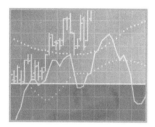

# STREAKS: GOOD AND BAD

TRADING IS DECISION MAKING: decision after decision after decision, endless decisions. Very few trading decisions are ever absolutely clear and certain. Virtually all have some degree of fuzziness and uncertainty. However, almost regardless of how hard you try, sometimes you will have consistently good results and other times consistently bad. In other words, traders tend to go through streaks, good and bad.

Naturally good streaks are more pleasant to live through, and superficially no real problem; however, they can, and usually do, tend to sow the seeds for future problems. Unfortunately, once a good streak ends, it is not so easy to get it going again. Therefore, it is important to be aware of the problems a good streak can cause.

Awareness is always a good first step to solving any problem. The main problem with good streaks is the longer they go on the more they tend to bring about a subtle, but profound, shift in a traders psyche or self-image. Good streaks tend to dull awareness, especially self-awareness.

A streak of successful trading invariably starts from a position of at least some humility. Good streaks start from a mental state of not attempting to know the future. They begin from a state of openness, of searching for truth, of unbiased clear observation, of seeing reality and then acting upon that seeing. Then, if the seeing has been clear and the action intelligent (meaning based on truths and natural laws), some success usually will occur and a good streak follow.

Humility means an absence of "self." When the search for truth and reality is conducted with intensity, then the self is naturally diminished. However, once this pure process of clear seeing followed by decisive action begins to produce concrete results (i.e., monetary rewards—money!), then a self-image begins to grow. This is where the problems usually begin. The fact is, it is simply very difficult to be truly humble after a period of protracted success. This is unfortunate. It is a problem because a minimum level of humility is required to see reality clearly.

Humility allows clear vision that enables the decisive action that produces success; however, success encourages an arrogance that distorts vision, which in turn impedes correct action, thus resulting in failure. Humility, clarity, decisive action, success: success, arrogance, distorted vision, ignorance, failure. Humility is the gateway to the path of success in trading, the humility to see, as absolute fact, that the future is unknown.

If fortunate enough to get into a good streak, try to keep emotions (and position size) under control. Try to avoid getting carried away with yourself. Maintain some humility. No matter how "hot" you get with your trading, the future will still be unknown. Regardless of how sure you are of the next market move, the truth is you do not know what is coming next. No matter how much you make, if you are to see clearly, you will still need to look with an open—meaning humble—mind, a completely not-knowing mind. Clarity of vision is essential for intelligent and decisive action, and humility is a prerequisite for clear vision.

Unfortunately, for most traders, bad streaks are far more common and frequent than good streaks. Moreover, while good streaks are frequently followed by bad streaks, the reverse is usually not true. Bad streaks tend to just continue. It does not seem fair; however, the truth is, while good streaks sow the seeds for bad ones, bad streaks tend to sow the seeds for just more of the same. Losing tends to be self-perpetuating in trading. So, what should a trader do when in a bad streak?

First, once you recognize you are in a bad streak, come to a complete and full mental stop by acknowledging it (the bad streak), even doing so publicly if possible (i.e., stating it to someone). Second, go back to the basics. This means take a fresh, clean and clear look at the chart and ask yourself: What is the trend? Up, sideways or down? Solidly up/down or shallow? How easy would it be to change the trend? What direction is the intermediate-term line (ML) pointing, up or down? Is it above zero or below? Continue this process all the way down the list of indicators. Simply look at each indicator clearly, objectively, without desire. Then methodically, one market at a time, get positioned with how the lines are indicating you should be at that moment (although, if a market is severely overextended, basis the location of the SL, it might be better to wait for the next trade in that market).

Losing streaks tend to fill a trader with doubt. Unfortunately, it is almost impossible to act decisively when full of doubt, and decisive action is necessary for successful trading. Therefore, if a losing streak has implanted too much doubt in you, just take a deep breath, swallow hard and simply have faith in the current line pattern. Cut down on the anticipation of the future line pattern and simply go with the present. In other words, when uncertain of what to do, position with present reality and expect it to continue; keep any anticipation to an absolute minimum.

The lines, the "Status," will put you on the right side of the market most of the time. When in a bad streak you want and need something of substance to hang on to, and this "something" is a solid Bullish or Bearish Status along with a solid concurrent mode. Bullish/Bearish Status and concurrent modes are real because they are based on the foundation of natural laws. Remember this when times are bad: A clear Status in a concurrent mode is an excellent life preserver to grab hold of when drowning in losses.

## BOTTOM LINE ON STREAKS

Streaks, good and bad, are almost inevitable in trading. We are human and so subject to getting carried away with ourselves, both positively and negatively. Awareness is our first line of defense for avoiding the inherent pitfalls produced by prolonged streaks, good and bad.

Try not to consider any one trade the be all and end all of your trading. There will always be another good trading situation somewhere ahead. Natural law guarantees this. Look at trading as a business and work at consistency of results; do not try to win the lottery on any one trade. Do not invest too much of either your ego or equity in any one trade. Work at maintaining some humility when successful. And when unsuccessful for an extended period, simply come to a full mental stop, go back to the basics, and make a fresh start.

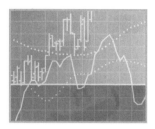

# THE COMMITMENT OF TRADERS REPORT

OF ALL THE DIFFERENT BITS AND PIECES OF INFORMATION I have come across during my thirty-plus years of trading, without a doubt the one that has cost me more money than any other has been the Commitment of Traders data. This simple information is exquisitely tempting in its promise, but all too frequently very destructive in its reality. However, if properly used, this data occasionally can be of some value.

Commitment of Traders data is collected by the government (the Commodity Futures Trading Commission, or CFTC) to assist in the prevention of market manipulation. To help identify attempts to manipulate markets, the CFTC requires all traders holding "large" positions in any futures market to report on their daily buying and selling activity in that market. Since the open interest of most futures markets is substantial, these reportable position limits are quite high. (The larger the open interest in a particular market, the more contracts would be needed to manipulate it.) For example, a trader needs to hold at least one hundred contracts of Beans, four hundred contracts of the Swiss Franc futures contract or one thousand contracts of Bonds before having to report daily activity. Therefore, only the truly big traders are required to file daily activity reports with the CFTC.

All futures trading accounts that reach reportable levels are designated as being either speculative or hedge. Commercial hedgers are those utilizing the futures market to hedge, or "lock in," a sale or purchase price of a commodity used in their business. Examples of commercial hedgers might be a mutual fund in the S&P Stock Index futures, a bank in the Interest Rate futures markets, a multinational corporation in the Currency markets, or a farmer in the Grain markets.

Using these daily activity reports, the CFTC is able to break the participants of each market down into three groups: (1) large speculators—traders holding positions in excess of reportable levels, these tend to be primarily futures funds; (2) commercial hedgers—businesses using the futures markets to "price" supplies and products, and; (3) small speculators—everyone else, meaning you and me. Then every Friday the CFTC releases a report showing the composition (large speculator, commercial, and small speculator) of each market as of the previous Tuesday's close.

The standard "logical" approach to using this information is the assumption that commercials must (should?) know more than speculators; therefore, if commercials as a group are heavily net long or short, then the "smart" action is to do the same. Bolstering this theory is the historical fact that when commercials do hit an "extreme" net position on one side of a market, invariably that market will *eventually* move in the direction of this commercial position. Unfortunately, the fatal flaw with this logic is there is no way to know when a net commercial position has reached *the* extreme for that particular price cycle. Plus there is the fact these "extremes" tend to vary on an absolute numerical basis and thus are not truly clear until after the fact.

Therefore, the problem with COT data is twofold: (1) "extreme" commercial positions tend to vary from one price cycle to the next and (2) the precise time when historical high commercial positions will affect a market is difficult to determine. However, fellow trader Bob Morss of La Jolla, California, had a very perceptive insight about COT data and was generous enough to share this insight with me (and through me, you).

History shows that commercials tend to "fade" (go opposite) sustained price moves until that move ends. Then, as the price moves in the opposite direction, they begin to fade that counter move until it in turn ends. Each pronounced price cycle usually requires a different "extreme" level of commercial "opposition" before it is finally turned back. Bob Morss observed that the key to determining a sustained price move has finally ended and a new directional move is under way is when commercials start to significantly reverse their existing positions (that had been built up as they "faded" the previous sustained move).

For example, if a market has been in a long downtrend and commercials have been steadily "fading" this move (i.e., buying into the sell-off by adding to their longs and/or reducing their shorts) and then they suddenly start to "meaningfully" do the opposite (i.e., reduce longs, increase shorts), this is a strong sign the market has ended its down move and has now started a sustained up move. What this Morss COT rule does is serve as a confirming tool to signal that the "extreme" commercial net position for that price cycle has been seen and thus indicates a new sustained, directional move is underway (in the new direction).

I have found that occasionally this sudden reversal of commercial activity occurs just before a true price reversal; however, most often this reversal of commercial activity occurs just after the price has started to reverse. The Morss rule's primary value seems to lie in its ability to confirm a price reversal. The important point is that it tends to be a reliable sign that an existing sustained price move has ended and a new sustained move in the opposite direction has begun.

Unfortunately, while the Morss rule works well in most markets, it does not work in all markets. It tends to work best in most of the traditional commodity markets and most of the Currencies; however, it works less well in markets such as the Stock Indexes and the Yen. It also works more on a broad picture basis since occasionally minor countermoves (in commercial net positions) have to be filtered out. In other words, the Morss rule is a general rule for general use; therefore, use it lightly and carefully.

To best use Commitment of Traders data it is necessary to know how to "read" it, meaning learn the Morss rule. However, Morss rule timing is more general than precise, with the more pronounced the movement of both price and commercial commitments, the more effective its signals tend to be.

However, it is essential not to overweight the COT data, even when applying the fairly reliable Morss rule. **ONLY** use COT data as background input for trading decisions. I have found that even if the Morss COT rule is giving a clear bullish or bearish signal, it should only be followed if and when a legitimate case to do so can also be made basis the lines and chart.

## BOTTOM LINE ON COMMITMENT OF TRADERS DATA

Consider Commitment of Traders data and Morss rule COT signals to be "tie breakers"—as a plus or minus in making a decision. Use COT data and the Morss rule to "encourage" trades, not determine them; use them to "confirm" trades, not dictate them. My basic rule on COT data is when a clear, heavy net commercial position *agrees* with the trend/momentum lines, then *really* believe the lines. When a clear, heavy commercial position *disagrees* with the lines, then tend to ignore the COT data and go with the lines anyway. In other words, COT data just adds to or subtracts from the line pattern.

On the following pages are four price charts with weekly COT data (courtesy of Commodity Price Charts, 250 S. Wacker Drive, Suite 1150, Chicago, IL 60606 - www.pricecharts.com). Look at them and judge for yourself the validity of the Morss rule and the overall "benefit" of the COT data. However, remember these are weekly charts, not daily, and a week can be a very long time when trading the futures markets. Finally, never forget that in the end we are trading *price*, not levels of commercial and speculator participation. It is not "who" is buying and selling that is ultimately most important; it is at "what" price trades are occurring that really counts.

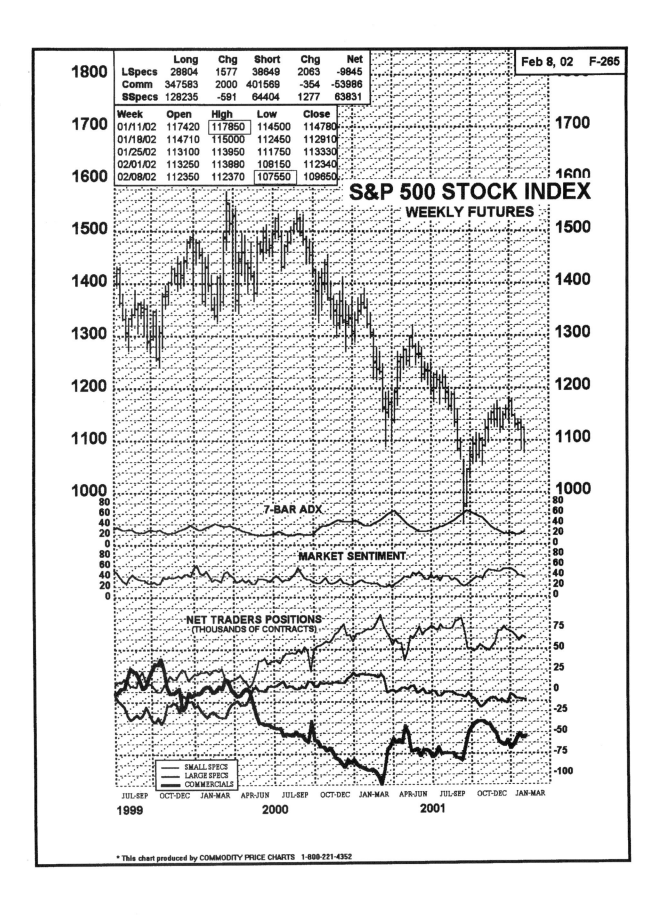

| | Long | Chg | Short | Chg | Net |
|---|---|---|---|---|---|
| LSpecs | 28804 | 1577 | 38649 | 2063 | -9845 |
| Comm | 347583 | 2000 | 401569 | -354 | -53986 |
| SSpecs | 128235 | -591 | 64404 | 1277 | 63831 |

| Week | Open | High | Low | Close |
|---|---|---|---|---|
| 01/11/02 | 117420 | 117850 | 114500 | 114780 |
| 01/18/02 | 114710 | 115000 | 112450 | 112910 |
| 01/25/02 | 113100 | 113950 | 111750 | 113330 |
| 02/01/02 | 113250 | 113880 | 108150 | 112340 |
| 02/08/02 | 112350 | 112370 | 107550 | 109650 |

Feb 8, 02   F-265

**S&P 500 STOCK INDEX**
WEEKLY FUTURES

7-BAR ADX

MARKET SENTIMENT

NET TRADERS POSITIONS
(THOUSANDS OF CONTRACTS)

SMALL SPECS
LARGE SPECS
COMMERCIALS

JUL-SEP   OCT-DEC   JAN-MAR   APR-JUN   JUL-SEP   OCT-DEC   JAN-MAR   APR-JUN   JUL-SEP   OCT-DEC   JAN-MAR

1999           2000                    2001

* This chart produced by COMMODITY PRICE CHARTS  1-800-221-4352

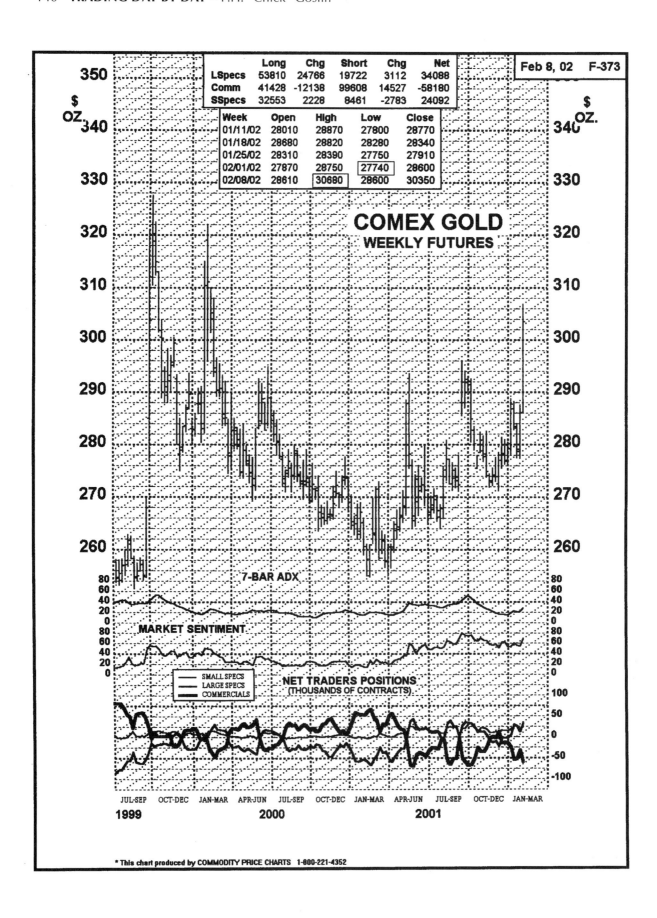

| | Long | Chg | Short | Chg | Net |
|---|---|---|---|---|---|
| LSpecs | 53810 | 24766 | 19722 | 3112 | 34088 |
| Comm | 41428 | -12138 | 99608 | 14527 | -58180 |
| SSpecs | 32553 | 2228 | 8461 | -2783 | 24092 |

| Week | Open | High | Low | Close |
|---|---|---|---|---|
| 01/11/02 | 28010 | 28870 | 27800 | 28770 |
| 01/18/02 | 28680 | 28820 | 28280 | 28340 |
| 01/25/02 | 28310 | 28390 | 27750 | 27910 |
| 02/01/02 | 27870 | 28750 | 27740 | 28600 |
| 02/08/02 | 28610 | 30680 | 28600 | 30350 |

Feb 8, 02   F-373

**COMEX GOLD**
**WEEKLY FUTURES**

7-BAR ADX

MARKET SENTIMENT

SMALL SPECS
LARGE SPECS
COMMERCIALS

**NET TRADERS POSITIONS**
(THOUSANDS OF CONTRACTS)

JUL-SEP   OCT-DEC   JAN-MAR   APR-JUN   JUL-SEP   OCT-DEC   JAN-MAR   APR-JUN   JUL-SEP   OCT-DEC   JAN-MAR

**1999**           **2000**              **2001**

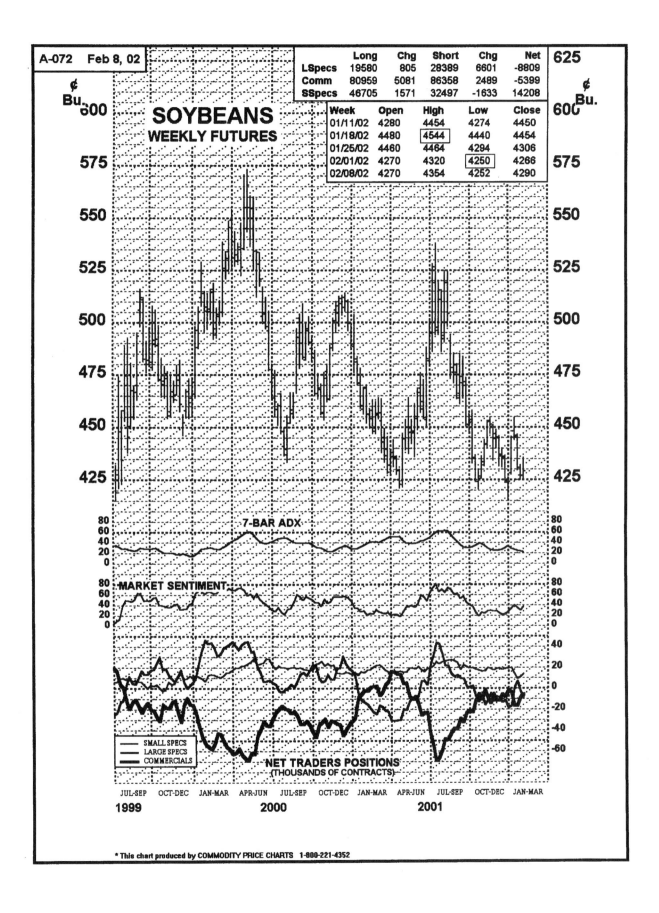

| | Long | Chg | Short | Chg | Net |
|---|---|---|---|---|---|
| LSpecs | 19580 | 805 | 28389 | 6601 | -8809 |
| Comm | 80959 | 5081 | 86358 | 2489 | -5399 |
| SSpecs | 46705 | 1571 | 32497 | -1633 | 14208 |

| Week | Open | High | Low | Close |
|---|---|---|---|---|
| 01/11/02 | 4280 | 4454 | 4274 | 4450 |
| 01/18/02 | 4480 | 4544 | 4440 | 4454 |
| 01/25/02 | 4460 | 4464 | 4294 | 4306 |
| 02/01/02 | 4270 | 4320 | 4250 | 4266 |
| 02/08/02 | 4270 | 4354 | 4252 | 4290 |

A-072   Feb 8, 02

¢ Bu.

SOYBEANS
WEEKLY FUTURES

7-BAR ADX

MARKET SENTIMENT

SMALL SPECS
LARGE SPECS
COMMERCIALS

NET TRADERS POSITIONS
(THOUSANDS OF CONTRACTS)

JUL-SEP   OCT-DEC   JAN-MAR   APR-JUN   JUL-SEP   OCT-DEC   JAN-MAR   APR-JUN   JUL-SEP   OCT-DEC   JAN-MAR

1999        2000                              2001

* This chart produced by COMMODITY PRICE CHARTS  1-800-221-4352

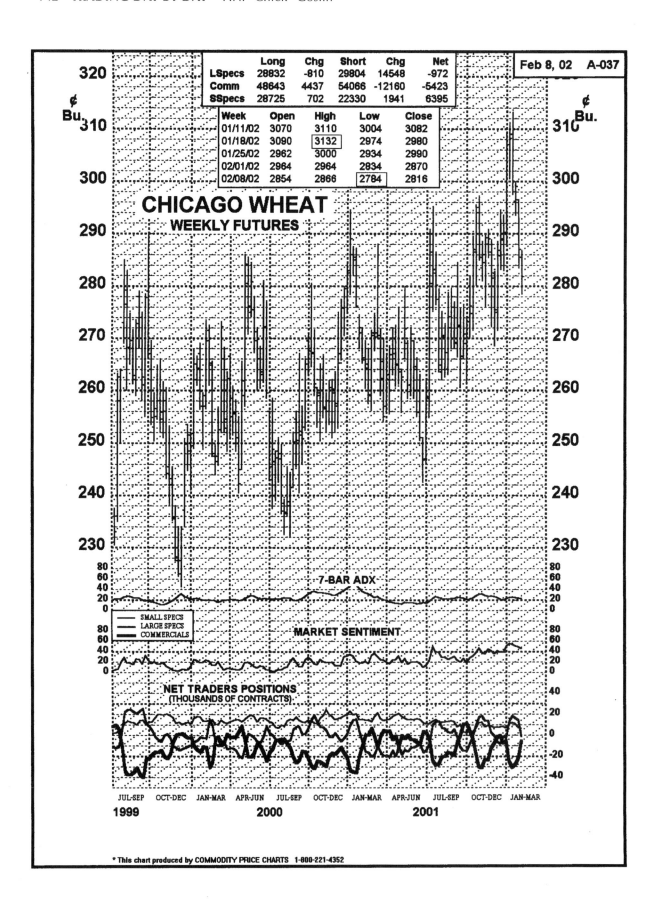

| | Long | Chg | Short | Chg | Net |
|---|---|---|---|---|---|
| LSpecs | 28832 | -810 | 29804 | 14548 | -972 |
| Comm | 48643 | 4437 | 54066 | -12160 | -5423 |
| SSpecs | 28725 | 702 | 22330 | 1941 | 6395 |

| Week | Open | High | Low | Close |
|---|---|---|---|---|
| 01/11/02 | 3070 | 3110 | 3004 | 3082 |
| 01/18/02 | 3090 | 3132 | 2974 | 2980 |
| 01/25/02 | 2962 | 3000 | 2934 | 2990 |
| 02/01/02 | 2964 | 2964 | 2834 | 2870 |
| 02/08/02 | 2854 | 2866 | 2784 | 2816 |

Feb 8, 02    A-037

**CHICAGO WHEAT**
**WEEKLY FUTURES**

7-BAR ADX

SMALL SPECS
LARGE SPECS
COMMERCIALS

MARKET SENTIMENT

NET TRADERS POSITIONS
(THOUSANDS OF CONTRACTS)

JUL-SEP  OCT-DEC  JAN-MAR  APR-JUN  JUL-SEP  OCT-DEC  JAN-MAR  APR-JUN  JUL-SEP  OCT-DEC  JAN-MAR

**1999**          **2000**          **2001**

* This chart produced by COMMODITY PRICE CHARTS  1-800-221-4352

# OPTIONS

OPTIONS ARE ONE OF THE GREATEST and most costly frauds ever perpetrated on the trading public.

Options have limited risk for the buyer and unlimited risk for the seller. Therefore, it is only natural that individual speculators tend overwhelmingly to buy rather than sell them. Unfortunately for the individual trader, the buy side of options has a significant built-in disadvantage. The very nature of options, as currently set up, is such that the odds are inherently stacked against the buyer (primarily small speculators) and in favor of the seller (usually big, institutional money).

The fundamental problem with buying options is they are a "time" depreciating asset. If you buy or sell a futures contract (or a stock) and a week later it closes unchanged, you will be even. However, if you buy a call or put option and a week later the market the option is written on closes unchanged, you will have a loss. When you own an option, every day the option's underlying market (futures, stock, etc.) fails to move in your direction, the option will lose value. Therefore, since time is constantly eroding the value of an option, this means time is always working for the seller (i.e., big money) and against the buyer (i.e., small money). What this time erosion factor means is that when purchasing an option you not only have to get the "direction" and the "timing" right, you also need the underlying asset to make a substantial move.

Merely getting direction and timing right is difficult enough in trading. When you add in the need for a decent sized move (in order to cover the cost of the option), the probabilities of success shrink significantly. In other words, the built-in liabilities in buying options turn the nominally fifty-fifty up or down game of trading into something closer to an eighty-twenty (or worse) bet against you. No matter how good you are at trading, these are extremely difficult odds to overcome on any kind of consistent basis.

All right then, since the options game is naturally slanted against the buyer and in favor of the seller, why not sell options? Unfortunately, the basic nature of the options game places a high "theoretical" risk in selling each individual option. In addition, when done on a limited basis, there are also high "costs" in trading options (i.e., high margins and commissions). This combination makes it too risky, as well as too difficult, for the average trader to profitably sell options consistently. To take proper advantage of the odds, as well as gain the necessary economy of scale to successfully sell options, an account needs to be capitalized with *at least* several hundred thousand dollars (and preferably several million). Very few individual traders have this level of speculative capital to devote solely to an option selling program.

The net overall result of the option business is the annual legal transfer of hundreds of millions (billions?) of dollars from small individual traders to large corporations, trading funds and brokerage houses. In other words, I consider options to be a colossal, albeit legal, fraud perpetrated by the options industry on individual traders. Amazingly, incredibly, this giant ongoing fraud has been blessed with a Nobel Prize in Economics. The recipients of this Nobel Prize, and the committee that awarded it, should feel profound and enduring shame; however, I doubt they do. In the rarefied air of academia and Nobel Prizes, shame rarely shows its face, no matter how appropriate.

I have always understood Nobel Prizes to be in recognition of producing at least some moral good; unfortunately, the truth in this case is there has been great moral harm and very limited, if any, moral good. A Nobel Prize awarded for facilitating the legal transfer of trillions of dollars from those with little to those with much is an award for extreme cleverness, not moral good. However, maybe I am mistaken about Nobel Prizes in Economics; maybe next year they will award the Nobel Prize in Economics to the inventor or developer of a more profitable slot machine. Should they do so it would be no different from the Nobel awarded for the pricing of options.

## THE BASIC TERMS USED IN OPTIONS

1 ~ A *call* is a bet on rising prices.

2 ~ A *put* is a bet on falling prices.

3 ~ The *premium* is the cost of the option.

4 ~ The *strike* price is the agreed upon potential purchase price (if a call) or potential sale price (if a put) of the option's underlying asset.

5 ~ The *expiration date* is when the option expires.

6 ~ *Volatility* indicates recent (and presumably, projected) degree of price fluctuation.

7 ~ *Delta* is the percentage daily move the option (put or call) will make in relation to the daily move of the underlying asset (be it individual stock, stock index, financial future, commodity future, etc.).

8 ~ An *in-the-money* call option will have a strike price below the current market price of the asset; an *in-the-money* put option will have a strike price above the current market price of the asset.

9 ~ An *out-of-the-money* call option will have a strike price above the current market price of the asset; an *out-of-the-money* put option will have a strike price below the current market price of the asset.

10 ~ *At-the-money* options have a strike price at the current market price of the underlying asset.

11 ~ *Intrinsic value* is the dollar amount an option is "in the money" (i.e., intrinsic value is the difference between the strike price of the in-the-money option and current market price of the underlying asset). Therefore, in-the-money options have intrinsic value and out-of-the-money options do not have any intrinsic value.

## THE PRICING OF OPTIONS

The basic problem with options is that they are essentially arbitrarily priced. Option prices are in effect set by the sellers. Option prices are determined primarily according to predetermined mathematical formulas (developed by the Nobel laureates referred to earlier). In other words, option prices are not really set by free market auctions between buyers and sellers.

There are three factors option sellers use to determine the "appropriate" selling price of an option: intrinsic value, time value, and volatility. Add these three together—intrinsic value (if any) plus time value (adjusted by volatility)—and you have the basic formula for calculating option prices.

Naturally, the critical part of using this type of arbitrary pricing formula is the specific dollar value awarded to time and volatility. Set the dollar values for time and volatility too low and the sellers of options will be at a disadvantage; set them too high and the buyers will be at a disadvantage. Not surprisingly, since those in the option industry overwhelmingly sell options rather than buy them, the option pricing formulas have been set up to produce prices that are "too high." The prices of options are arbitrarily set to inherently favor the sellers (who also happen to be those who control the options industry) and against the buyers (who happen to be the individual customers of the option industry). This is the basic problem with options: the arbitrary, mathematical, formula-produced prices of options are invariably too high.

What I mean by this is that the actual payout on options is too low in relation to true odds. For example, if past history (statistics) shows that a 100-point move in the S&P over a 20-trading-day period occurs say about twenty-five times a year, this would mean that the odds of a move of this magnitude starting on any one specific day would be about ten-to-one (i.e., 250 trading days a year versus the twenty-five times a year a 20-day, 100-point move would begin)—actually the true odds for a move of this magnitude would be twenty-to-one since both directions (up and down) should be factored in because a buyer not only has to get the timing of the hundred point move right, but also its direction. However, an option bet that this hundred point move will occur would pay you significantly less than these twenty-to-one odds. In other words, the built-in disadvantage of option buying is that even if you are right on your option bet, your profit will not be anywhere near what the true odds dictate it should be. The pricing formula ensures that payoffs are measurably less than the true odds—just as casinos ensure that payoffs on most bets are significantly less than true odds. Once again, this means that the option game is tilted clearly in favor of the sellers.

The futures and stock "game" is a fifty-fifty up or down situation (minus costs, of course). The options game is more like a casino bet where the odds, mathematically, clearly favor the house. Buying options is not a fifty-fifty game; it is more like eighty-twenty against the buyer.

The sellers of options (i.e., the option industry) argue that this tilt (in favor of the seller) is necessary to compensate for the theoretical unlimited risk involved in selling options. However, the truth is that over time, as long as enough of a wide variety (different strike prices and expiration dates) of options are sold, there is no real risk in selling them—the biased statistical pricing formulas make sure of that.

On a big picture basis there is no more risk on the sell side of options than there is in selling life insurance. When selling life insurance the key is to utilize accurate actuarial formulas and then make sure you sell enough of a wide variety of policies. Do this and there will be no real risk. Similarly, simply rig the pricing formulas of options high enough and then sell enough of them (at a wide range of strike prices, expiration dates, and in a variety of markets) and there will be no real risk in selling them.

This is exactly what the clever noble laureates did for the options industry. They gave the industry a pricing formula that could be easily rigged to permanently favor the sellers. This was an extremely profitable "gift" for the industry; however, this "gift" has unfortunately cost the trading public untold billions (trillions?). To repeat, the net result of options has been, and continues to be, the transfer of huge sums of money from the trading public to the options industry.

There are some who will argue that none of this is so. They will argue that being long or being short options are equal propositions, virtually identical to being long or short futures, i.e., a fifty-fifty proposition. In addition, they will argue that options are an honest proposition on par with buying stocks and futures. These arguments are clearly wrong and a couple of simple, real-life observations prove it.

First, there are many trading funds whose sole purpose is to sell (i.e., short) options; on the other hand, I do not believe there exists, or has ever existed, a single fund whose sole purpose was to buy options. The reason for this is simple: no one in the fund (or brokerage) industry is so foolish as to believe a fund solely devoted to buying options could ever be a profitable business. Therefore, by their actions, those in the option industry proclaim very clearly that selling (shorting) options is inherently better than buying them, meaning the options game is set up to favor the sellers (i.e., the options industry) over the buyers (i.e., the trading public).

Second, simply read a NYSE brokerage firm's customer option agreement. At most major brokerage houses a customer will not be permitted to make an option trade (buy or sell) until he or she has submitted a completed detailed option agreement. These agreements are written in dense "legalese," but in essence simply say: "You, the customer, by signing this agreement, acknowledge that we, the brokerage house, have warned you explicitly that you have little, if any, chance of making money in options, that you will almost certainly lose all you invest in options, and that you will hold us free of any and all liability for your foolishness in going into the options game." Compare the option agreements brokerage houses require customers to sign to all other investment agreements. The reason the option agreements are written so defensively is that brokerage houses have been sued too many times by those trading in options and so now protect themselves in advance.

......................

In reality, options are no more or no less than "insurance" policies on price moves. Buying options as an investment strategy is no more likely to produce consistent profits than would buying individual life, fire, or earthquake insurance policies. Naturally, some insurance policies return more in benefits than they cost, but as a general rule they do not. Insurance policies are bought to protect against the unexpected, adverse event. If options were marketed solely as insurance against unusual price moves, then they would be marketed honestly. However, options are marketed as trading vehicles on a par with futures and stocks, and this is a fraud.

So, when you buy an option (either a Put or Call), realize that all you are doing is buying an insurance policy on the possibility of an unusual price move. When you buy an out-of-the-money option, realize you are essentially buying a limited-time disaster (i.e., fire, flood, earthquake) policy with very little likelihood of this disaster happening. When you sell an option (either a Put or Call), realize that you are selling one insurance policy against an unusual move, and the odds and risk are the same as if you sold one disaster (fire, flood, earthquake) policy. The point being that selling thousands of insurance policies can be a consistently profitable business, but selling one, or only a few, insurance policies is a pure *gamble*.

I am well aware that there are hundreds, maybe thousands, of option "experts" who will vigorously argue that what I have said here is not true. In addition, they will proclaim there are numerous fancy techniques (spreads, delta neutral, etc.) for trading options profitably. However, no matter how elaborate the option strategy, its success or failure will always boil down to getting "direction" and "timing" right. Success or failure in trading always comes down to direction and timing, regardless of the technique used.

Using options to make your direction and timing bets is just making the process far more complicated and difficult than it needs to be. I have found that those who are incapable of getting direction and timing right are those who are most attracted to marketing the option game to the trading public. If you are adept at direction and timing in trading, there is no need to waste time, effort and money on options. If you are not adept at direction and timing, then focusing on options will do little more than limit an already almost guaranteed loss, and this is little consolation.

Obviously I have exaggerated "some" here, but not too much. For the overwhelming majority of traders, avoiding options completely will add to their net results. Should you absolutely insist on buying options, make a point to stick to in-the-money options, and the deeper in the money, the better (and then make sure you remember to take profits when they are good). There are some advantages to buying in-the-money options, but even here I believe the disadvantages outweigh the minor advantages.

## BOTTOM LINE ON OPTIONS

Insurance has a place for protecting against loss of property and life; it has no real place in your trading business. Therefore, do not buy options. The odds and risk/reward ratio are too slanted against the buy side of options to justify buying them. And, on the other hand, being in the business of selling insurance only makes sense when done on a large scale basis. Therefore, unless you have a couple of million dollars (or more), as well as the time and energy to work at it every day, do not sell options either. In other words, just ignore options completely. Act as if they do not exist. Your bottom line will be the better for it.

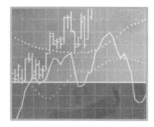

# PAPER CHARTS VS. COMPUTERS

WHEN I STARTED OUT IN THIS BUSINESS thirty years ago there were no personal computers, which meant anyone trading technically had to use paper charts. So, I started on paper charts and have stuck with them ever since. However, today the overwhelming majority of traders use computer charts.

Maybe it is just a question of habit, but I definitely prefer paper charts. Frankly, I do not understand the appeal of computer charts, and in fact find much not to like. The problem is computers can do *too* much, meaning they provide too many indicators. I believe the individual trader needs to keep the game of trading as simple as possible. Remember, we cannot "out complex" our competition in this game. The more complicated you make it, the more of a natural disadvantage you will have.

We are trading price. All you need to trade price are some reasonably reliable indicators of the trend and momentum of this price. In addition, you only need these indicators to cover a small variety of time periods—short term, intermediate term, and long term is sufficient. SMR's paper charts provide all of this, so they provide all that is needed to trade successfully.

The objective when looking at a chart is to see the truth of what is there, the reality. The greatest obstructions to seeing the reality of a chart are our expectations and desires. We tend to see what we expect and hope to see. I believe it was William Blake who said to see *through* your eyes, not *with* them. If so, what he meant by this (as applied to trading) was to let the chart come in through your eyes and imprint itself on your brain, rather than your brain reaching out to the chart and imprinting your expectations and desires on it.

To see what a chart is saying, it is necessary to have your mind fully alert, but blank—meaning completely awake, but empty. You cannot see what is on the chart if you look with a brain full of hopes and wishes. Therefore, to see accurately you must look at the chart with humility and openness.

I believe it is easier for this purity of vision to happen with paper charts than computer charts. Paper charts are more passive; computer charts, more active. However, this is just my opinion; had I started with computer charts, possibly I would consider paper charts severely lacking, even primitive.

If you prefer computer charts and still want to use SMR's specific trend/momentum indicators, they are available from CQG (www.cqg.com). The CQG software lets you make all sorts of projections as well as produce charts with oscillators covering any time period—minutes to months. No question it is very impressive. So, if computer charts fit you better than paper ones, then by all means go with the computer. Of course, virtually every charting software on the market can create any kind of momentum oscillator as well as compute any type of trend-moving average.

Were I to ever start using computer charts, there are a couple of features I would want.

First, I would want the software to provide, on a daily basis, a breakdown of all markets in terms of relative strength—strongest to weakest, best uptrends to best downtrends. There are many different ways to measure this big-picture relative strength. My preference would be to measure basis the average closing price of the past three days versus average closing price of the five days from forty-six to fifty days earlier.

Once having this daily list, I would look to the strongest markets for potential buying situations and to the weakest for potential shorting situations. In trading you always want to be looking for good reasons to go long the strongest markets and short the weakest. Therefore, it would be helpful to be reminded daily about which markets were currently the strongest and weakest.

Second, I would want my trading software to signal me any time a market in an uptrend was on the low price of the past three days and/or the high price of the past six days, and vice versa for downtrending markets. Any time a price is in a clear uptrend and is trading at its lows of the past three days, some case can be made to be a buyer; so it would be helpful to be reminded of this. In addition, any time a price in an uptrend is on the highs of the past six days, it might be time to consider taking profits; so it would be helpful to be reminded of this. (Of course, the same would be true of markets in downtrends—reminded when price was on highs of past three days and lows of past six days.)

## ARE REAL-TIME QUOTES NECESSARY FOR SUCCESS?

No. I have had several brokers mention to me that their clients who do not get real-time quotes tend to do better in the long run than the ones who do. The reason is simple: real-time quotes tend to produce over trading. When trading, it is important to keep the proper distance from intra-day price moves since many are "false" moves.

Naturally, if you are day trading, then real-time quotes are probably a necessity. However, if you are position trading on a several-day to several-week basis, then I believe real-time quotes do more harm than good. Following either the ten-minute updates of futures prices on CNBC or simply checking with your broker several times a day should be more than sufficient.I do believe it is usually a good idea to check each market about ten to fifteen minutes before its close to see if there is anything particularly unusual going on, i.e., a price that would materially change the technical picture. Otherwise, I feel that almost all traders will do best in the long run if they limit most trading decisions to after the market has closed. Unplanned, spur-of-the-moment trading decisions tend to have a poor record, regardless of how "good" and urgent they may appear to be at the time.

# PRICE ACTION

BY "PRICE ACTION" I MEAN both the action of the price during the day (whether intra-day pressure was primarily up or down) and action in relation to what the technical indicators were "saying." Of these two meanings of price action, the second is by far the more important.

Intra-day price action is significant, but it can be deceiving. What counts is where a price is, not how it got there. Occasionally, a price can push in one direction most of the day only to reverse and quickly retrace the entire earlier move, and more, in much less time. Closing price is the most important of the day; how that price came to be is significant, but less important.

How a price acts in relation to what the trend/momentum lines indicate it *should* act can be extremely significant. For example, if a market is in a solid concurrent mode to the upside, yet the price fails to move up over a several-day period, this is usually a sign that there is something "wrong"—meaning the buy signal will probably not work, or if it works it will not work very well. Therefore, it is always very important to compare actual action (i.e., movement) of the price with what the lines indicate this price action *should* be. A day or two of poor price action is acceptable, but persistent (i.e., several day, to a week) of bad price action is not.

# CHARTS

ON THE FOLLOWING PAGES YOU WILL FIND the charts of nine different markets covering the first ten trading days of 2002. The markets covered are, in order: March Cocoa, March Sugar, March Japanese Yen, March Swiss Franc, March 30-Year Treasury Bonds, March S&P 500 Index, February Gold, March Soybeans, and March Chicago Wheat (all in the year 2002). These nine markets cover a broad spectrum of the futures markets and so provide a good representative sample.

Please be aware that I selected this time period in advance. I did not select it after the fact. Late in December 2001 I asked SMR to provide me with daily charts covering this time period. I expected and hoped that the first ten trading days of the year would provide some decent price moves and was confident the natural laws of trading would apply well regardless of what happened. I am confident that the same results reflected herein would be achieved over any randomly selected time period. Natural laws are consistent; they work in virtually all situations.

It would have been easy to look backwards and "cherry pick" a ten-day period where the lines and prices moved exceptionally well together, but this would have been somewhat dishonest. I felt it would be better to select (somewhat at random) the time period in advance. This approach has the effect of being as close to a "real time" ten-day sample as is possible within the constraints of a book.

However, keep in mind that "reading" the charts in this book is quite different from doing so in real time. First, what can be done in minutes here takes days in real time. This means many, many more hours of time for doubt to enter your mind and possibly affect your decisions. In addition, there is the great difference between "paper," or intellectual, trading and real-money trading. Paper trading is to real-money trading as walking across a plank one foot off the ground is to walking across the same plank twenty or thirty feet above ground level. Finally, in real-time trading you look at the charts of many different markets each day; here on these examples you follow them one at a time for ten days.

Again here, as in the earlier charts on Cocoa, the commentary at the top of each page (with the date) is what I wrote after the close of that day (in real time). These commentaries are taken (virtually) verbatim from the daily market letter I was publishing at the time. I have made a few, very minor, grammatical corrections to make them read better; however, I have not made any changes to make my "read" of the market situation look better. What is important here is that this ten-day sample should enable you to see how the natural laws and trading rules laid out earlier in this book work in real time in real futures markets.

(**NOTE:** *I have also included the charts of 15 February 2002 for each of these markets, along with some commentary so as to show what happened from 15 January to 15 February.*)

# March 2002 Cocoa (Jan 2)

## REAL-TIME COMMENTARY

**1/2 (Wednesday, first trading day of the year):** Mar Cocoa - Status - Bullish/Neutral. Trend solidly up and ML sideways, but should turn up tomorrow so on verge of going to clear upside concurrent mode. Line pattern now in between bullish and neutral so can make case for either long or sidelines. Tough call here at moment since really need close over 1325 to turn both lines and chart solidly positive, however now very close to turning both at least slightly positive. Action slightly negative on minor down side reversal day, but not down enough to change picture materially negative. So, picture remains essentially the same as has been past few days in that can make good case for light "anticipation" longs; however, prefer to wait for picture to be more solidly positive before go to a full long position. Bottom line: Lines in between sidelines and long, but continue to prefer light "anticipation" longs with stops 1275 (preferably on close or later in day basis) for now. (Note: I had been suggesting anticipation longs for several days.)

......................

## AFTER-ACTION CRITIQUE

Status at moment is in between Bullish and Neutral. Trend is solidly up so that counts for +1 point; ML is below zero, so while this counts for -1/2 point we do not count it because trend is up (remember, we only count points that are with the trend), and since ML sideways can either count 0 or +1/2 point; SL is up so this counts for +1. Therefore, if count ML as up, Status is Bullish (+2 1/2 points); if count ML as sideways, then Status is Neutral (since need ML to be either up or above zero to "confirm" trade). Sometimes the point-count total comes out "in between" due to a line being sideways. In cases like these (as here) it just boils down to a decision, and have to look at big picture to help come to this decision. In this case have trend very solidly up so bias should be to upside; however, since momentum line pattern is a little on mixed side here at moment, this temporarily tempers strong uptrend.

I evidently decided to split the difference in this case and go for "light" anticipation longs while waiting for the pattern to clarify. A day or two of sideways-type movement would turn picture obviously positive here since it would turn ML clearly up (because will be taking off progressively lower SL numbers for next week or so). If look at where SL was three weeks ago, will see it was at zero and then moved down to minus twenty-two before moving back up above zero. SL spent a little over a week below zero (ten to fifteen days ago); therefore, if SL now holds at zero for next few days, the ML will turn up. Remember, the ML is about a three-week moving average of the SL, so always have to compare where SL is now (and will most likely be next few days) with where SL was between three and two weeks ago. Since SL will almost certainly be higher during the next few days than it was three and two weeks earlier, this means ML will almost certainly be clearly pointing up very soon.

Since a day or two of sideways (or higher) type action would turn pattern clearly bullish, I saw no reason not to be lightly long in anticipation. A day or two sideways in SL would set up potential third higher low in SL and this also would be positive.

01/02/2002

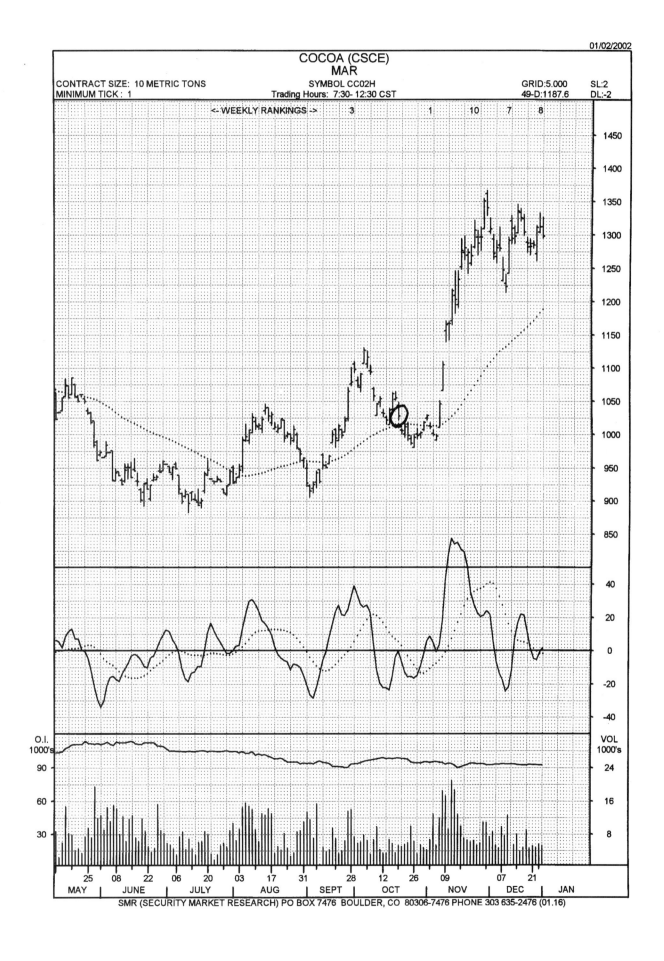

COCOA (CSCE)
MAR

CONTRACT SIZE: 10 METRIC TONS
MINIMUM TICK : 1

SYMBOL CC02H
Trading Hours: 7:30- 12:30 CST

GRID:5.000
49-D:1187.6

SL:2
DL:-2

<- WEEKLY RANKINGS ->    3       1     10    7    8

SMR (SECURITY MARKET RESEARCH) PO BOX 7476  BOULDER, CO  80306-7476 PHONE 303 635-2476 (01.16)

# March 2002 Cocoa (Jan 3)

## REAL-TIME COMMENTARY

**1/3 (Thursday):** Mar Cocoa - Status - Neutral (to Bullish). Trend solidly up and ML now slightly up so market in concurrent mode to upside. However, slight turn down in SL turns Status back to Neutral. Action slightly negative on minor down day, but price still well within bullish parameters. Mentioned couple days ago that few days of sideways-type action would set up market well for buy signal and have now had that. What need now is a moderate (or better) up day and would have all three lines up and pattern would become solidly positive. Therefore, currently set up well for upside, just need to get it started and if do "should" be able to produce sustained upside action. Bottom line: Lines (temporarily?) back to saying sidelines but continue to prefer "anticipation" longs here (and would view move above 1315 as solidly positive and enough to get fully long). On other hand, a move, and especially a close, below 1275 would turn picture too short-term negative to stick with longs.

......................

## AFTER-ACTION CRITIQUE

Status was back to Neutral since the SL had turned back down slightly; however, the clear turn up in ML put market in concurrent mode to upside. Therefore, overall picture was positive to slightly mixed and next moderate move (up or down) would tell tale.

If look back over chart, will see had a series of three up surges starting with the one at end of July that turned trend from down to up. What is most noticeable about these three surges is how they coincided with the up cycles in the ML and how the down cycles in ML coincided with dips/pauses in the ongoing uptrend. The picture here at moment was very similar to the one had at first week of November. At that time had trend up, ML in good up cycle, and SL making series of higher lows. Once SL turned up from a clear third higher low, the market exploded to upside and produced a major, sustained up move (covered in detail earlier). The current momentum line pattern was not quite as solid as it was in early November, however the trend here was much stronger. Since trend was so strong and this market was one of the strongest on board, it only made sense to give upside the benefit of doubt and stick with anticipation longs. In addition, the stop point was once again quite close (just under 1275) so risk level was low. The reason I selected this for a stop level was that a close down there would get SL moving down too sharply, and therefore not only would have kept Status Neutral but also would have produced a lower low in SL, which would have been clear negative (since had just put in a lower high on SL).

Therefore, this market was right at moment of decision as next fifteen or twenty point move would have tilted momentum either clearly up (and if so would have wanted to be and go long) or clearly down (and if so would have wanted to go to sidelines—trend would have been up so could not have gone short, but momentum would have been too negative to be long). However, since market was in clear concurrent mode to upside at moment and trend solidly up, should have given longs the edge. Therefore, I saw "anticipation" longs as fully justified here. Could have been either fully long and taken risk or been lightly long with idea of adding on even minor up move next day. This was just a trading decision and when have these sometimes make right one, sometimes wrong; however, either way should have had some longs on here.

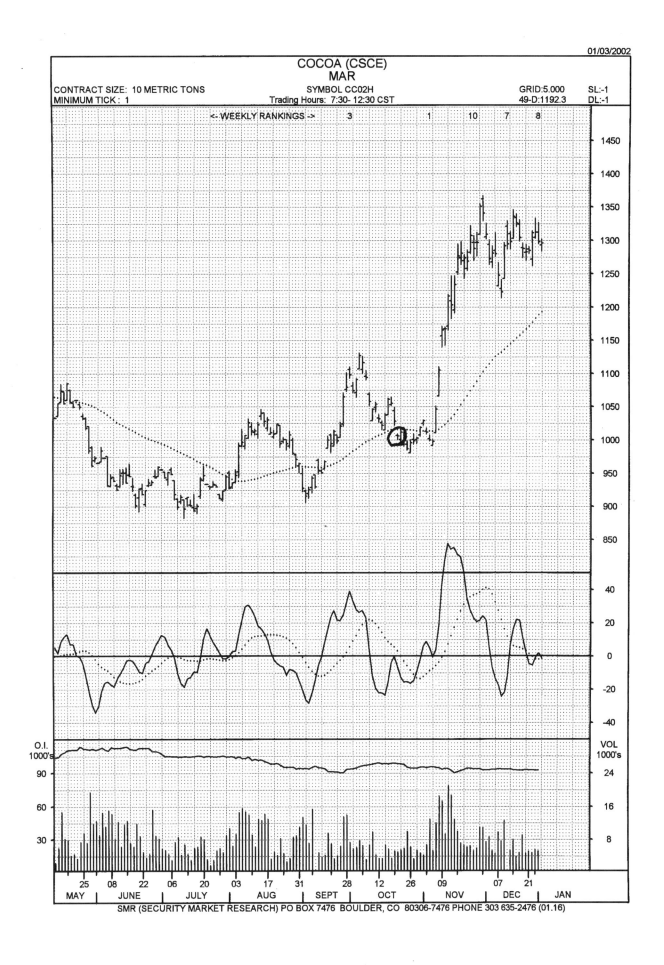

01/03/2002

COCOA (CSCE)
MAR

CONTRACT SIZE: 10 METRIC TONS  SYMBOL CC02H  GRID:5.000  SL:-1
MINIMUM TICK : 1  Trading Hours: 7:30- 12:30 CST  49-D:1192.3  DL:-1

<- WEEKLY RANKINGS ->  3  1  10  7  8

SMR (SECURITY MARKET RESEARCH) PO BOX 7476 BOULDER, CO 80306-7476 PHONE 303 635-2476 (01.16)

# March 2002 Cocoa (Jan 4)

## REAL-TIME COMMENTARY

**1/4 (Friday):** Mar Cocoa - Status - Bullish. Trend and ML both up so market in concurrent mode to upside. Action very positive today on big, breakout-type day to upside. Trend clearly up with basically zero chance of turning down any time soon. ML on solid up cycle with little chance of this changing for at least week or so. Plus, SL has now turned up from third higher low and this always a positive, and especially when happens with the trend. If look at chart will see this market has been cycling very well with ML. The ML has been on three-week down cycle and has just turned up, indicating past patterns suggest "should" have at least couple weeks of upside pressure. So, all signs positive indicating odds favor even higher prices ahead. Bottom line: Can be long with stops now in 1300 to 1325 area on close only basis.

......................

## AFTER-ACTION CRITIQUE

Status was back to solidly Bullish since had all three lines up, plus ML at zero (and on way to above zero, so could count point total as either +2 1/2 or +3). Market also remained in concurrent mode to upside and this was now very solid. Therefore, anticipation longs was the right action here previous couple days. Interesting how current pattern and pattern in early November turned out to be so similar. However, while trend was much stronger to upside at this point, the momentum line pattern was a little more solid in November (since back then had three weeks of below zero SL numbers to be "taking off," while this time would soon be "taking off" a week of relatively high SL numbers, meaning ML up cycle not as solid this time). Regardless, patterns remarkably similar; we will see how similar the results were.

While this market has given an exceptionally good illustration of how important it is to pay close attention to concurrent vs. crosscurrent mode (i.e., the cycles of the ML within a clear uptrend), you will see as we move along in other markets that this is not that unusual. I believe paying attention to concurrent vs. crosscurrent mode is just about the most important factor in trading this trend/momentum method.

I did not mention it at the time (in daily letter), but this big up move fully qualified as a non news related (there was no specific news event that triggered this big up move), with the trend up spike, and so basis the spike rule it should have been considered a continuation spike. I chose to raise the stop level to as high as 1325 since if this upside breakout type move was for "real," then the price should not come back down much, if at all. In addition, a move back below 1325 would have had the clear look of a "false" breakout and these can be very negative chart patterns, especially if they occur at contract highs.

Therefore, the correct position here was very clear: long with stops 1325 or slightly lower, and then just sit back and watch to see what happened.

01/04/2002

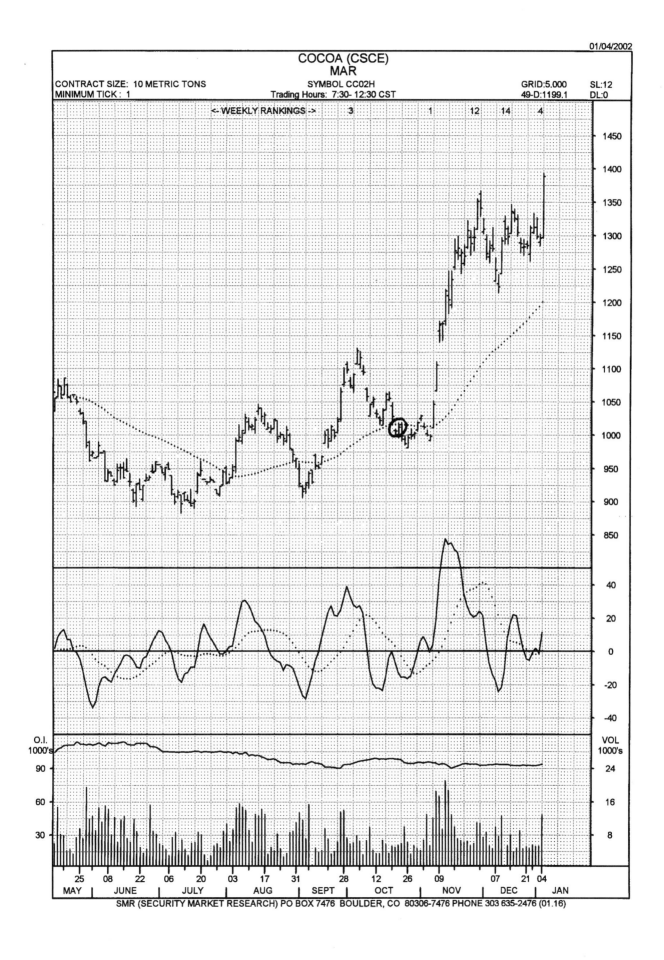

COCOA (CSCE)
MAR

| CONTRACT SIZE: 10 METRIC TONS | SYMBOL CC02H | GRID:5.000 | SL:12 |
| MINIMUM TICK : 1 | Trading Hours: 7:30- 12:30 CST | 49-D:1199.1 | DL:0 |

<- WEEKLY RANKINGS ->     3        1     12    14     4

SMR (SECURITY MARKET RESEARCH) PO BOX 7476  BOULDER, CO  80306-7476  PHONE 303 635-2476 (01.16)

# March 2002 Cocoa (Jan 7)

**REAL-TIME COMMENTARY**

**1/7 (Monday):**   Mar Cocoa - Status - Bullish. Trend and ML both solidly up and so market remains in clear concurrent mode to upside. Action positive, but did see some lessening of upside momentum as not much in way of follow through to upside after big up day on Friday. Therefore, could see minor pause/dip here next few days even though overall pattern remains very positive. Now have well over 100 percent of margin profit on any buys from 1280 area and never anything wrong with taking some partial profits when this the case, but odds clearly favor higher. Bottom line: Can be long with stops still just under 1325.

........................

**AFTER-ACTION CRITIQUE**

Status was solidly Bullish here with plus three points (all three lines solidly up and ML above zero). Market was also in good concurrent mode to upside since both trend and ML were clearly up. Only negative in picture here was, as mentioned in daily letter, the relatively disappointing up day. If look at up surge in early November, the market actually picked up speed for the first three days, and only then started slowly losing upside momentum. Here, on other hand, the second day of this two-day up surge/breakout was up much less than first day. Note how I cautioned that this indicated "could pause/dip here next few days," meaning I definitely had some concerns due to lack of sustained upside pressure.

What we are doing here is using three reasonably reliable indicators of past and current price energy flows: long, intermediate, and short term. While each of these lines moves somewhat independently, they are joined at the hip. Each of these indicators is either directly or indirectly related to price movement. If the price moves persistently and significantly up, eventually all three lines will move up behind it. The price is directly contained in the short-term line (the SL). The short-term line is contained within the intermediate-term line (the ML), and then both these lines are contained within the trend. The lines are like a snake: the head (SL) moves first and is followed by the midsection (ML), which in turn drags the tail (trend) behind. Study the marks left in the dirt by a snake and you will be able to anticipate its *most likely* next directional move; however, to do so you need to look at head, middle and tail, and then combine them into an overall picture. Once the current direction and speed are observed, it is only logical to expect these to be more likely to continue than change.

Therefore, what we have here at the moment is a "snake" that lunged forward only to suddenly and unexpectedly slow down. Odds favor it continuing forward, but the sudden drop in forward momentum is disturbing (because it's not what "should" have happened).

When traders talk about price action, this is what they usually mean: Whether or not the market acted as it "should have"—meaning did it follow its existing price energy flow? Frequently (usually?) it is the unexpected price action that is the most revealing. It is the "dog that did not bark" that is the most worthy of attention. In other words, this market should have been up more and it bothered me that it was not.

# March 2002 Cocoa (Jan 8)

## REAL-TIME COMMENTARY

**1/8 (Tuesday):** Mar Cocoa - Status - Bullish (to Neutral). Trend and ML both still solidly up so market remains in concurrent mode to upside. Action slightly negative as gave back yesterday's minor up. Mentioned yesterday that market had shown some sign of lessening of upside energy and so minor dip possible (likely) and could therefore make case to take partial profits. Can still make case to take partial profits (if have not already done so) since SL and price now both near recent highs and always have some down side vulnerability when this the case. Normally when market in strong concurrent mode can override high SL and price, but since bull move "old," prefer to take some profits. However, since underlying pattern (i.e., concurrent mode) so positive, would retain at least some longs. Bottom line: Can be long with stops still essentially out of range (just under 1325).

........................

## AFTER-ACTION CRITIQUE

Status remained solidly Bullish here since all three lines were up and ML was well above zero (so had plus three points). Market was still in solid concurrent mode to upside. In checking back, notice that my suggestion to take some partial profits was more subtle than the above commentary indicated; however, I write letter shortly after market closes and am sure, as evening wore on, I became increasingly concerned about previous day's action and so remembered being more negative than letter stated.

Now had had two days in a row of relatively negative action. The point here was if you asked me after close two days earlier (after the big up spike day) if I would have considered it positive or negative action if price was unchanged two days later, no question I would have said that would be very disappointing or negative action. Action of first three days of this up surge was very different from the first three days of the November up surge. Action of this up surge was more like action of the late September up surge. The mini up spike at the end of September (from 1025 to 1065) did not have much in way of follow through the next few days, although current trend/momentum pattern was much more positive (all three lines more positive here than in late September).

While I had been suggesting anticipation longs starting around the 1280 area (late December), the correct "official" entry point for this trade was closer to 1300. Regardless, this trade had gone slightly beyond the 100 percent of margin profit point (using roughly a $1000 margin). Therefore, with the action disappointing and both price and SL on recent highs, I saw taking partial profits here as correct action and have to agree with this now also. If only trading one contract, would have definitely taken profits here. Reason is that when you are trading with a small amount, the first job is to make money. Focus on maximizing profits only when you have enough equity to do multiple positions, because then can hold a few contracts for potential maximization of profit.

Overall pattern was still clearly positive here so could not argue for total liquidation of longs. A situation like this does not have an absolute "correct" answer (as to whether to take profits on all longs, or hold on to small long position). This is simply a trading decision. However, it is never wrong to be positioned on long side when trend/momentum solidly positive, and was solid here.

01/08/2002

COCOA (CSCE)
MAR

| CONTRACT SIZE: 10 METRIC TONS | SYMBOL CC02H | GRID:5.000 | SL:45 |
| MINIMUM TICK : 1 | Trading Hours: 7:30- 12:30 CST | 49-D:1214.8 | DL:8 |

<- WEEKLY RANKINGS ->     3        1      12     14      4

SMR (SECURITY MARKET RESEARCH) PO BOX 7476  BOULDER, CO  80306-7476 PHONE 303 635-2476 (01.16)

# March 2002 Cocoa (Jan 9)

## REAL-TIME COMMENTARY

**1/9 (Wednesday):** Mar Cocoa - Status - Bullish. Trend and ML both up and so market still in clear concurrent mode to upside. Action positive on minor upside reversal. SL turned down slightly; however, this is no serious cause for concern when in solid concurrent mode to upside. Past few days has look of minor bull flag which would expect to see break to upside. A couple more days of sideways-type action here would set up another buying opportunity, but for now prefer to stick with reduced level of longs. If pushes up from here, then will simply make less. If dips slightly or sideways next few days, will be able to justify reinstating some of longs taken off past couple days. Bottom line: Can be long with stops still 1325.

....................

## AFTER-ACTION CRITIQUE

Status was still Bullish because trend and ML were still up (uptrend +1, ML above zero +1/2 and on up cycle another +1/2, for a total of +2 points). Market was still in concurrent mode to upside, but not a very solid one. If you look back to where the SL was ten to fifteen days earlier, will see that would be taking off some high numbers (in +20 area). Therefore, with SL currently at +40 and headed down, this means it would not take very much in way of downside price movement next couple days to turn market back to crosscurrent mode and Status back to Neutral.

I was overestimating the positive picture here and believe this was because I had very high hopes for this trade. If you look back on the chart, will see that had three clear up surges. Each of these up surges was progressively stronger (made a bigger up move, gave less of it back). Therefore, as soon as had the big up spike (four days ago here), I naturally started thinking this move would be even bigger still. In other words, I started calculating something like this: first surge went up about 150 points, second surge 225 points, third surge picked up 350 points, and so this one should be good for 450 or even 500 points. Once I started to think about big profits ahead, I did not want to let go of that possibility. Therefore, I was perfectly willing to grab hold of any positives and at the same time excused away any negatives.

If you go by the "rules" as I have laid them out in this book, then the correct action in a situation like this one was to take partial profits (liquidate at least three-quarters of position) if holding multiple positions, or get out of all positions if holding only one or two contracts. The fundamental profit rule is that whenever the profit on a trade reaches 100 percent of margin, then you must find a good reason not to take profits. There was "some" reason not to take profits here (market still in concurrent mode and Bullish Status); however, there were also clear reasons to take profits (price and SL on recent highs, price action disappointing/negative). You cannot make money trading unless you take profits. In the long run I believe virtually all traders will do better if they tilt toward taking profits when "good" (according to rules), with the only exception being when cannot find any reason at all (other than size of profit) to do so. Note how in the November up move there was no technical reason to take profits until very late in move. However, both here and in first two price surges on chart there were a number of reasons to take profits (besides size of profit). Therefore, in situations like this one I believe the best tactic was to take profits on all but a token amount (or on all contracts if only trading one or two), regardless of what happens.

01/09/2002

COCOA (CSCE)
MAR

CONTRACT SIZE:  10 METRIC TONS
MINIMUM TICK : 1

SYMBOL CC02H
Trading Hours: 7:30- 12:30 CST

GRID:5.000
49-D:1222.7

SL:40
DL:11

<- WEEKLY RANKINGS ->         3         1     12     14     4

SMR (SECURITY MARKET RESEARCH) PO BOX 7476  BOULDER, CO  80306-7476 PHONE 303 635-2476 (01.16)

# March 2002 Cocoa (Jan 10)

## REAL-TIME COMMENTARY

**1/10 (Thursday):** Mar Cocoa - Status - Bullish (to Neutral). Trend and ML both up so market remains in concurrent mode to upside. Action negative on moderate downside reversal as made new highs early, but sold off sharply very late in day to close on four-day lows. Today's chart action called a "key reversal" since made new contract highs and closed lower. Some consider this type of one-day reversal significant; however, one time I checked a big bull move and found it had over a dozen downside key reversals over a several month up move. When a key reversal occasionally does prove significant it will stand out on the charts, whereas the ones that do not "work" simply get buried in a larger advance and therefore are little noticed. This market has already had two key reversals over past seven weeks. One meant nothing as price immediately moved higher while second one (five weeks ago) did produce week long sell-off before market subsequently moved to new highs (that key reversal came when ML was on verge of turning down so it had a different technical background). On "line basis" and price chart the picture here still fully justifies longs. However, today a good reason why like to take some partial profits when reach 100 percent of margin (or more), as has been case here past few days. Doing this makes holding the remainder of longs much easier here. Bottom line: Can be long with stops still just under 1325 (preferably on close-only basis).

.....................

## AFTER-ACTION CRITIQUE

Status was still Bullish since both trend and ML were still up (had +2 points at moment).Market also remained in concurrent mode to upside, but this was now getting shaky since another down day and SL would fall below where it was three weeks ago and turn the ML down (thus putting market in crosscurrent mode).

I am writing this "critique" three weeks after the fact, so it is still fairly fresh in my mind. The market opened near its highs on this day and after about thirty minutes or less started down and kept going until it closed on lows. I remember early in day being a little sorry I had taken partial profits, but then by the time market closed I was sorry I had not liquidated all positions. This is a typical thought process traders go through. One minute a trader can be sorry he is not holding more contracts, then the next minute he can be wishing he was not in at all, or at least had a smaller position. It seems to me these types of thoughts are normal and pretty much unavoidable; however, the important point is not to let random hopes and wishes like these have anything at all to do with your decision making process and ultimate action.

To be successful at this very difficult game you need to be as cold-blooded as possible when it comes to decision time. Wishes, hopes, wants, desires, fears, dreads, whatever—none of these have anything whatsoever to contribute to good decision making. In fact they are all hindrances to clear seeing and acting. Feel these emotions all you want when watching the markets move; however, when it comes time to see the current situation clearly and then act on what you see, banish all these thoughts and feelings from your mind. Send them into the other room. They have no role to play in the seeing and acting of trading. They are only spectators; do not let them play the game.

01/10/2002

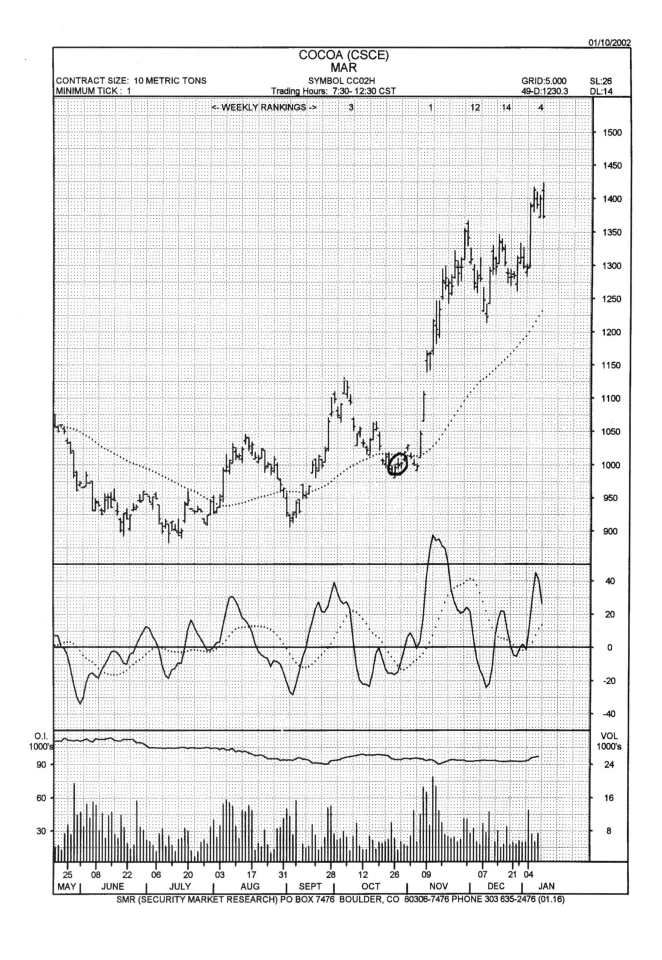

COCOA (CSCE)
MAR

CONTRACT SIZE: 10 METRIC TONS     SYMBOL CC02H     GRID:5.000     SL:26
MINIMUM TICK : 1     Trading Hours: 7:30- 12:30 CST     49-D:1230.3     DL:14

<- WEEKLY RANKINGS ->     3     1     12     14     4

SMR (SECURITY MARKET RESEARCH) PO BOX 7476  BOULDER, CO  80306-7476 PHONE 303 635-2476 (01.16)

# March 2002 Cocoa (Jan 11)

**REAL-TIME COMMENTARY**

**1/11 (Friday):** Mar Cocoa - Status - Bullish/Neutral. Trend still solidly up, but ML now sideways and so market now just barely concurrent. Action slightly negative on minor down day—closed on lows of day and did not show much in way of upside energy. Market now at key point since if cannot move up on Monday, line pattern will go to neutral. So far, with trend up, the spike of a week ago has more the look of a temporary (?) upside exhaustion move than a continuation spike. Therefore, would put any longs here on fairly strict probation for Monday (meaning it's either up or out, and longer it goes unchanged or lower on day the more willing would be to liquidate longs). Bottom line: Can still be long, but if unchanged or lower after first thirty to sixty minutes of trading (or even sooner) would go to sidelines.

.....................

**AFTER-ACTION CRITIQUE**

I let my upside desires override reality a little here. Actually Status had already turned Neutral since the ML was sideways and most likely would be down in another day (SL would go down next day unless price was up very sharply—1400 or higher—and so ML would turn down also). Therefore, only had plus one point (+1) from the uptrend and plus a half point (+1/2) from the ML being above zero, which meant the Status was Neutral and the market in crosscurrent mode.

Desires distort vision in this game. As I remember at this time I was still holding out a slim hope for a big up move in this market. What I was hoping for was a solid up day, which would have turned the SL up for a third higher low and thus would have created a very bullish picture. I still "thought" this market "should" have been on its way to another upside thrust, similar to the earlier ones. Therefore, I was still hanging on to some longs. This was a case of desire distorting fact. It was a case of trading on hope, not reality. When a trader trades solely on hope, then he or she usually has no hope.

This was more likely a time to be fully out of the market than a time to "put longs on strict probation." Anything less than a good (at least twenty points) up day would have turned the pattern too neutral to justify sticking with longs. A week ago here had a breakout day to the upside; new contract highs were made on a ninety-point up day. All trend and momentum indicators became solidly positive. In addition, the big up day clearly should have been a continuation spike. Yet, in spite of all these bullish factors the market never traded more than about twenty-five points higher than the spike day's close. In fact, five days later it was thirty points lower. By any definition, this was negative action.

Anything was possible, but when the only scenario that justified being long was the next day being a big up day and the current short-term momentum was clearly down, then being long was going against the odds. The more intelligent action here would have been to be fully on sidelines. If the market had subsequently moved back up to 1390-1400 area, then could have gone back long. The situation here was just too iffy to justify longs. It would have been better to give up first thirty or forty points of any up move from this point than to be long here against the odds.

If you want to walk away winner, then only be positioned when odds are in your favor.

01/11/2002

COCOA (CSCE)
MAR

CONTRACT SIZE: 10 METRIC TONS
MINIMUM TICK : 1

SYMBOL CC02H
Trading Hours:  7:30- 12:30 CST

GRID:5.000
49-D:1237.9

SL:14
DL:14

<- WEEKLY RANKINGS ->      1        7        2      4    36

SMR (SECURITY MARKET RESEARCH) PO BOX 7476  BOULDER, CO  80306-7476  PHONE 303 635-2476 (01.18)

# March 2002 Cocoa (Jan 14)

## REAL-TIME COMMENTARY

**1/14 (Monday):** Mar Cocoa - Status - Neutral. Trend still clearly up but ML now on down cycle so market in crosscurrent mode. Action very negative on big gap lower—opened and closed near lows of day. Move (and especially close) back at 1300 gives past week or so of action (in high 1300's) the look of both a "false" upside breakout and an "island" reversal, and both these chart patterns frequently signal major tops. Intermediate price swings over past several months have been accurately marked by the cycles in ML and this has now turned down, so this also a clear negative. Additional negative is that this ML cycle is turning down clearly below previous high ML. Therefore, picture too negative now to justify longs, but trend still up so cannot make any kind of legitimate case for shorts. Although, if had to be in here now, would be short with stops at 1350 since all indicators but trend are now negative, and the trend is in a position to weaken. (Taking profits at 100 percent of margin was best idea here this time since if waited for lines to turn neutral, lost all profit.) Bottom line: Sidelines.

......................

## AFTER-ACTION CRITIQUE

Status was now solidly Neutral since only had one point for the uptrend and half a point for the ML being above zero. The SL was well below where it was around three weeks earlier as well as below all levels of prior three weeks; therefore, for time being there was little likelihood of the ML turning up. The basic expectation for crosscurrent patterns is for choppy, sideways-type price action. Therefore, the picture in this market was now very fuzzy and the correct position clear: sidelines.

What happened here over past week was upside exhaustion. The upside ran out of energy, so the price did a slow roll over to the downside. Evidently, over the weekend enough longs decided to run for cover and enough shorts decided to attack, that by time got around to New York opening (Cocoa trades actively in London, so in a sense New York session is second half of an international market day) the market was already sharply lower and under heavy selling pressure.

One day, one night, one hour, and sometimes even a few minutes can make a big difference in this game. As soon as the technical picture becomes clear that it is the time to exit a market, then it is usually best to just do so—at the market. When the odds on a trade shift from favorable to unfavorable, then there is no reason to stay in the position. The temptation to hold on a little longer in the hope it might do better than expected should be resisted. If you are trading based on natural laws and rules derived from those laws, then make sure you do so. If you want to make bets against the odds, then go to Las Vegas since all bets are against the odds there. Remember, in trading all trades pay the same regardless of their true odds for success; therefore, might as well only trade when the odds are favorable.

By mistakenly hanging around one day too long on some contracts on this trade, I turned an excellent trade (over 100 percent of margin profit on all contracts) into a financially so-so one (100 percent of margin profit on some, minor profit on others), as well as a psychologically negative (disappointing) one.

COCOA (CSCE)
MAR

01/14/2002

CONTRACT SIZE: 10 METRIC TONS
MINIMUM TICK : 1

SYMBOL CC02H
Trading Hours: 7:30- 12:30 CST

GRID:5.000
49-D:1244.1

SL:-5
DL:13

<- WEEKLY RANKINGS ->    1    7    2    4    36

SMR (SECURITY MARKET RESEARCH) PO BOX 7476  BOULDER, CO  80306-7476  PHONE 303 635-2476 (01.18)

# March 2002 Cocoa (Jan 15)

## REAL-TIME COMMENTARY

**1/15 (Tuesday):** Mar Cocoa - Status - Neutral. Trend still solidly up, but ML now in minor down cycle and so market in crosscurrent mode. Action fairly positive as down sharply early but rallied even more sharply late and closed near day's high and slightly higher on day. Both SL and price now near recent lows and whenever trend clearly up can always make some argument to be/go long when this the case. However, both price chart and line pattern now very mixed (price chart showing some clear negatives, as outlined yesterday) and so cannot make good case to be/go long here at this time. Naturally, market will move, and based on past two days probably will make decent move, but any trade here at moment has both low odds and poor risk/reward and so prefer sidelines. Bottom line: Sidelines.

.....................

## AFTER-ACTION CRITIQUE

Status was now solidly Neutral since still only had the uptrend (+1) and ML above zero (+1/2) for with-the-trend points. Market also was now in fairly solid crosscurrent mode since there was little chance of the SL getting above where it was three weeks earlier for at least another few days; therefore, there was little chance of turning the ML up anytime soon.

Price action on this day was impressive since normal expectations would have been for it to have kept pushing lower. This was a good example of the power of a solid uptrend. It is difficult for a market to move sharply against a strong trend for very long, especially as price gets closer to the 50-day moving average. Solidly trending moving average lines invariably provide decent support/resistance. This is probably because so many traders pay attention to these and frequently use them for entry areas. Against-the-trend moves are like a "ball being pushed under water"; the farther the ball is pushed, the more energy that is required to keep pushing it, and then as soon as downside pressure eases, the ball will tend to "pop" up sharply. While this pop may not last, it does tend to be fast and can be surprisingly big.

In the previous letter I said something about shorting; this was a mistake. When the trend is this strong to the upside, you should post a sign on it that says: Do not even think about shorting. However, when markets are open and moving around significantly, somehow strange thoughts tend to enter a trader's mind; therefore, you have to be constantly alert to make sure these impulses do not translate into any action. Any and all action on initiating new trades should be done coldly and calculatingly, and according to the "rules." When the trend is clear, the basic trend rule applies: If you cannot trade with the trend, then do not trade at all.

We have now covered two and a half months of an active Cocoa market. If a trader had followed the rules as laid out in this book, he or she could have produced some substantial profits trading Cocoa over this period. Throughout this period a trader would never have had any position be a loser for more than a couple days. While this was a very good period for trend/momentum trading in this market, it was by no means particularly unusual. Markets tend to provide clues to their unknown futures, as this one did during this time period. It is our job as traders to see them, and then act on what we see. Understand the natural laws, see clearly, then act decisively.

01/15/2002

COCOA (CSCE)
MAR

CONTRACT SIZE:  10 METRIC TONS
MINIMUM TICK :  1

SYMBOL CC02H
Trading Hours:  7:30- 12:30 CST

GRID:5.000
49-D:1250.4

SL:-18
DL:10

<- WEEKLY RANKINGS ->

SMR (SECURITY MARKET RESEARCH) PO BOX 7476  BOULDER, CO  80306-7476 PHONE 303 635-2476 (01.18)

# March 2002 Cocoa (Feb 15)

**2/15 (Friday):** Mar Cocoa - For the week and a half after 1/15 this market simply chopped sideways, never getting far from 1350 level. It very briefly went to concurrent mode to upside; however, it was clear from the very high SL numbers would have been taking off from ten to fifteen days earlier that this would not stick, and it did not.

However, right around the first of February the market began to set up well for going long again. In the daily letter as of the close on Friday, 2/1, I wrote the following: "Bottom line: Lines say sidelines but as long as does not open weak on Monday (below 1340) could make case to start going long 'in anticipation' of lines turning positive again soon (or can use buy stop at 1371 to initiate new longs), a close under 1325 would be too negative to stick with longs so could use this for stop."

The above was written the day the market closed at 1350 and one day before the 50-point up move to 1400. Up until that day I had been suggesting "sidelines" as the best position because the ML was still too far away from being in position to turn solidly up. However, by the first of February there were about fourteen days of SL numbers of +10 or lower, plus were coming up on a week where would be taking off very low SL numbers, which meant the ML would almost have to turn up in few days. (Remember, the ML is about a three-week moving average of the SL. Therefore, to estimate the ML's next directional move, it is necessary to compare current SL levels with those of ten to sixteen days earlier.) In addition, the SL tends to move in roughly one week cycles, up and down. In the preceding two weeks it had had a good up move (from -25 to +10) for six days, followed by a straight sideways week. In other words, the previous week "should" have been a down-cycle week for the SL; instead, it went sideways and this was a sign of internal strength.

Markets tend to ebb and flow. They tend to "breathe in and out, up and down." I consider it a sign of strength when a market holds well during what would normally be a short-term down period. Therefore, on 1 February I started "anticipating" that the line pattern would soon go to a clear Bullish Status as well as a sustained period of concurrent mode, which is why I suggested anticipation longs.

Regardless of whether a trader bought early on 1 February (around 1350) or waited for the next day (after the close at 1400), the market had a nice up move and so could have easily picked up another 75 or 100 percent of margin profit, depending on where entered the trade.

A long-term trader could have entered this market on long side as soon as the price had its first big up day (the close at 1045) in early November, then would have just stuck with the longs all the way through the ups and down. The only time a long-term trader would have had to even begin paying close attention was in early February when there was a slim chance the trend would turn down. Other than that brief period, he or she would have just held long positions without stops. While doing this would have produced very good profits, it would have required great patience as well as solid discipline in the face of the periods of price weakness. Whether a trader uses a day-by-day trading approach or a long-term trading approach is solely a question of personal preference and self-knowledge. And only the individual trader can make that choice.

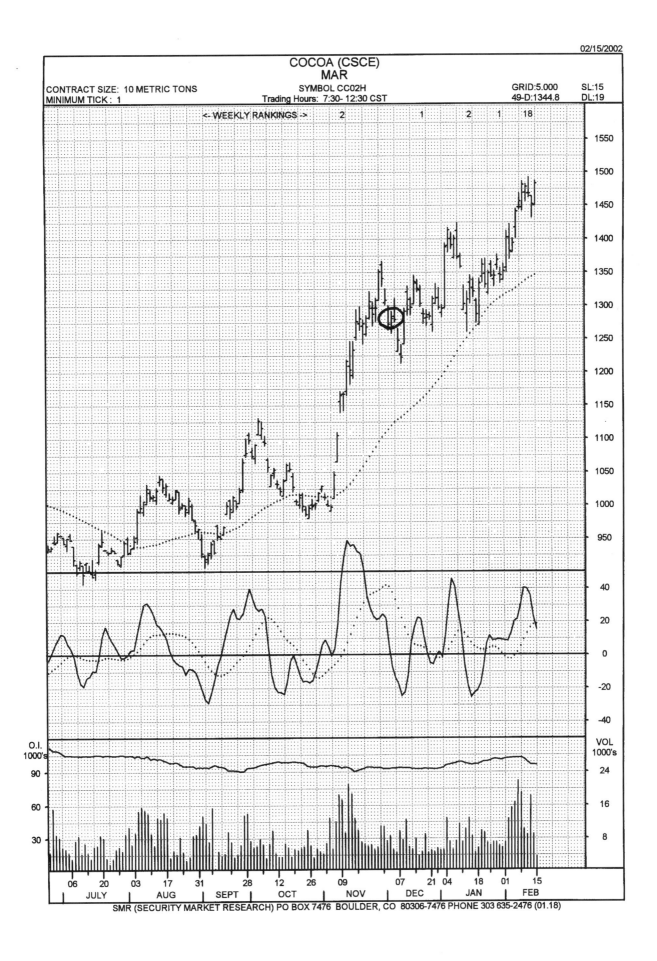

02/15/2002

COCOA (CSCE)
MAR

CONTRACT SIZE: 10 METRIC TONS
MINIMUM TICK : 1

SYMBOL CC02H
Trading Hours: 7:30- 12:30 CST

GRID:5.000
49-D:1344.8

SL:15
DL:19

<- WEEKLY RANKINGS ->

SMR (SECURITY MARKET RESEARCH) PO BOX 7476 BOULDER, CO 80306-7476 PHONE 303 635-2476 (01.18)

# March 2002 Sugar (Jan 2)

## REAL-TIME COMMENTARY

**1/2 (Wednesday, first trading day of year):** Mar Sugar - Status - Bullish. Trend still up and ML now also up so market now in concurrent mode to upside. Action quite positive as market up sharply and has now remade all it lost on big sell-off several weeks ago. This market has history of making spike-type bottoms and tops and did the same this time. Unfortunately, when it makes these spike-type bottoms it takes a long time for line pattern to turn back to positive, which means do not get buy signal until market has already moved up substantially from a low. Question here is whether pattern is positive enough to justify going long with price on such a big rally? Naturally would have preferred buying at better price but see picture as good enough to go lightly long here with idea of saving some buying power to add if do get minor couple day dip sometime over next week or so. Bottom line: Can go long with stops just under 7.30 for now.

......................

## AFTER-ACTION CRITIQUE

Keep in mind what we are doing here; we are in the futures trading business. The business of futures trading is a game, an up or down intellectual numbers game. In spite of the fact that this game is a fifty-fifty proposition, up or down, the truth is the overwhelming majority (90 percent or more?) of players lose. We acknowledge we cannot compete in this game relying on information and knowledge (of fundamental supply and demand); therefore, we do waste time and energy trying. Since we accept that we know nothing about any market, this means we have to rely on the natural laws of trading. The first law of trading is the future is unknown; therefore, we do not waste time and energy predicting. The second law of trading is continuation is more likely than change; therefore, we observe and measure price energy flows. The third law of trading is prices fluctuate; therefore, we need a business plan for taking profits and losses.

The three SMR lines are our tools for measuring price energy flow. The three-point system is the gauge, the compass, and speedometer for price movement. Our job as the "action" part of our personal trading company, i.e., the trader, is to pay attention to reality—what is actually happening—and then act on what we see (based on our reasonably reliable indicators of price energy flow). Trade on what you *see*, not what you think.

Now, let us look at Mar Sugar as of the close 2 January 2002. We see that the trend is now solidly up (price is significantly higher than it was nine and ten weeks ago). We see that the inter-mediate-term momentum indicator (ML) is just turning up and is in position to make a sustained up move (SL is above where it was three weeks earlier, and since will be "taking off" low SL numbers for the next couple weeks, this means the ML "should" continue up for at least next couple weeks). We see that both SL and price are on recent highs, meaning price not very "attractive" for buying. However, we know that whenever trend and ML are solid in one direction, the odds clearly favor at least some short-term continuation. So, our job as the trader in this trading business is to get positioned here. We do this by trying to buy at unchanged for the first half hour or so, and if unable to do so, then we cancel and buy at the market. In addition, since the price is "high," we will spread (i.e., "scale") our buys over the next couple of days.

01/02/2002

SUGAR #11 (CSCE)
MAR

CONTRACT SIZE:  112,000 lbs.          SYMBOL SB02H                    GRID:0.020      SL:25
MINIMUM TICK :  0.01              Trading Hours: 8:30-12:20 CST            49-D:7.2      DL:-11

<- WEEKLY RANKINGS ->          6          6      30      40      4

SMR (SECURITY MARKET RESEARCH) PO BOX 7476  BOULDER, CO  80306-7476 PHONE 303 635-2476 (01.16)

# March 2002 Sugar (Jan 3)

## REAL-TIME COMMENTARY

**1/3 (Thursday):** Mar Sugar - Status - Bullish (to Neutral). Both trend and ML fairly solidly up and so market in concurrent mode to upside. Action slightly negative on minor downside reversal; however, after five good up days a minor dip is not particularly negative. A couple day dip here would actually set up a better buying opportunity as price is a little over extended to upside at moment. Plus, the line pattern will get more positive as move on here next few days. So, could have minor pause next few days but overall pattern positive enough to be long here as well as go long on additional minor dip. Bottom line: Can be (and go long on further dip) with stops in 7.20 to 7.30, preferably on close basis.

...................

## AFTER-ACTION CRITIQUE

There was no problem buying at unchanged since the market opened slightly lower; therefore, now have partial long position with stop at least below 7.30. This stop level was chosen because price "should not" have gone there (dropped that much) if the upside was "good" here (meaning, when in solid concurrent mode if should see that much of a dip, especially on the close, it would be strong sign trade was not going to work). Prefer to use a close-only stop here because I would want to hold through a quick, early drop; however, I would not want to hold on to any longs if this market *closed* below 7.30 (because that would be "too" weak).

As the "trader" of your trading business it would be your job here to get more fully positioned. A $25,000 account could hold up to three contracts of Sugar in a situation like this. Therefore, if account size was large enough for more than one contract, a trader could put an order in to buy additional contracts at unchanged or slightly lower here. The first chart support level here was 7.50 since this level was just above a minor rally high of two weeks earlier. There was fairly solid support in 7.40 area since that was the top of some earlier trading congestion. For the price to go down all the way through that trading congestion and out the other side (below 7.30) would have taken quite a bit of downside energy, especially when going against trend and intermediate-term momentum; therefore, this area was a good place for any stops.

If a trader had a big enough account to buy a large number of contracts (15 or more), the approach would be to buy on a scale down basis to the 7.50 area, maybe slightly lower (and spread out buying over couple days). However, in this situation I would not buy any contracts any lower than that level since it would begin to be "too weak."

Approaching this trading situation in this manner puts the trader in position to benefit from the most likely continuation of existing price energy flows without risking too much of his equity. Remember, the basic idea is to identify clear price energy flows and then position *with* these price energy flows until they either change direction or show signs of being about to change direction.

This is trend/momentum trading. Then, once positioned, a trader needs to follow sound business practices by taking profits and losses in a businesslike manner—meaning follow the account diversification and allocation rules, as well as the profit taking rules.

SUGAR #11 (CSCE)
MAR

CONTRACT SIZE: 112,000 lbs.
MINIMUM TICK : 0.01

SYMBOL SB02H
Trading Hours: 8:30-12:20 CST

GRID:0.020       SL:36
49-D:7.2         DL:-10

<- WEEKLY RANKINGS ->      6        6      30    40    4

8.90
8.70
8.50
8.30
8.10
7.90
7.70
7.50
7.30
7.10
6.90
6.70
6.50

40
20
0
-20
-40

O.I.
1000's

180
120
60

VOL
1000's

45
30
15

25    08    22    06    20    03    17    31    28    12    26    09    07    21
MAY    JUNE         JULY        AUG         SEPT        OCT         NOV         DEC         JAN

SMR (SECURITY MARKET RESEARCH) PO BOX 7476 BOULDER, CO 80306-7476 PHONE 303 635-2476 (01.16)

# March 2002 Sugar (Jan 4)

**REAL-TIME COMMENTARY**

**1/4 (Friday):** Mar Sugar - Status - Bullish (to Neutral). Trend and ML both up and so market remains in concurrent mode to upside. Action neutral on quiet, sideways day; however, see sideways for few days as a positive at moment since price was a little overdone to upside. Have now had two minor days down within an overall bullish pattern; therefore, this qualifies as a "dip" can buy into. SL on recent highs and always have some downside vulnerability when this the case, but can override this when are in a solid concurrent mode to upside, and this is the case at moment. Nothing in COT that would prevent sustained up move from here. Bottom line: Can be and go long with stops still in 7.20 to 7.30 area.

....................

**AFTER-ACTION CRITIQUE**

Market opened at 7.60 and had a low of 7.56 so would have had no problem buying more at unchanged or slightly lower. Therefore, if you were trading a $25,000 account, would now be long two contracts with an average price around 7.65 (with stop still down just below 7.30). Therefore, you would be risking around 40 points ($440, plus commission) per contract. Since both price and SL are still on recent highs (indicating market remains a little overbought), it would probably be prudent (i.e., businesslike) to hold off on buying any more at the moment. Since this market was in a fairly solid concurrent mode to upside, meaning upside odds quite good, $1000 was a perfectly acceptable risk (on two contracts) on this trade for a $25,000 account.

My experience with line patterns like this one are that even when they do not work (price does not continue), they will at least chop around up in this general area for few days or a week. It would be very rare to see the price move straight back down when have a pattern that is clearly positive like this one.

Once positioned and with stops in place, our job then becomes one of simply "observing." Naturally, a trader would have desires here (we would want the market to go up!); however, these desires would have nothing to do with our job as the trading business's observer. Therefore, when it comes time to "look" at what the market is doing, send your desires elsewhere. Emotions, desires, wishes, fears—none of these play a part in the "seeing" of what is happening.

So, what should a trader be looking for here? Primarily for any signs of greater than expected price weakness. By this I mean that, in this situation, trading down to 7.50 or slightly lower the next day would be nothing out of the ordinary. Trading down to that level would still be well within bullish parameters. However, trading much below 7.50 (around 7.45 or lower) and spending any more than a few (ten, fifteen) minutes under 7.50 would begin to become worrisome. Preferably, I would prefer not to see price dip much at all here. Ideally (for bullish picture), the more and the faster it moved up the better; however, as an observer, what you are looking for are downside warning signs. Sideways and upside action will take care of themselves when you are long; what you want to be alert to are any downside warning signs.

Now we simply watch to see what the market does from here.

SUGAR #11 (CSCE)
MAR

01/04/2002

CONTRACT SIZE:  112,000 lbs.
MINIMUM TICK :  0.01

SYMBOL SB02H
Trading Hours:  8:30-12:20 CST

GRID:0.020
49-D:7.3

SL:43
DL:-8

<- WEEKLY RANKINGS ->    5    10    28    19    9

SMR (SECURITY MARKET RESEARCH) PO BOX 7476  BOULDER, CO  80306-7476  PHONE 303 635-2476 (01.16)

# March 2002 Sugar (Jan 7)

## REAL-TIME COMMENTARY

**1/7 (Monday):** Mar Sugar - Status - Neutral (to Bullish). Trend and ML both remain solidly up so market still in concurrent mode to upside. However, with slight turn down in SL, the line pattern has turned temporarily (?) back to neutral; however, it "should" turn back to positive soon. Two-day dip ended today with minor upside reversal. Therefore, in spite of line pattern being back to neutral, continue to see longs (either existing or new) as fully justified here. Bottom line: Lines say sidelines, but prefer to stick with longs with stops still just under 7.30.

....................

## AFTER-ACTION CRITIQUE

The Status was back to Neutral since only had +1 1/2 points: uptrend equals +1 and ML on up cycle equals +1/2. The rest of points are against trend. However, just because the Status back to Neutral is no reason to liquidate long positions. Market was in a very solid concurrent mode to upside and odds were good it would go back to Bullish Status soon.

The point system is a guide, not an absolute law. If you can look at the chart (as you could here) and see that the Status has a high probability of quickly turning back to Bullish, then there is no need to get out when/if it turns to neutral temporarily. Think of the lines as lane lines on a highway. In most situations you want to stay inside the lines; however, there are times when it is appropriate to drive outside the lines. Think of the Status as speed limit signs on the highway; *usually* you want to stay around the speed limit, however there are times when the appropriate speed may be higher than the speed limit.

Your job as manager of your trading business is to bring all your reasonably reliable technicals together and combine them with prudent business practices. However, every situation is a little unique, so each situation can require a little different course of action.

The seeing and reading of the market is the *art*. The deciding and acting part is the *business*. An individual trader needs to be both an artist and a businessperson; both are necessary for great success. However, the truth is that a mediocre artist with an excellent business manager has a much better chance for financial success than the opposite. The world is full of financially successful mediocrities as well as exceptionally talented financial failures. If your measurement of success in trading is the monetary result, then the most important part of trading for you will be the business part—the management of the money.

A certain level of artistic understanding and talent is a prerequisite; however, ultimate financial success is overwhelmingly dependent on good business practices. Good businesspeople act in a cold (emotionless) and calculating way because this is what works best in business. Therefore, study and learn the art of trading as best you can, but remember that your final monetary success or failure will be determined by how you manage your account—how many you buy and sell, and when you sell or buy them back. There are no prizes for seeing and calling the markets right; there are only prizes for trading them right. The more artistic talent you have the better; however, if it is money you seek, then focus maximum energy on correct business action because that is where the money is.

01/07/2002

SUGAR #11 (CSCE)
MAR

CONTRACT SIZE: 112,000 lbs.          SYMBOL SB02H                    GRID:0.020      SL:39
MINIMUM TICK : 0.01              Trading Hours: 8:30-12:20 CST           49-D:7.3       DL:-6

<- WEEKLY RANKINGS ->        5        10      28     19      9

SMR (SECURITY MARKET RESEARCH) PO BOX 7476  BOULDER, CO  80306-7476  PHONE 303 635-2476 (01.16)

# March 2002 Sugar (Jan 8)

## REAL-TIME COMMENTARY

**1/8 (Tuesday):** Mar Sugar - Status - Neutral (to Bullish). Trend and ML both solidly up so market remains in concurrent mode to upside. Action positive on small but steady up day with the close back on recent highs. Pattern technically neutral, but it will go back to positive in day or two and overall picture remains good enough to be/go long here. Always a positive sign when dips are limited to a couple of days as well as minor in depth, and this case here so far. Bottom line: Lines say sidelines, but picture still positive enough to fully justify longs with stops now in 7.30 to 7.40 area.

.....................

## AFTER-ACTION CRITIQUE

Status is Neutral because have only one and a half with-the-trend points (+1 for trend and +1/2 for ML in up cycle). However, since the SL way above where it was three weeks ago (remember ML is about a three-week moving average of SL), the ML will go above zero in couple days and so pattern will go back to Bullish Status soon. Therefore, remain close enough to Bullish Status to be long here, especially since the market is in such a solid concurrent mode.

If you look back over past eight months of chart, you will see that the intermediate-term price cycles have coincided quite well with the cycles of the ML—much as the Cocoa chart did earlier. I have found that many—if not most—of the storable commodities have this tendency. The reason for this is that once supply is known, once crop has been harvested, then the prime variable in supply/demand equation is demand, and demand is normally very susceptible to intermediate-term time cycles. Usage of these commodities is not hand-to-mouth, meaning inventories are maintained. This means buying pressures are flexible on a short-term basis. For the short term, buying can be moved backward and forward fairly easily depending on price levels. This buying flexibility tends to produce fairly rhythmic price cycles. Therefore, whenever trading a storable commodity (i.e., a commodity that once harvested can be kept in storage for long periods of time without deteriorating), it is a good idea to give the ML a little extra weight in your seeing and acting.

What we had here at this moment was a market where the current price energy flows were clearly to the upside. We used the minor dip of previous couple days to put on moderate long positions. Price moved up a little so we moved our stop up a little also (since would not want to see price back below 7.50, and especially not below 7.40).

The bad news about trading is the future is unknown, which means we cannot predict it. However, the good news about trading is continuation of price energy flows is more likely than change. Therefore, if we can identify these flows and then position with them, we have a decent chance to succeed at betting on this unpredictable future. This is exactly what we have done here. Now it is just a matter of continuing to keep stops in and maintain close, clear observation of the price action on a day-by-day basis.

01/08/2002

SUGAR #11 (CSCE)
MAR

CONTRACT SIZE:  112,000 lbs.
MINIMUM TICK :  0.01

SYMBOL SB02H
Trading Hours:  8:30-12:20 CST

GRID:0.020       SL:36
49-D:7.3         DL:-4

SMR (SECURITY MARKET RESEARCH) PO BOX 7476  BOULDER, CO  80306-7476 PHONE 303 635-2476 (01.16)

# March 2002 Sugar (Jan 9)

## REAL-TIME COMMENTARY

**1/9 (Wednesday):** Mar Sugar - Status - Bullish (to Neutral). Trend and ML both remain solidly up so market continues in concurrent mode to upside. Action quite positive on persistent upside intra-day pressure with close on day's highs and new recent highs. As expected, line pattern turned right back to positive. All indicators remain positive here with no warning signs at moment; therefore, see no reason to take any profits yet. Bottom line: Can be long with stops now just under 7.50.

.....................

## AFTER-ACTION CRITIQUE

From a bullish standpoint, it was about as good a day as could expect. Market gapped higher and held that gap, then closed on highs up decently—25 points, or half the old limit. In the "old" days, price could not trade more than 50 points up or down in one day, and even today, when have no daily limits, 50 points is still about most ever see in one day; therefore, 25 points up is a good one-day move in Sugar.

From a business perspective, as soon as initiate a position it is a good idea to note where the 50 and 100 percent of margin profit points would be. As a general rule I measure these percentage points from the "official" line entry price. In this case that would be 7.72, or the closing of the day when the Status switched from Neutral to Bullish (2 January in this case). Had the price gapped higher the morning after the signal day, then I would use that opening price as starting point for the trade. However, in practice, if you get in better than the official signal price, I see nothing wrong with using your entry point as the starting point of the trade (would have been 7.65 in this case). Regardless, in practice most traders should adjust these profit points somewhat based on conditions.

Trading is decision making, daily multiple decisions. Even when no action is taken, this is still a decision. When playing a game with as many variables as this one has, and it has a tremendous number of daily variables, you have to accept that perfection is impossible. All we can do is try to get in at approximately the right price and time.

A good way to give yourself a solid chance to position well is not to be too insistent on getting in at the best—the most perfect—time and price. Sometimes (much of the time?) a little sloppiness works best in trading. It is OK to try limit orders when positioning; however, if the overall pattern is fairly solid, then keep these limits reasonable, and in end just make sure to get in fairly soon. When the odds clearly favor one direction, then it is your job as the "trader" to get positioned in that direction. You are allowed some discretion, but not at the expense of failing to position. When the odds and risk/reward are more marginal (trend more indecisive, etc.), then you can and should be pickier (meaning you can insist on getting a good price and if cannot, then just pass on the trade).

In this case, pattern was clearly positive the previous five days, so a trader needed to get long. If we calculate the entry point on this trade to be in 7.65 to 7.70 area, and use a margin of $900 to $1000, then the 50 percent of margin profit point would be in the up-45-point area (plus or minus a few points), or somewhere around 8.10 to 8.15. The 100 percent of margin profit area would be just over 8.50. However, all signs were positive at moment, so there was no need to take any profits yet.

01/09/2002

SUGAR #11 (CSCE)
MAR

CONTRACT SIZE: 112,000 lbs.
MINIMUM TICK : 0.01

SYMBOL SB02H
Trading Hours: 8:30-12:20 CST

GRID:0.020
49-D:7.3

SL:38
DL:-1

<- WEEKLY RANKINGS ->    5    10    28    19    9

SMR (SECURITY MARKET RESEARCH) PO BOX 7476  BOULDER, CO  80306-7476  PHONE 303 635-2476 (01.16)

# March 2002 Sugar (Jan 10)

**REAL-TIME COMMENTARY**

**1/10 (Thursday):** Mar Sugar - Status - Bullish. Trend and ML both solidly up so market remains in concurrent mode to upside. Action slightly negative on minor down day; however, one minor down day does not cancel out two weeks of solid up. Minor dip/brief pause here would not be surprising as market has had big up move over past two weeks, but overall pattern remains solidly positive so odds favor higher prices ahead and indicate any dip should be shallow and brief. Bottom line: Can be long with stops still just under 7.50 for now.

....................

**AFTER-ACTION CRITIQUE**

Even though SL turned down, Status was still Bullish since trend was up and ML was both up and above zero (this added up to two points with trend). Since neither trend nor ML had any chance of turning down anytime soon (in both cases were taking off numbers much below current levels), market was going to remain in Bullish Status for at least next several days. Stop could be inched up a little more without too much risk (of it being hit on momentary downside aberration).

This day was clearly on disappointing side since day before the picture was solidly positive and so could have reasonably expected another good up day. Daily action like this would be the type of downside warning action an observant trader would pay attention to—because it was unexpected and negative. However, the overall pattern was still very solidly positive, so there was still no need to take any precautionary action (other than move stop up slightly).

If you look two weeks back on this chart, you will see a situation where a trader could have made a case to be buyer on a "faith-in-trend" basis. The trend was solidly up and the price was making its first dip in a strong, new bull market. Anytime the trend is solidly up and both price *and* SL are at recent lows (or vice versa, trend down and price *and* SL are on recent highs), then a trader can make a legitimate case to put on light with the trend positions in "anticipation" that the line pattern will turn Bullish/Bearish soon.

The basic idea in trading is to sell higher than buy, buy lower than sell. The most reliable and persistent line (price energy flow) is the trend. When the trend is solid (meaning clear and with virtually no chance of turning any time soon, i.e., next few weeks) and both price and SL are at recent counter trend lows/highs (depending on direction of trend), a trader can always make some kind of case to position with the trend. However, when you do position in a situation like this, you have to keep quantity small because you cannot use stops (or if you do use a stop it has to be very generous one). I call this type of positioning a "faith-in-trend" or an "attractive-price" position.

This faith-in-trend or attractive-price entry method tends to work very well; however, it can be very nerve-wracking because you are positioning when short-term momentum is still clearly moving against your position. In other words, you are just guessing that a counter-trend move will soon end and thus may have to endure some pressure against your position. Unfortunately, every once in a while price will just keep moving counter trend until the trend actually changes, and when this happens the losses can be quite large. Therefore, this faith-in-trend/attractive-price entry method of positioning with the trend should be used with some care.

SUGAR #11 (CSCE)
MAR

CONTRACT SIZE: 112,000 lbs.
MINIMUM TICK : 0.01

SYMBOL SB02H
Trading Hours: 8:30-12:20 CST

GRID:0.020
49-D:7.3

SL:37
DL:3

<- WEEKLY RANKINGS ->     5        10        28    19     9

SMR (SECURITY MARKET RESEARCH) PO BOX 7476 BOULDER, CO 80306-7476 PHONE 303 635-2476 (01.16)

# March 2002 Sugar (Jan 11)

## REAL-TIME COMMENTARY

**1/11 (Friday):** Mar Sugar - Status - Bullish. Trend and ML both up so market remains in concurrent mode to upside. Action moderately negative on weak close, but two days down within an overall positive pattern is an acceptable dip and one which can justify buying. Have had several surges up and down in this market past few months and always possible have started a down one past two days; however, the overall pattern remains positive and so continues to fully justify longs here. Bottom line: Can be (and go) long here with stops still 7.50 (preferably on close basis).

...................

## AFTER-ACTION CRITIQUE

This was a good example of how the future really is unknown. Couple of days earlier all signs were green and it looked like full speed ahead to upside; however, now the price is back almost to entry point. Therefore, psychologically have gone from wondering how big profit would be, to a fear will end up taking a loss. Moreover, the moves of past few days have been moderate, whereas in volatile markets they are substantially faster and bigger. When traders talk about how trading can be an emotional roller coaster, this is what they mean (and previous two days here a mild example).

However, the picture here was still clearly positive since the market remained in solid concurrent mode to upside with price still well within bullish parameters. By "bullish parameters" I mean no important chart support levels had been violated; in fact, the price was only back to the top of first support level (top of recent congestion area or just above 7.70). In addition, both price and SL had been at recent upside extremes, so a minor dip/brief pause was not out of line, i.e., not particularly negative. However, no question the action had been disappointing for longs the prior two days, and this means now had minor downside warning.

Trading is like a voyage down an unexplored river; we can know where we have been and where we are but we cannot know what lies around the next bend. All we can do is understand the laws of the river, pay close attention to what is happening, and then work at being positioned with the primary energy flow of the river.

Interesting to note on chart how the line pattern gave some clear upside warning signs back in early October when the market made its lows. The ML turned up a day or two after the contract low day, so the market switched to a crosscurrent mode very soon after contract lows and stayed there until the trend turned up. In addition, notice how had a very clear bullish divergence (between price and SL) at the same time. Both price and SL made first lows around September 21, then two weeks later on second lows price made a sharply lower low (at 6.10) but the SL did not since it turned up from much higher low (-35 around October 10, compared to -64 two weeks earlier around September 21). Once you know what to look for and how to read the signs, you should find that markets almost always give some warning signs before good moves. Sometimes these signs come before market moves, sometimes a little after a move starts; however, there are invariably some indications.

Past two days somewhat unpleasant, but nothing to do here except just stay long with stops still just under 7.50 level.

01/11/2002

SUGAR #11 (CSCE)
MAR

CONTRACT SIZE:  112,000 lbs.
MINIMUM TICK : 0.01

SYMBOL SB02H
Trading Hours: 8:30-12:20 CST

GRID:0.020
49-D:7.4

SL:26
DL:6

<- WEEKLY RANKINGS ->

SMR (SECURITY MARKET RESEARCH) PO BOX 7476 BOULDER, CO 80306-7476 PHONE 303 635-2476 (01.18)

# March 2002 Sugar (Jan 14)

## REAL-TIME COMMENTARY

**1/14 (Monday):** Mar Sugar - Status - Bullish (to Neutral). Trend and ML are both still up so market remains in concurrent mode to upside. Action on negative side though as now have had three days of steady down with very little in way of intra-day upside energy. This market has had a series of steady up moves, followed by steady down-type moves; therefore, it is always possible are now on a steady down. Line pattern remains clearly positive enough to fully justify being (and going) long here and so far price dip not big enough to change this. However, would not want to see another down day since if did then SL would pick up a little too much speed to downside. So, "should" turn back up soon (i.e., tomorrow), but if does not, then picture would become very "iffy." Bottom line: Can be (and go) long here with stops now 7.60 on close basis and/or just under 7.50 on regular basis (entered after first half hour).

. . . . . . . . . . . . . . . . . . . .

## AFTER-ACTION CRITIQUE

Price closed just below entry point on trade and so were now sitting with a small loss. Therefore, had a little conflict here since the line pattern was still clearly positive, yet the price action had been very poor for such a good pattern. When I look at daily price action, I am looking both at pure intra-day up/down action (positive and negative) as well as price action in relation to line pattern. When the line pattern is clearly positive but the price moves persistently opposite (i.e., down), this tends to be a negative sign for the near term (next few days to week). Therefore, this day had all around negative price action since intra-day action was negative and overall action was negative in relation to its existing positive line pattern.

However, no significant chart-price support levels had been violated yet, although were now close to doing so. In addition, the line pattern was still positive since it was still in concurrent mode to upside and Bullish Status. Therefore, I was willing to give longs another day here, and believe this was correct. However, notice that I tightened up stop a little by cutting time after opening before entering regular stop. Sometimes—and this was such a case—it is best not to enter stops until after the open. The reason for this is that when a market is on a counter-trend dip, the selling pressure tends to build up overnight so will frequently get an early surge to down-side; however, once this early dip is over, counter-trend selling can run out of steam. On other hand, if the price holds around these early lows for an hour or more (the later in day still on lows the more negative it is), then this tends to be a negative sign. In this case I was willing to go without a stop for the first half hour or so of the day, but recent action was now negative enough so that I was unwilling to go too long without having downside protection in place, i.e., the persistent negative action had increased the downside risk. Therefore, unless price turned up quickly, this position would either be stopped out or pattern would turn too neutral/negative to legitimately justify sticking with longs.

Sometimes market moves start out looking great and for a while are going exactly according to "plan," only to suddenly reverse. There was no warning here the up move would not continue when prices were on highs several days earlier. However, when price had no follow through to upside even with picture solidly positive, this was a clear warning sign the up move was not so solid. Problem is it is difficult to act on a minor warning sign like that. Correct action here now was to be prepared to enter stops shortly after open since now have some meaningful downside risk.

01/14/2002

# March 2002 Sugar (Jan 15)

**REAL-TIME COMMENTARY**

**1/15 (Tuesday):** Mar Sugar - Status - Bullish (to Neutral). Trend and ML still up and so continue to be in concurrent mode to upside. Action moderately positive as only slightly lower early and closed on highs of day. Both price and SL have dipped moderately past few days and so "should" be ready to move up again (assuming upside still good here). Therefore, would view any failure to be up tomorrow as a clear negative. Bottom line: Can be long with stops either 7.60 on close basis or regular basis entered anytime after first half hour or so.

...................

**AFTER-ACTION CRITIQUE**

Good up day here, but was not out of the woods yet. The three-day dip was a little too big and went on a little too long for comfort. Have usually found that markets in solid trending moves usually do not give much in way of good entry prices, meaning they do not move counter trend for far or long. The rule seems to be the more solid the move, the less chance the market will give you to get in at attractive prices.

Therefore, when a market with solidly positive underlying technicals (i.e., in solid concurrent mode) like this one suddenly moves a surprising distance counter trend, this is frequently a warning sign that current trend move may be in trouble. In daily letter I said "…would view any failure to be up as a clear negative." I probably should have emphasized this more in letter by putting this trade on "probation."

By "probation" I mean give the trade an "up or out" ultimatum for the next trading day. Act on the basis that you will only hold the trade if it performs well; in other words, if it gives you any trouble (is lower for almost any amount of time), get rid of it. "Probation" on a trade can be strict or minor, but the basic idea is the same.

Situation in March Sugar here indicated it was a good time to put any longs on probation. Action had been somewhat negative. The trend was still solidly up but the ML was now beginning to move within the margin-of-error to turn down. Since the SL had been above zero for ten days and was now just below zero, this meant the ML was starting to have the potential to turn down within five days. In addition were now in position for a bearish divergence between price and SL (since the price is much closer to its recent high than SL). Therefore, definitely have some negative warning signs now, so either have to put any longs here on tight leash, i.e., probation, and/or move stop up fairly tight. Placing stop at 7.60 possibly a little too low since even a move under 7.70 next day here would probably have been too negative to stay long.

Therefore in a case like this, if had multiple positions, would now be ready to take small profits on some fairly quickly (unless price forced me to stay in, meaning up quickly and decently). This trade was not working out anywhere near as nicely as it started out; however, in this game we have to take what market gives us; we cannot ever try to force a trade against price action. All we can do is follow the price energy flow wherever it happens to take us. We have to be apolitical. If the "bull" party is winning, then we join the bulls; however, if situation changes and the "bear" party starts to win consistently, then we need to switch parties. Long side still justified here, but now needs to prove it or else.

(**NOTE:** *To see how market worked out over next month, turn page.*)

# March 2002 Sugar (Feb 15)

**2/15.** As you can see this market underwent a dramatic shift from bullish to bearish in the few days after 1/15. In the letter of 1/16 I wrote: "...should put any longs on moderate probation (meaning either it closes at least moderately—10 points or more—higher or would get out). Bottom line: Can be long with stops now just under 7.70." And as it turned out, any longs were stopped out the next day (on the big down day that closed just under 7.50).

That big down day changed the picture since it turned the SL down for a third lower high (always a sign upside energy losing momentum) as well as put the ML on verge of what looked like could be a sustained down cycle. However, at the time, the trend was still clearly up, which meant the trend was still too positive for shorts, while rest of the picture was too negative for longs. Then for the next three days the market chopped around some, but since all this choppy trading was below 7.50 (the close of the big down day), this was a negative sign. A good bull market usually will not keep giving good entry prices like this one was doing at that time. If look back at the dip during the middle of December, will note that price did not give repeated chances to buy at or near the lows of that dip. Counter-trend moves that are "false" (i.e., will be quickly reversed back with trend) tend to be "touch-and-go" type moves—meaning they may move toward the 50-day moving average, but once the counter-trend move is over they do not linger. Counter-trend moves that persist tend to continue to persist.

Next the price sold off and closed just under 7.00. This thirty-five-point down day turned the trend sideways to down, which in turn turned the Status from Neutral to Bearish and the mode from crosscurrent to concurrent to the downside (meaning it produced a sell signal).After this big down day I wrote the following: "Trend now down and so with ML also down market now in concurrent mode to downside. Action quite negative on solid down day with zero upside energy and close on lows of day. Price now at low of past ten weeks so virtually all longs now sitting with losses. ...Minor rally would set up good shorting opportunity... Bottom line: Can go short here and on any rally with stops in 7.40 to 7.50 area." The next three days had plenty of chances to short in the 7.10 area. Since an 80-point move covered a 100 percent of margin, regardless of whether measured from 7.00 or 7.10, the market subsequently produced slightly more than a 100 percent of margin profit on shorts before the line pattern turned back to Neutral and the mode back to crosscurrent (in the 6.25 area).

A long-term trader would have had some problems during the time period reflected by this chart. He would have had nice profits on shorts (initiated late July), but by the time trend turned back up in early November, most of those profits would have been given back. Then he would have had some profits on longs only once again to give them all back when trend turned right back down in late January. Then he would have good profits again, but unfortunately, as I write this, these also would have been taken back. Long-term trading keying off a 50-day moving average will invariably produce good profits; the difficult part of this type of trading is knowing when to take these profits, since when trend finally turns, it tends to do so fairly quickly and dramatically, thus much of hard-earned long-term profits tend to disappear. Therefore, there are trade-offs when decide to trade either long term or short term. Each has its benefits and drawbacks. It is up to each individual to choose his or her best "time style" for trading.

02/15/2002

SUGAR #11 (CSCE)
MAR

CONTRACT SIZE: 112,000 lbs.
MINIMUM TICK : 0.01

SYMBOL SB02H
Trading Hours: 8:30-12:20 CST

GRID:0.020    SL:3
49-D:7.2      DL:-31

<- WEEKLY RANKINGS ->    43    43    44    44    39

SMR (SECURITY MARKET RESEARCH) PO BOX 7476 BOULDER, CO 80306-7476 PHONE 303 635-2476 (01.18)

# March 2002 Yen (Dec 31/Jan 2)

(**NOTE:** *Here I have reprinted both 12/31/01 and 1/2/02 commentaries.*)

## REAL-TIME COMMENTARY

**12/31/01 (Tuesday):** Mar Yen - Status - Bearish. Trend solidly down and ML moderately down; therefore, market remains in good concurrent mode to downside. Had minor day-and-a-half rally before downside pressure came back in. Market somewhat oversold but down move has been so persistent recently that this (being so persistently oversold but unable to rally) usually indicates will get substantially oversold before see meaningful bounce. Remains weakest of group and so best bet for any shorts. When a market has gone down as steadily and as much as this one has past month or so, can be almost certain first rally (and several after that one) will fail quickly. Takes a long time for a market that's been this weak to be able to do much on upside. So odds continue to favor even lower prices ahead here. In past, when get persistent weakness in a major currency, would normally expect to start seeing some government intervention; however, in this case appears Japanese government wants Yen lower so this should not be major risk here for time being. Bottom line: Can be short with stops essentially out of range (could use 77.00 for short-term trading stop if prefer).

## REAL-TIME COMMENTARY

**1/2/02 (Thursday):** Mar Yen - Status - Bearish (to Neutral). Trend solidly down but ML is now only very marginally down; therefore, market still in concurrent mode to downside but getting quite shaky. Action today negative but not overly so as was set up for good down move but did not really go down much. Current sell signal came in around high 77.00 area and so at current prices has produced 100 percent of margin profit. Have had several signals in a row each of which have produced a 100 to 150 percent of margin profit followed by minor sideways pauses. Way overdue for some kind of upside action here as market has been pushing slowly but steadily lower for over three months with only two moderate rallies. On line basis, market now in better position to maintain a decent rally than at any time since down move started over three months ago. Tough call here as showing some reluctance to keep pushing much lower, lines only marginally negative and market at profit objectives. Therefore, can continue to justify shorts but would not argue with taking profits and especially if price unchanged or higher tomorrow a.m. (as would be sign selling pressure running out of gas). Bottom line: Can be short but would cover if higher tomorrow a.m. (and or can use tight stop of 76.30).

.....................

## AFTER-ACTION CRITIQUE

This chart is good example of reliability of trend, and especially in a major currency. Once firmly established, trends in currencies have a strong tendency to continue. As mentioned earlier, currencies are among the most reliably trending of markets. This market has been in concurrent mode to down side for a month and a half, and price has pushed steadily lower. Couple of weeks ago ML went sideways, so mode then was slightly indecisive; however, overall it has been concurrent. Now the ML was in position to turn up easily and stay in up cycle for a while, so the concurrent mode was weakening. Therefore, I was still bearish here but was ready to get out on any signs of strength.

01/02/2002

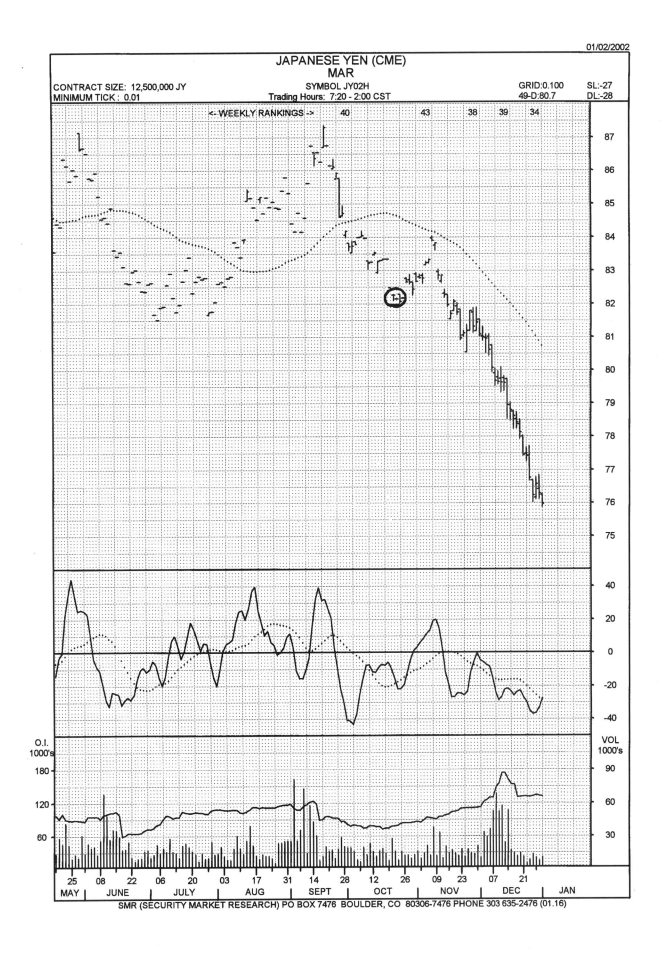

JAPANESE YEN (CME)
MAR

CONTRACT SIZE: 12,500,000 JY
MINIMUM TICK : 0.01

SYMBOL JY02H
Trading Hours: 7:20 - 2:00 CST

GRID:0.100
49-D:80.7

SL:-27
DL:-28

<- WEEKLY RANKINGS ->    40        43        38    39    34

SMR (SECURITY MARKET RESEARCH) PO BOX 7476  BOULDER, CO  80306-7476  PHONE 303 635-2476 (01.16)

# March 2002 Yen (Jan 3)

## REAL-TIME COMMENTARY

**1/3 (Thursday):** Mar Yen - Status - Bearish/Neutral. Trend solidly down, but ML now flat so market in between concurrent and crosscurrent. Pattern also now in between bearish and neutral and so can indicate either short or sidelines. Getting a little support in this area, but on bigger picture this just looks like a temporary pause in ongoing down move. Line picture now such that it would be much easier to turn mode to solidly crosscurrent and status from fairly solidly bearish to neutral, so technical picture not as negative as has been. However, it is highly unlikely have seen even an intermediate-term low here because when a market has been pushing to downside so persistently for so long it takes quite a bit of price stability and some time to pass before market makes any kind of bottom. Therefore, on short-term basis the picture here is close to fifty-fifty, but longer term odds still clearly favor downside. Bottom line: Lines in between short and sidelines and so for now prefer sidelines; however, would be prepared to go short again should price rally moderately next couple days.

......................

## AFTER-ACTION CRITIQUE

Status was in between Bearish and Neutral here because had either -1 1/2 or -2 points (due to a sideways ML). In situations like this, when Status is in between, it is simply a trading decision since lines can support either short or sidelines. In this case you should be able to see why I decided to go to the sidelines. Other than the solid downtrend, the short-term picture had turned more neutral than negative. ML was sideways and based on where SL had been previous three weeks (-22 to -38) were much more likely to see an up cycle in ML than down for the next few weeks. Remember, ML is about a three-week moving average of the SL, and since we would be dropping off very low numbers from the SL for the next three weeks, this meant the ML was more likely to move up than down.

If you look back over this chart you will see that the ML did a reasonably good job of identifying the intermediate-term price cycles. It did not change directions too often. Sometimes it was a little early on directional turns, and other times a little late; however, it kept consistently within its margin-of-error of up to five days.

Notice also how the price tended to make sustained (several weeks or more) with-trend moves when the market was in concurrent mode as well as how it tended to move in a more choppy, sideways manner when it was in crosscurrent mode. Remember, the trend is like the current of the river of price energy and the ML (intermediate-term momentum line) is like the tide cycling in and out (with and against the trend). It is only natural that the river of price energy would tend to flow more downstream (with trend) when current and tide are in concurrence rather than at crosscurrents. Since the objective is to be positioned with price flow, we should always focus on being positioned when both long-term and intermediate-term price energy flows are in concurrence.

Situation here was simply a trading decision since could have justified sticking with shorts and could make equal case to go to sidelines. Since 100 percent of margin profit had been reached and pattern was turning indecisive, I believed sidelines was the better choice.

01/03/2002

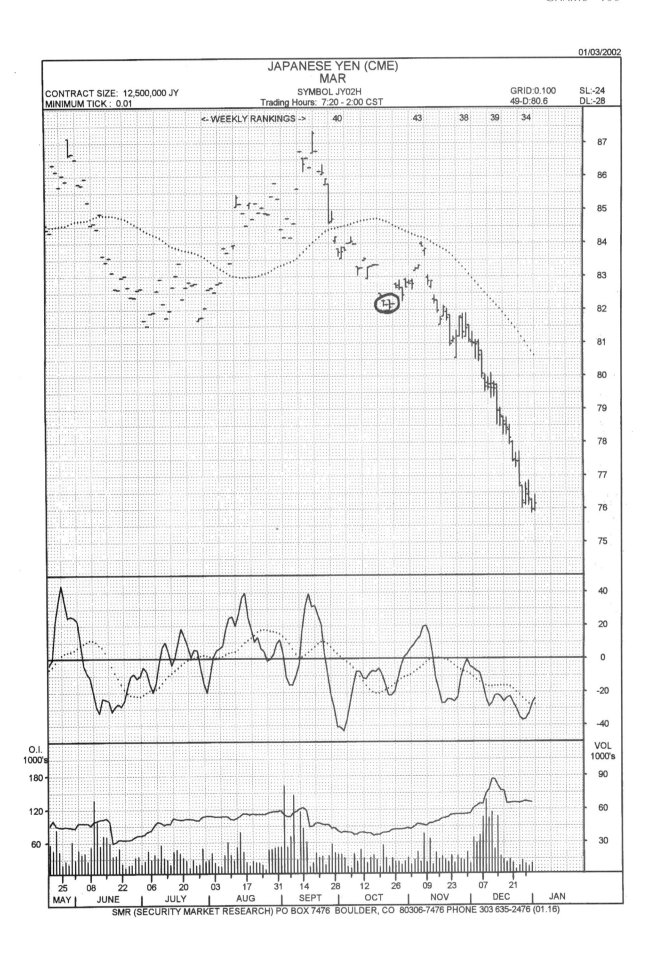

JAPANESE YEN (CME)
MAR

CONTRACT SIZE: 12,500,000 JY
MINIMUM TICK : 0.01

SYMBOL JY02H
Trading Hours: 7:20 - 2:00 CST

GRID:0.100
49-D:80.6

SL:-24
DL:-28

# March 2002 Yen (Jan 4)

## REAL-TIME COMMENTARY

**1/4 (Friday):** Mar Yen - Status - Neutral. Trend solidly down but ML now turning into what could easily be a sustained up cycle so market now in crosscurrent mode. This usually means sideways, more choppy-type action now more likely rather than continuation of recent sustained down move. Action fairly positive today as gapped higher and held these gains all day with little in way of downside pressure. So, seeing signs have reached some minor support level. However, it would be extremely unusual if have made any kind of bottom here since when have such an extended down move almost always takes quite a bit of time and positive action first (before bottoms). Almost always have to put in at least one bullish divergence before make even inter-mediate-term bottom. Therefore, question here is when to start going short again. Any price above 76.80 on Monday would be third day up as well as highs of past six days within a very strong downtrend and can always make case to be/go short when this the case. Only problem in selling in this area is short-term momentum pushing up and no way to know when this will run out of steam and no clear chart stop point. COT (Commitment of Traders situation) not a factor here. Bottom line: Lines say sidelines; however, can make case to go short again any price 76.80 or higher Monday.

..................

## AFTER-ACTION CRITIQUE

The basic idea of the "Status" is to provide a daily mathematical position indicator. It tells you, in terms of prevailing trend and momentum, the current status of the market. However, the Status is just a starting point for looking at the chart because it only tells us the present situation; what we want is to be positioned with the most likely (immediate) future trend/momentum. Therefore, we always have to be looking a little ahead to see how easy or difficult, likely or unlikely, it will be for the Status to change.

At this moment the only way Status would turn back to Bearish (from current Neutral) was if SL turned back down. (Have minus one and one half points at moment and only way to get to minus two points is for SL to turn back down.) However, since trend is so strong to downside it is almost certain that this rally will not last long; therefore, a trader would be perfectly justified in trying to anticipate when and where price would turn down again. The question is how to go about doing this.

Remember my definition of a "rally" in a downtrending market: a two or more day move against the trend and/or a price on the highs of past three days. Naturally, this is just a general rule; however, when dealing with an unpredictable future, by necessity we can only develop and use general rules. Another way to measure where and when an against-trend rally might be about to run out of steam is by the location of the SL. As a general rule, once the SL has come back up to minus ten or higher, after having been on recent lows, we can conclude that the market is no longer overextended to downside, i.e., it has "rallied" off its recent lows. Therefore, going by both the "rally" measuring devices (i.e., the price and the SL), I could make a decent case to try to anticipate top of rally by initiating shorts anywhere in 76.80 area on the next day of trading here.

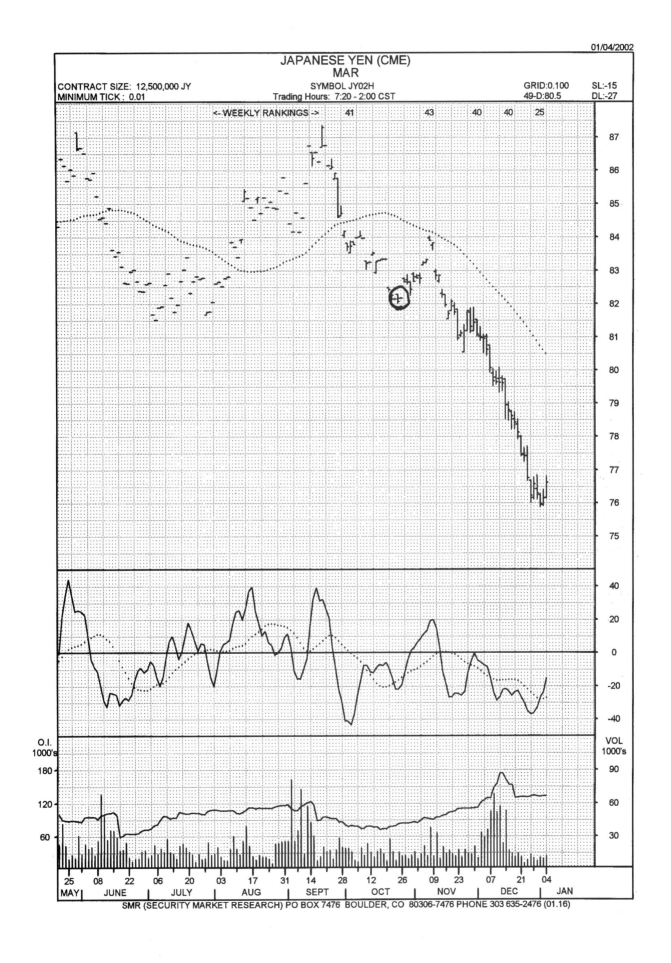

01/04/2002

JAPANESE YEN (CME)
MAR

CONTRACT SIZE: 12,500,000 JY
MINIMUM TICK : 0.01

SYMBOL JY02H
Trading Hours: 7:20 - 2:00 CST

GRID:0.100
49-D:80.5

SL:-15
DL:-27

<- WEEKLY RANKINGS ->   41      43      40      40      25

# March 2002 Yen (Jan 7)

**REAL-TIME COMMENTARY**

**1/7 (Monday):** Mar Yen - Status - Neutral (to Bearish). Trend solidly down but ML now on minor up cycle so in minor crosscurrent mode. Action slightly negative due to minor down day, but more so because minor early rally ran out of steam quickly. SL now getting close to zero, so market no longer oversold. Now have had six days of sideways here and this has clear look of a bear flag which should eventually break to new lows. Would be extremely unusual if this type of pattern marked any kind of meaningful (or even intermediate-term) bottom and so odds still clearly favor lower prices. Main question here is when and where to start going short again. Anytime trend this strong to downside and momentum line pattern neutral, can make decent case to initiate new shorts any time price around highs of past few days, and that is case now. Bottom line: Lines say sidelines but can continue to make decent case for "anticipation" shorts in area of past week's highs (76.70 or higher); however, cannot use stops for now as just no clear stop point on charts.

..................

**AFTER-ACTION CRITIQUE**

The currency markets trade essentially around the clock. As soon as the futures market closes, then the "after market," or Globex, trading starts. Generally I prefer to stick to trading during the regular futures market hours; however, I will use (and recommend using) the after market (i.e., Globex) both to get in and out of trades. Therefore, in a case like this one, if you had decided to try to short the Yen at 76.80, then it would make sense to put in limit orders in the "after market" to do so. Then, if unable overnight, merely reenter order in the regular market. As I recall (am writing this a month after the fact), in this case it was possible to short at 76.80 in both the overnight market and in regular market.

Shorting the Yen here is what I call an "anticipation" trade. It is done in "anticipation" of the SL, or short-term, momentum turning back with the trend. The stronger the trend the quicker you should be to try anticipation trades. Counter-trend moves, especially when the trend strong as it is here, tend to end quickly and with little warning. As I mentioned earlier, in almost all cases when a market has been in such a strong and long-lasting downtrend, it will usually produce at least one (and usually more) price/SL divergences before making any kind of lasting bottom. Since this market has not done that yet, shorting this minor rally should have been a fairly safe "anticipation" trade.

The future is unknown, so there was no way of knowing whether shorting here at 76.80 was a good idea. It is easy in a case like this one to try to get a better (higher) price to go short, after all, 76.80 was not even a hundred points off the contract lows. However, my feeling in a case like this one is this: Trading is a competition. While there was no way of knowing if 76.80 was going to be the best price to sell over the next few days, it was absolute that 76.80 was close to the best price of the past six days. Therefore, in this tough competition, if you shorted at 76.80, you would be selling at a higher price than every single seller of the past six days! We trade futures, not "pasts"; therefore, while selling at the best price of the past six days is no certainty of success in the future, it is a very good place to start.

01/07/2002

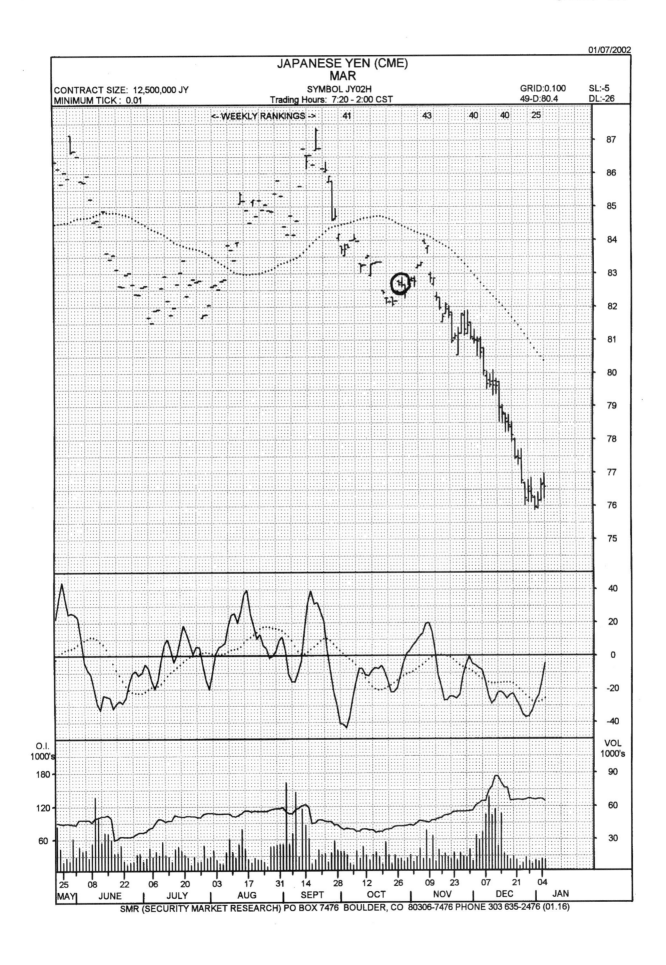

# JAPANESE YEN (CME)
## MAR

CONTRACT SIZE: 12,500,000 JY      SYMBOL JY02H      GRID:0.100    SL:-5
MINIMUM TICK : 0.01      Trading Hours: 7:20 - 2:00 CST      49-D:80.4    DL:-26

<- WEEKLY RANKINGS ->    41    43    40    40    25

SMR (SECURITY MARKET RESEARCH) PO BOX 7476 BOULDER, CO 80306-7476 PHONE 303 635-2476 (01.16)

# March 2002 Yen (Jan 8)

## REAL-TIME COMMENTARY

**1/8 (Tuesday):** Mar Yen - Status - Neutral (to Bearish). Trend solidly down but ML now on fairly solid up cycle so market remains in crosscurrent mode. Action quite negative on big down day, but all downside made overnight and zero follow through in day session, so this mitigated some of negative action. Had a week of the 76.00 area holding as a support level and broke through this decisively today; therefore, if price should move back above 76.00 now (and especially on close basis), would have minor false downside breakout and this would signal temporary bottom. Have mentioned that would be highly unusual to make any kind of lows without at least a single bullish divergence and have not had that yet; however, now set up for just such a divergence and will get one if have any upside from here next few days. Lines will go "officially" negative again tomorrow, but now lines running a little behind so would not short here regardless of lines. If shorted "in anticipation" yesterday (as suggested and as could have done fairly easily), would prefer taking profits unless keeps pushing down, as would see any close around this level tomorrow as being too positive to stick with shorts (since would set up good bullish divergence and with market now in solid crosscurrent mode have to expect more sideways, choppy action rather than trending). Bottom line: Lines say sidelines, but will go to negative after tomorrow; however, would not short here, and if short from higher, would either cover now or would cover on any failure to keep pushing lower tomorrow.

....................

## AFTER-ACTION CRITIQUE

Since SL was essentially sideways here it would have probably been more accurate to say Status was in between Bearish and Neutral, rather than just Neutral as I said at time. As a general rule, can use the strength/weakness of trend as the plus or minus factor when Status is "in between." In this case, with the trend so solidly down, should have maintained a prevailing bias to downside, both when looking at chart and when acting.

One question that might come up here is why bother covering shorts a few days previously when trend was so solid to downside and there were no meaningful upside warning signs. This is simply a question of individual trading style. A long-term trader would have gone short sometime in early to mid-October when the trend turned down (somewhere in 82.00 to 83.00 area), and would still be holding these shorts. With the trend so solidly down and having been clearly down since October, there would be absolutely no reason for a long-term trader to be even thinking about covering in this area (or at any time over the past several months). Furthermore, a long-term trader would be holding shorts here with no stops (virtually impossible to turn trend up any time soon since to do so price would have to go above where it was ten weeks ago, and can see by circle that is very long way above where it is now). Therefore, a long-term trader would have to be prepared to absorb a major loss of equity (and profit on trade) if the unusual happened and price turned up from here (i.e., if this was a bottom). A short-term trader is not willing (both by choice and nature) to run that risk. Therefore, the short-term trader prefers to act on reasonably reliable indications that price will move counter trend for a "while." Since there is no way to know how long this "while" will be, a short-term trader has to get out and get back in fairly frequently.

01/08/2002

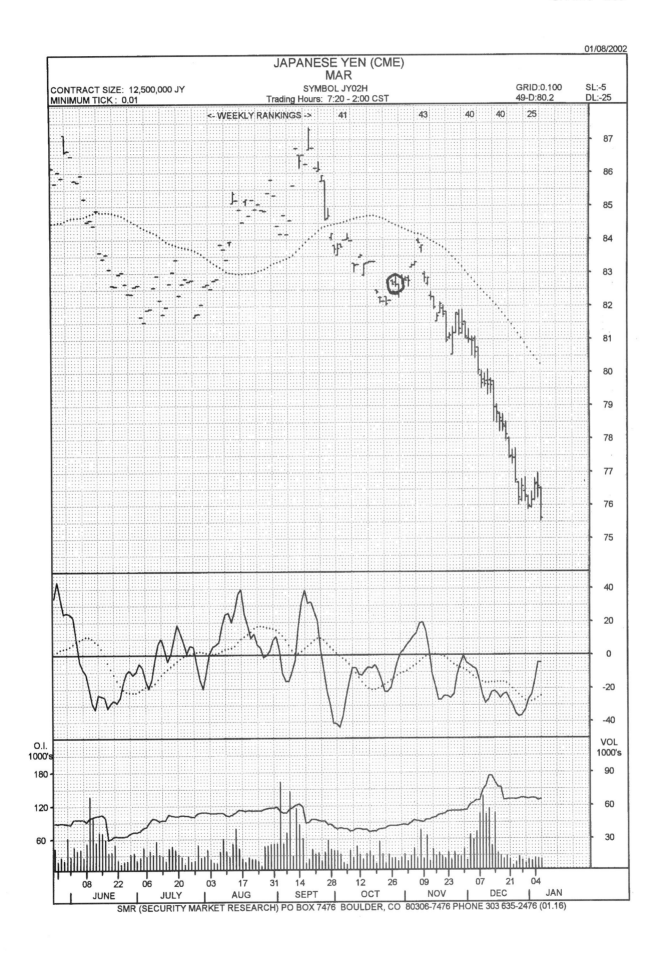

JAPANESE YEN (CME)
MAR

CONTRACT SIZE: 12,500,000 JY
MINIMUM TICK : 0.01

SYMBOL JY02H
Trading Hours: 7:20 - 2:00 CST

GRID:0.100
49-D:80.2

SL:-5
DL:-25

<- WEEKLY RANKINGS ->   41   43   40   40   25

SMR (SECURITY MARKET RESEARCH) PO BOX 7476  BOULDER, CO  80306-7476 PHONE 303 635-2476 (01.16)

# March 2002 Yen (Jan 9)

### REAL-TIME COMMENTARY

**1/9 (Wednesday):** Mar Yen - Status - Bearish (to Neutral).Trend down but ML up so market in crosscurrent mode and this usually indicates more choppy, sideways-type action. Action neutral on unchanged day. SL turned down so this gives line sell signal, but it is a crosscurrent sell and these only tend to last two to five days and have already had two days down. Now set up for potential bullish divergence and this first potential positive on technical basis in long time. Therefore, can fully justify shorts here, but since market now in crosscurrent mode, prefer not to short here on lows, and if short from high 76.00 area, prefer to cover. Bottom line: Lines say can go short, but prefer not to short here, and if short from higher, prefer to take profits; however, based on lines, can justify shorts, and stops on any shorts here can be just above 76.00.

.....................

### AFTER-ACTION CRITIQUE

This is a good example of how "anticipating" can get you in at a much better price than waiting for the line pattern (i.e., the Status) to "officially" turn from Neutral to Bearish. The problem or risk in anticipating is you will sometimes get in too soon. Sometimes the anticipated quick turn back down in short-term momentum does not occur and the price just keeps rallying. In those cases, waiting for the line pattern to turn would work better, which means it is a trade off. However, I believe that in the long run a short-term trader has to anticipate at least a certain amount in order to succeed.

Looking back over this chart it can seem obvious that a trader had to be short, and the sooner short the better. It can look like once short there was never any real pressure to cover since even the rally of few days earlier here was minor (less than 100 points off contract lows). However, while the entirety of the past several months of relentless down action here can be seen at a glance, actually living through it took many months. Every day of this time period the Yen was moving up and down intra-day. Every minute of this time span a trader who was short would have felt constantly on edge. The future is unknown, and anyone with any experience in trading knows all too well that no matter how solid a directional move may appear at the moment, the situation can change rapidly and dramatically.

Frequently a novice trader will do quite well because he or she has not been burned by any big sudden, surprise moves against them. Therefore, the beginner trader will just sit with a clear, ongoing move without much fear of it suddenly reversing; while on the other hand, the experienced trader will always be at least a little on edge. Therefore, if you have not traded much, do not get the idea that riding a clear down move like this one here is in any way "easy." It is not, no matter how obvious it may appear that this market has simply been following the second natural law of price movement: Continuation is more likely than change.

Since price had moved down so much here and had given so many good sell signals in a row, I was getting increasingly nervous about how much more could go down before had a meaningful pause or rally, and therefore was happy to take quick, solid profit.

01/09/2002

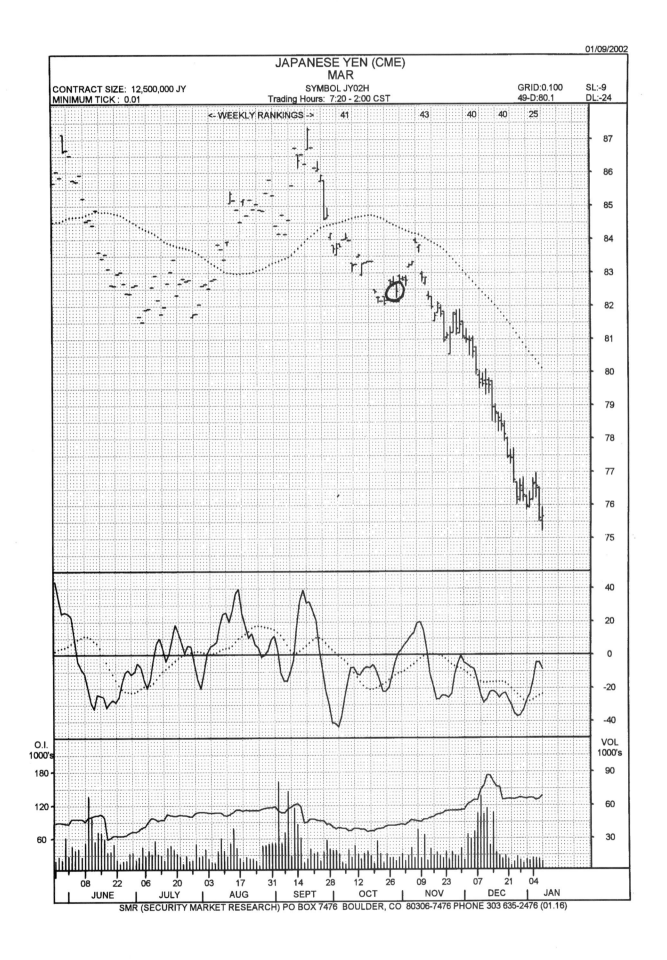

# March 2002 Yen (Jan 10)

## REAL-TIME COMMENTARY

**1/10 (Thursday)**: Mar Yen - Status - Bearish (to Neutral). Trend down but ML up so market in fairly solid crosscurrent mode. Action neutral on second unchanged day in row, but when go sideways during crosscurrent sell signal, this sideways is a little positive. Crosscurrent signals (sell here) usually only last two to five days and this one now three days old, so beginning to push it on time basis here. Therefore, based on lines, can be/go short here, but since in crosscurrent mode and action mixed, prefer to stick to sidelines for time being. Bottom line: Lines say can be/go short with stops just above 76.00 on close basis, but prefer sidelines.

.....................

## AFTER-ACTION CRITIQUE

The suggested stop point of 76.00 (in previous day's letter) for a trader deciding to stay short would not have worked well since price rallied up to 76.20 and then turned back down. A better stop would have been at 76.50 since a move back up there would have completely made back the big down move of couple of days earlier and this would probably have shown a little too much short-term strength to stick with shorts. Believe the reason I chose such a tight stop was because ML was in good up cycle and was also set up well for a more reliable-type bullish divergence. Price had made a slightly lower low than previous low a week earlier, but the SL was in the -10 area and this was a long way from the week or so earlier low of -38. Therefore, if both price and SL turned up from here, this would have produced a good bullish divergence. Remember, when price and SL diverge, the rule is to believe the SL.

Since the trend was so solid to downside, I was probably unnecessarily quick in covering shorts. However, at the time the margin on Yen was in low $2000 area, so a 100 percent of margin profit would have been about 160 points. Therefore, a 120-point profit (sell at 76.80 and cover at 75.60) would have been about a 75 percent of margin profit.

Again, looking at the chart here is completely different from actually having a position on in real time. The risk here is merely intellectual; in real time the risk is real. This was a market that had been going steadily down for a long time and now for the previous two weeks had been going more sideways. Therefore, it was only natural that I, and other traders, were getting nervous about further down moves. However, the "official" line-pattern sell signal came at 75.60 (close two days ago when SL turned down again), and when trend this negative, unlikely any sell signal would produce much, if anything, in way of loss.

So odds still clearly favored downside here, but since market was now in crosscurrent mode, my preference then (and agree now) was that when/if can take a quick 75 percent profit on a crosscurrent signal, there is nothing wrong with taking it. Whether or not to be short here was basically just a trading decision as could have made decent case either way. Trading is decision making, all the time; even not acting is a decision. Sometimes decisions work out well, other times they do not. My feeling is when the question is close as to whether to take good profit or to stay in, I believe as a general rule should take profits. Remember, this is a business, and in business the only way to make money is to take profits.

So, could have been short here or on sidelines; either decision was fully justifiable.

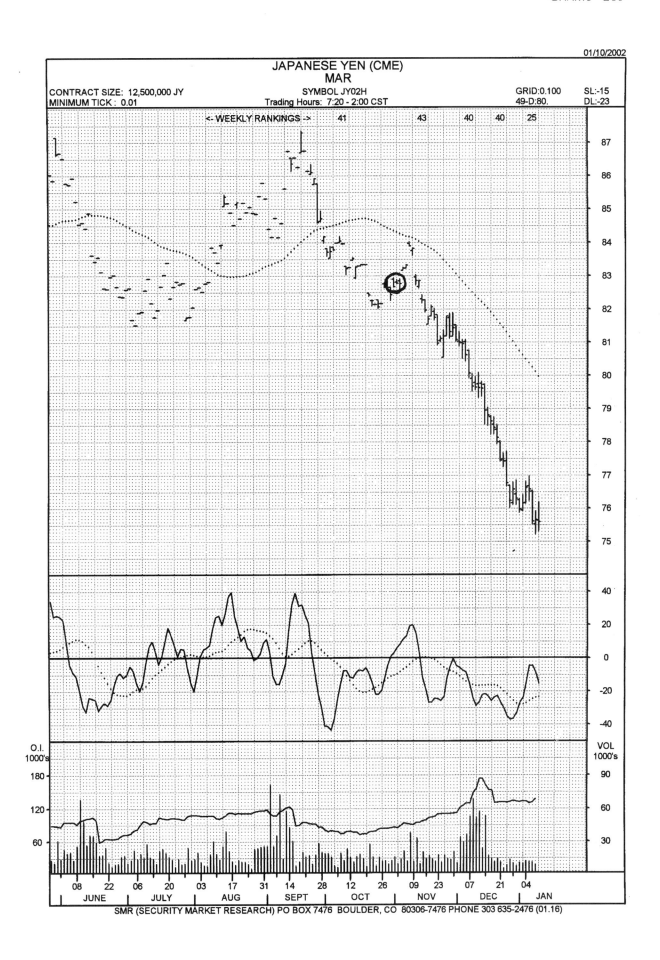

01/10/2002

JAPANESE YEN (CME)
MAR

CONTRACT SIZE: 12,500,000 JY
MINIMUM TICK : 0.01

SYMBOL JY02H
Trading Hours: 7:20 - 2:00 CST

GRID:0.100
49-D:80.

SL:-15
DL:-23

<- WEEKLY RANKINGS ->   41   43   40   40   25

SMR (SECURITY MARKET RESEARCH) PO BOX 7476 BOULDER, CO 80306-7476 PHONE 303 635-2476 (01.16)

# March 2002 Yen (Jan 11)

## REAL-TIME COMMENTARY

**1/11 (Friday):** Mar Yen - Status - Neutral (to Bearish). Trend down but ML up so market in cross-current mode and this usually indicates will see choppy, sideways action (and so far this is exactly what have been seeing). Action slightly positive on moderate up day. SL turned up from higher low and so with price having made lower low now have put in minor bullish divergence. However, divergences of this type (when against such a strong trend) usually only produce couple of days of upside, at most. Unlikely have seen any kind of significant bottom here yet, but prefer to stick with sidelines for while longer, although should see another decent shorting opportunity fairly soon. In other words, short side still the side to trade here and it should just be a question of when and where. Bottom line: Sidelines.

....................

## AFTER-ACTION CRITIQUE

Turn up in SL changed the Status back to Neutral. So the line-pattern sell signal at 75.60 couple of days earlier would have produced a 40-point loss (using today's close as exit point). However, anticipating turn down in short-term momentum and then taking quick profit would have produced 120-point gain. This good result is not a matter of "guessing." Rather, both getting in around 76.80 and out around 75.60 would have been simply following basic trading rules I have laid out in this book.

Mentioned in previous day's commentary that crosscurrent price moves only tend to last between two to five days. Naturally this is a generalization, but I have found it to work fairly well. I never see anything wrong with trading a market when it is in crosscurrent mode; however, I believe it is best to apply against-trend trading rules to crosscurrent trades as well. This means when you do crosscurrent trades you should keep positions smaller than otherwise (i.e., than when do concurrent trades) and should be quicker to take profits. In addition, believe it is a good idea to let the strength or weakness of the trend direct how aggressively you do any crosscurrent trades. The more solid the trend, the more aggressive you should be on being in when mode crosscurrent.

Now had a more reliable-type bullish divergence between price and SL here. Since the trend was so solid to downside, it was unlikely that a single bullish divergence would produce too much to the upside. However, combine this bullish divergence along with the good up cycle in ML, plus signs of support building on price chart in 75.50 to 76.50 area, and this was enough to send a short-term trader to the sidelines for time being.

A long-term trader would still simply be just sitting with his short positions here since trend was so solidly down. A long-term trader does not even want to think about getting out (i.e., taking profits) until a legitimate case can be made that a trend reversal could be imminent. And there were absolutely no signs that was the case here.

So at the moment a long-term trader would have been short with no plans of covering, but a short-term trader would have been on the sidelines with no plans of going short until had some signs short-term momentum was about ready to turn down again.

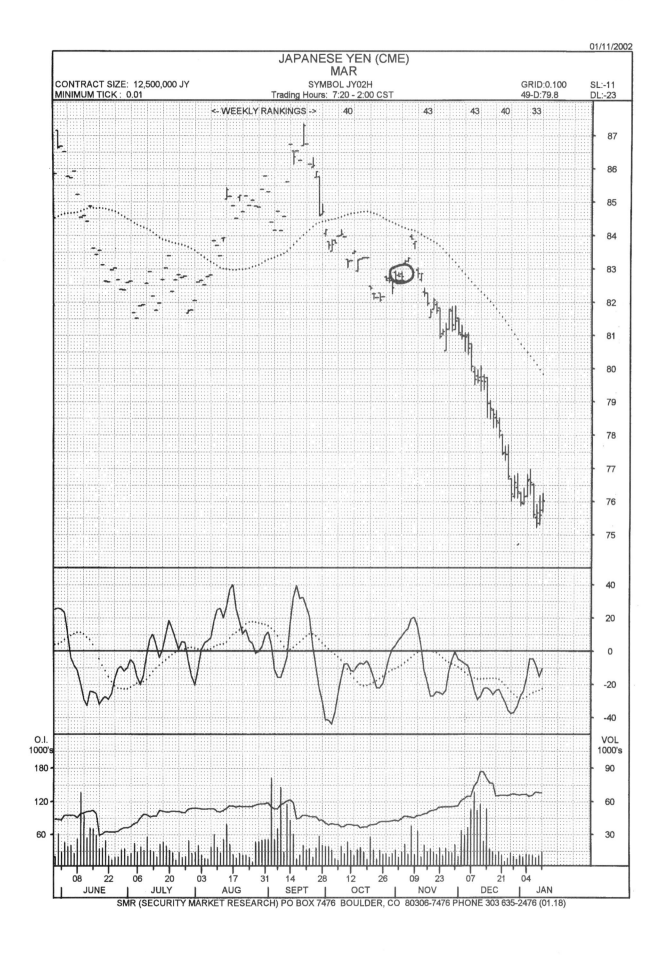

# March 2002 Yen (Jan 14)

**REAL-TIME COMMENTARY**

**1/14 (Monday):** Mar Yen - Status - Neutral (to Bearish). Trend solidly down but ML moderately up so market remains in crosscurrent mode. Action neutral on fairly quiet, unchanged day. Currently have a minor bullish divergence here, but against-trend divergences of this type rarely produce much in way of upside (either in terms of time or price) and this one has now had two days of minor up (and this frequently all get out of this type of divergence when trend as solid as is here). Any time trend as solidly down as it is here, time always favors the down side; therefore, can always make some case for going short when/if have any kind of rally or sideways for few days. So can make some case for "anticipation" shorts here, especially if trading around these levels again tomorrow. Bottom line: Lines say sidelines, but can begin to make case to go back to short side again "in anticipation" as long as trading below 76.35 tomorrow a.m. (no clear chart stop points at moment).

......................

**AFTER-ACTION CRITIQUE**

With price on four-day minor rally and around highs of past four days, could have made some case to go short in "anticipation" of SL (short-term momentum) turning back down soon. Again this was simply a trading decision. The lines said sidelines since Status was Neutral, but when trend this negative, can use almost any excuse to be/go short. Like week earlier, while no way to know if this will be best price to sell at over next few days, do know this is about best price of past few days and that is a good start.

I mentioned in daily letter that would only short if price was under 76.30. What I meant by this was that any price above that level would indicate upside short-term momentum would be a little too strong to anticipate quick turn down. When short-term trading there are many times when should not position when offered a "better" price than expected since this frequently is a sign counter-trend move has more to go and so it is too soon to get in.

Shorting here would be on the aggressive side; however, when trend is this solid to downside, being aggressive is fully justified. Over time, being overly aggressive when positioning with solid trends will pay off far more than it costs. Stubbornness is not a particularly good trait for a short-term trader; it is much better to be fairly flexible. However, being stubborn about positioning when trend is solid is always a good trading trait. In trading, if you are going to be stubborn about anything, make it being stubborn about being positioned with strong trends. Remember, let the trend decide whether you are bullish or bearish a market, and the more solid the trend the more bullish or bearish you should be. Therefore, in this case a trader should have been extremely bearish on the Yen, regardless of what he or she knew about the fundamental situation.

At any one time a person could spend weeks, even months, studying the fundamental supply/demand situation searching for the "correct" value of dollar versus Yen. It is much simpler, and more reliable, to just let the trend be your guide.

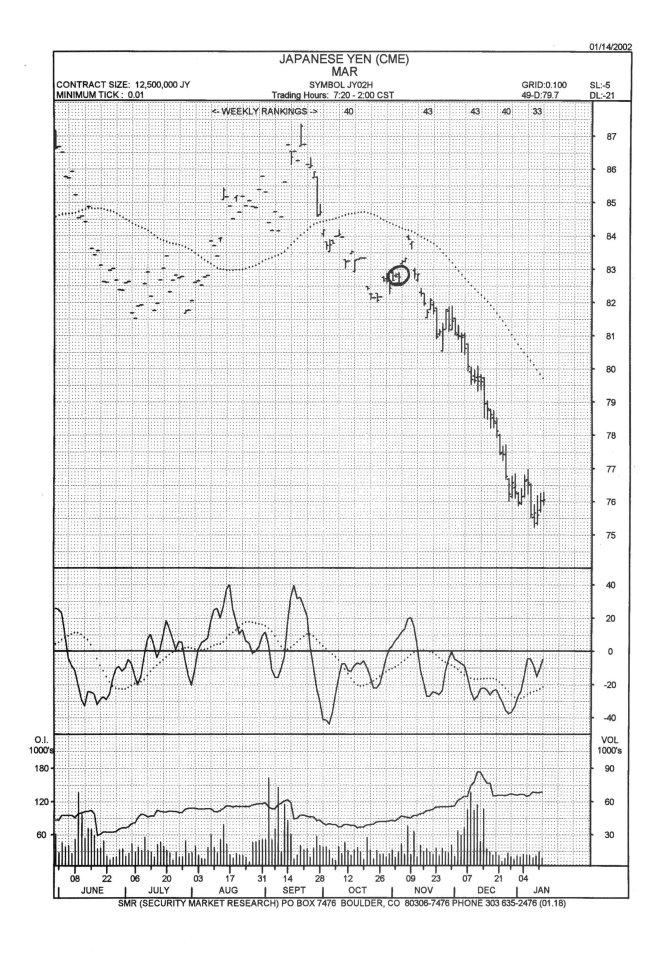

01/14/2002

JAPANESE YEN (CME)
MAR

CONTRACT SIZE: 12,500,000 JY
MINIMUM TICK : 0.01

SYMBOL JY02H
Trading Hours: 7:20 - 2:00 CST

GRID:0.100
49-D:79.7

SL:-5
DL:-21

<- WEEKLY RANKINGS ->      40          43          43      40      33

SMR (SECURITY MARKET RESEARCH) PO BOX 7476  BOULDER, CO  80306-7476  PHONE 303 635-2476 (01.18)

# March 2002 Yen (Jan 15)

## REAL-TIME COMMENTARY

**1/15 (Tuesday):** Mar Yen - Status - Neutral. Trend solidly down but ML moderately up so market remains in crosscurrent mode (which usually means will see more sideways, choppy-type action rather than trending). Action moderately positive on decent up day with gap higher, and more impressively, held this gap all day. Market has "feel" that selling pressure has at least temporarily dried up here, but trend still solidly down so could reappear in earnest at any time. Still on minor bullish divergence, but these rarely produce too much on upside in either time or distance and so pushing it a little here already (since on three-day rally). When trend this negative to downside, market can head lower at any time, but both action and technicals a little too positive at moment, so probably best to wait awhile longer before looking to go short again. Yesterday mentioned could justify initiating shorts if opened under 76.30, but opened higher and held slightly above that level all day. What I meant by this is felt any price above this level would have been a little too positive to short, but if opened at that level or lower, then would be sign upside energy weak and so could have shorted. Now have situation where probably best to see some negative action before shorting again. So, could justify shorts on close (or a move, if after first hour or two) below 76.10. Bottom line: Sidelines, but could justify going short on close below 76.10.

.....................

## AFTER-ACTION CRITIQUE

Now just have a situation here where could be almost certain price will head back down again, just a question of when and from where. If a trader had shorted around 76.00 in overnight market and could have made legitimate case to do so, now would just have to sit with losses without stops. The only problem with this approach here was the market could (future is unknown) rally substantially without materially changing overall negative situation since trend would still be solidly down. As rule would be very reluctant to use a stop on shorts here since when trend this solid to down side the one thing do not want to do is be buying (even if only covering shorts) at recent highs, and that is what would have been doing if put buy stops much above current price.

On price chart basis, this market was showing some positives here since had some support at 76.00, broke through that briefly, and then moved back above it; therefore, could have made an argument that move below 76.00 was a minor "false" breakout to downside. Also it was somewhat positive that price had made back all it lost on the big down day week earlier and this was also minor chart sign of some downside exhaustion. At moment had both some positive signs on chart as well as some positives on momentum-line patterns (ML in good up cycle, SL has made higher low/high and have bullish divergence between price and SL). Therefore, on short-term and intermediate-term basis, picture here was now indecisive.

However, on long-term basis, price energy flow remained solidly down and, as kept repeating in daily letter, when downtrend this solid, the downside pressure can reappear at any time and without any warning signs from momentum indicators.

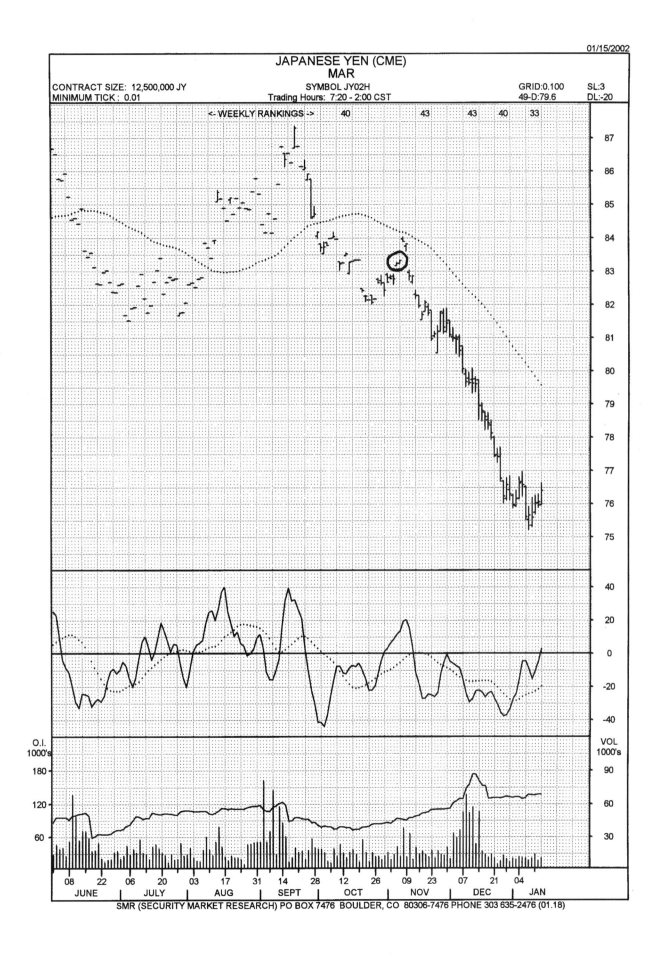

01/15/2002

JAPANESE YEN (CME)
MAR

CONTRACT SIZE: 12,500,000 JY
MINIMUM TICK : 0.01

SYMBOL JY02H
Trading Hours: 7:20 - 2:00 CST

GRID:0.100
49-D:79.6

SL:3
DL:-20

SMR (SECURITY MARKET RESEARCH) PO BOX 7476 BOULDER, CO 80306-7476 PHONE 303 635-2476 (01.18)

# March 2002 Yen (Feb 15)

**2/15.** I was a little early on starting to give up on short side here as market produced another good trade on short side in the week or so following 1/15. Whether a trader shorted on the next day's (1/16) close just above 76.00 or waited for the next day when picture clearly turned negative (SL turned solidly down from just above zero), he would have made anywhere from 75 to 100 percent of margin profit over the next week. Once the SL turned up slightly on 1/25 (in 74.65 area) then Status turned back to Neutral and waiting for that point would have reduced the profit more toward the 50 percent of margin level.

In is interesting to note how the concurrent and crosscurrent modes so accurately indicated what type of price action would see in this market during the time period reflected by this chart. While the price did continue to push some lower after the market switched from concurrent to crosscurrent just after the first of the year, the price action definitely became more two-sided. Normally, when a market has had as pronounced a trending move as this one had for the two months between early November and early January, then when it does go from concurrent to crosscurrent, the price will tend to keep pushing lower for a while. A "body" in such a solid trending move needs some time to first slow down its descent before it can actually stop.

The "easy" money in good trending trades invariably occurs during concurrent mode phases. While the odds will always favor a solid trend, when intermediate-term momentum is moving opposite this solid trend it is only natural to expect to see more choppiness. Remember, the trend is like the current of a river (the river of price energy) and the ML (the intermediate-term momentum indicator) is like the tide. When current and tide are pushing solidly in the same direction, the surface flow of water (price) will tend to be smooth in that direction; however, when current and tide are moving at cross purposes, it is only natural to see choppy water (price action).

A long-term trader would have been whipsawed some back in the August/September period on this chart (going from short to long and then back to short again) and would have been fortunate to break even during that time period. However, once the trend turned down in mid to late October (assuming he rode through the brief rally up to 84.00), it would have been very smooth sailing until the price reached the 76.00 area, and even then there was never much in the way of upside movement. However, keep in mind that looking at this solid trending move after it is over makes getting and staying short look easy, i.e., obvious. Believe me, it is not. Every day of this down move being short felt very precarious since it "seemed" that the market "had to" rally soon as it just "could not" keep going lower forever. "Feelings" are an extremely unreliable indicator as to what price will do next; the lines (i.e., reality) and natural laws are far superior.

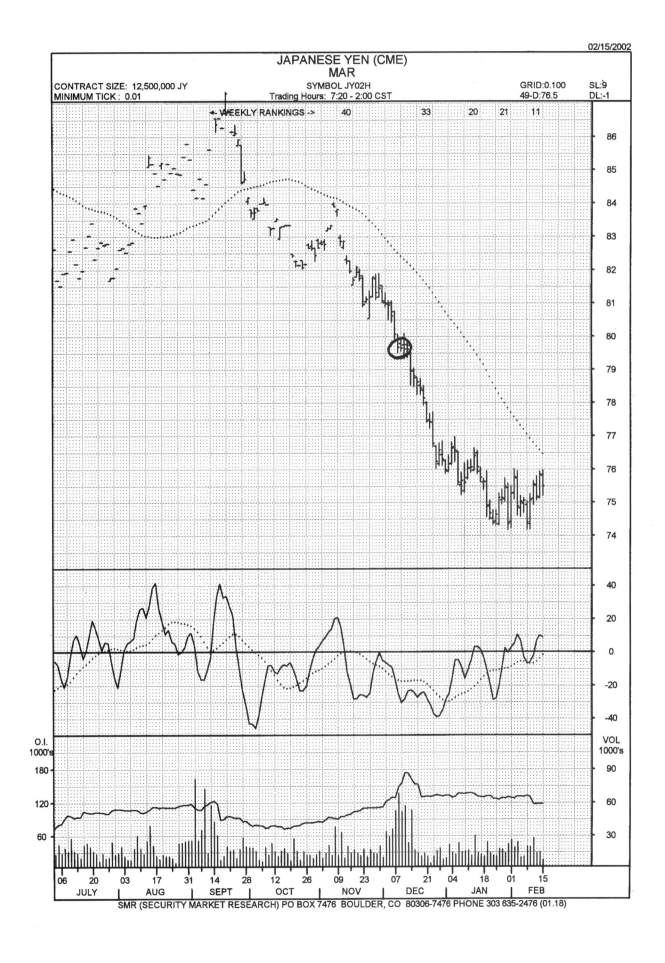

02/15/2002

JAPANESE YEN (CME)
MAR

CONTRACT SIZE:  12,500,000 JY
MINIMUM TICK :  0.01

SYMBOL JY02H
Trading Hours:  7:20 - 2:00 CST

GRID:0.100
49-D:76.5

SL:9
DL:-1

SMR (SECURITY MARKET RESEARCH) PO BOX 7476  BOULDER, CO  80306-7476 PHONE 303 635-2476 (01.18)

# March 2002 Swiss Franc (Dec 31/Jan 2)

## REAL-TIME COMMENTARY

**12/31/01 (Monday):** Mar Swiss - Status - Bearish (to Neutral). Trend now somewhat indecisive but still slightly negative. With ML still solidly down, market remains in concurrent mode to downside. Rally off week ago spike low has been surprisingly strong but has still not violated upside parameters so overall picture remains negative. How much of past week or so of down and back up action due to holiday market and/or tomorrow's currency switch in Europe hard to tell, so will just keep following lines. Lines still justify being short here in spite of today's big up. COT data continues to indicate downside move more likely than up from here. So pushing upside limits but prefer to give shorts a little more time and distance. Bottom line: Can be and go short here with stops in 60.80 to 61.00 area (regular stops, close only would be too risky now)—if trading above 60.50 for more than 30 minutes or so Wednesday, could justify getting out at market since if downside still good here, should not see much strength from here.

## REAL-TIME COMMENTARY

**1/2/02 (Wednesday):** Mar Swiss - Status - Bullish (to Neutral). Trend sideways but on strict basis can now call it up (since price above where was ten weeks ago and above ten-week moving average). ML now also sideways but will turn up after tomorrow regardless of what price does. SL pattern, which had been clearly negative, is now positive, since coming back all the way from its sharp down is a positive. Misread the "news" here as did not give switch to Euro currency enough weight. From trading perspective, this just not a big deal since have been trading Euros for several years, but it is big deal when actually switch the monetary paper. Now believe it quite possible European Central Bank intervened in markets and pushed Euro (and by connection Swiss) lower week or so ago and then used this artificial dip as spring board to push Euro right back up into currency switch day. Naturally they (European powers that be) would want to make sure Euro was not weak, and preferably was strong, on switch day since paper money is only held up through confidence, and only logical they would do everything they could to bolster public confidence in their new currency. In addition, they would be much more interested in doing this now, when actually switching paper, than several years ago when switched for business purposes only. So misread the impact of this event. Now ignoring all this, what do lines and chart say as of this moment? On price chart basis, when get a big down spike like had week and a half ago and regain all of it, this usually indicates solid strength and is normally a sign price will continue moving higher. On line basis, the pattern is now Bullish and will get more so after tomorrow (since SL will keep moving up). Therefore, technicals now marginally positive and justify longs (in both Euro and Swiss), and with fundamentals also positive, this means can justify longs (but have had so much whiplash here past few months, understandable if prefer to pass here for time being). Bottom line: Can go long with stops now in 60.00 to 60.25 area.

....................

## AFTER-ACTION CRITIQUE

I have included commentaries from both last day of 2001 and first day of 2002 here for continuity and because it was unusual move.

01/02/2002

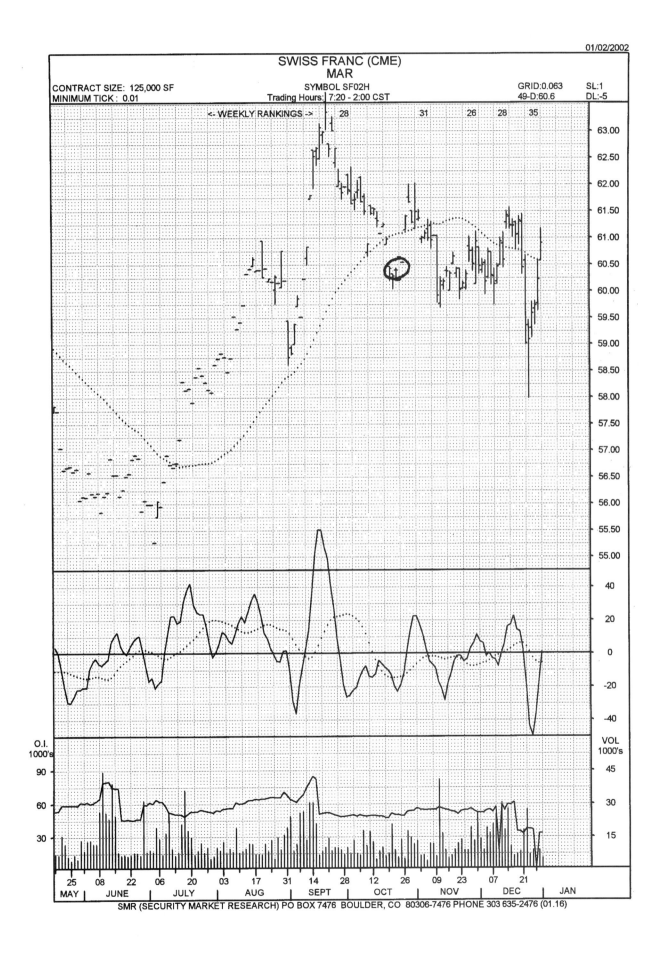

SWISS FRANC (CME)
MAR

CONTRACT SIZE: 125,000 SF
MINIMUM TICK : 0.01

SYMBOL SF02H
Trading Hours: 7:20 - 2:00 CST

GRID:0.063
49-D:60.6

SL:1
DL:-5

<- WEEKLY RANKINGS ->    28    31    26    28    35

# March 2002 Swiss Franc (Jan 3)

## REAL-TIME COMMENTARY

**1/3 (Thursday):** Mar Swiss - Status - Bullish (to Neutral). Trend sideways to marginally up and ML also sideways to marginally up so market very marginally concurrent to upside. SL on positive side but now getting a little overextended to upside. So picture here technically positive but on bigger picture probably closer to neutral. Continue to have background factor of currency switch in Euro, which would expect to be a supportive factor for both Swiss and Euro for at least next couple of weeks (as European governments obviously want to build confidence in new Euro currency and holding value up versus other currencies a step in that direction). Therefore, on straight-line basis, can justify being/going long here, but very marginal so hard to argue with passing on any longs (or shorts) for now. Bottom line: Lines say can be/go long with stops in 60.00 to 60.25 area, but hard to argue with sidelines.

.....................

## AFTER-ACTION CRITIQUE

It was very volatile couple of weeks for this market. Unusual to get such a big with-trend, non-news-related spike (as did here week earlier) only to have it quickly and completely retraced. When this market closed at 59.00 week earlier, it "should" have continued lower. A couple days of minor up or sideways (after down spike) would not have been out of line, but once it pushed back above 60.00 (three days earlier here), this was a clear sign something was "wrong" with short side. Also, when price moved, and especially closed, back above 60.00, it gave the earlier decisive break to 59.00 a clear appearance of a "false" downside breakout. Therefore, when stuck with short positions on the close above 60.00 (60.25), this was a mistake. The problem was I had been a little too sure the big down-spike day (close at 59.00) was start of sustained down move, so was taken by surprise when price did the reverse of expected.

The move (week ago here) down to 59.00 should have been a prelude to a sustained down move, instead the exact opposite occurred. Always have to keep an open mind about future price movements in this game. The future is truly unknown. No matter how seemingly likely the future might appear to be from time to time, in reality it is unknown. The natural laws of trading and reasonably reliable trend/momentum indicators can only provide "most likely" future outcomes; they can never provide certainty. I have found that price action that is persistently (more than day or two) out of line with what "rules" indicate "should" be happening invariably turns out to be clear warning sign that this time is an exception.

If look back on chart to the end of August, will see a big one-day down spike. This down spike was clearly against the trend, and the rule is, against-trend spikes tend to be quickly reversed. However, that spike happened on no real news and so this made me respect it more. Therefore, at the time I did not act (buy) on the dip. Rules are not perfect. All they do is provide general guidance based on a "most-of-the-time" basis. Although when dealing with spikes, the trend rule should carry more weight than the news rule. If had gone on that basis, then could have made case to buy that one-day down spike, even though pattern was solidly neutral and mode was solidly crosscurrent.

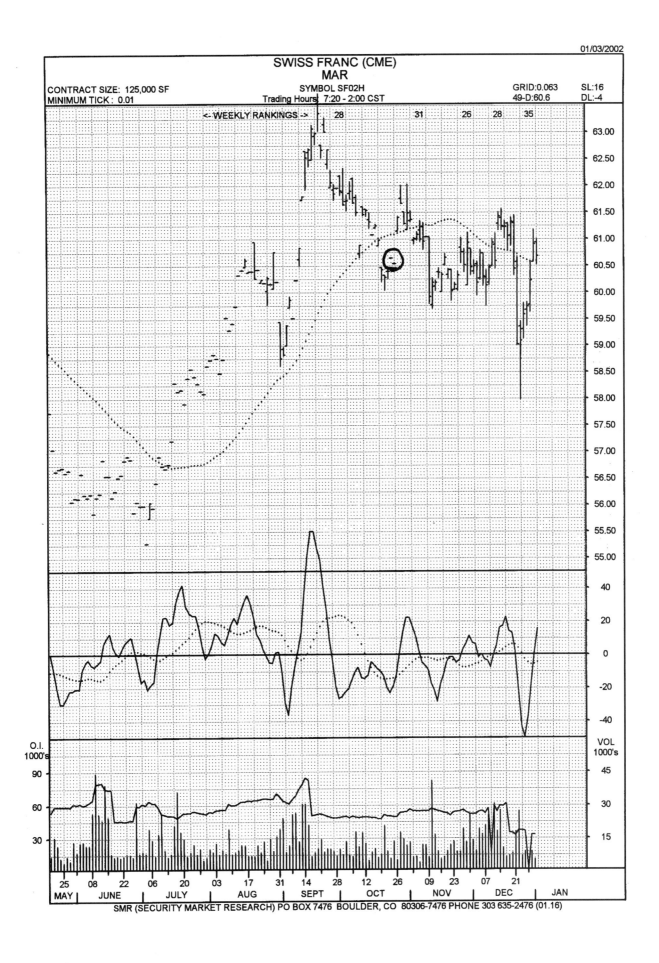

SWISS FRANC (CME)
MAR

01/03/2002

CONTRACT SIZE: 125,000 SF
MINIMUM TICK : 0.01

SYMBOL SF02H
Trading Hours 7:20 - 2:00 CST

GRID:0.063
49-D:60.6

SL:16
DL:-4

<- WEEKLY RANKINGS ->   28   31   26   28   35

SMR (SECURITY MARKET RESEARCH) PO BOX 7476  BOULDER, CO  80306-7476  PHONE 303 635-2476 (01.16)

# March 2002 Swiss Franc (Jan 4)

## REAL-TIME COMMENTARY

**1/4 (Friday):** Mar Swiss - Status - Bullish/Neutral. Trend sideways, ML on minor up cycle, SL positive but overextended to upside, price chart neutral to marginally positive, COT basically neutral (can make some argument for either direction)—so picture about as neutral as can get. However, still see upside as having better chance; therefore, if had to be in, would be long, not short. Action today fairly positive as held up well in face of some weakness in Euro. Can make case introduction of Euro may prompt some extra demand for Swiss as easy to see why some might want to switch some new, and thus naturally at least somewhat questionable, Euros for some old, well-established Swiss. On SL line pattern, the current "V" shaped pattern usually positive once get SL to pause briefly. Bottom line: Sidelines probably best as pattern very neutral, but see odds as favoring upside.

......................

## AFTER-ACTION CRITIQUE

Trend here was nominally up because price was slightly higher than it was ten weeks earlier; however, it was probably more accurate to consider trend indecisive. So it was a tough call here as could have made some arguments for being/going long; however, on big picture basis it was a little too neutral, so sidelines were probably best.

Normally, this big of a false downside spike will produce a fairly decent upside move because it tends to be a sign that just do not have sustained downside selling pressure in market. From a momentum-line basis, a couple more days of sideways-type action here, which would have turned SL down briefly, would have given a better setup for being/going long here, but markets do not always cooperate.

As a short-term trader, restraint is one personal characteristic that is important to possess. Some refer to this as "discipline," but I believe the more accurate word is "restraint." There are many active futures markets to trade. Each of these markets opens every day and their prices move around. A trader is going to have constant thoughts about this or that market moving up or down. He or she is also going to feel constant impulses to buy or sell this or that market. It is important to be able to separate the better situations from the not so good.

In this situation in Swiss Franc it would have been easy to envision the price moving sharply higher from here; however, it was also fairly easy to conjure up a mental picture of it moving lower. The point is that markets are always there and moving. The trick is to only act when picture quite clear or can make legitimate case it is on verge of becoming quite clear. The truth is at this time the picture was not very clear. In daily letter a day earlier I suggested longs, but in daily letter here I leaned more toward sidelines. Sometimes, frequently, a day of sideways action will give me (and other traders) a chance for a more sober look and this will sometimes result in different ideas of what to do, as it did in this case.

If you position one day and then the next decide that the argument for this position really was not very convincing, then just get out (regardless of profit or loss).

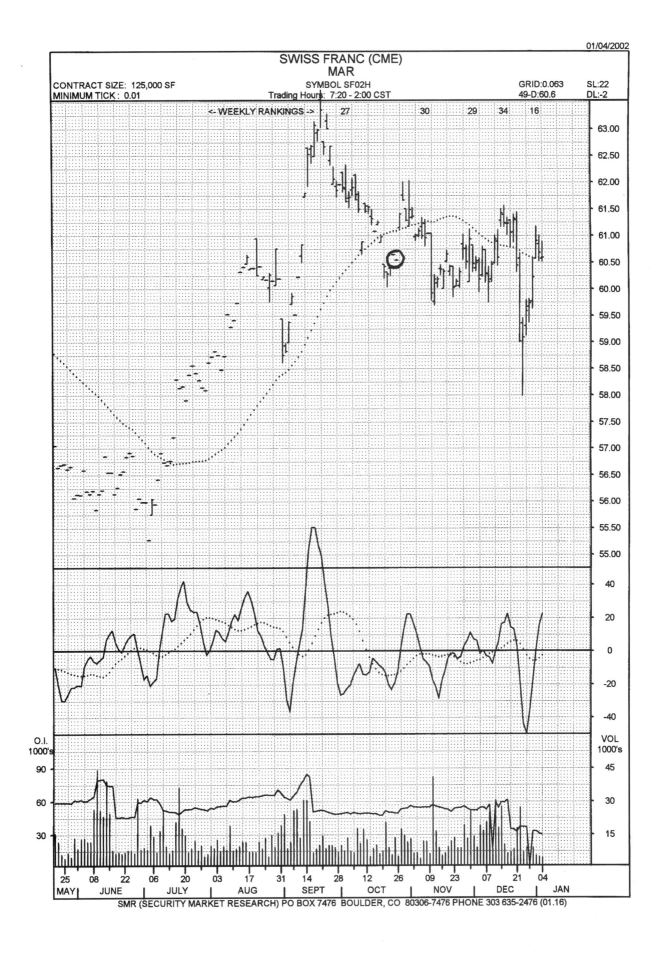

01/04/2002

SWISS FRANC (CME)
MAR

CONTRACT SIZE: 125,000 SF
MINIMUM TICK : 0.01

SYMBOL SF02H
Trading Hours: 7:20 - 2:00 CST

GRID:0.063
49-D:60.6

SL:22
DL:-2

<- WEEKLY RANKINGS ->    27      30    29    34    16

SMR (SECURITY MARKET RESEARCH) PO BOX 7476 BOULDER, CO 80306-7476 PHONE 303 635-2476 (01.16)

# March 2002 Swiss Franc (Jan 7/8/9)

**REAL-TIME COMMENTARY**

**1/7 (Monday):** Mar Swiss - Status - Neutral (to Bullish). Trend indecisive and with ML at zero and essentially sideways the market here is in very indecisive mode. SL turned down slightly after a big, week-long up move and so this line also neutral (to slightly positive). Action also neutral on fairly quiet sideways day. So picture about as solidly neutral as can get here at moment. However, still see slight upside tilt to picture here, so if had to be in, would still be long with stops in 60.00 area. Bottom line: Sidelines.

**REAL-TIME COMMENTARY**

**1/8 (Tuesday):** Mar Swiss - Status - Neutral. Trend indecisive as is ML so background technicals indecisive. Action slightly negative as continued to work slightly lower. So on straight line basis cannot make any kind of solid case for position here, in either direction. However, still see overall pattern as slightly more positive than negative and so if had to be in here would still be long, not short. Can make case past four days of slight working lower is simply bull flag, which should break to upside eventually. Also, usually find "V" type of SL pattern (as have here now) tends to indicate higher prices ahead are more likely than down. However, picture is still too mixed to justify positions so sidelines looks best. Bottom line: Sidelines.

**REAL-TIME COMMENTARY**

**1/9 (Wednesday):** Mar Swiss - Status - Neutral. Trend sideways to marginally down, ML sideways also and so market in indecisive mode. Action continues slightly negative as pressure light but persistent to downside. Since the big up on introduction day for Euro (first day of year), both Euro and Swiss have been drifting lower. Pattern here now closer to turning negative than positive, but overall remains solidly neutral and so difficult to make good enough case for positions in either direction at moment. 60.00 level is clear chart support level so move below there, especially on close, would be clear negative. Picture now has slight tilt to downside so could make minor case for "anticipation" shorts with stops in 60.70 area, but too mixed for me so prefer to stick to sidelines. Bottom line: Sidelines.

(**NOTE:** *To conserve space and because no material change from previous two days, have combined three days into one here.*)

....................

**AFTER-ACTION CRITIQUE**

Continued to be more accurate to call the trend here sideways rather than either up or down. Since trend was sideways could not have either Bullish or Bearish Status, so Status remained Neutral.

However, on strict line basis, trend was down here at moment (so this one point) and ML was just below zero and flat (so had half point there), and since SL was down (had another point) could have argued that Status was really Bearish, so going short would have been justified. However, trend was so indecisive it remained a close call, and when it is this close hard to argue against sidelines.

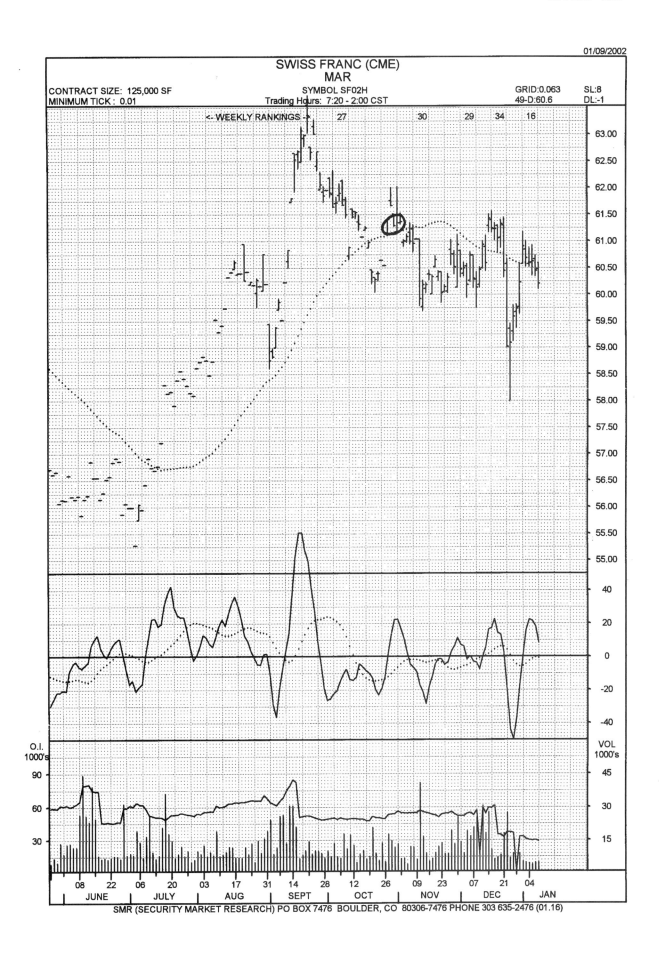

01/09/2002

SWISS FRANC (CME)
MAR

CONTRACT SIZE:  125,000 SF          SYMBOL SF02H                    GRID:0.063      SL:8
MINIMUM TICK : 0.01          Trading Hours: 7:20 - 2:00 CST              49-D:60.6       DL:-1

<- WEEKLY RANKINGS ->     27          30       29     34     16

SMR (SECURITY MARKET RESEARCH) PO BOX 7476  BOULDER, CO  80306-7476  PHONE 303 635-2476 (01.16)

# March 2002 Swiss Franc (Jan 10/11/14)

## REAL-TIME COMMENTARY

**1/10 (Thursday):** Mar Swiss - Status - Neutral. Trend sideways to marginally down, ML sideways also and so market in indecisive mode. Action continues slightly negative as pressure light but persistent to downside. Since the big up on introduction day for Euro (first day of year), both Euro and Swiss have been drifting lower. Pattern here now closer to turning negative than positive, but overall it remains solidly neutral and so difficult to make good enough case for positions in either direction at moment. 60.00 level is clear chart support level so move below there, especially on close, would be a clear negative. Picture now has slight tilt to downside so could make minor case for "anticipation" shorts with stops in 60.70 area, but too mixed for me so prefer to stick to sidelines. Bottom line: Sidelines.

## REAL-TIME COMMENTARY

**1/11 (Friday):** Mar Swiss - Status - Bearish (to Neutral). Trend marginally down to sideways and ML slightly down so market remains in marginal concurrent mode to downside. Action on positive side on minor up day. Very mixed picture here as lines currently slightly negative, but would only take one moderate up day to turn picture back to neutral, and when look at overall picture would still rather be long than short (in spite of line pattern). Can make case slow, steady down of past week and a half just a drawn out bull flag which is now poised to break to upside. Also, have had SL making fairly rhythmic week-long swings up and down and have just concluded a week long moderate down move. So on straight line basis shorts marginally indicated but on overall basis see picture as more positive than negative. When picture this confused, sidelines probably best; however, if opens above 60.50 Monday, could make case to go long with stops in 6030 area. Bottom line: Lines say can be short, but sidelines looks best.

## REAL-TIME COMMENTARY

**1/14 (Monday):** Mar Swiss - Status - Bearish (to Neutral). Trend and ML both still marginally down so market remains in very mild concurrent mode to downside. Action neutral on another quiet, sideways-type day. So lines continue to very marginally indicate can be/go short here but still see overall pattern as too mixed to make good enough case for shorts. Also can continue to make almost as good a case for longs as shorts here since would only take one moderate up day for overall pattern to turn positive enough for longs. SL has been making one-week swings up and down past month or so and has now been on minor down swing for a little over a week, and so this a minor positive. When a market is in a sideways pattern like this one has been in for past several months, it's always tempting to try to position here (either way) as a guess about which direction will break out; however, in long run will come out better if just stick to sidelines until technicals give clear indication since frequently just get whipped around when try to guess next breakout direction. Bottom line: Sidelines.

.....................

## AFTER-ACTION CRITIQUE

Have combined previous three days here since no material change. Always tempting to guess here, but as said above, sidelines best when so mixed.

01/14/2002

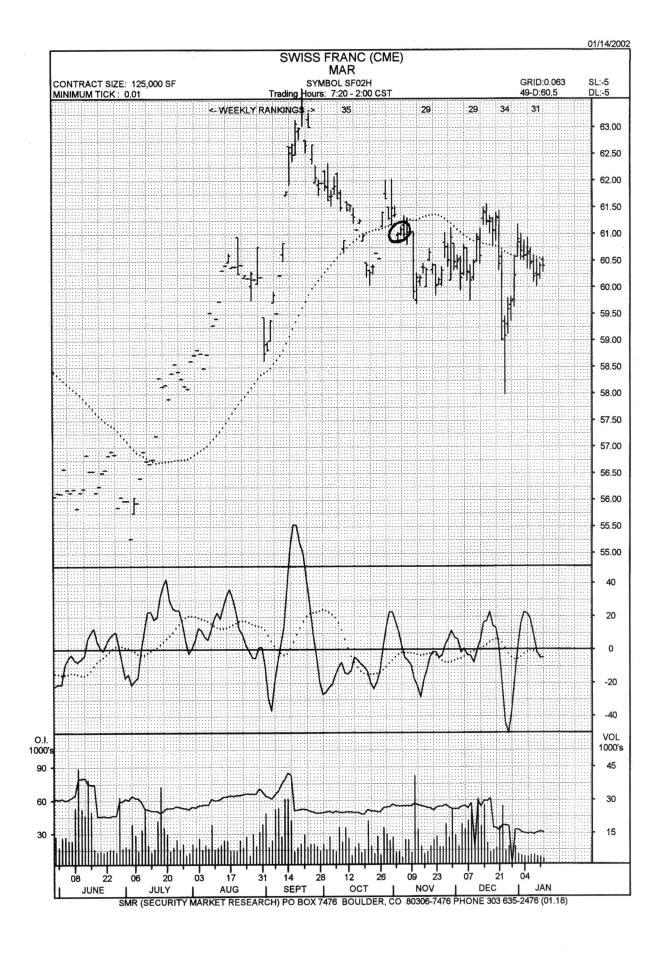

SWISS FRANC (CME)
MAR

CONTRACT SIZE:  125,000 SF
MINIMUM TICK :  0.01

SYMBOL SF02H
Trading Hours:  7:20 - 2:00 CST

GRID:0.063
49-D:60.5

SL:-5
DL:-5

<- WEEKLY RANKINGS ->     35          29          29      34      31

SMR (SECURITY MARKET RESEARCH) PO BOX 7476  BOULDER, CO  80306-7476  PHONE 303 635-2476 (01.18)

# March 2002 Swiss Franc (Jan 15)

**REAL-TIME COMMENTARY**

**1/15 (Tuesday):** Mar Swiss - Status - Bearish (to Neutral). Trend and ML both marginally down so market remains in marginal concurrent mode to downside. Action negative on minor downside breakout-type day. Overall picture remains quite mixed here as all three lines on "iffy" side, although all three currently down. Since what looked like "artificial" rally on day of Euro introduction (first day of year), this market (and Euro) have been under light but persistent downside pressure. May have underestimated downside potential here since today's minor downside breakout gives downside decent chance, but still see overall picture as too mixed to make solid case for shorts. However, now have fairly clear stop point, which did not have before today. Bottom line: Lines say can be short with stops now in 60.40 to 60.50 area.

....................

**AFTER-ACTION CRITIQUE**

It is easy to see in retrospect (one month later) that I was fighting the lines a little here. While pattern had been only very marginally negative for previous few days, it had been negative and was now quite clearly negative. However, I had been expecting (hoping?) to get breakout-type day to upside (a close above 61.00) instead of downside as had here. The reason (for looking for upside rather than down) was that a close above 61.00 would have produced a more solid pattern since ML would have been on a very solid up cycle (since would have been taking off some very low SL numbers for week or so) and SL would have turned up from a sharply higher low. Always have to be careful not to let a natural desire for line and price chart symmetry override reality. What counts in end is movement of price, and sometimes this goes opposite to symmetrical development of line patterns, as did here.

The choice of a 60.40-60.50 area for stops on any shorts here was on basis a move back up to that level would signal another, although smaller, false breakout to downside and would not want to stay short if this happened since would be a sign of too much strength. So had been looking (and itching) to go long and suddenly price gave an opposite signal. Since we are trading price and not momentum line patterns, then price has to rule. Plus at moment had all three reasonably reliable trend/momentum lines pointing down so line pattern had turned negative and so could have fully justified being/going short, and could not justify in any way being/going long. However, since I was still skeptical I decided to wait for at least one more day to see if this one day minor downside breakout proved to be one day aberration.

This one-day down move is a little too small to call it a clear down "spike," but can make some case to do so. On spike rule basis, since trend down and there was no news to prompt the down move, then odds should have favored continuation to downside. (With-trend spikes and spikes that happen on no news tend to continue, and so both parts of spike rule indicated lower prices ahead.) Now had all three lines down and spike rule in accordance as well; therefore, while none of these indicators were solid at moment, all signs were negative and so shorts were clearly justified.

01/15/2002

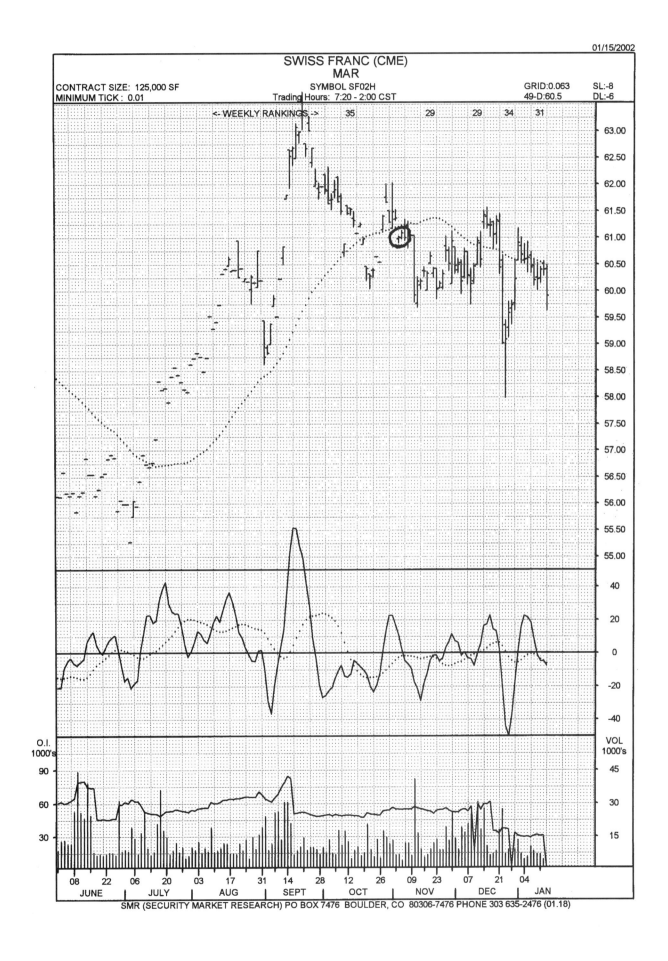

SWISS FRANC (CME)
MAR

CONTRACT SIZE: 125,000 SF
MINIMUM TICK : 0.01

SYMBOL SF02H
Trading Hours: 7:20 - 2:00 CST

GRID:0.063
49-D:60.5

SL:-8
DL:-6

# March 2002 Swiss Franc (Feb 15)

**2/15:** This market continued choppy for four days before turning down solidly. Within a couple of days of 1/15 the Status turned back to Neutral and mode back to crosscurrent, but it then turned right back to negative again. Once price closed back in 59.75 area again, the SL turned back down (from a lower high, always a short term negative) and so shorts were justified again. The mode did not turn back to concurrent until after the big (110 points, from 59.80 to 58.70) down day. However, since it was possible to count back three weeks and see that were going to be taking off some high numbers on SL very soon, then anticipating a return to concurrent mode to downside was relatively easy.

On 1/24 (the close of the day before the big down move) I wrote the following in daily letter: "Mar Swiss - Status - Bearish. Observations: Trend and ML both slightly down so market in concurrent mode to downside. Action slightly negative, but more due to inability to move up any than to minor down. Longer hold around recent lows the more solid yesterday's minor downside breakout becomes. Have all three lines marginally down at moment with each in good position to pick up speed to downside; therefore, even though price not particularly attractive for initiating new shorts here (since on recent lows), price still fairly close to stop points and picture increasingly negative, so see doing so as worth the risk. Bottom line: Can be and go short here with stops in 60.25 to 60.40 area (preferably not entered until after midday)."

Since margin at this time equaled about a 160-point move and if figured entry point on shorts was in high 59.00 area (anywhere from 59.70 up to 60.00), then a move down to low 58.00 area (anywhere from 58.10 up to 58.40) would have produced a 100 percent of margin profit. However, would have had to be very quick taking profits since once price did go below 58.50 (basically would have had to have had resting buy orders 160 points below entry level) it did not linger there. At the time, the market was in a solid concurrent mode to downside, so would have been easy to overstay welcome on shorts and end up having to cover in 59.00 area once Status switched back to Neutral and mode back to crosscurrent. Regardless, any shorts at this time would have produced profits, just a question of how much.

A long-term trader would have gone long this market back in July when trend turned up (around the 58.25 area) and had some very nice profits only to end up losing most of those by waiting for trend to turn down again in late November (around the 60.25 area). Then he would have had to ride through a month or so of choppiness and a 100-point move against before price dropped back to current 59.00 area. So once again long-term trading would have produced very good profits only to have most taken back on the trend change. This is the difficult part of long-term trading: trend changes that take back large amount (if not all) of profits. Unfortunately, in this case, when price was at its highs in September (in 63.00 area), there were no line pattern warning signs of imminent downside reversal. Sometimes prices just stop going up and turn down, and vice versa. As a trader, all can do is follow the movement of price and lines and make adjustments to positions as go along. A trader has to be like a canoeist paddling down an unexplored river: cannot fight the current and tide; can only pay close attention and act on the ever changing reality he or she encounters.

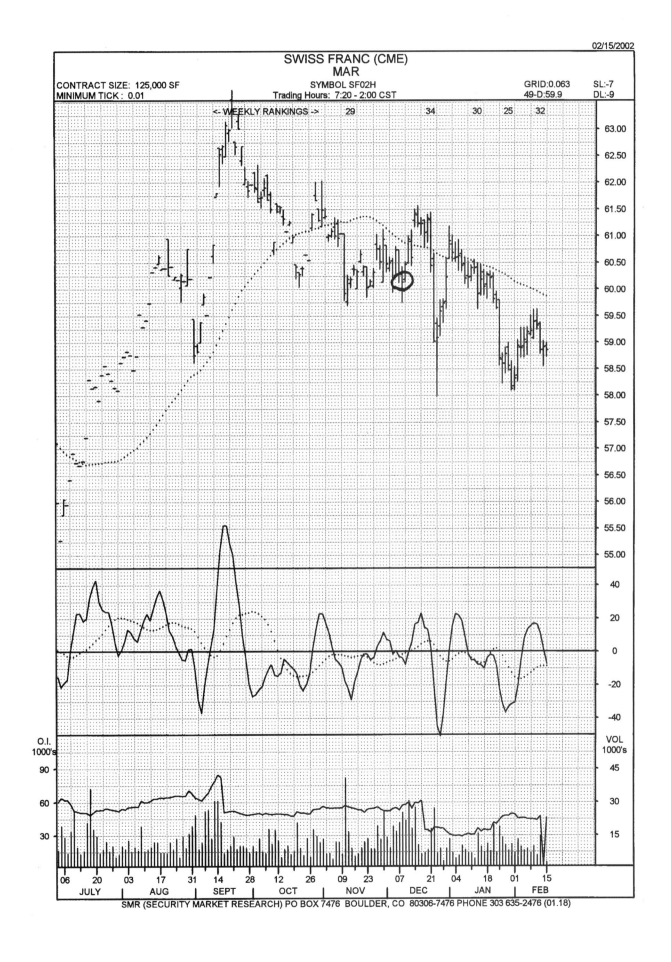

# Relative Strength Example

(**NOTE:** *Following is a slightly edited—for clarity—excerpt from my daily market letter of 12/21/01. Suggest you go back and take a look at the preceding charts of the Swiss and Yen and see how they looked on December 21. Then take a look at what they did between 12/21/01 and 2/15/02. See how the clear difference in relative strength in the third week of December turned out to be such a good indication of these two markets' relative price movement over the ensuing couple months.*)

(**From 12/21/01 market letter**): Have been a little off past couple weeks. Made mistake of trying to trade a few markets against the trend (primarily stocks) and this always throws me off. Have always found trading against the trend to be like a "drug" since it tends to be habit forming— more do it, the more want to do it. This is because when do go against the trend and are wrong (as usually will be), then tend to think it was just a matter of being a little off on timing, so tend to keep trying. Better just not to trade against the trend unless the market is within margin-of-error (two weeks/ten days) of changing trend, and only then when all other indicators are clearly pointing in direction of presumed new trend. We have also had, and continue to have, over the past few weeks a number of markets actually changing trend directions, as well as a number coming close and then failing. Trend changes are always toughest times to trade since price tends to get to a key pivot point and then either pushes through and trend changes or market cannot quite turn trend and price moves quickly back in direction of prior existing trend. When a market is at pivotal point of either turning its existing trend or not, it tends to put traders on edge more than normal (of course are always at least somewhat on "edge" in this game).

Human nature—our natural instinct when trading—tends to work against successful trading. For some reason virtually all traders, myself included, are always more interested in positioning in markets where the trend looks like it's about to change or the trend has just changed. In other words, the prospect of buying near lows and shorting near highs has a real pull on us. However, we tend not to be anywhere near as attracted to positioning with markets that have been in well-established trends for a long time (i.e., months).

A perfect recent example of this has been the Swiss versus Yen. The Yen has been in a clear downtrend for months, but I (and am sure many others) have had a hard time sticking with and pushing the short side. The Swiss has been essentially sideways the past few months, yet I (and am sure many others) have been eager to guess that its next major move would be up. For some reason, buying in anticipation of a new uptrend in the Swiss has had a strong pull on me (and others), while being/going short the Yen has had almost the opposite effect. Simply getting in and staying in an "old," already well-established, trending market almost seems to repel most traders. For some reason it seems to be human nature (natural) to be more afraid that an existing trend is about to change and less afraid a potential new trend will not actually materialize (become well established).

We seem to lose interest quickly in the well-established move, yet are endlessly eager to fully anticipate the next potential trending market. These feelings (fear the existing clear trend will suddenly change and fear a new move will start without us) are imbedded deep within (me, and I expect most others) as they seem to overpower us no matter how much empirical evidence to the contrary we may see.

The past week or so in Swiss and Yen (week of 12/14/01 to 12/21/01) have been a perfect example of this. I've been stubborn about getting long Swiss and jumpy about being short Yen during a time period when the exact opposite was what the trends clearly were indicating. Not surprisingly, the strength of the existing trends in Yen and Swiss have proven once again that "continuation is more likely than change."

I know of no way around these harmful natural tendencies other than simply resolving to force myself to follow the "rules." This means follow the natural laws of trading. This does not mean I cannot position in new trends when and if I can make decent case a new trend is about to start. However, it does mean to focus most attention on the old, well-established trending markets rather than constantly chasing first one potential trend change after another.

If you have ever seen film footage of lions hunting, you will see the young lions charge into a herd and chase one potential juicy prey after another, only to end up catching nothing. The older, more experienced lions act very differently. They single out the most vulnerable prey, focus solely on one of those, and then pursue their chosen target relentlessly and single-mindedly until successful.

Traders should act the same way. Potential new trending markets will always look the "juiciest" because they appear to offer the most potential; however, these potential trend beginnings are also the most difficult to catch and have the biggest kick when wrong, whereas the old, well-established trending markets (where one side is clearly in trouble and thus very vulnerable) will always provide the most reliable "meal," so this should be where we focus most of our attention and the bulk of our trading equity.

Remember, there are no "degree-of-difficulty" bonus points in trading. This is not Olympic diving or gymnastics where the more difficult the "trade" the greater the points. Buying the low or selling the high or positioning just at the moment of a trend change does not pay any more than taking a chunk out of the middle of a well-established trend. Everyone likes to say they caught "the" low or high in a market, but that is just "bar talk." Nobody brags about consistently taking modest chunks out of the middle of a trending market because that is not exciting or special; however, the truth is the middle of moves is where the most reliable profits are. Therefore, if we want to survive and prosper in this very tough game of trading, we need to force ourselves to constantly attack the weakest "prey." And that will always be the losing side of a well-established trending market.

# March 2002 Bonds (Jan 2)

## REAL-TIME COMMENTARY

**1/2 (Wednesday):** Mar Bonds - Status - Bearish (to Neutral). Trend solidly down but ML on fairly solid up cycle so market in solid crosscurrent mode. However, major downside reversal day today and this turned SL back down, which gives sell signal. Market down sharply and quite easily today with no news to speak of, and this always a very negative sign (and especially when trend so solidly down). Turn down in SL also produces a minor bearish divergence and these always more negative when market in solid downtrend. So now have good sell signal basis the lines, but it is a crosscurrent sell and these less reliable (but countering this is fact market in such solid downtrend). Had thought (and charts looked like) would get some upside pressure here near term but markets "sometimes" surprise, and when surprises come with strong trend should respect them, i.e., act on any signals. Bottom line: Can go short with stops in 101.00 to 101.08 (preferably on close basis).

......................

## AFTER-ACTION CRITIQUE

Status was Bearish because had trend down, ML below zero, and SL down for total of minus two and a half points. One potential problem for short side though was ML being on a solid up cycle, which means market in strong crosscurrent mode. Other than that, overall picture was quite negative since trend so strong to downside and chart quite negative with past three weeks of sideways having the clear look of a bear flag (which would usually break to downside). Normally would prefer not to go against such a strong crosscurrent mode, but rest of picture was quite negative, so felt it was worth a shot.

Could have made case for anticipation shorts the previous two days when price was in 101.16 area (around recent highs and SL slightly above zero, so was not over extended to downside). However, I did not do so in this case due to solid up cycle in ML and the SL having just turned up and was on a series of higher lows.

Trading is decision making. Most (all?) trading decisions involve some degree of uncertainty. "Anticipation" type trades involve a little more uncertainty than usual because you are trying to anticipate a change in short-term energy flow. As a general rule, though, whenever price is around "best" recent levels (past few days to past few weeks), you can make some case to position with the solid trend. The only problem when do this is usually do not have a close, clear stop point, so either have to use a dollar stop (i.e., pick amount willing to risk and place stop accordingly) or go without stop. However, as long as short-term momentum is not moving too strongly against trend (SL not going straight up/down and gaining speed), then when/if a counter-trend move offers the "best" recent price, you can always consider positioning (with the trend). I call this type of trade a "faith-in-trend" trade.

The choice of using just above 101.00 as stop point was based on idea that if breakout from current bear flag imminent, then the price should not go back up to 101.00 area. When markets are starting sustained moves, they rarely go back and give those who missed getting in at good price one last chance to do so. As a rule, the more times a seemingly "good" price is available to buy or sell, the less likely it really is "good."

01/02/2002

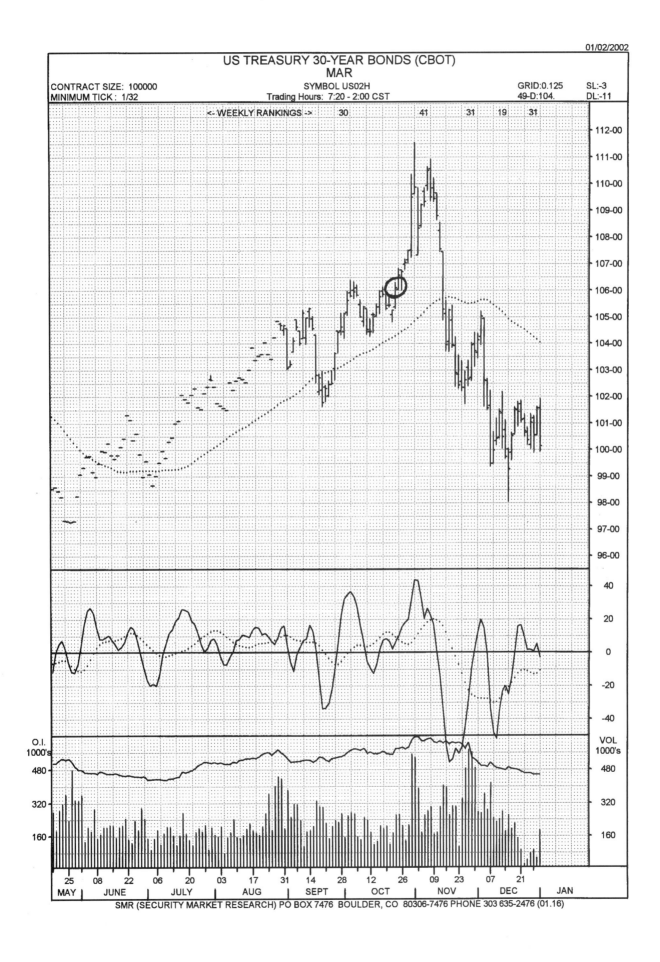

## US TREASURY 30-YEAR BONDS (CBOT)
### MAR

CONTRACT SIZE: 100000  
MINIMUM TICK : 1/32  

SYMBOL US02H  
Trading Hours: 7:20 - 2:00 CST  

GRID:0.125  
49-D:104.  

SL:-3  
DL:-11  

<- WEEKLY RANKINGS ->    30    41    31    19    31

# March 2002 Bonds (Jan 3)

## REAL-TIME COMMENTARY

**1/3 (Thursday):** Mar Bonds - Status - Bullish (to Neutral). Trend solidly down but ML almost as solidly up so market in crosscurrent mode and will remain so for another week or so. Action slightly positive on minor up day but price still well within bearish parameters. Past four weeks on price chart has look of broad bear flag, which should eventually break to downside. Have major report tomorrow a.m. (monthly employment report) and this can affect this market. It's expected to be bullish for Bonds (show weak economy) but market not acting much like will be. Report may decide near-term move but trend so negative odds continue to heavily favor downside, and so any upside (if get any) should just be temporary. Bottom line: Can be short with short-term trading stops 101.00 to 101.08 (but would not enter stops until an hour or so after report).

......................

## AFTER-ACTION CRITIQUE

A nothing day here, but if market was in process of breaking out to downside of recent sideways pattern (bear flag), then it "should" have been down decently. Instead it was up slightly and never even traded lower on day. I should have given the relatively negative action a little more weight, especially with market in such a strong crosscurrent mode (ML on such a solid up cycle). However, I had made my decision for short side and was in no mood to be deterred.

It takes a lot of psychic energy to keep your mind fully open at all times. It is unpleasant to be constantly on edge and alert to something going "wrong" (i.e., against expectations). It is much more comforting to just say to yourself this market is now going lower or that market is now going higher so I can position and then forget any other decisions for a while. To be a consistently successful trader, it is necessary to always be looking for warning signs. We have to always be alert to the unexpected action; always pay extra attention to the dog that does not bark.

I also seem to have forgotten here that crosscurrent trades should be treated the same as against-trend trades—get out quicker. As a rule, should only expect crosscurrent trades (i.e., price moves) to only last somewhere from two to five days. In other words, when doing a crosscurrent trade, have to have finger on trigger to get out almost as soon as put trade on.

However, trend was very solidly down here, so shorts were still justified. Again, being or not being short here was simply a trading decision. Can make some case either way.

Interesting to note the big up spike at end of October from 107.16 up to 109.16 followed a day later by move up to intra-day high of 111.16. This big up spike was prompted by government suspension of 30-year Bond sales. While with the trend, the spike was therefore clearly news related, so was at least somewhat suspect. I have found that many with-trend, news-related spikes tend to have large but relatively short-lived with-the-trend moves. Also interesting to note how Status turned from Bullish to Neutral and market moved to crosscurrent mode (around the 108.25 area) only a few days after top, so if were following the lines would not have been caught in the big down move.

01/03/2002

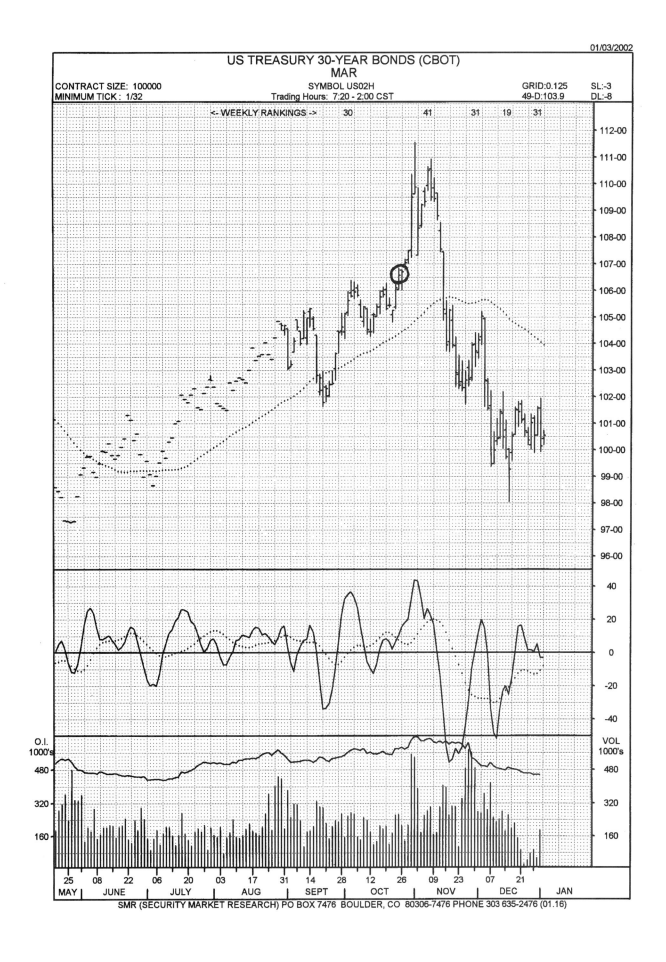

## US TREASURY 30-YEAR BONDS (CBOT)
### MAR

CONTRACT SIZE: 100000
MINIMUM TICK : 1/32

SYMBOL US02H
Trading Hours: 7:20 - 2:00 CST

GRID:0.125
49-D:103.9

SL:-3
DL:-8

<- WEEKLY RANKINGS ->   30   41   31   19   31

# March 2002 Bonds (Jan 4)

**REAL-TIME COMMENTARY**

**1/4 (Friday):** Mar Bonds - Status - Bearish (to Neutral). Trend solidly down but ML clearly up so market remains in crosscurrent mode (and will continue so for at least several more days). However, when trend is as solidly down as is here, can fully justify being short when pattern negative and is at moment. Action slightly negative as down sharply early but came back to close only down ten points. Since in crosscurrent mode, may be in line for some more sideways to up action, but doubt have meaningful upside. COT essentially neutral, so no hindrance to move in either direction. Bottom line: Can be short with short-term trading stops just above 101.00 (if get stopped out have to be ready to get back short within few days).

....................

**AFTER-ACTION CRITIQUE**

The government releases regularly scheduled statistical reports. Most of these reports have little or no market impact. However, some can and usually do produce sharp market moves. One of these is the monthly employment report which is released at 8:30 a.m. (Eastern) on the first Friday of every month. This report is viewed as an indicator of recent economic strength or weakness, so tends to produce sharp moves in both the interest rate and stock markets.

For the most part I do not see any problem with going into this report, and other important reports, with positions. While risk is always greater when important reports are released, trading is a risky business and reports are simply another risk. Over time I believe reports do not really affect the natural laws of pricing. Very rarely a report will produce a trend-altering move; however, most of the time reports are quickly forgotten and the short-term moves they produce quickly dissipate. Since some reports can produce big, fast moves, I will usually pull any stops until the market has had an hour or so to absorb the news. While this does increase risk, it tends to avoid getting stopped out on some short-term aberrational moves. In addition, I have found that prices tend to make several up and down moves immediately after reports are released before finally settling on a direction for the rest of the day. Therefore, it is usually best not to act too quickly after a report, but instead let the market settle down some first (give it about an hour or so after report). This tendency is more true of interest rate and stock markets than agricultural commodities.

Even with the intra-day gyrations after the monthly employment report (market traded decently above and below previous day's close), this market ended only slightly lower on day. The chart and line situation remains about same as past couple of days. Trend still solidly down, but ML almost as solidly up so market still in strong crosscurrent mode (and now have had three days of this crosscurrent mode move, which indicates move getting a little "old"). SL clearly down now, but since have three days in row of prices in this area, would not take too much to upside to turn it right back up.

So, picture basically same as has been: Are on a decent looking crosscurrent sell signal, but so far price not taking advantage of this chance to breakout to downside.

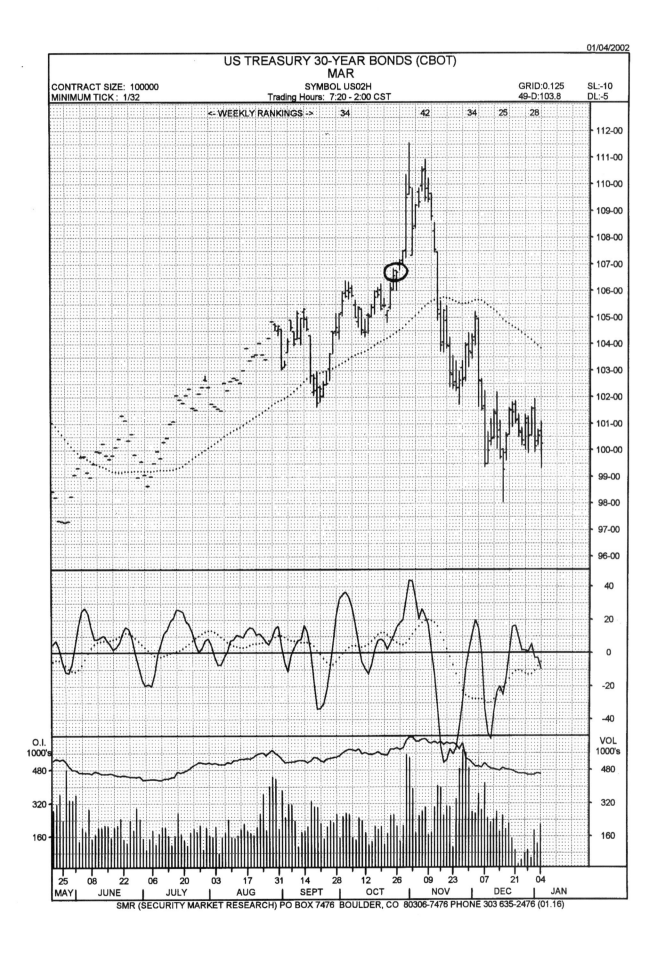

01/04/2002

US TREASURY 30-YEAR BONDS (CBOT)
MAR

CONTRACT SIZE: 100000
MINIMUM TICK : 1/32

SYMBOL US02H
Trading Hours: 7:20 - 2:00 CST

GRID:0.125
49-D:103.8

SL:-10
DL:-5

<- WEEKLY RANKINGS ->    34        42        34      25      28

SMR (SECURITY MARKET RESEARCH) PO BOX 7476 BOULDER, CO 80306-7476 PHONE 303 635-2476 (01.16)

# March 2002 Bonds (Jan 7)

## REAL-TIME COMMENTARY

**1/7 (Monday):** Mar Bonds - Status - Neutral. Trend solidly down but ML now solidly up so now in strong crosscurrent mode. Action solidly positive on good up day with no downside pressure and a close on day's highs. ML on good up cycle again and on verge of moving above zero; therefore, this line is positive for time being. SL turned up sharply from clear third higher low and this also a short-term positive. In spite of trend being solidly down, momentum picture now too positive to be short here anymore. Trend too negative to be/go long, momentum too positive to be/go short. Bottom line: Sidelines.

......................

## AFTER-ACTION CRITIQUE

This was good example of the perils of crosscurrent trades, and peril highest when crosscurrent strong (ML moving solidly against trend). Status was back to Neutral as only had trend and the ML slightly below zero as negatives—meaning the net-with-trend points equaled minus one and a half. In addition, the ML was on verge of crossing to positive territory, so were close to having everything positive except the strong downtrend, as additional short-term positives now had a clear third higher low on SL and a modified double-bullish divergence (between price and SL).

With both Status going back to Neutral and stop level being hit, could not justify being short anymore. Basic situation here now was solidly neutral since, as noted at the time, trend too negative for longs, momentum too positive for shorts.

Starting in early November, this market topped out and suddenly collapsed. Incidentally, this collapse was not accompanied by any particularly negative news, so it was a non-news-related collapse. As with price spikes, any sustained move that occurs without any obvious news-related cause should be respected as they tend to continue. As a rule, the more difficult it is to find an explanation for a sustained move, the more likely the move will keep going. Conversely, the more obvious the reason for a big move, the less likely it will be to continue (such as big rally in late October due to government suspension of 30-year Bond sales).

Take a look back on chart during the second half of November. The major two-week price collapse moved the price down to 102 area. Then the price staged a five-day bounce-back rally. At the time, I suggested shorting into this rally because the trend had turned clearly down, so I saw that rally as a good example of the "sell-the-first-rally-in-a-new-bear-market" rule (and vice versa for first dip in new bull market).

This type of trade, where are selling into a counter-trend rally on scale basis (over time, meaning short some every day after rally underway), can be very effective; however, it does have higher risk since have to go without stops for at least a while. I do not recommend this scale up shorting (or with trend scale down buying) approach unless have good nerves because the market can push against you for a while and this can get uncomfortable. However, almost invariably the price will move back with trend, and when it does, the move is usually fast and big (as happened here).

01/07/2002

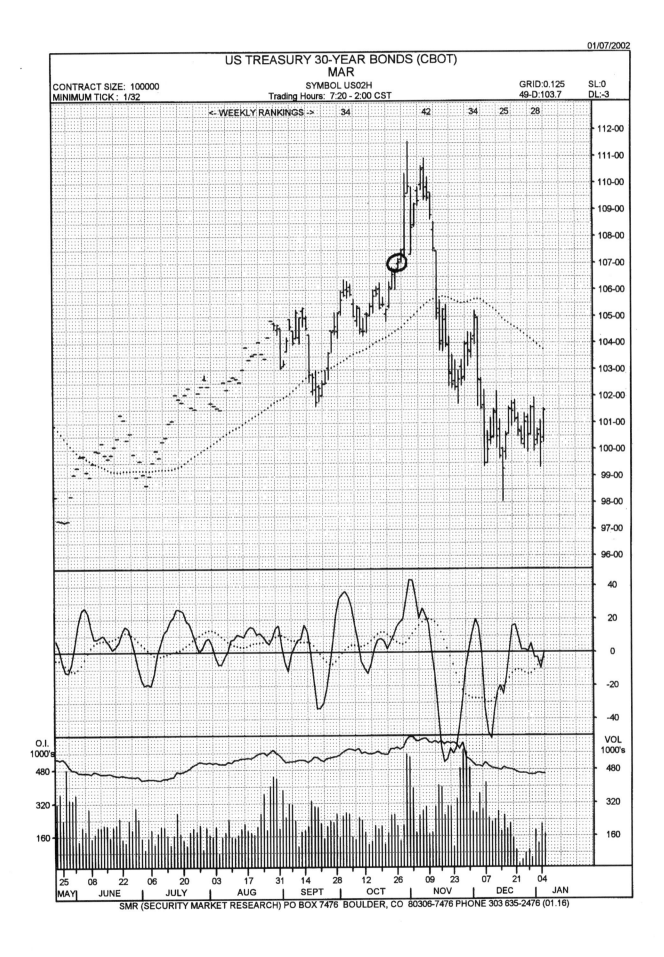

US TREASURY 30-YEAR BONDS (CBOT)
MAR

CONTRACT SIZE: 100000
MINIMUM TICK : 1/32

SYMBOL US02H
Trading Hours: 7:20 - 2:00 CST

GRID:0.125
49-D:103.7

SL:0
DL:-3

<- WEEKLY RANKINGS ->   34   42   34   25   28

# March 2002 Bonds (Jan 8)

## REAL-TIME COMMENTARY

**1/8 (Tuesday):** Mar Bonds - Status - Neutral. Trend solidly down but ML just as solidly up so market in crosscurrent mode. Action neutral on fairly quiet, unchanged day. Basic situation here remains unchanged from yesterday in that trend way too negative to consider longs but momentum pattern still too positive to make good enough case to be/go short. However, time always favors the trend and especially when as strong as it is here at moment. Past month of broad sideways trading range has the clear look of big bear flag, which should eventually break to downside. Another sideways-type day tomorrow and will be able to start to make case for "anticipation" shorts here again, but at moment pattern is too mixed to justify doing so at moment. Have a monthly inflation report Friday a.m. and this one has a slim chance of being a bearish surprise. Have had several months of clear signs of strength in commodities across the board; however, this has been disguised in monthly inflation reports due to major sell off in energy markets. Crude complex no longer going down and actually has moved up some past month or so. Therefore, this month inflation may start to show up in government reports. So could justify starting to go short here again if closes under 101.20 area (or so) tomorrow. Bottom line: Sidelines.

...................

## AFTER-ACTION CRITIQUE

Quiet, unchanged day, so basic situation was unchanged; trend still too negative for longs, momentum too positive for shorts. The temptation to short here in area of recent highs was very strong though, and this was due to continued very solid downtrend.

Obviously, I started to look ahead here and began to anticipate a turn down in both SL and ML over the next few days. What I figured was if this happened (both SL and ML turned down), then the picture would become solidly bearish again, and since trend was so negative I would definitely want to be short. However, I was certain neither of these lines would turn down the next day; therefore, shorting the next day here would have been a little bit of anticipating the anticipation. In other words, suggesting shorts here was pushing it some since it was too soon to realistically expect Status to turn back to Bearish yet. Another point for concern about shorting here was the fact price once again was back at recent best levels, and as mentioned earlier, in this game you have to be wary of getting too many chances to get in at a particularly "good" price.

The suggestion to wait until made sure market did not close much higher was a good one. The reason for waiting was if the market closed much more than a few points higher, then the possibility of turning the SL down the next day would diminish significantly. So, as tempting as this price was for going short, the correct action here was to wait until at least an unchanged or lower close before doing so, and even then possibly wait until at least next day. In looking at chart now (month later) can see too many warning signs about upside potential to justify shorting at this moment (and trend too negative to even consider longs). Therefore, correct action here really was to stick to sidelines for at least another day, regardless of what happened the next day.

01/08/2002

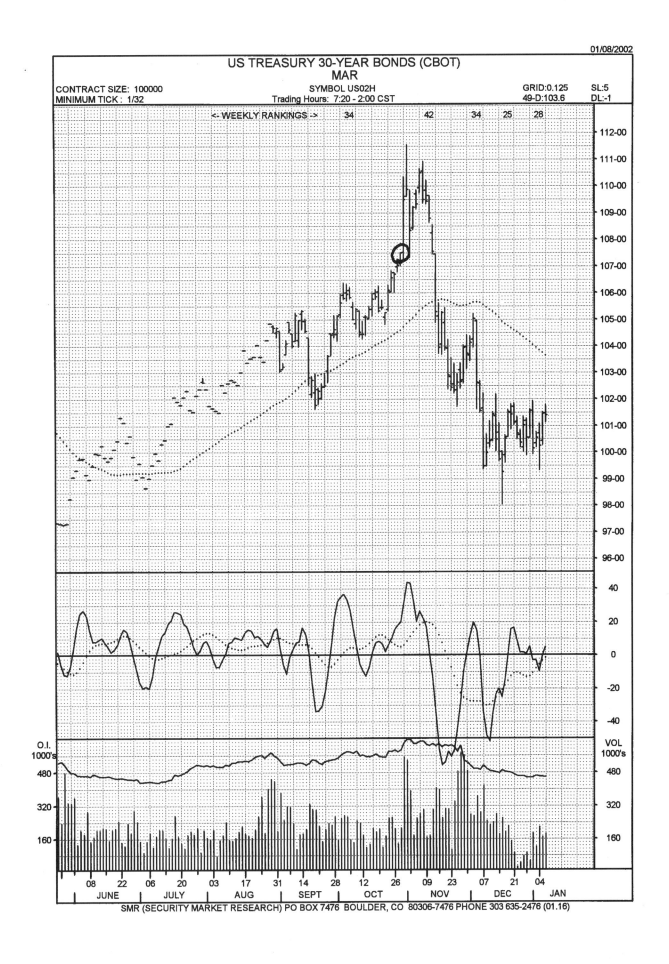

US TREASURY 30-YEAR BONDS (CBOT)
MAR

CONTRACT SIZE: 100000
MINIMUM TICK : 1/32

SYMBOL US02H
Trading Hours: 7:20 - 2:00 CST

GRID:0.125
49-D:103.6

SL:5
DL:-1

<- WEEKLY RANKINGS ->

SMR (SECURITY MARKET RESEARCH) PO BOX 7476  BOULDER, CO  80306-7476  PHONE 303 635-2476 (01.16)

# March 2002 Bonds (Jan 9)

**REAL-TIME COMMENTARY**

**1/9 (Wednesday):** Mar Bonds - Status - Neutral. Trend down but ML up so market remains in crosscurrent mode. Action positive as overcame persistent downside pressure to close unchanged. ML currently positive but now within margin-of-error for it to turn negative. Price and SL now both near recent highs and any time trend as solidly down as is here this means can see sustained downside pressure come back into market at any time. So question here now is how much more counter-trend upside pressure will see before trend reasserts itself. Any price 101.24 or higher tomorrow would be highs of past month in a solid downtrending market and so would qualify as "attractive" price for initiating "anticipation" shorts. Have PPI (producer price index) report Friday a.m. and believe this report has decent chance to be a bearish (for bonds) surprise since seeing so much upside pressure in commodities. Feel general market (interest rate markets and stocks) extremely complacent about inflation risk at moment and thus very vulnerable to any negative surprises. Therefore, would see any further upside tomorrow as opportunity for "anticipation" shorts, but have to go without stops for time being (through Friday). Bottom line: Lines say sidelines, but can now make decent case for "anticipation" shorts anywhere from today's close up to 102.08 area, no stops for now though.

......................

**AFTER-ACTION CRITIQUE**

Unchanged day left situation same as had been prior couple days, but now it had clear look of approaching a moment of truth. A close back below 101.00 would probably turn SL down and in so doing would tilt entire technical picture clearly negative enough to be short. Since going long was out of question due to the strong downtrend, therefore the only question was whether to try any "anticipation" shorts.

Since I had been bearish for some time, due to the strong downtrend I opted for anticipation shorts. However, if take a cold look at picture here, can see that many of upside warning signs have mentioned earlier were still present. ML not only was still on solid up cycle but also was now clearly above zero. The "confirming rule" is that need to have ML either cycling in direction want to trade or have it on side want to trade, and neither was the case here. In addition, had that clear third higher low on SL and have seen many times where a series (three or more) of higher lows in SL can produce bigger than expected rallies. The third warning was the price giving so many chances to sell a solidly downtrending market at four week highs.

The truth is that in this case trying anticipation shorts here was a little too aggressive, just a few too many upside warning signs. In a case like this it is probably better to wait for some more time or price confirmation (some weakness in order to make sure SL and ML would actually turn down soon) before trying shorts. However, trading happens in real time. It is always hard to see situations clearly all the time when under the real pressures of trading.

It is so easy to be influenced by hope in this game. It is so easy to look a little too far ahead when anticipating—one day ahead is usually enough and best. Regardless, I went short.

01/09/2002

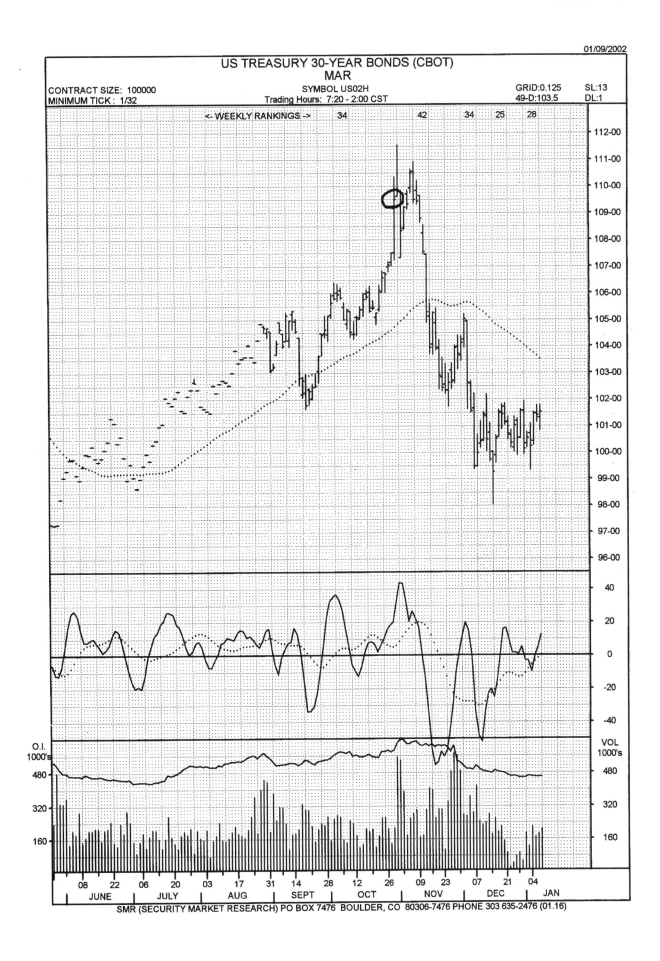

# March 2002 Bonds (Jan 10)

## REAL-TIME COMMENTARY

**1/10 (Thursday):** Mar Bonds - Status - Neutral. Trend solidly down but ML still clearly up so market remains in crosscurrent mode. Action very positive on solid up day and close on day's highs and at five-week highs. Can make case today an against-trend, non-news-related up spike and these have mixed record as against-trend spikes invariably short-lived, but have to respect spike more when comes on no real news, as did today. Bonds are a fairly good trend following market and trend still solidly down here so have to keep giving downside better chance. Downtrending ten-week moving average now in 103.16 area and market has rallied up close to this level, which usually turns out to be good place to initiate new with-trend positions. So market definitely stronger than had expected today (and past few days), but overall pattern still clearly negative since trend solidly down, although now will need move back under 101.16 to turn both chart and line pattern legitimately negative enough to be/go short. However, most of time in this type of situation, initiating with-trend positions proves to be good idea in week or so, but at moment being/going short here strictly a "faith" (belief that trend will eventually reassert itself and push prices back down) trade and these can be trying since no real stop point (never a good idea to buy at recent highs in solid downtrending market, and any stop triggered above here would be doing just that). Have PPI (inflation) report tomorrow and expectations are for zero inflation, but continue to believe may show surprising increase. Bottom line: Lines say sidelines, but see being/going short here as decent bet although no clear chart-stop point, so either have to go without stops or just pick "dollar" stop point (choose how much willing to risk and then place stop there) or use "fail-safe" stop up somewhere in 104 to 105 area.

......................

## AFTER-ACTION CRITIQUE

A very big up day that was quite decisive. Obviously, I misread this market badly here. There were plenty of warning signs that shorts were at risk, but I was carried away by hopeful, although low probability, scenarios (i.e., a close below 100.00, but got the opposite instead). Market was now very solidly in Neutral Status and crosscurrent mode, meaning virtually impossible to turn back to Bearish or concurrent to downside any time soon. Then I compounded error by sticking with shorts instead of just biting the bullet (taking the loss) and going to sidelines.

When momentum is this strong to upside, regardless of trend and attractive price, you simply cannot justify being/going short. Staying short when momentum this solid to upside is trading on "hope," not anticipation. Unfortunately, when trade only on hope, usually have no hope. Most of the time a solid trend will bail out almost any with the trend trade; however, as an individual trader, you simply cannot afford to be on wrong side for very long. Therefore, in a case like this one, no matter how strong the trend was to downside and regardless of how "attractive" the price might have appeared, if short, the correct action was to take the loss and go to the sidelines.

Your first order of business in trading is to survive. There will always be a good probability trade ahead. Probability for downside here the next few days was very low; therefore, the correct action was to just get out—at the market. When "stuck" in a bad trade, and I was here, do not get cute; get out (i.e., do not try to save a few dollars by getting a slightly better price to get out; just get out!).

01/10/2002

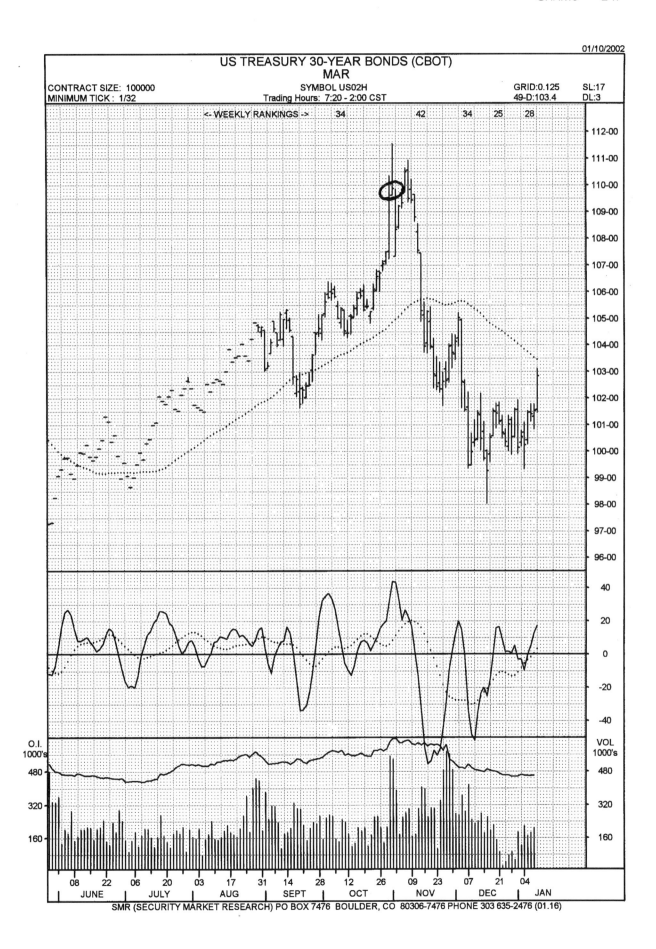

US TREASURY 30-YEAR BONDS (CBOT)
MAR

CONTRACT SIZE:  100000
MINIMUM TICK : 1/32

SYMBOL US02H
Trading Hours: 7:20 - 2:00 CST

GRID:0.125
49-D:103.4

SL:17
DL:3

<- WEEKLY RANKINGS ->     34        42        34     25     28

SMR (SECURITY MARKET RESEARCH) PO BOX 7476  BOULDER, CO  80306-7476  PHONE 303 635-2476 (01.16)

# March 2002 Bonds (Jan 11)

## REAL-TIME COMMENTARY

**1/11 (Friday):** Mar Bonds - Status - Neutral. Trend solidly down but ML clearly up so market in crosscurrent mode. Action positive on good up day, but had small feel of blow-off-type day to upside since market did not move up much after Greenspan bullish comments became public. So on straight line basis, sidelines still indicated, but whenever trend this solid to downside and both price and SL are at recent extreme highs, can make decent case to be/go short on "attractive" price basis (best recent price in solid downtrend). In addition, can make argument big up of past two days primarily due to expected and actual bullish comments from Fed Chairman Greenspan; therefore, can make case past two days simply an against-trend, news-related up spike, and these almost always quickly reversed. Against a strong trend, spikes caused by specific news events (and especially when this event is Fed Chairman comments) have extremely good record of turning out to be false moves that are quickly reversed. So it is painful to be short here and may feel scary to go short here since momentum so strong to upside, but past records on "fading" (shorting here) this type of move very good, so continue to view shorts here as worthwhile. Bottom line: Lines say sidelines, but continue to prefer being and going short here although still no clear chart-stop point (but a move, and especially close, above 104.16 would start to be too much on upside to stick with shorts).

..................

## AFTER-ACTION CRITIQUE

Another good up day that I tried to talk away. In this game we trade price, not indicators. When obviously wrong on price, give up; do not stick with bad trade simply because "most of time" trend will reassert itself. It might be different case here if had real possibility for either Status to turn back to Bearish or market to go to concurrent mode sometime next day or two; however, in this instance there was simply no chance of either of these happening any time soon. To get either Bearish Status or a concurrent mode to downside, the SL would have had to go below zero, and at moment it was plus twenty-six and picking up speed to upside. Therefore, unless price absolutely collapsed, the SL would not go below zero for at least week or so, meaning being short here in "anticipation" of this was simply dead wrong (no matter what price did from here).

In trading it is important to focus energy on trading "correctly." By correctly I mean according to probabilities based on natural laws. We cannot control the outcome since the future is unknown; however, we can control how we act in preparation for this unknown future. Strive to trade intelligently (follow the "rules") rather than trying be "right." In the long run I believe it is better to take the correct action and end up being wrong than to take the incorrect action and be right. Not good to reinforce incorrect action. Work at conditioning intelligent action regardless of situation and result. Sticking with shorts here may have turned out to have been the right action; however, regardless of this, doing so was incorrect (because upside momentum was just too strong with little chance of this changing soon).

I made a lot of mistakes in this market over previous week, mistakes I should have been able to avoid. Knowing is not enough in this game. Have to do!

01/11/2002

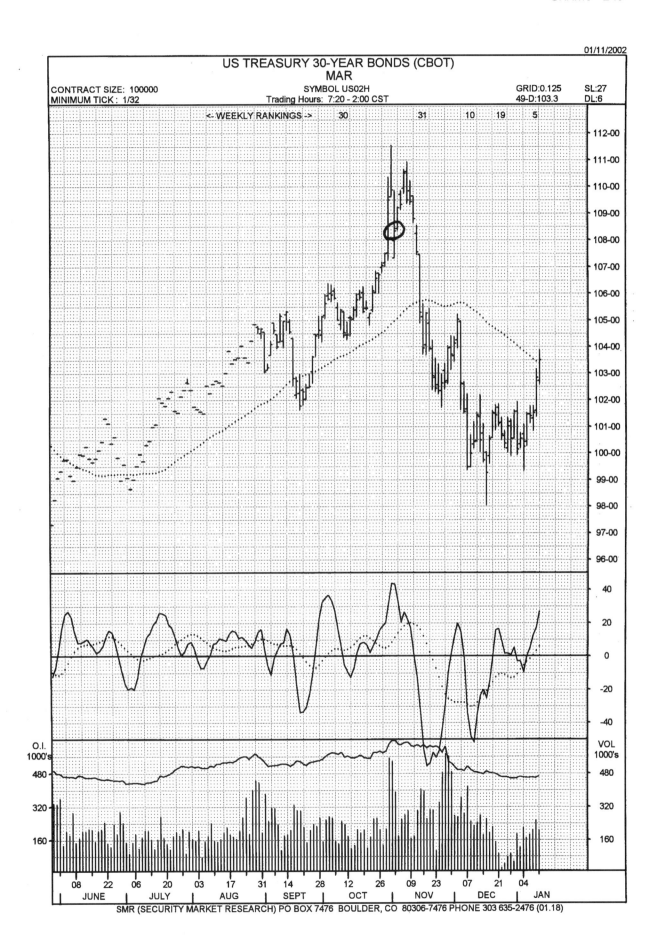

US TREASURY 30-YEAR BONDS (CBOT)
MAR

CONTRACT SIZE: 100000
MINIMUM TICK : 1/32

SYMBOL US02H
Trading Hours: 7:20 - 2:00 CST

GRID:0.125    SL:27
49-D:103.3    DL:6

<- WEEKLY RANKINGS ->

SMR (SECURITY MARKET RESEARCH) PO BOX 7476  BOULDER, CO  80306-7476  PHONE 303 635-2476 (01.18)

# March 2002 Bonds (Jan 14)

## REAL-TIME COMMENTARY

**1/14 (Monday):** Mar Bonds - Status - Neutral. Trend down but ML up so market remains in crosscurrent mode. Action neutral to slightly negative on minor downside reversal. On straight line basis picture too mixed to be in here since trend too negative to be/go long but momentum too positive to be/go short. However, anytime trend as solidly down as is here at moment and both price and SL on recent highs (as are at moment), can always make case for light shorts on "attractive" price basis. Although unless sell off sharply now, it will be difficult for lines to turn negative again for at least another week or two. Clearly made mistake suggesting anticipation shorts here several days ago as rally just too strong. Should have respected third higher low in SL and up cycle in ML more than did. So far Greenspan effect (fading Greenspan comment inspired day or two moves) working marginally, but unless sells off sharply next day or two, should disregard this factor (if not sooner, since these types of considerations simply not reliable enough to trade off of). So lines say sidelines and unless down sharply and quickly tomorrow, would have to agree with that now, regardless of down-trend and high price and SL. Bottom line: Lines say sidelines; if short on "attractive" price basis, would now use stops just above 104.00 since any continuation of up move from here would be sign market just too strong to be short in spite of trend.

......................

## AFTER-ACTION CRITIQUE

I finally came to my senses and realized the error of my ways. This was not a situation where I would want to be or go short. Remember the "mistake" rule: Once you realize you have clearly made a mistake and should not be in a trade, then just correct this immediately by getting out at the market. Do not try to save a few points by getting a slightly better price; just take your medicine, get out, and move on to the next good probability trade. Staying in "bad" trades is twice wrong: First, when "stuck" in a market, by definition you are fighting price energy flow and odds favor this flow continuing; Second, "bad" trades tend to monopolize a trader's time, attention and, most importantly, energy. Bad trades are like rotten apples in a barrel; they tend to contaminate the good ones.

As soon as price closed above 102.16 (couple days ago here), this left a big four-week "island" down below (from 99.16 up to 101.16), and these types of chart formations frequently signal meaningful bottoms. Therefore, in addition to the very strong momentum indicators I disregarded the previous few days, I also had the price chart showing clear positive signs. However, at least I finally realized I had been wrong sticking with shorts and acted to correct this. It is OK to be wrong; just do not stay wrong for long. As individual traders, our resources are—by definition—limited; therefore, we have to make sure to conserve them. The "market" has unlimited resources; fight it for too long and it will always beat you.

The correct action here was sidelines. The trend remained too negative to consider long side, but momentum was still too positive to be/go short. That was the situation back a week ago, and was still the situation here. Sidelines was correct then and was still correct. When you make a mistake try to learn from it, resolve to do better, and then go on with your trading life.

01/14/2002

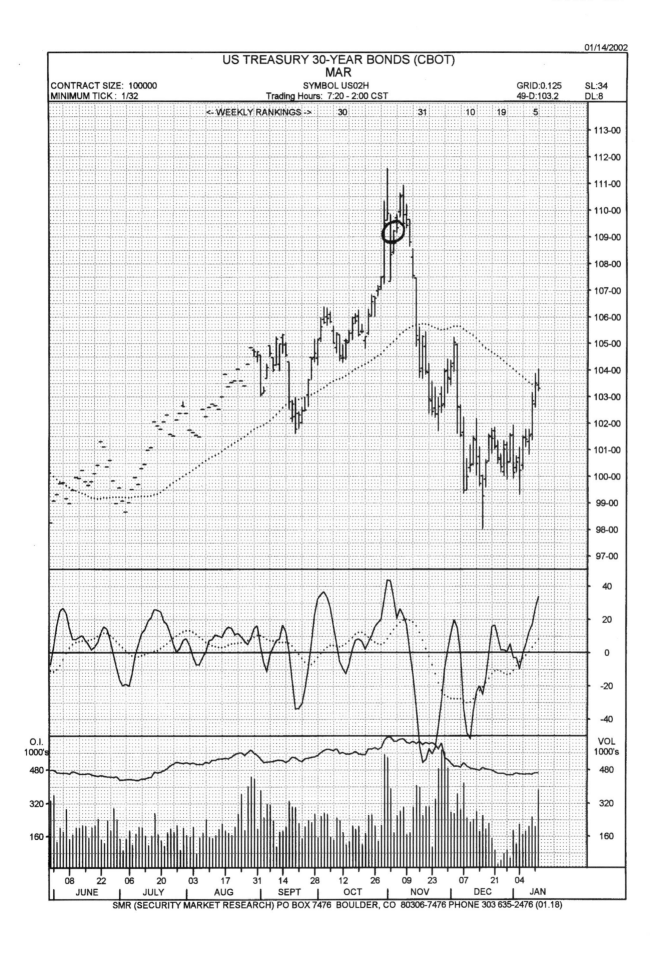

US TREASURY 30-YEAR BONDS (CBOT)
MAR

| CONTRACT SIZE:  100000 | SYMBOL US02H | GRID:0.125 | SL:34 |
| MINIMUM TICK : 1/32 | Trading Hours: 7:20 - 2:00 CST | 49-D:103.2 | DL:8 |

<- WEEKLY RANKINGS ->    30         31      10      19      5

SMR (SECURITY MARKET RESEARCH) PO BOX 7476  BOULDER, CO  80306-7476  PHONE 303 635-2476 (01.18)

# March 2002 Bonds (Jan 15)

**REAL-TIME COMMENTARY**

**1/15 (Tuesday):** Mar Bonds - Status - Neutral. Trend down but ML up so market remains in crosscurrent mode. Action quite positive as made and closed at new recent highs. Picture very mixed here at moment since trend still clearly down and both price and SL on recent highs, but ML on solid up cycle and action persistently positive at moment. Have misread this market past few days since once it closed near 103.00 area it left an "island" down below and turned momentum too positive to consider shorts. If downside is still any good, should start to see some weakness, but will now take quite a bit on downside (both in terms of time and price) to turn pattern legitimately negative enough to go short again. So picture here at moment is that trend still too negative to justify longs, but momentum (and action) too positive to justify shorts. Bottom line: Sidelines.

......................

**AFTER-ACTION CRITIQUE**

Normally when have a market in as strong a downtrend as had here, will not see much in way of sustained upside price energy. However, when you are going on probabilities and not certainties, this means there are going to be a fair number of exceptions, and this was one. However, it is important to point out that since price closed at 101.16 (six market days earlier on this chart), the Status had been Neutral and the mode had been crosscurrent; therefore, the lines had been right. What I really did wrong was my over anticipating a change back to Bearish and Concurrent mode to downside.

When anticipating, have to keep it under control. As a rule, do not want to anticipate more than a day or two ahead. Anticipate much more than that and you are counting on too much. It is a little like driving down the highway; do not want to look too far ahead, just a little.

Over the years I have found that when I take a bad "hit" (not only a loss but miscalculations all around) such as took in this market at this time, it is best to just leave that particular market alone for a while. It is almost impossible to wipe the psychological slate clean after a bad experience in a market, and the leftover baggage will tend to distort vision and affect action on the next trade in that market. Therefore, if you know in advance that you will most likely not see clearly and act decisively, then it is best to leave that market alone for a while. One great factor of trading is there are many different markets to trade. They are all open every day. Leaving one market alone for a while is no sacrifice; in fact, after a bad experience, doing so is a gift to yourself.

After a bad experience like prior week or so here, I would not make a trade in Bonds until—and unless—the overall picture was quite clear. Therefore, since situation remained the same as had been past week or so—trend still too negative for longs, momentum too positive for shorts—it was no problem putting this one aside for a while.

01/15/2002

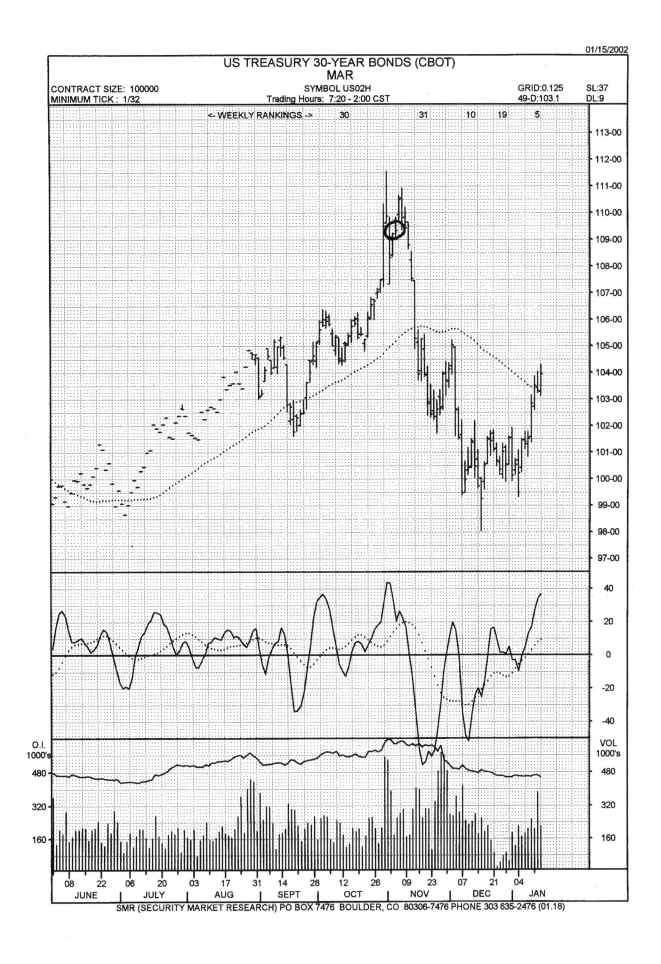

US TREASURY 30-YEAR BONDS (CBOT)
MAR

CONTRACT SIZE:  100000
MINIMUM TICK : 1/32

SYMBOL US02H
Trading Hours: 7:20 - 2:00 CST

GRID:0.125
49-D:103.1

SL:37
DL:9

<- WEEKLY RANKINGS ->

SMR (SECURITY MARKET RESEARCH) PO BOX 7476  BOULDER, CO  80306-7476  PHONE 303 635-2476 (01.18)

# March 2002 Bonds (Feb 15)

**2/15:** Sticking to the sidelines for the next month or so was the right idea. While there were several moderate momentum moves over this time period, a trader would have had to be fairly nimble to profit from them. The most reliable indicator during this essentially non trending period was the SL. It made a couple of week-and-a-half swings in both directions, with each one corresponding to about a two-point move in the price. While this is a good move for a short-term trade in this market, actually capturing profits of that size would not have been as easy as it might look. All but the most aggressive and focused traders are better off just passing on a market when its trend and intermediate-term momentum are as indecisive as they were the past month here.

A long-term trader would have had some difficulty here. While the market made a sustained up move from the first of July until mid-November, once it topped out it sold off fast and dramatically. Waiting only a day or two too long to liquidate long-term long positions would have cut profits substantially. I have found long-term traders tend to get locked into their positions when the trend has lasted a long time. It is not easy to hold for months on end through all sorts of price gyrations and then suddenly have the energy and guts to liquidate on a major sell off, and especially just a few days after the price was substantially higher. It is a rare trader who in a few days can shift from being a committed, stubborn long (for over a half year) with market acting as bullish as can be to suddenly running for the sidelines with the market in total collapse. The temptation is great to hold on for another day or so in hopes of getting a better price to liquidate longs. From my observations, once a trader does not get out when he "should" (i.e., as soon as trend and line pattern turn in the other direction), it becomes extremely difficult to then get out at an even worse price in the days that follow.

I believe if you are going to use the long-term (based on trend) trading approach, then it is necessary to pay particular attention to the cycles of the ML. If long-term trading, I believe a trader needs to get out of most or all his positions whenever the ML turns solidly against the trend. Even when this turns out to be a "false" signal (i.e., down move in price does not turn the trend), my experience is you will not miss much, if any, of trending move. However, when an against-trend cycle in ML does result in an eventual change in trend, you will save substantial amount of profits. In other words, I believe long-term traders should primarily be "concurrent mode" traders rather than just "trend" traders. While this will involve more in-and-out trading, I believe it will also produce substantially better results as well as make trading somewhat easier from a psychological point of view. If convinced or adamant about the trend move, then simply reduce with-trend positions instead of liquidating entire holdings. When in concurrent mode, go to maximum position, and when market goes to crosscurrent mode, reduce to a minimum position, then as price moves against trend can gradually rebuild your long-term, with-the-trend position. Point is I simply do not believe just sticking with long-term moving averages is a good enough approach. I believe you have to add in intermediate-term momentum.

This was about as poor a read and trading of a market as I tend to do. I included it here solely as a good example of how easy it is to get off track, even when a trader knows the "correct" way to trade. Knowing is never enough; you also must act on what you know.

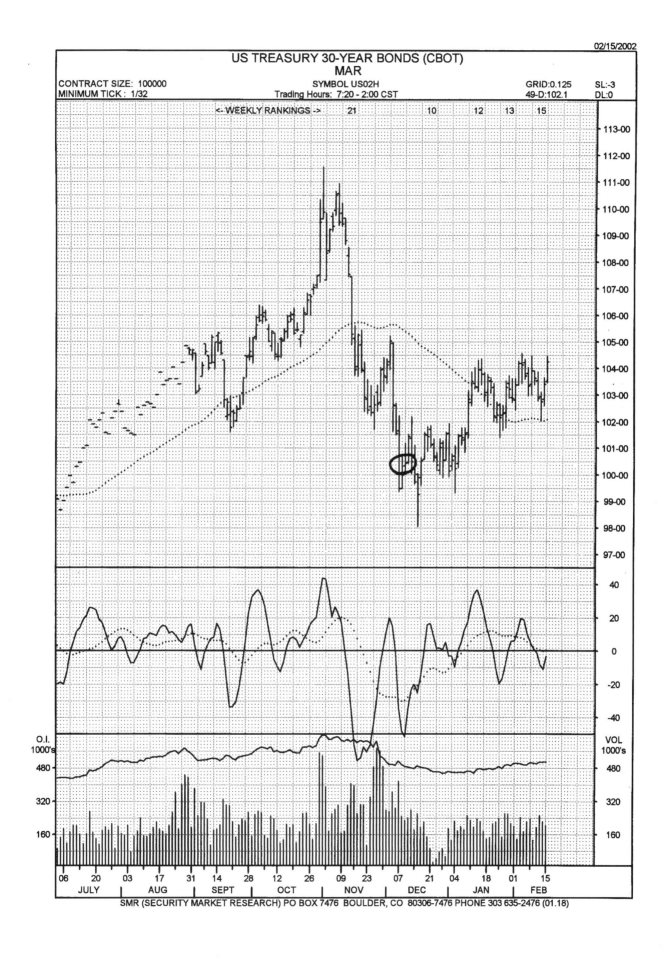

SMR (SECURITY MARKET RESEARCH) PO BOX 7476 BOULDER, CO 80306-7476 PHONE 303 635-2476 (01.18)

# Put/Call Ratios on Stock Market

WHILE I STRONGLY ADVISE AGAINST BUYING OPTIONS, what option buyers are doing can be helpful in timing stock market trades. The simplest way to measure the activity of option buyers is by the daily volume in puts and calls. Some option experts have elaborate formulas for measuring not only option volume but also the comparable prices of puts and calls. However, I have found that in options, as in most of the rest of trading, "simple" works best for the individual trader. Simply tracking daily option volume has been a reasonably reliable indicator of extreme activity (and thus potential turning points) in the past, and I expect it will continue to be in the future.

Options are traded on both individual stocks and on stock indexes. Over the years I have found the data on individual stocks tends to be more reliable at measuring extremes than those on stock indexes, although when both are in agreement reliability does increase. The basic way to measure put/call activity is to compare the daily volume of puts to calls, i.e., the "put/call ratio." The put/call ratio is devised by dividing the volume of puts on all individual stocks by the volume of calls. For example, a put/call ratio of .50 would indicate there were 50 puts traded for every 100 calls. Every day the Chicago Board of Options Exchange (CBOE) compiles and publishes the total volume of options (puts and calls) traded on all individual stocks. The basic put/call ratio "theory" is to watch this volume activity, and whenever it gets "too extreme" in one direction, then treat this as a sign of imminent price reversal. What this means is that if an unusually high number of calls are being traded, then you should expect the price to go down, and vice versa.

Polls of American voters have consistently shown that they hold their individual Member of Congress in higher regard than the Congress as a whole. The data on put/call ratios is the same. On individual stocks, invariably more calls than puts will be bought and sold (i.e., traded); however, the exact opposite is true on stock indexes (invariably more puts than calls will be traded). Therefore, individuals generally are more positive on specific stocks than they are on the market as a whole. What this means is that there will almost always be more calls than puts traded on individual stocks, but there usually will be more puts than calls traded on the stock indexes.

While I have not kept detailed statistics of put/call ratios, I have been following them for long enough (twenty-plus years) to devise parameters as to what is extreme and what is neutral. For individual stocks (reported daily on the CBOE Web site as the put/call ratio) I consider a .70 ratio to be neutral—.70 means there were 70 puts traded for every 100 calls. I have found the "extremes" of the put/call ratio to be .50 or lower, or .90 or higher. In other words, whenever the CBOE put/call ratio reaches .50 or lower, this indicates that an extreme number of calls are being traded versus puts, which in turn is an indication that bullishness has reached an extreme (and presumably unsustainable) level. Conversely, whenever the CBOE put/call ratio reaches .90 or higher, this indicates an extreme number of puts are being traded versus calls, which in turn is an indication that bearishness has reached an extreme (and presumably unsustainable) level.

I have found that once the put/call ratio hits an extreme it will rarely stay there for more than a couple days. The reason for this is simply that prices will invariably reverse direction after a couple of days of extreme put/call ratios, and once this happens it will change the extreme market psychology that produced the high number of puts or calls being traded in the first place. The basic theory of why the put/call ratio works is that option buyers are habitually wrong. While historical data shows this to be true, it is important to know why this is so.

Traders buy options (puts or calls) as a substitute for the actual stock (or future). Buyers of calls tend to be those who cannot afford to buy the actual shares, or prefer not to commit the funds to buy more shares (since options are much "cheaper"—100 shares can be controlled with much less money). For example, someone may already own 1000 shares of IBM but not have enough funds to buy another 100 shares. Therefore, if they become very bullish (usually due to the price moving up) and want to own more, what they will do is buy some call options instead. So, when an excessive number of calls are being bought (i.e., traded), this is an indication that there is not much real or underlying buying power or demand left for the actual shares, and as a result the price will soon start to go down.

The opposite is true on the downside with puts. Say this same individual is long-term bullish on IBM but due to recent weakness in the market in general and/or IBM in particular he becomes fearful of potential near-term weakness. Rather than sell any of his shares, what he might do instead is buy some puts. In doing this he will have protected himself from any further downside action, i.e., he will have taken out "insurance" on the downside and thus have no need to actually sell any of his shares. Therefore, when an extreme number of puts have been bought (i.e., traded), this indicates that much fewer actual shares of stock will be sold and thus selling pressure will naturally begin to decrease. As a result the price will turn up.

Another group of option buyers are those traders with insufficient funds to buy the underlying market. Naturally, since options are inherently a "bad" trade (as mentioned earlier, when you buy an option you are starting the trade with a handicap), people with substantial funds will simply buy or sell the underlying market and ignore the options. Therefore, by definition, many (most?) option buyers have little capital. And again, by definition, traders with little capital tend to be unsuccessful traders, and unsuccessful traders tend to be wrong more than right.

Therefore, if you combine the fact that buyers of options tend to be poor traders along with the fact that the buying of puts and calls tends to lessen either selling or buying pressure for the underlying market (be it individual stocks, stock indexes or futures markets), then you have the reasons why extremes in the put/call ratio tend to be reliable indicators that an existing big price move is close to ending and turning in the other direction, at least temporarily (i.e., for the next few weeks or month). So, whenever extreme levels of put or call buying are seen, it is wise to take a more sober look at the current technical situation and look for reasons to take profits and go to the sidelines temporarily (or, if very aggressive, go the other way).

## BOTTOM LINE ON CBOE PUT/CALL RATIOS

.70 is a neutral number; .90 or higher is a bullish number and indicates bearishness at extreme and most likely unsustainable levels; .50 or lower is a bearish number and indicates bullishness at extreme and most likely unsustainable levels. In Index Options, doing 50,000 more Puts than Calls is about neutral. Anytime do more Calls than Puts it is bearish, and 100,000 or more Puts is bullish.

## THE STOCK MARKET IS DIFFERENT FROM OTHER MARKETS

While superficially the same as other futures markets, there is no doubt that the stock market is different. The primary difference is the imbalance between the forces seeking higher prices and those seeking lower prices. In every commodity market there are powerful producers or suppliers of that commodity desiring higher prices as well as powerful consumers or users of that commodity seeking lower prices. However, in the stock market all of the powerful forces are on the side seeking (hoping) for higher prices.

The companies whose shares are traded on the stock exchanges naturally want their stock prices to go up. The brokerage industry also wants higher prices because bull markets produce more business than bear markets. In addition, there are thousands of mutual funds who almost exclusively want prices to go higher (although there are a few "bear" funds as well as hedge funds which from time to time go short). Finally, and possibly most importantly, there is the federal government that also wants stock prices to go up. Politicians tend to be reelected much more easily when stock prices are moving up than when they are going down. In addition, higher stock prices tend to produce a "wealth effect" that adds to economic growth, and naturally any government prefers growth to contraction. On the other side of the ledger, the only "forces" desiring lower stock prices are traders who might happen to be short at any one time. Therefore, the balance of power between those seeking higher stock prices and those desiring lower prices will always be overwhelmingly in favor of the bulls.

There is also a natural tendency for stock prices to rise over time due to the fact that in a growing economy (and the U.S. economy has always grown over time), corporations, and the value of their shares, will also grow. These forces seeking higher prices, plus the natural tendency of prices to rise over time, are important factors to keep in mind when trading the stock futures indexes. Therefore, if you are going to have a built-in bias on stocks, it is better for it to be bullish rather than bearish.

There is one other outside factor to consider when trading the stock index futures and that is the increasing circumstantial evidence that the government actively intervenes in the stock market whenever there appears to be any chance of a confidence-shattering "crash." I have no way of "knowing" whether the Federal Reserve and/or U.S. Treasury come in and buy S&P and/or Dow futures whenever the stock market appears to be on the brink of collapse; however, I do know that for many years it is apparent that this indeed does happen. I, and most other close observers, feel certain this happened in the day or two after the market crash in October 1987. I believe that this first stock market intervention was so successful that starting around 1994 (about the time the veteran of Wall Street, Robert Rubin, became Secretary of the Treasury) it became a standard procedure, and has been used increasingly since.

Published reports (in the *New York Post* and *London Guardian*, among others) have called the Treasury Department unit that apparently does these periodic stock market interventions the "plunge prevention team." This has a ring of truth to it since it would be typical of the government to use this kind of euphemism. The government would never call such a unit the "crash prevention team." Instead they would use a more neutral word, like "plunge."

There is no question that all governments periodically intervene in the currency markets. There is also no question that the government periodically intervenes in the interest rate markets. This is one way in which the Federal Reserve adds and subtracts liquidity from the financial system. Therefore, it is only logical that it would be in the national interest to make sure the U.S. never again experiences a truly confidence shattering stock market crash, and one way to prevent this would be to intervene in the stock futures.

Now, it is perfectly understandable why politicians and government bureaucrats would like to act in this manner, i.e., intervene in markets to ensure stability. No doubt the vast majority of Americans feel this type of behavior is not only acceptable but also correct. The problem for us individual traders is that this type of activity totally disrupts the natural flow of price movement. In addition, I believe in the long run it is probably counterproductive. However, politicians consider the "long run" the next election cycle and so see little or no problem in "fixing" things just enough to get them successfully through the next election.

Before the advent of the futures markets, government intervention in the stock market would have been very difficult, if not impossible. However, with futures it is extremely easy. Heavy and aggressive buying of S&P and Dow futures at critical times could easily turn a selling panic into a sharp short-covering rally. It would only be necessary to maintain this buying for a day or two before the feeling of panic passed and natural momentum forces took over. Then, once the market had stabilized, the government could gradually liquidate their long futures positions and stand by ready to intervene in the next selling panic. Of course, this type of government intervention would never be able to prevent an eventual decline in stock prices; however, there is no question it could easily dictate the nature of the decline (i.e., its timing and speed).

Personally, I wish they (the government) would just leave the markets alone and let natural forces play themselves out; let nature take its course. However, what I believe is not important; what is important is reality. While I cannot "know" the truth of this probable periodic government intervention in the stock futures markets, I can say that there have been many instances where this is exactly what appeared to happen.

It is unfortunate that this type of information (the fact, and timing, of government intervention in the stock market) is shared among only a privileged few, and I have no doubt these few use this information for personal profit; however, it is hard to see how government intervention of this nature could ever be publicly acknowledged. So, when and if short the stock futures indexes and the hint of panic is in the air, be forewarned; the U.S. government might be about ready to save it. When—and if—they do come in to save it, they do so with great vigor (by buying seemingly limitless blocks of hundred contracts at a time in the S&P and Dow). This buying runs the futures to good-sized premiums over the cash, which in turn prompts program traders to come in and simultaneously sell futures and buy the actual stocks. This in turn pushes the actual stock prices up. Once both futures and stock prices start to reverse to the upside, then momentum traders start to cover shorts and go long, which also boosts stock prices.

The final net result is that heavy buying of the futures by the government's "plunge prevention team" can and will fairly easily turn a potential selling panic into a sharp, bear-market rally—and only those doing the business will know what really happened (and they have no incentive to publicize this government activity since they profit so much from it).

# March 2002 S&P (Jan 2)

## REAL-TIME COMMENTARY

**1/2 (Wednesday):** Mar S&P - Status - Neutral (to Bullish). Trend still clearly up but ML slightly down so market remains in crosscurrent mode. However, action today quite positive as came back well from early weakness, and while did not make back all lost on Monday, came close. So pattern remains neutral but now tilting back to upside and if holds here (or higher) next few days, will get decent "line" buy signal (as would go to concurrent mode to upside). Have favored short side past couple of days but have to cancel that after today since when going against trend have to be ready to "run" quickly whenever get any solid with-trend action, and had that today. Very tough call here at moment since recent action and line pattern (past few weeks) has been very indecisive as just cannot get anything sustained in either direction. My personal "bias" is to downside since hard for me to believe have made major bottom in stocks, but personal bias rarely beats the "lines" and lines much closer to being solidly positive here than vice versa. If can avoid selling off much over next few days, pattern will go to concurrent to upside, and whenever this the case odds clearly favor upside. Therefore, would cover any against-trend shorts as can now make decent case for "anticipation" buys (but still couple of days from getting "official" buy). Bottom line: Lines say sidelines and recent action so mixed hard to argue with this, but can make case for "anticipation" longs with stops in 1142.00 to 1144.00 area.

......................

## AFTER-ACTION CRITIQUE

Before I get into day-by-day review here, take a look back on chart to late August and you will see where the market gave a clear "line"-pattern sell signal in the 1175.00 area (basis March, although was trading the September contract at the time). I had been pushing the short side for a couple of months (after trend turned clearly down), and once SL turned down, pressure remained consistent to downside for a couple weeks. Therefore, when 9/11/2001 came along, the market was in a solid Bearish Status and concurrent mode to downside. While the tragic events of 9/11 were obviously not predictable in this case, following the trend and momentum would have had you positioned in the right direction. Stock market was closed for several days after 9/11, but when it reopened it quite naturally gapped sharply lower. This was a "with-the-trend, news-related" down spike and so would have been expected to continue for at least a while. Prices pushed sharply lower for five market days before turning up. At its lows the existing Bearish Status had produced profits in excess of 200 percent of margin. It is also interesting to note that on the last two days of the sell-off (9/20 and 9/21) the CBOE put/call ratio climbed to extreme high levels (1.20 area on both days, which are as high as have seen in many years). However, at the time I tended to disregard this and suggested sticking with shorts. Unfortunately this proved to be the wrong advice. Regardless, within a few days after the lows on 9/21 the Status turned back to Neutral and the mode turned to crosscurrent (since SL was moving up and ML turned up). Therefore, if going strictly by the line patterns, would have covered shorts for big profits, and if had allowed the extremely bullish put/call ratios (and the profits being in excess of 200 percent of margin) to prompt covering of shorts, the profits would have been even greater (and would have occurred almost exactly on the lows). The events of 9/11 were tragic, but life goes on. And if you are going to be a trader, you have to deal with any events that affect markets, regardless of personal feelings. What is significant here, from a trading standpoint, is that the basic laws and rules applied even in this extreme case.

01/02/2002

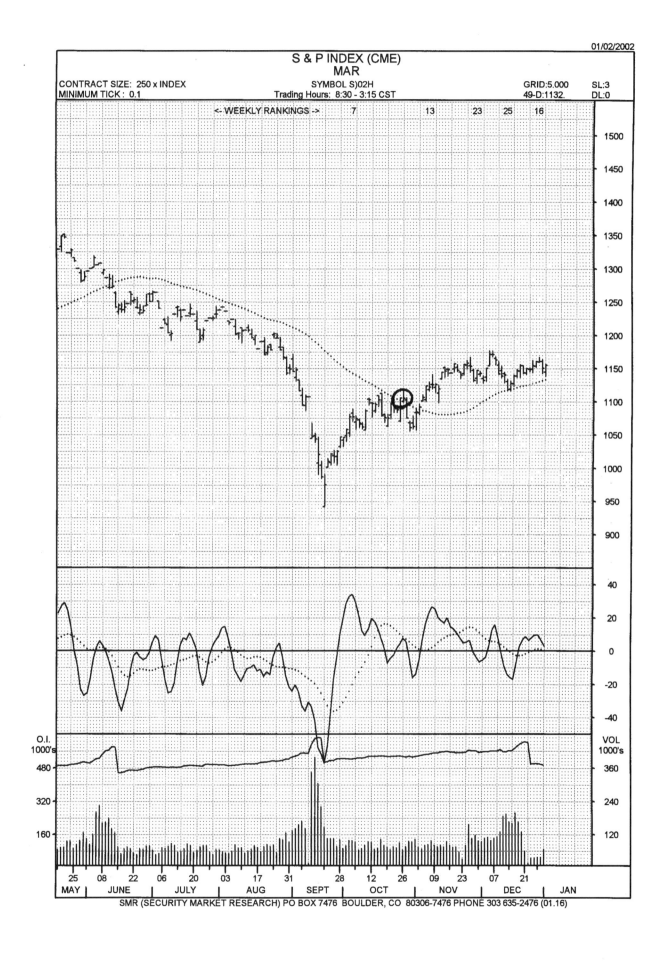

# March 2002 S&P (Jan 3)

**REAL-TIME COMMENTARY**

**1/3 (Thursday):** Mar S&P - Status - Neutral (to Bullish). Trend somewhat up but ML sideways so market still in crosscurrent mode; however, on verge of going clearly concurrent tomorrow as long as not down sharply. Action quite positive again today on good up day with virtually nothing in way of intra-day downside pressure. Price now back up in area where up move has failed several times over past several months, so at a key chart point. On straight line basis have trend mildly positive and other two lines sideways, but all three are on verge of being clearly to upside if can get any kind of decent strength tomorrow. Have major monthly report (employment) and this report can move market. Expectations are for it to show continued weakness in economy (show increasing amount of unemployment), but have always found markets tend to "know" what reports will be in advance and today's positive action indicates report will be benign, and even if negative (for stocks), effect will be temporary. At moment market looking beyond any short-term weakness in economy, and until this changes, negative reports will most likely not have any kind of lasting effect. Bottom line: Lines still say sidelines but continue to prefer "anticipation" longs with stops now 1155.00 (not entered until at least an hour after open to avoid any short-term extreme reactions to report).

......................

**AFTER-ACTION CRITIQUE**

Now let's go to the day-by-day review. The trend here was clearly up, although not solidly so. The reason I expected the market to go to solid concurrent mode very soon was that I could look back three weeks earlier to where the SL was and see that for next week would be taking off numbers below zero. Therefore, unless price turned down sharply here (and thus turned the SL down sharply), the ML would be in an up cycle for a "while." I had suggested anticipation longs in the previous day's letter and stuck with that recommendation here. Interesting to note that would have been able to buy at unchanged on this day, and this would have been just about as good an entry price as could have gotten.

Another positive here was the SL was turning up from a definite higher low and this is always at least a short-term positive. Therefore, while none of the three trend/momentum indicators were solidly positive here, all three were close to being up and so anticipation longs would have been fully justified.

The monthly unemployment report is released on the first Friday of every month. This is a major report and can produce sharp moves immediately after its release. While some traders prefer to go to the sidelines for major reports, I have found that most of the time the market will continue to move in current direction of trend/momentum, regardless of what reports say. Furthermore, even when a report does produce some counter-trend/momentum action, this move will usually be temporary. (Remember the spike rule: Against-the-trend, news-related market moves tend to be quickly retraced.) I selected the 1155.00 area for the stop point since a move to that level would have retraced all of this day's gain and would have been quite negative action because it would have set up the potential for a quick turn back down in the SL (and this would have been "too" negative).

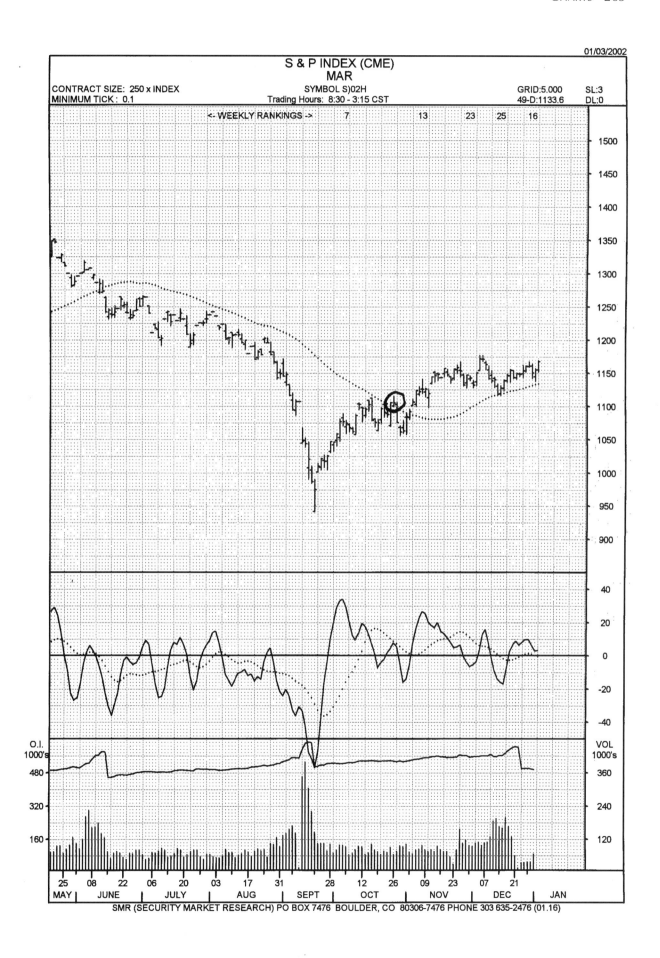

01/03/2002

S & P INDEX (CME)
MAR

CONTRACT SIZE: 250 x INDEX
MINIMUM TICK : 0.1

SYMBOL S)02H
Trading Hours: 8:30 - 3:15 CST

GRID:5.000
49-D:1133.6

SL:3
DL:0

<- WEEKLY RANKINGS ->      7        13        23    25    16

SMR (SECURITY MARKET RESEARCH) PO BOX 7476  BOULDER, CO  80306-7476  PHONE 303 635-2476 (01.16)

# March 2002 S&P (Jan 4)

**REAL-TIME COMMENTARY**

**1/4 (Friday):** Mar S&P - Status - Bullish. Trend and ML both now up so market in concurrent mode to upside. SL turned up from a higher low, which is a positive. Action fairly positive although the high's were made early and action not so positive after that; however, market did close on firm side. On a straight line basis picture fairly positive, so fully justifies being long here. Still have some doubts about upside potential in this market, but all three lines up and no signs of any kind of top so have to give upside more chance. COT slightly more negative than has been, but nothing extreme. Bottom line: Can be long with stops still 1155.00.

........................

**AFTER-ACTION CRITIQUE**

Evidently no negative reaction to the monthly employment report. As I recall, all signs of a weak economy at this time were being discounted since any weakness was still being attributed to a reaction to the 9/11 atrocity.

Therefore, the technical picture at this time was clearly positive (all three lines moderately up, with nothing overdone to upside). In checking back, the put/call ratios were running solidly neutral here as were in the .67 to .78 area and were doing around 50,000 more puts than calls in the index options. All of this meant could fully justify being long. I continued to use the same stop level since a move back down to that level would have been far too negative to stay long. Since the buy signal had just kicked in, the trade was nowhere near the 50 percent of margin profit area.

It is interesting to note if look back to last week of October (right at ten week ago "circle" on the chart), you will notice that the market was still in a downtrend, ML was on a good down cycle, and SL had made three lower lows—meaning the line pattern was solidly negative. However, after only two days down, the market steadied and then started to move up. The point here is that when have a clearly negative technical picture, yet the price does not move as "should" (i.e., according to the line pattern), then you should consider this a definite warning sign and be prepared to get out of the trade fairly quickly. When I look at the daily price "action" of a market, I am looking at two things: first, whether the intra-day pressure was primarily up or down, as well as whether it closed nearer highs or lows; and, second, looking to see how price acts in relation to what the trend/momentum lines indicate it should act. At the end of October this market had a solidly negative line pattern with neutral put/call ratios (I checked), yet the price could not move down; in fact it moved up. At the time I considered this surprisingly positive action as very meaningful and indicating that the market had essentially finished with downside for the time being (and this indeed proved to be the case). Therefore, always look both at how a market price acts on straight positive/negative basis and how it acts in relation to how the lines and/or price chart indicate it "should" act. Once again, it is usually the unexpected price action that tends to be the most meaningful.

01/04/2002

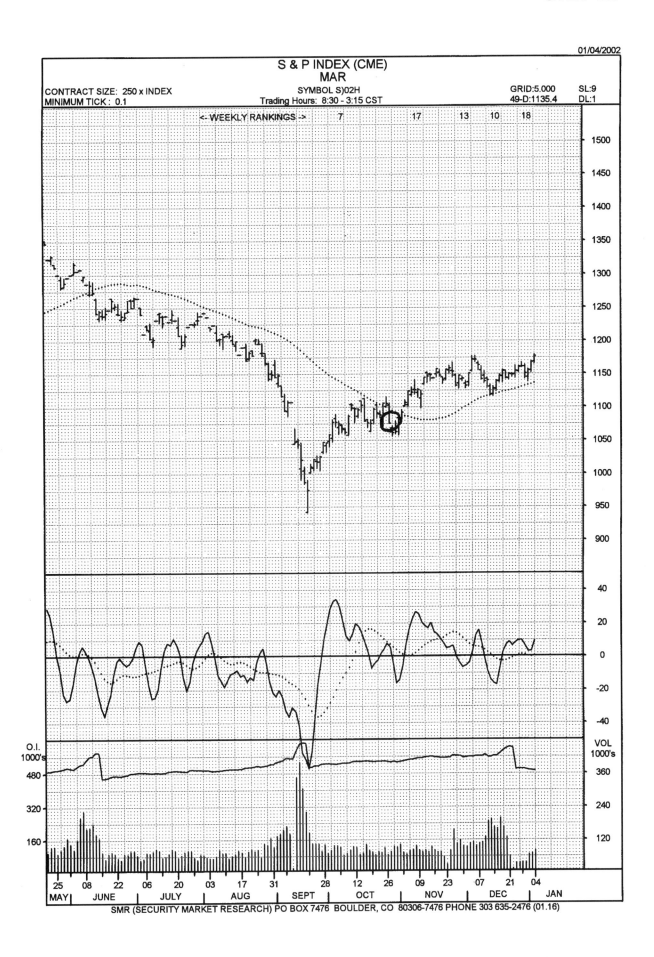

# S & P INDEX (CME)
## MAR

| CONTRACT SIZE: 250 x INDEX | SYMBOL S)02H | GRID:5.000 | SL:9 |
| MINIMUM TICK: 0.1 | Trading Hours: 8:30 - 3:15 CST | 49-D:1135.4 | DL:1 |

<- WEEKLY RANKINGS ->    7    17    13   10   18

1500
1450
1400
1350
1300
1250
1200
1150
1100
1050
1000
950
900

40
20
0
-20
-40

O.I.
1000's

480

VOL
1000's

360
240
120

160
320

| 25 | 08 | 22 | 06 | 20 | 03 | 17 | 31 | 28 | 12 | 26 | 09 | 23 | 07 | 21 | 04 |
| MAY | JUNE | | JULY | | AUG | | SEPT | | OCT | | NOV | | DEC | | JAN |

SMR (SECURITY MARKET RESEARCH) PO BOX 7476 BOULDER, CO 80306-7476 PHONE 303 635-2476 (01.16)

# March 2002 S&P (Jan 7)

## REAL-TIME COMMENTARY

**1/7 (Monday):** Mar S&P - Status - Bullish (to Neutral). Both trend and ML up so market remains in moderate concurrent mode to upside. SL up but not yet able to make clear higher high so pattern still only moderately positive. Action today on negative side but not decisively so. Market was vulnerable to minor downside pressure and so far that is all had today; however, would not want to see any pick up in downside energy tomorrow. Still have some doubts about how much this market can move up from here since the uptrend from lows of late September has been somewhat labored, plus still have a question of how good a bottom was made. However, at moment all three lines up and none of them over extended to upside, so odds still favor higher. Not a pattern would be heavily long, but clearly positive enough to be long (although would not go long right here as do not see risk/reward or odds as good enough). Bottom line: Can be long with stops still 1155.00 (preferably on close basis).

........................

## AFTER-ACTION CRITIQUE

Action on this day was clearly a little negative since had all three lines up so "should" have been up, and was down instead. Also, the down day took back all made on previous good up day and this never a good sign. As mentioned above (in daily letter), the failure of the SL to make a decisive higher high (than the previous high a week earlier) was also a somewhat negative sign. However, markets do not move in perfect accord with the lines and so always have to give them some leeway—meaning, while had some cause for concern about long side here, so far these concerns were not really enough to get out of longs.

The concerns I had at the time about the solidness of the uptrend were primarily related to the fact that the uptrend was clearly not as strong as the preceding downtrend had been weak. When a market makes a true reversal of trend, its angle of ascent (when go from downtrend to up) will usually be at least as great, or preferably greater, than the angle of descent of its preceding downtrend. In this case the opposite was true; therefore, this provided some cause for concern about the solidity of this uptrend.

If look back on chart at the period after September 21, you will see that the turn up in the SL was extremely sharp. (It went from a low of about -65 to a high of about +32 in slightly less than two weeks.) This was a clear sign that the down move was over for at least the next few weeks. (Although I did not fully recognize it at the time, I was too bearish.) In addition, if the market had still been solidly bearish, the SL should not have moved much, or at all, above zero. It is also important to note how after the lows were made on September 21, the ML turned up sharply. I have usually found that the price will not move much against a solidly cycling ML, regardless of what the trend may be. This is why I suggest treating any with-trend trades that are against a solidly cycling ML (such as the crosscurrent sell signal given when the SL turned down from +32 around the first of October) as very short-term and less reliable. Interesting to note that that sell signal only produced a minor down move and only lasted for a few days. While not perfect, the lines will almost always give good clues about what is coming over next; the trick is to be able to read these clues as they happen in real time, and then act on what you see.

01/07/2002

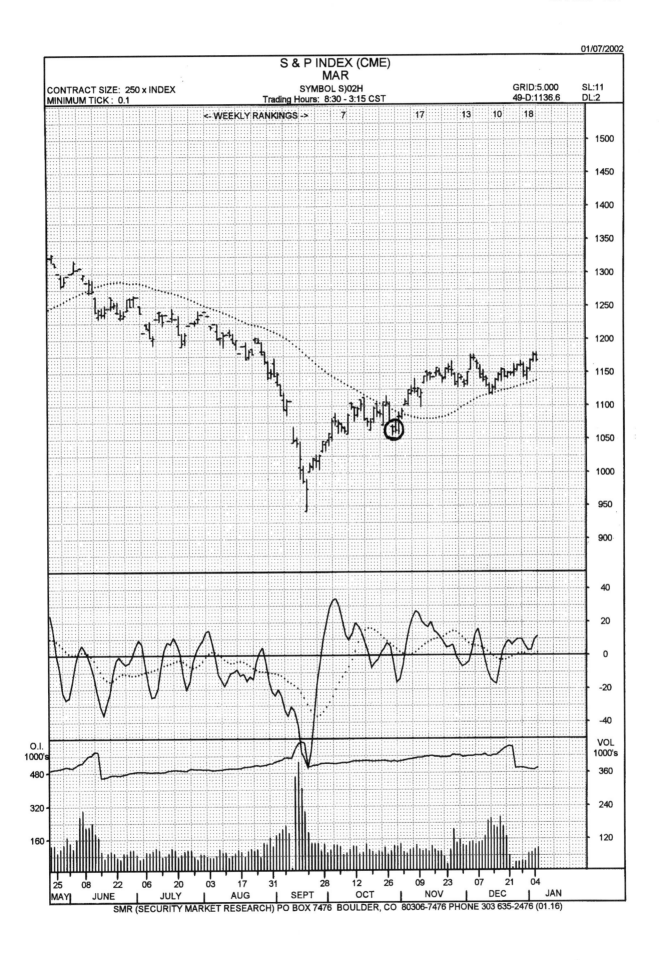

# March 2002 S&P (Jan 8)

## REAL-TIME COMMENTARY

**1/8 (Tuesday):** Mar S&P - Status - Bullish (to Neutral). Trend and ML both slightly to moderately up so market remains in concurrent mode to upside. Action slightly negative on second minor/moderate down day in a row. If upside still solid here, then should not see much, if any, pressure to downside tomorrow. Longer go sideways to only slightly higher here the less positive pattern becomes and the closer get to being in position for pattern to turn clearly negative. This market has had plenty of chances to break out decisively to upside past couple months and each time has been unable to do so. See this as sign market just does not have much in way of upside potential from these levels. Therefore, if long, would use any upside tomorrow to liquidate as see downside risk increasing and would view any failure to move up decently tomorrow as clear negative sign. Bottom line: Can be long with stops still just below 1155.00; however, would liquidate any longs if fails to close above 1170.00 tomorrow and could use any rally tomorrow and next day to get out (and if not in, would not get in here).

.....................

## AFTER-ACTION CRITIQUE

I have usually found that when a market is in a good trending move, then it will usually not move more than a couple days against this trend. Therefore, with the market down two days in a row here I was becoming increasingly concerned about upside chances. Also, I did not like the fact the SL had turned down from the same level it had hit a week earlier. As mentioned at the time, I was bothered by the fact this market had had many good chances to move up above the clear chart resistance in the 1170-1175 area, yet had persistently been unable to do so. I believe markets have "windows of opportunities," first for one direction and then the other. When a market persistently fails to take advantage of these technical "windows," it tends to be a clear warning sign.

An additional cause for concern here was that now had two and a half weeks of an SL in zero to plus ten area, which meant we were getting close to being within the margin-of-error for the ML to turn down. If you count back on the chart will note that price had now been in 1125.00 area or higher for seven and a half weeks; therefore, if it failed to move up soon, the trend would also begin to get within its margin-of-error to turn down.

So, while longs were still justified here, the situation was now much more tenuous. In a case like this the best action would have been to put any longs on some kind of "probation"—meaning to get out unless the price action was positive.

The point is that neither the trend nor the ML were very positive at the time and you should always judge action and short-term prospects through the prism of the trend and ML situation. If both the trend and ML had been solidly up here, I would have been much more tolerant of a couple of minor down days and/or a slight turn down in the SL. However, they were not, so caution was in order. Since trading is about making money and the only way to do this is by taking profits, in a situation like this one I would not argue in the least against taking small profits and going to the sidelines. When a pattern is tenuous, be quicker to take profits, regardless of their size.

01/08/2002

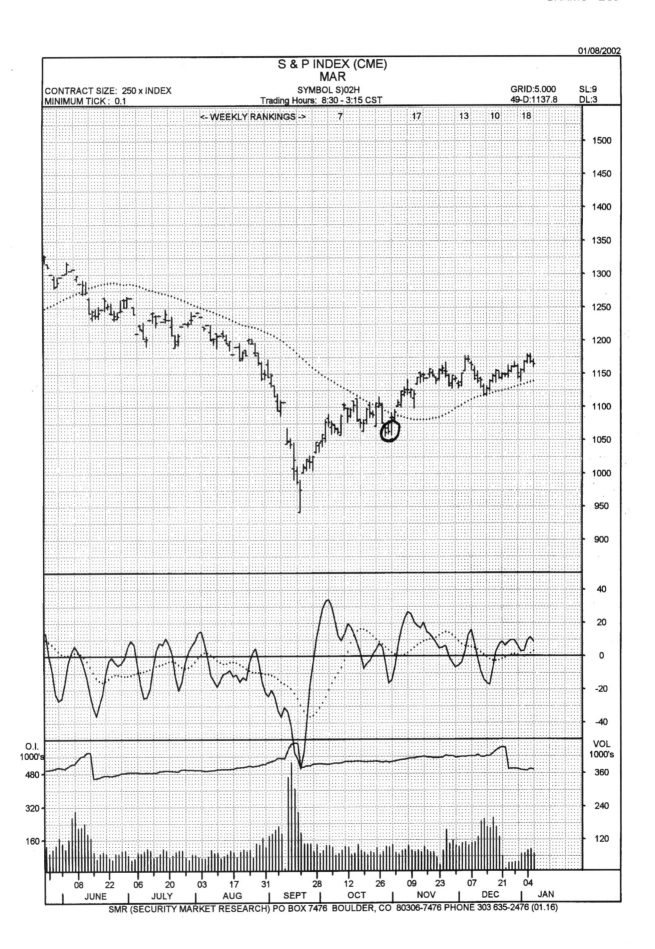

# S & P INDEX (CME)
## MAR

CONTRACT SIZE: 250 x INDEX
MINIMUM TICK : 0.1

SYMBOL S)02H
Trading Hours: 8:30 - 3:15 CST

GRID:5.000
49-D:1137.8

SL:9
DL:3

<- WEEKLY RANKINGS ->     7          17      13    10    18

SMR (SECURITY MARKET RESEARCH) PO BOX 7476 BOULDER, CO 80306-7476 PHONE 303 635-2476 (01.16)

# March 2002 S&P (Jan 9)

**REAL-TIME COMMENTARY**

**1/9 (Wednesday):** Mar S&P - Status - Bullish (to Neutral). Trend and ML both slightly up and so market still in concurrent mode to upside; however, unless rallies soon, will go back to cross-current in day or so. Action quite negative today on rather big downside reversal as was up nicely early but sold off hard late and closed on lows. Mentioned yesterday that would view any rally today as good opportunity to get out of any longs and had plenty of chances early today to sell any longs above 1170.00. Technical picture still positive, but getting very shaky. In a few days could even start to be able to make some case for "anticipation" shorts since ML close to turning down and trend will soon be within margin-of-error to call it down (if sell off any more from here). Therefore, like upside here less and less every day and so would not be long anymore. Still cannot make case for shorts, but short side looking more attractive by day. If downside "good" here, and very well could be, then should not see price back above 1170.00; therefore, if wanted to "jump the gun" on shorts, could use this as stop level. Bottom line: Lines say can still be long, but should go to neutral after tomorrow—prefer sidelines.

......................

**AFTER-ACTION CRITIQUE**

This was the third day in a row down, and a bad down day, since it was a big reversal day (meaning made highs early, but then closed lower). What was particularly negative here on a price chart basis was the failure once again to break through the clear chart resistance level at 1175.00. Again, this would not have been so negative were it not for the fact that the underlying technicals (i.e., trend and ML) were so marginally up. Always have to keep the current pattern of the trend and ML, and their strength or weakness, foremost in mind when assessing daily action of both price and SL. What might be insignificant when trend and ML are solid may be very significant when they are tenuous (as was case here).

Therefore, it should be fairly clear why I was now uninterested in the long side, and in fact was looking in the other direction (i.e., to the short side), in spite of the trend still being up. Always have to be looking ahead to where the three lines, and particularly the trend and ML, will most likely be in a few days. Remember, we trade "futures."

To go short at this point would have been a definite stretch in terms of the line patterns; however, we do not trade trend/momentum lines, we trade price. I make it a point in my daily letter not to recommend going against the trend, but when and if I feel a case can be made, I will hint at doing so (as did here). I believe it is up to the individual trader to decide for himself or herself if they want to make a trade against the trend. In the long run I believe most traders will do better if they do not trade against the trend; however, when and if you have a clear and close stop point, there is nothing wrong with doing so, assuming, of course, you can make a legitimate case the lines will be turning in your direction within a few days, as could have here. When you do go against trend you will always be getting in at a "good" price, but the trade-off is that the odds for success will be somewhat less.

01/09/2002

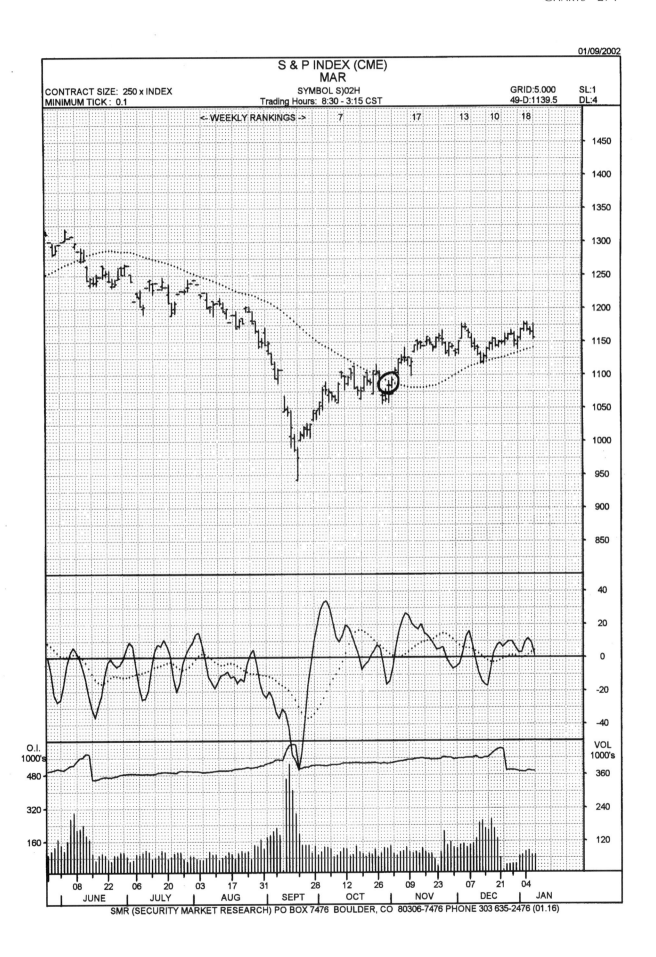

# S & P INDEX (CME)
## MAR

CONTRACT SIZE: 250 x INDEX     SYMBOL S)02H     GRID:5.000    SL:1
MINIMUM TICK : 0.1     Trading Hours: 8:30 - 3:15 CST     49-D:1139.5    DL:4

<- WEEKLY RANKINGS ->    7    17    13   10   18

SMR (SECURITY MARKET RESEARCH) PO BOX 7476 BOULDER, CO 80306-7476 PHONE 303 635-2476 (01.16)

# March 2002 S&P (Jan 10)

## REAL-TIME COMMENTARY

**1/10 (Thursday):** Mar S&P - Status - Bullish (to Neutral). Trend and ML both slightly up so market remains in slight concurrent mode to upside. Action slightly positive on minor up day but nothing significant on technical basis. ML close to turning back to minor down cycle and so pattern very close to going back to Neutral Status. Markets tend to have "windows of opportunity" for one direction and then the other. Have usually found that when a market has had abundant opportunities to move in one direction (as this one has had to upside here past couple months), yet persistently is unable to do so, then it is usually a sign just marking time until technicals set up for try at making decent move in other direction. Believe this may be just what is happening with stocks at this time. This is normally a strong period for stocks since a substantial amount of pension, profit sharing, etc. type money tends to come in during January. So far this year, late December/early January period has been markedly unimpressive on upside. So see longer go sideways here the more likely; next meaningful move will be to downside. Have PPI report tomorrow a.m. and believe this has chance to be a bearish surprise (for stocks). With p/e ratios historically high, believe any official signs of increasing inflation could be extremely negative for stocks, especially with signs interest rates moving up also. This is because can only support high p/e ratios if both interest rates and inflation low, and any solid signs both these changing could trigger beginning of major down move for stocks. Therefore, in spite of lines being positive here, see overall pattern as too mixed and downside risk as too big to be long at moment. Bottom line: Lines say can be long but see too many negatives, so prefer to stick to sidelines.

......................

## AFTER-ACTION CRITIQUE

This was an inconsequential day; however, when both trend and ML are up (regardless of how marginally), any persistent failure to move up is a negative sign.

Focused on the PPI (producer price index, or wholesale inflation) report here and usually do not do this as have always found reports extremely difficult to predict. And even if do get report right, will not necessarily get price movement correct. Prices do not always move in the direction reports indicate they should.

On a straight line (i.e., technical) basis, the sidelines looked best here; however, if trading very aggressively, could have still made some case for against-trend shorts here with stops in 1170.00 to 1175.00 area. I have usually found that in the S&P most of the time have to be willing to risk at least ten full points, and sometimes closer to twenty. (Twenty points would be $1000 on an e-mini contract and $5000 on the full contract.) Sometimes, when the price is at a key chart point, then stops can be placed closer than I place them here; however, in this market (the S&P) ten points can be just "noise," so have to be willing to risk at least that much.

Therefore, had a situation here where if the upside was still "good" then the price should have moved up quickly and decently, and the longer it failed to do so the more negative the line pattern became.

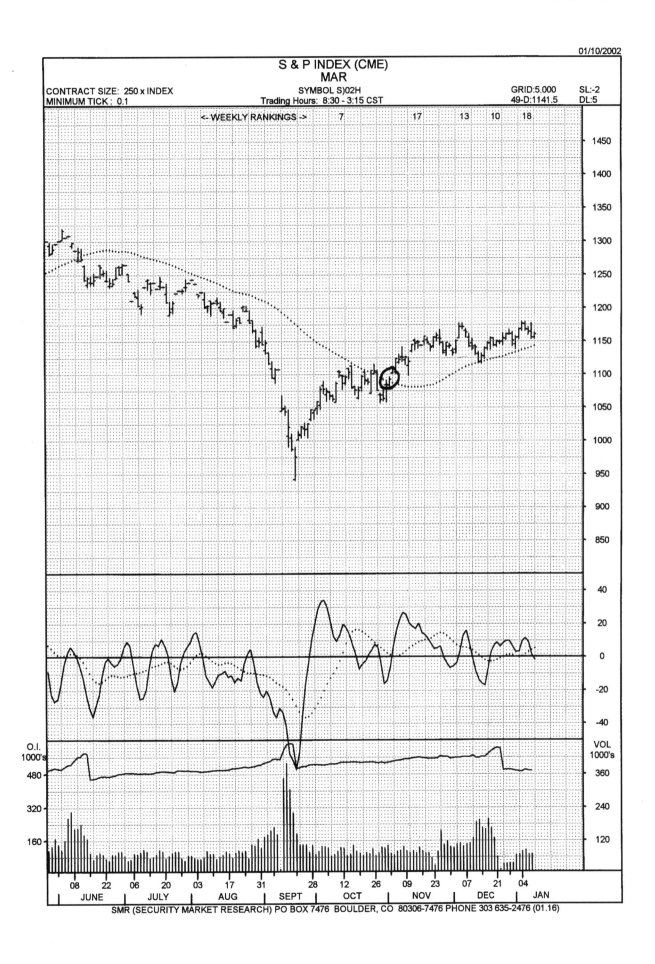

# March 2002 S&P (Jan 11)

## REAL-TIME COMMENTARY

**1/11 (Friday):** Mar S&P - Status - Neutral (to Bullish). Trend slightly up but ML now flat to down so market now more in crosscurrent mode. Action negative again on moderate down day and fourth down day out of past five. Market down today partly due to Greenspan comments that economy still on shaky ground. Since Greenspan's infamous "irrational exuberance" comment several years ago when Dow was in 7000 area, virtually every one-day spike caused by his comments has been quickly reversed. This is type of news event that always receives a great deal of news coverage and gets analysts all excited, but in reality changes nothing (or at most very little). Basically he said the economy was still shaky, so the Fed may or may not cut interest rates some more at next meeting. Stock market supposedly did not like idea economy is not on solid road to improvement and so sold off, but reality is same as was yesterday—the economy is or is not improving at good rate, i.e., Greenspan comments did not change existing reality. In other words, this is psychological news event and these rarely have lasting impact on prices. On negative side, action of stocks still very sluggish during time period when both lines and seasonals indicate should have been strong, and this a clear negative. So picture now is that trend still a little too clearly up to legitimately consider shorts yet, but action too persistently negative to justify longs either. Bottom line: Sidelines.

......................

## AFTER-ACTION CRITIQUE

There was no significant change in the technical picture after this day, but the continued inability to move up (instead was moving down) remained a clear negative sign.

I usually do not pay much attention to chart trend lines. I prefer to watch the ten-week moving average line. However, in this case the price was now down to both the uptrending ten-week moving average line and the price chart's uptrend line; therefore, it was probably at a key support level—meaning any further weakness from here would be a serious negative sign.

Incidentally, throughout this time period the put/call ratio continued to run in the neutral area with no days at either bullish or bearish extreme levels. Therefore, the put/calls did not give any clues as to future price direction. Usually will not see extreme put/call ratios unless price is on a sustained and sharp move, and that had definitely not been the case at this time (movement was more sideways than up or down).

So, as long as the trend was up, and still was here, the upside had some chance; however, with both the trend and ML so tenuous here, it was only logical to be getting increasingly skeptical about upside chances.

In letter (above) mentioned the pattern of Greenspan comment inspired moves being quickly reversed. While the move on this day was minor, if go back over the years and check on this, you will see that this has been the case in almost every instance. I consider any market moves prompted by any government official or politician's comments to be very suspect. Words, regardless of who speaks them, rarely change reality.

01/11/2002

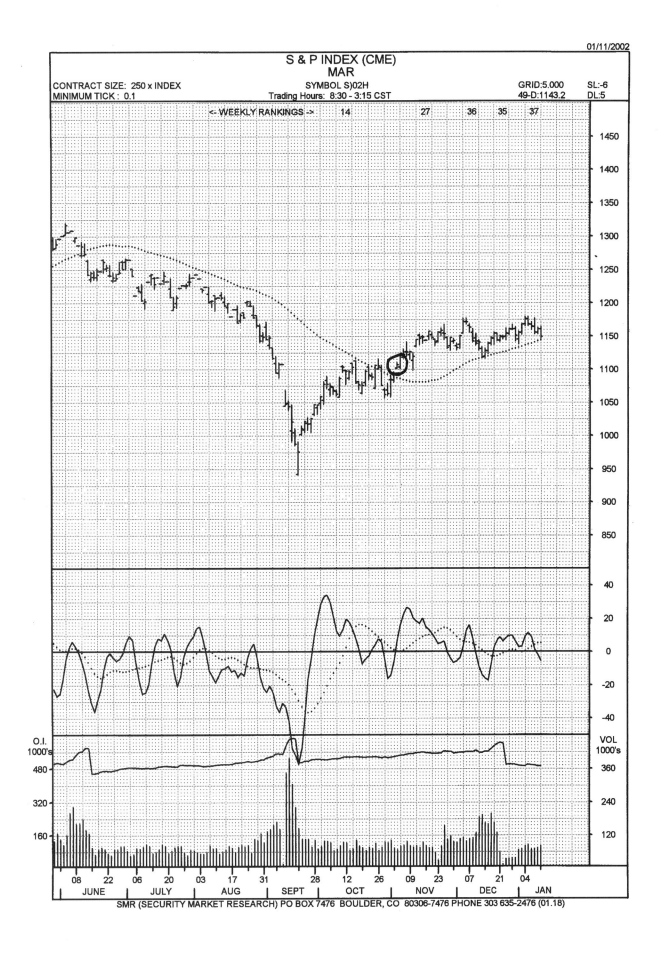

S & P INDEX (CME)
MAR

CONTRACT SIZE:  250 x INDEX          SYMBOL S)02H          GRID:5.000      SL:-6
MINIMUM TICK : 0.1          Trading Hours: 8:30 - 3:15 CST          49-D:1143.2   DL:5

<- WEEKLY RANKINGS ->          14          27          36     35     37

SMR (SECURITY MARKET RESEARCH) PO BOX 7476  BOULDER, CO  80306-7476  PHONE 303 635-2476 (01.18)

# March 2002 S&P (Jan 14)

## REAL-TIME COMMENTARY

**1/14 (Monday):** Mar S&P - Status - Neutral. Trend slightly up but ML now slightly down so market in crosscurrent mode. Action negative as recent persistent downside pressure continued virtually all day today. Action of stocks continues to be quite negative since are still in what should be a fairly solidly positive seasonal time period. Now getting very close to being able to make legitimate case are within margin-of-error to call trend down. Also, now in position for sustained down cycle in ML. In addition, have made clear lower low in SL and this continues pattern of past few months of making lower highs/lows. So every day adds to argument this market has made significant top and now most likely just a question of how and when will turn down with real energy. Only "positive" here at moment is trend still slightly up, and so with both price and SL on recent lows could have minor rally or pause near term. However, the longer goes without any upside energy the more likely will turn sharply lower without any interim rally. If continue to show inability to rally next two, three days then would see downside odds as increasing significantly. So feel should give up on long side now and only look for where and when to go short (and can make minor case to do so now, and longer fails to rally the better the case would become). Bottom line: Sidelines (but getting closer and closer to making good case for shorts here, with stops on any shorts in 1155 to 1160 area).

....................

## AFTER-ACTION CRITIQUE

This was another small down day. However, the size of the down day was not as significant as the fact the market had been persistently unable to move up in spite of trend being marginally up. The fact that ML was now in position for sustained down cycle (since now had three weeks of SL numbers above where SL was now) was also now a solid negative. Add in the fact the SL was making lower lows/highs and can see why I was continuing to become increasingly negative about future price moves.

You can also look back to where price was ten weeks earlier (circle on chart) and see that would now not take much to downside to turn the trend down. In fact, a move below 1125.00 would have put price on lows of previous ten weeks and this would have meant that everyone who had bought over the prior ten weeks would have been a loser. This in turn meant could then have expected to see selling above the market since longs with losses would have been willing to sell if given a chance to get out even. There is an old trader/broker "joke" about how every trader's dream is to get out even. Unfortunately, there is a lot of truth to that joke. This is why when the price reaches a point where all the trading of the previous ten weeks is above (or below) where it currently is, then you can expect to see solid resistance at those levels (since will run into traders anxious and willing to get out "even").

So, now could have begun to make a legitimate case for "anticipation" shorts here. A trader would have been "anticipating" a turn down in the trend since the momentum line pattern was already negative enough to justify shorts—just needed the trend to turn "officially" down.

01/14/2002

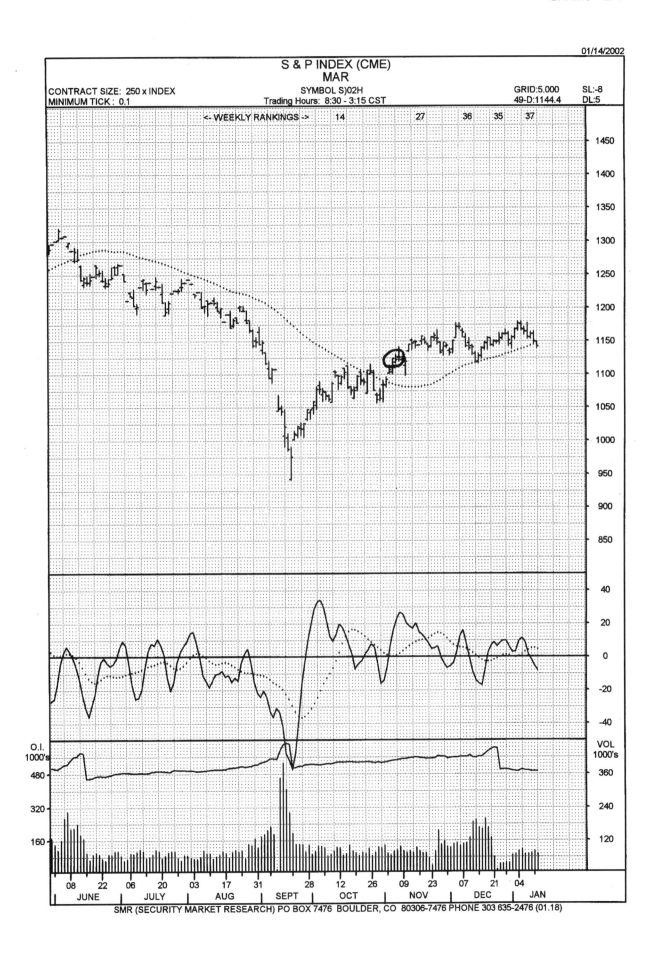

# March 2002 S&P (Jan 15)

## REAL-TIME COMMENTARY

**1/15 (Tuesday):** Mar S&P - Status - Neutral. Trend slightly up but ML slightly down so market in crosscurrent mode. Action slightly positive but nothing particularly impressive as was overdue for some kind of upside action and what had today lethargic at best. Continue to see overall picture as increasingly negative and enough so to justify some "anticipation" shorts, but since trend still up, cannot yet make legitimate case for shorts. Plus whenever have trend up and both price and SL on recent lows (as is case here), as a "rule" it is usually better to be buying rather than shorting. In addition, this an option expiration week and normally do not see major down moves in few days before option expiration day. So still prefer shorts to longs here but this strictly an "anticipation" trade and odds always a little lower when this the case. However, see downside potential here as substantial since if get much more to downside, will turn trend down and this would indicate past few months of up simply an unusually big bear-market rally as well as indicate new contract lows likely (and that a long ways down from here). Bottom line: Lines say sidelines, but still see no big problem with anticipation shorts here using stops just above 1155.00 for now.

...................

## AFTER-ACTION CRITIQUE

Had a small up day, but this did not change the increasingly negative picture of this market. On a straight line basis (going precisely by direction and location of the three trend/momentum lines), sidelines was still indicated here. However, due to the persistent inability of this market to move up when had the trend up, I was still clearly tilting to short side (in spite of the nominal uptrend).

Trading is decision making. The future is always unknown. As an individual trader with no access to any insider information (and not being on e-mail list of Chair of Federal Reserve and/or Secretary of Treasury for notification of imminent government intervention in market), all you or I can do is pay close attention to the trend/momentum indicators and the daily price action, and then act accordingly. All we can do is follow the natural laws of trading and then make our best bets based on the most likely future outcome. Sometimes these bets will be wrong, and when they are we have to do our best to exit market quickly. However, more often, if the trend/momentum indicators are reasonably reliable (and SMR's are), we will be right. Then we have to be prepared to take profits when "good," or when technical indicators start to give some clear warning signs that the current price energy flow is beginning to lose steam.

Trading is not easy; however, it can be done successfully. The first step is to learn how to read the indicators (i.e., the lines, charts, and price action). Then once you have acquired some confidence in your ability to "read" the markets, you have to be able to act on what you see (and this can be very difficult to do). Reading the markets without any money on the line is like walking across a one-foot-wide board when it is on the ground. Add in money and the board rises off the floor, and the more meaningful the amount of money, the higher the board rises off the ground (meaning the greater the fear). Turn the page to see how this market developed over the following month.

01/15/2002

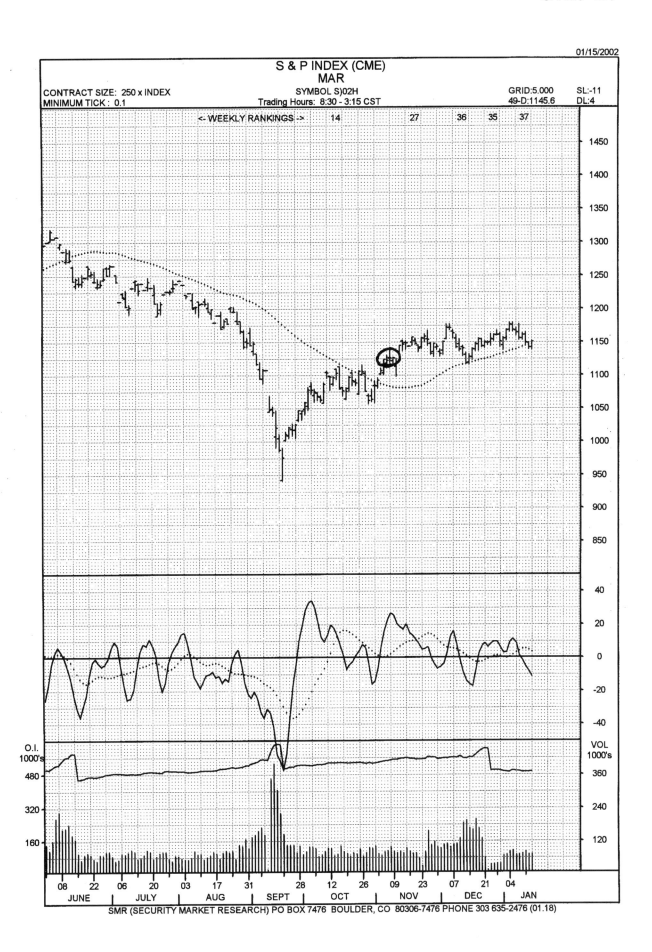

# March 2002 S&P (Feb 15)

**2/15:** Picture in this market had been slowly becoming clearly negative, and on 1/16 a moderate down move was enough to make it conclusively negative. In the letter of 1/16 I wrote the following: "Bottom line: Can now make legitimate case for shorts, so can justify being short and can make decent case to initiate new shorts on any rally up to 1135.00 area next day or so. Stops levels need to stay in 1150.00 area for now." Over the next week or so the market traded essentially sideways; however, it did give repeated chances to short in the 1135.00 area and the suggested stop point of 1155.00 did not come close to being hit. Throughout this period the market remained in concurrent mode to downside and the Status stayed Bearish (i.e., shorts continued to be fully justified). Then at the end of the month the market had a big down day.

The big down day on 1/29 (price went from 1135.00 down to just under 1100.00) qualified as a non-news-related, with-the-trend down spike, i.e., a "continuation" spike. However, after being decently lower early the next day, the price rallied sharply for a big one-day upside reversal. This market has a real habit of having these sudden, surprise upside reversals (for whatever reason), and this was one. The spike rule says the two days after a spike day can see some counter-spike move, but this was unusually large since it took the market almost back to pre-spike day levels. The strength of the bounce back caused me to suggest covering shorts after the second day up; this proved to be a mistake. However, I wrote the following after the close of 2/1: "Bottom line: Lines still justify shorts and agree (therefore, can go back short); however, market needs to be down Monday so would use close stop (1130.00 to 1135.00)." Subsequently, the market pushed lower for several days until it made slight new lows for move, then once again started a good rally. After the first good up day on 2/8 (move from 1080.00 to 1095.00) I wrote following: "Bottom line: Can still be short, but now need to put shorts on moderate probation (meaning longer it trades above 1100.00 after first half hour, the more should cover and go to sidelines); major stop on shorts still in 1110.00 and 1115.00 area." I was reluctant to give up on shorts, but can never argue with surprisingly strong price action (and especially strong upside action in stocks).

This was a tough period in this market due to fairly choppy action. Had several good chances for a sustained down move, but price just could not break through the support in the 1075.00-1080.00 area. Sometimes markets are just not "ready" to make a sustained with-the-trend move. In addition, when a market repeatedly fails to move when it has a good line pattern, then have to respect this.

Long-term trading would have produced substantial profits during July through end of September (up to the week or so after trading resumed post 9/11 atrocity). However, once again, long-term traders would have been better off covering as soon as the mode turned solidly to crosscurrent (at the end of September) instead of waiting for the trend to turn up. Once the trend turned up, longs would have produced minor profits over the next several months of slow up move; however, the turn down in trend would have erased them. Switching to sidelines both times the market went to crosscurrent mode would have produced slightly better results. Sometimes markets just do not get into a sustained trend; however, these times are only evident after the fact (as was case here during November through mid-February time period). As a rule, if you can break even during a sideways period, you should consider doing so a good result.

# Feb 2002 Gold (Jan 2)

## REAL-TIME COMMENTARY

**1/2 (Wednesday):** Feb Gold - Status - Neutral. Both trend and ML are sideways and very indecisive; therefore, the pattern remains quite mixed and so cannot make good enough case for either direction here at moment. Continue to find it hard to make any kind of fundamental case for a major up move in this market and cannot justify longs here unless pattern clearly positive, and this long way from case at moment. On the other hand, it would not take too much on downside to turn pattern quite negative and fully justify shorts. Bottom line: Sidelines indicated and probably best, but can make minor case for "anticipation" shorts with very tight stops (could go short with idea of not going home a loser and/or use regular stops at 281.00).

......................

## AFTER-ACTION CRITIQUE

Gold (like the stock market) is a market that tends to come with a lot of psychological baggage. Virtually no trader has a permanent built-in directional bias on markets like cocoa, cotton, oats, natural gas, and so on; however, many traders have built-in biases on the stock and gold markets. Any kind of bias is a liability when it comes to "seeing" the markets realistically, meaning seeing them as they are rather than as we want them to be.

I believe most traders would do much better if they did not know the specific markets they were trading. If there were some way to have your broker intercept your charts and replace the names at the top of each page with code numbers, I would recommend it be done. Then you would just say to your broker: "Buy 5 contracts of 'number 16' at the market." What this would do is take away any built-in bias you have for different markets. Having a belief a market "should" go up or down before you actually look at its chart is the equivalent of looking through distorting lens—you just cannot see it accurately.

This same type of bias can come about as a result of your personal trading history. A market you may have lost substantially in, or one that has given you big profits, can also produce a built-in bias. I have always found that "new" traders (those with little or no trading experience) frequently can look at a market more clearly than those who have been trading for many years. The longer we trade, the more specific individual markets tend to seem "too low" to sell or "too high" to buy; however, the truth is, for short-term trading purposes there is no "low" or "high." Over the next few days, weeks or months (and even years) the price of any market can always go lower or higher, regardless of its current historical level. Therefore, be extra alert looking at the charts of markets where you have a directional bias and/or a meaningful past trading history. Bias is the enemy of seeing clearly, and seeing clearly is a prerequisite for correct action.

This market was solidly neutral at this moment and so probably it was best to just look for better (clearer) opportunities elsewhere. However, on a short-term basis it did have the potential for a third lower high on the SL (if it would have turned down from here) and this is usually a reasonably reliable near-term negative. Therefore, in "anticipation" of this possibility, a trader might have gone lightly short here "hoping" for a close of 276.00 or lower, which would have turned the chart clearly negative.

01/02/2002

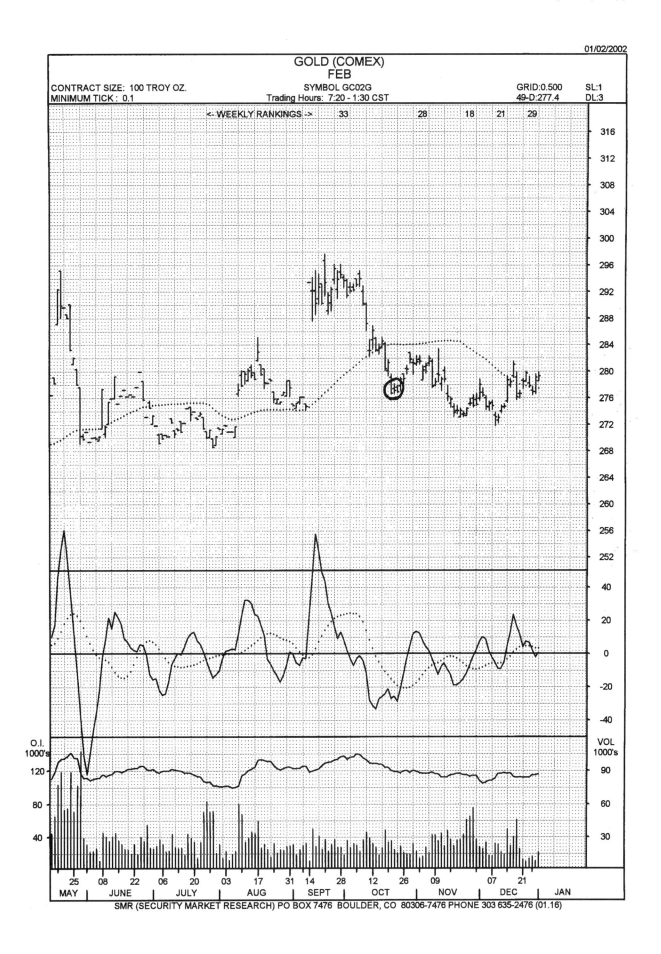

GOLD (COMEX)
FEB

CONTRACT SIZE: 100 TROY OZ.
MINIMUM TICK : 0.1

SYMBOL GC02G
Trading Hours: 7:20 - 1:30 CST

GRID:0.500
49-D:277.4

SL:1
DL:3

<- WEEKLY RANKINGS ->    33    28    18    21    29

O.I.
1000's

VOL
1000's

SMR (SECURITY MARKET RESEARCH) PO BOX 7476  BOULDER, CO  80306-7476  PHONE 303 635-2476 (01.16)

# Feb 2002 Gold (Jan 3)

## REAL-TIME COMMENTARY

**1/3 (Thursday):** Feb Gold - Status - Neutral. Trend and ML both sideways so market in cross-current mode. Action slightly negative as upside energy ran out of steam, although did firm up a little late. This one remains clearly least positive/most negative of group and so is least attractive for longs and most attractive for any shorts. On a straight line and chart basis the picture is too mixed to justify positions in either direction at moment; however, if had to be in here, would still prefer shorts to longs as would only take minor to moderate down day to turn picture negative enough to justify shorts. So could continue to make some case for "anticipation" shorts here. Bottom line: Sidelines (although can make some case for anticipation shorts with stops in 280.00 to 281.00 area—preferably on a late-in-day or close basis).

....................

## AFTER-ACTION CRITIQUE

If you look back on this chart to the period from early September to early October, you will see a good example of how a series of three lower highs in the SL tends to be a sign of imminent price weakness. What this indicates is that the upward energy price flow is losing steam. A price that does not have the energy to keep moving up will always be vulnerable to moving lower, at least temporarily.

Notice also how while the SL was making the series of three lower highs (Sept/Oct) simultaneously, the price was making a series of three higher highs. This was a classic example of a "double-bearish divergence" and these tend to be quite reliable as short-term indicators. Someone looking only at the price chart (without the momentum lines) would have tended to view that three and a half week period of trading range between 290.00 and 296.00 as simply a pause before eventually pushing higher. However, once you add in the SMR oscillators, then a trader could easily have seen clear warnings that a period of weakness lay immediately ahead.

In addition, right when the SL turned up for two days around October 5, the ML started moving into position for a sustained down cycle, and this was another clear negative warning sign. Remember, the ML is about a three-week moving average of the SL; therefore, if you count back from the day the SL turned up (around Oct 5), you will see that three weeks earlier the SL had been shooting up to extreme levels (as high as +78). Therefore, since these numbers were almost certainly going to be substantially lower than the SL numbers that were going to be coming off the ML moving average over the coming week, this meant the ML would be heading down significantly over the near term.

So, just before the sharp price break from 294.00 to 277.00 in mid-October, the SMR oscillators were flashing very clear downside warning signs, and these warning signs were coming in spite of the trend and price chart still having a superficially very bullish look. I like to think of the SMR oscillators as reliable indicators of a market's internal "health." Sometimes a market can look very healthy (i.e., bullish) on a basic price chart; however, once you add in the oscillators, a completely different picture can appear. Just as heart-monitoring machines can show that a superficially healthy person is in imminent danger of heart failure, so too oscillators can reveal imminent problems for a market.

01/03/2002

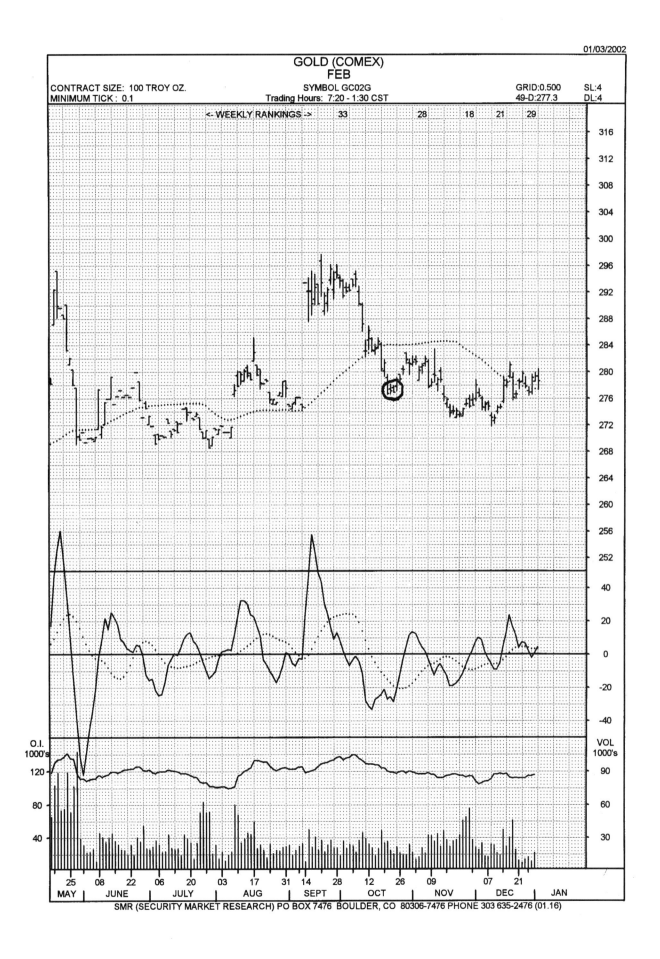

GOLD (COMEX)
FEB

CONTRACT SIZE:  100 TROY OZ.
MINIMUM TICK :  0.1

SYMBOL GC02G
Trading Hours:  7:20 - 1:30 CST

GRID:0.500
49-D:277.3

SL:4
DL:4

<- WEEKLY RANKINGS ->    33    28    18    21    29

SMR (SECURITY MARKET RESEARCH) PO BOX 7476  BOULDER, CO  80306-7476 PHONE 303 635-2476 (01.16)

# Feb 2002 Gold (Jan 4)

**REAL-TIME COMMENTARY**

**1/4 (Friday):** Feb Gold - Status - Neutral. Trend and ML both remain indecisive/sideways and SL pattern also neutral, meaning all indicators essentially neutral. Price action also neutral on another fairly quiet, sideways day, but market is holding up reasonably well and that is always a positive for gold (since it has been weak for so long). However, Gold remains clearly least positive of group and so least attractive for any longs and best bet for any shorts. COT slightly bearish, but nothing significant. While picture solidly neutral and sidelines probably best here, still have situation where it would be easier to go to a solidly negative pattern than vice versa. Bottom line: Sidelines.

......................

**AFTER-ACTION CRITIQUE**

While I definitely have some built-in biases on various markets, I find my real "bias" is toward potentially "solid" line patterns. Take this chart for example. What I was looking (hoping?) for here was one good down day (a close of 276.00 or lower), which would have turned the SL down decisively. (Remember, the SL is a short-term oscillator determined by prices of the past couple weeks, particularly the past few days.) One good down day here would have turned the SL down decisively, and if the SL had moved below zero from there, it would have resulted in a very negative line pattern. This is what I meant when I wrote the above "real-time" comments.

If you look at this chart you will see how the SL had been making a long series of higher lows (starting around October 12). Just as the series of lower highs on the SL in September was indicating a lessening of upside energy, so too this series of higher lows in SL was indicating a lessening of downside energy. However, now the SL had started to show some lower highs as well, thus it was forming what the technicians at SMR refer to as a "coil." These long, tightening coils in the SL tend to come at turning points for markets. They indicate a market is moving toward a decisive breakout point, either up or down. Therefore, since a reasonable case could have been made for both upside and downside here at this moment, taking a position at this point would have been essentially a guess about the direction of this imminent breakout. In addition, the price action of the previous several days was another indication of this indecisiveness since the price remained stuck in very tight range.

It is always very tempting to try to guess "right" about the next price move (i.e., guess which way market will break out of a tight range) by going long or short so as to get a head start on next move. However, the more professional action is simply to sit on the sidelines patiently waiting for the market to show its hand first. Remember, as individual traders we have to operate on the assumption we have no knowledge of impending moves. This means all we can do is look for clear signs of current trend/momentum and then bet for this to continue rather than change. Taking a position in a situation like this one would have been just guessing. And when you guess, you are abandoning all natural laws and tendencies, thus giving up any edge you might have in trading.

Therefore, as tempting as taking a position here (either short or long) might have been, the intelligent or professional action was clear: sidelines.

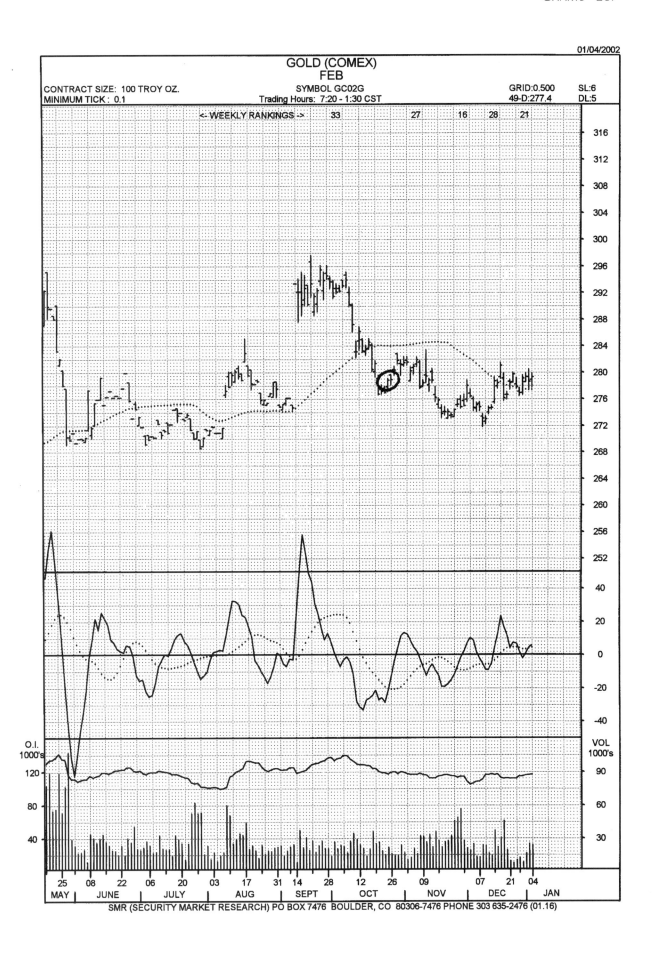

01/04/2002

GOLD (COMEX)
FEB

CONTRACT SIZE: 100 TROY OZ.
MINIMUM TICK : 0.1

SYMBOL GC02G
Trading Hours: 7:20 - 1:30 CST

GRID:0.500
49-D:277.4

SL:6
DL:5

<- WEEKLY RANKINGS -> 33  27  16  28  21

SMR (SECURITY MARKET RESEARCH) PO BOX 7476  BOULDER, CO  80306-7476  PHONE 303 635-2476 (01.16)

# Feb 2002 Gold (Jan 7/8)

**REAL-TIME COMMENTARY**

**1/7 (Monday):** Feb Gold - Status - Neutral. Trend and ML both basically sideways so solidly neutral there. SL also meandering sideways, so no clear indications there either. This market remains clearly weakest/most negative of group and so best (only) bet for downside. However, past week and a half does have look of bull flag which would expect to break to upside. So picture not clear enough here for position in either direction at moment, but overall probably still slightly more negative than positive. If pattern was a little more positive here, would be more confident of longs in Silver, but maybe will be after tomorrow. Bottom line: Neutral.

**REAL-TIME COMMENTARY**

**1/8 (Tuesday):** Feb Gold - Status - Neutral. Trend and ML both sideways so market remains in very indecisive pattern. Action neutral on another quiet, sideways day. Can make small argument for either shorts or longs here since would only take minor (two dollar or more) move in either direction to turn pattern either bullish or bearish enough to legitimately justify positions. Remains clearly least positive/most negative of group and so only one can make any case for shorts. Bottom line: Sidelines.

...................

**AFTER-ACTION CRITIQUE**

(Have combined two days here.) Past two days of this market were continuation of previous couple weeks of a tight trading range. Therefore, the situation remained unchanged with the price chart and oscillator line patterns such that it would have taken only one minor (two dollars or more) day in either direction to turn patterns either clearly positive or clearly negative. A close of 276.00 or lower would have put price on the lows of previous week and produced a minor downside chart breakout, while a close of 282.00 or higher would have done the reverse on upside. The trend also was so indecisive at the time that just a small one-day move would have turned the trend either up or down.

It would be hard to design a chart as much on the "edge" between being clearly positive or negative than this one here. Therefore, the correct (i.e., intelligent, professional) position here remained sticking to the sidelines. While guessing right by going either long or short here would have been a tremendous help if correct, the problem was it would have been an even bigger "hurt" if wrong. This was because if I had guessed wrong (i.e., gone long and had market sell off sharply the next day, or vice versa), then I would have had to both get out of the existing wrong position and then would have had to turn around and put on the correct position. In other words, I would have had to quickly reverse my position. While in theory reversing a position sounds easy, my experience (both as a broker and trader) is that it is quite difficult to do in practice and most traders are not very good at doing it. Making a complete shift in one's position (instantly switching from being long to short, or vice versa) just involves too much fear of being wrong. Therefore, it is best in situations where the patterns are indecisive to wait for the market to show a clear directional price energy flow before positioning.

The precious metals group (Gold and Silver, as well as Platinum to a somewhat lesser extent) is quite reliable in terms of relative strength, meaning once one of the group becomes clearly more positive or negative than another, this tends to continue.

01/08/2002

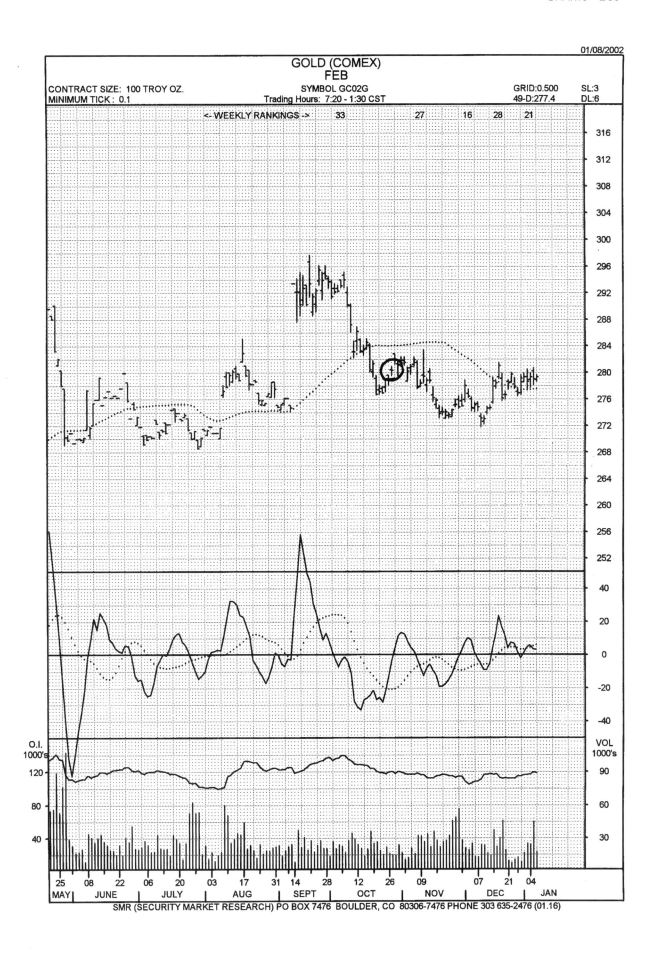

# Feb 2002 Gold (Jan 9)

## REAL-TIME COMMENTARY

**1/9 (Wednesday):** Feb Gold - Status - Bullish. Both trend and ML now clearly up, so market now in concurrent mode to upside. Action quite positive on breakout-type day to upside. First time in several months this market has been in upside concurrent mode and bullish status. Today's up has clear look of a with-the-trend, non-news-related up spike and rule is these tend to continue. Mentioned yesterday that would only take two dollar move (or more) to turn pattern solid (either direction) and got more than that to upside today. So can now make solid case to go long here. This market the all-time world champion of "false" upside moves, but when the lines turn solidly positive on a with-trend, up spike, should give it a chance in spite of past history—plus most of past false up moves have produced decent moves before failing, so have some upside potential. Bottom line: Can go long with stops 279.00 on close-only basis.

...................

## AFTER-ACTION CRITIQUE

Obviously the indecisive situation here was now, at least temporarily, resolved. This chart picture here is an excellent example of a "with-the-trend" up spike. My definition of a "spike" is a one day market move that clearly stands out on the price chart, and there is no question that is the case here. Remember the "spike" rule: non-news-related (meaning moves with no obvious "news" explanation), with-the-trend spikes tend to continue; therefore, based on the spike rule, this one-day up spike should be the beginning of a sustainable move.

On a line pattern basis, this up move had turned a very indecisive, neutral pattern into a solidly positive one. Status had gone from Neutral to Bullish. At this time had trend up (+1 point), had ML above zero (+1/2) and pointing up (another +1/2), and had SL pointing up (+1), which added up to a total of +3 points, or a solidly Bullish Status. In addition, with the SL turning up again, the long series of higher lows on SL had continued. I have found that every time the SL turns up from a higher low (or turns down from a lower high) the market has an increased chance of making a sustained move in that direction. It is a little like rocking a car stuck in a rut; each time you rock the car back to a higher starting point the odds increase that that time will be the one that breaks it out of its rut. Plus, the SL was now higher than its previous high (of few days earlier) and so this ended the short-term pattern or minor lower highs and thus canceled that particular technical negative.

The problem I have found most traders have with a situation like this one is an inability to act quickly. Keep in mind that you are looking at these charts in a compressed time frame. It only takes a few minutes to take in one day when reading it here. However, there is an enormous difference "psychologically" between looking at the chart patterns here in this book and actually living through them. When involved in trading, even just one trading day can feel very long. Many, many different trading thoughts will pass through a traders mind in one day, and the more experienced the trader the more of these thoughts. Many (most?) traders will be lulled to sleep in a sideways pattern like the one had here for previous several weeks or months. Then suddenly, after a long period of inactivity, it was necessary to act boldly and decisively—and this is much easier said than done.

01/09/2002

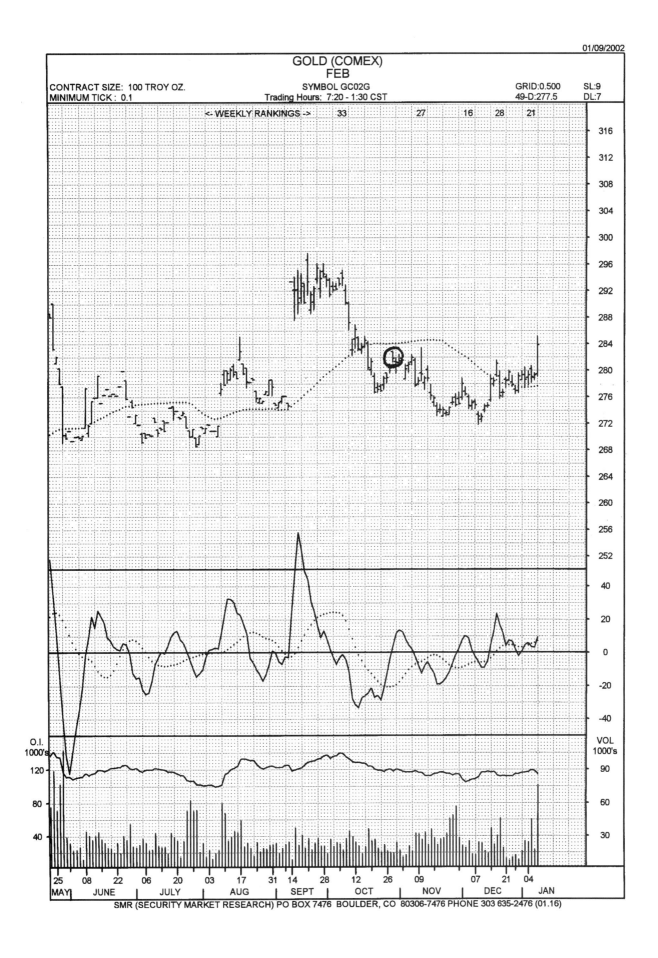

GOLD (COMEX)
FEB

CONTRACT SIZE: 100 TROY OZ.
MINIMUM TICK : 0.1

SYMBOL GC02G
Trading Hours: 7:20 - 1:30 CST

GRID:0.500
49-D:277.5

SL:9
DL:7

<- WEEKLY RANKINGS ->    33    27    16    28    21

SMR (SECURITY MARKET RESEARCH) PO BOX 7476  BOULDER, CO  80306-7476 PHONE 303 635-2476 (01.16)

# Feb 2002 Gold (Jan 10)

## REAL-TIME COMMENTARY

**1/10 (Thursday):**  Feb Gold - Status - Bullish. Trend and ML both solidly up now, so market in strong concurrent mode to upside. Action positive on gap higher and close above middle of day's range. Could have bought at unchanged until late in overnight session, and whenever have a breakout-type day like had here yesterday, feel getting in unchanged is good idea and so would definitely try do so in evening session if can. The point is, if you want to position around unchanged the next morning, then it only makes sense to try to do so in overnight market first. Gold market has long history of brief false up moves, but whenever lines and chart solidly positive (as are here now), regardless of what market has done in past, should go with lines (i.e., get long here). One other background negative here is COT data, which shows commercials slightly net short and most of time major up moves here tend to happen when commercials solidly net long; however, price trumps all other factors and price action here clearly positive enough to be and go long. PPI report tomorrow and has chance to show bullish surprise since have had sustained period of strength in commodities, and this could show up in report. Bottom line: Can be (and still go) long with stops in 279.00 to 280.00 area (preferably on close-only basis).

...................

## AFTER-ACTION CRITIQUE

I find it is much more difficult to see clearly and act decisively during the market day then when the market is closed (i.e., in evening). It is simply much easier to see a stationary target accurately than a moving one. During trading hours prices are moving, however in the evening they are either stationary or, if the market has after hours trading, at least quieter. Therefore, it would have been much easier after a market like this one had closed (previous day here) to see that it had clearly broken out to the upside. During the trading day it is fairly easy to overlook the significance of what is happening. However, after the close, when your brain has quieted some, then a breakout of this nature should be fairly obvious. Once the situation was obvious (i.e., the market had made a clear upside breakout), there was no need to wait for the next morning to position if you could do so in the overnight market—as could have been done here. Waiting for the next morning would have meant having to buy over two dollars higher, and doing this might have increased the risk (i.e., the distance from the stop) enough to have actually stopped a trader from making the trade.

Situation here now actually was even more bullish than the previous day. With upward momentum so strong now could conclude that the SL would go to a clear higher high than the peak of two and a half weeks earlier (a positive), which meant the ML should continue in solid up cycle for some time to come. Plus, having another good up day added to argument the previous day's up spike was a continuation spike. Therefore, at this time the technical picture here was solidly positive. All trend/momentum indicators were solidly positive (and becoming increasingly so), plus both the spike rule and price chart were clearly bullish.

I selected the 279.00 to 280.00 area for stops since a move back to those levels would have been extremely negative. Such a move would have given the previous two big up days the look of a "false" upside breakout, which can be very negative sign. In other words, in a situation like this one you want to give a market every chance to "continue" its current clear price energy flow and only get out if have extremely negative action.

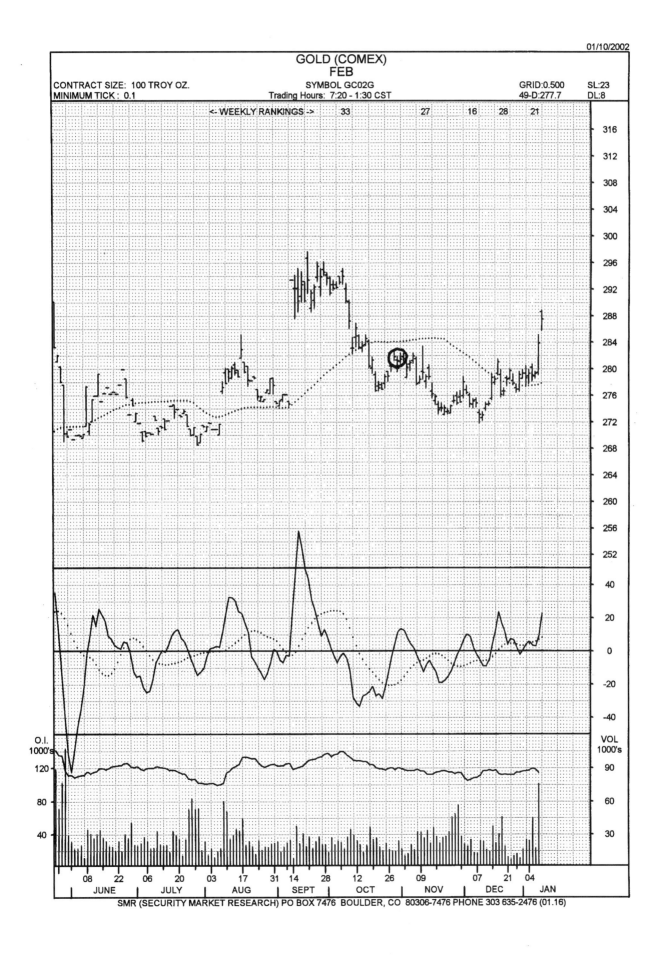

01/10/2002

GOLD (COMEX)
FEB

CONTRACT SIZE: 100 TROY OZ.
MINIMUM TICK : 0.1

SYMBOL GC02G
Trading Hours: 7:20 - 1:30 CST

GRID:0.500
49-D:277.7

SL:23
DL:8

<- WEEKLY RANKINGS -> 33 27 16 28 21

SMR (SECURITY MARKET RESEARCH) PO BOX 7476 BOULDER, CO 80306-7476 PHONE 303 635-2476 (01.16)

# Feb 2002 Gold (Jan 11)

## REAL-TIME COMMENTARY

**1/11 (Friday):** Feb Gold - Status - Bullish. Trend and ML both solidly up so market in good concurrent mode to upside. Action positive even though unchanged on day. This market has such a history of giving back gains quickly, any time can hold good gains it's a positive. So far Wednesday's up spike acting like continuation spike (which it was indicated to be on Wednesday) and this a positive sign also. So see no reason to liquidate any longs and can still make good case to initiate new longs. Gold is now better bet than silver for any new longs as gold now more positive. Bottom line: Can be long with stops just under 280.00 for now.

..................

## AFTER-ACTION CRITIQUE

I have usually found that when a market makes a clear chart breakout and the line patterns turn solidly in that direction as well, then the sooner a trader positions in that direction the better. Think about a situation like this one here as a case where the "train" (i.e., the price) was sitting in the station with engine running for a few weeks. Your challenge is to bet on which direction it will move next. Rather than guessing while the train is still stationary, instead wait for it to start moving clearly in one direction; then, depending on the speed it moves, time the placement of your bet. If it suddenly races out of the station (as it did in this case), it is only logical to expect it to keep going in that direction for at least the near term. Therefore, in a case like this it only makes sense to jump on board quickly rather than hoping the train will suddenly decide to come back a little to pick you up at a slightly better entry point. Once trend/momentum become obvious, just get aboard, i.e., position at the market.

I noted in the daily commentary that gold was now more positive than silver. When considering relative strength, it is usually better to buy the more positive market when going long and short the more negative market when going short. However, if the technical picture of a market turns solidly bullish or bearish (as this one did a few days ago), do not let the fact that another market in its group (silver in this case) is somewhat more positive prevent you from positioning in this one as well. Price comes first in terms of importance, then momentum-line pattern, then spike rule, and only then relative strength within the group. Do not let some minor deficiency in relative strength stop you from making a trade that is clear in terms of price action, line pattern, and spike rule (all of which are more important factors than relative strength).

I continued to use the 280.00 level for a stop here since I wanted to keep giving this solidly positive picture plenty of chance to work. At this time the only "negative" in this picture was the fact that both price and SL had now reached recent (previous several weeks) extreme highs. Whenever this happens, a market will have some downside vulnerability (meaning some short-term downside risk). However, this concern can be overlooked when both trend and ML (i.e., concurrent mode) is very solid, and that was now the case here. Therefore, a trader should have been long this market by now, and if not already long, then he or she should have been buying at the market here. In addition, he or she would have had to be willing to risk a move down to 280.00 for the time being.

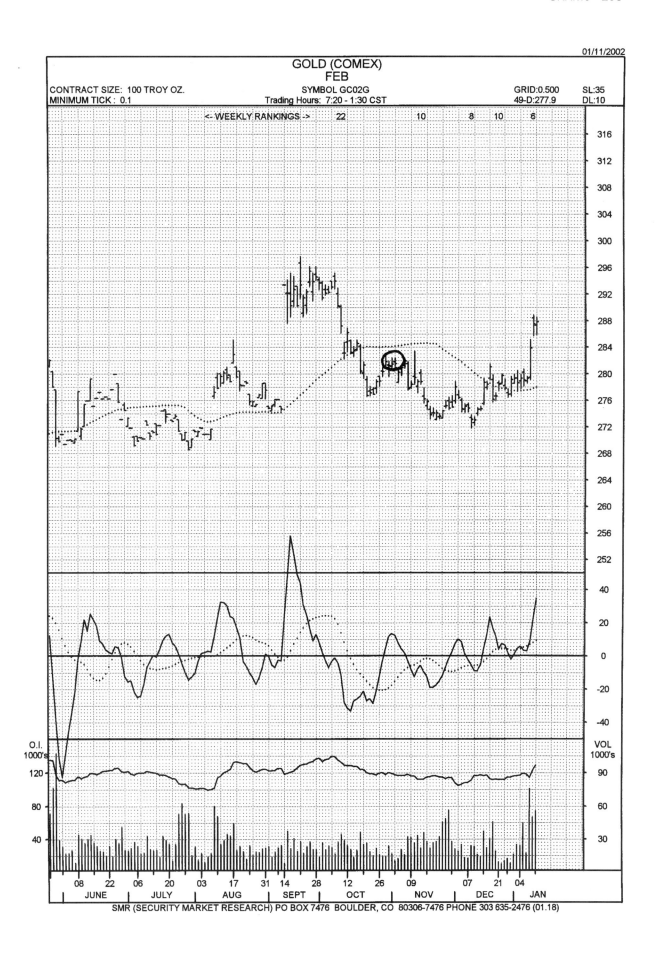

# Feb 2002 Gold (Jan 14)

### REAL-TIME COMMENTARY

**1/14 (Monday):** Feb Gold - Status - Bullish (to Neutral). Trend and ML both moderately up and so market still in concurrent mode to upside. However, action on negative side as never traded higher on day and closed on day's lows as well as on lows of past three days, and this never positive sign. Normally would consider current line pattern and price chart as positive enough to be long here, but with both Silver and Platinum turning at least short-term negative as well as Gold having such a long history of not being able to hold any good gains, can make case to liquidate any longs and go to sidelines. So tough call here at moment since technicals say can stick with longs, but history and other two precious metals indicate upside potential not there anymore so sidelines better bet. Bottom line: Lines say can still be long with stops at 280.00, but prefer to go to sidelines for time being as group now too negative for near term.

......................

### AFTER-ACTION CRITIQUE

On a line and chart basis, actually there was no reason to give up on this trade yet. Looking at it now (almost two months later) it is clear that in a situation like this you just have to "suck it up" and take whatever the market might give you. However, in real life it is not so easy to just sit tight for as long as no serious warning signs exist, and they really did not here. My problem with being long this market at this time was its long history of sharp up moves that invariably turned out to be very short-lived.

Earlier I mentioned my belief that most (all?) traders would do better if they did not know what market a chart represented. When starting out in trading a trader has no contamination from the past; however, the longer one trades, the more past experiences tend to color and distort current vision. Therefore, the more you can keep your vision pure, meaning free of past experiences and bias, the more likely it is you will see the present accurately. We need to see the past and present accurately in order to extrapolate forward the most likely future. Therefore, regardless of what happened from this point forward, there was really no reason to give up on being long here.

The Status was still solidly bullish here since both trend and ML were clearly up. The previously existing positive pattern in the SL continued to exist since this line was still making hew highs and lows. Therefore, this was just a situation where the price action on this day was disappointing, but even so it was still a long way from being fatal to any upside chances.

Two items I have not mentioned much up to this point are volume and open interest. Over some thirty years of trading I have never been able to see anything reliable in the patterns of either volume or open interest. Some market technicians place great importance on one or both of these factors, however I have never seen anything worthwhile in them. Every time unusually high volume or unusual changes in open interest have signaled something meaningful, there have been at least as many, if not more, times they have produced false signals. We trade price, not volume or open interest. I believe paying attention to volume and open interest just detracts from focusing on the essential, which is price.

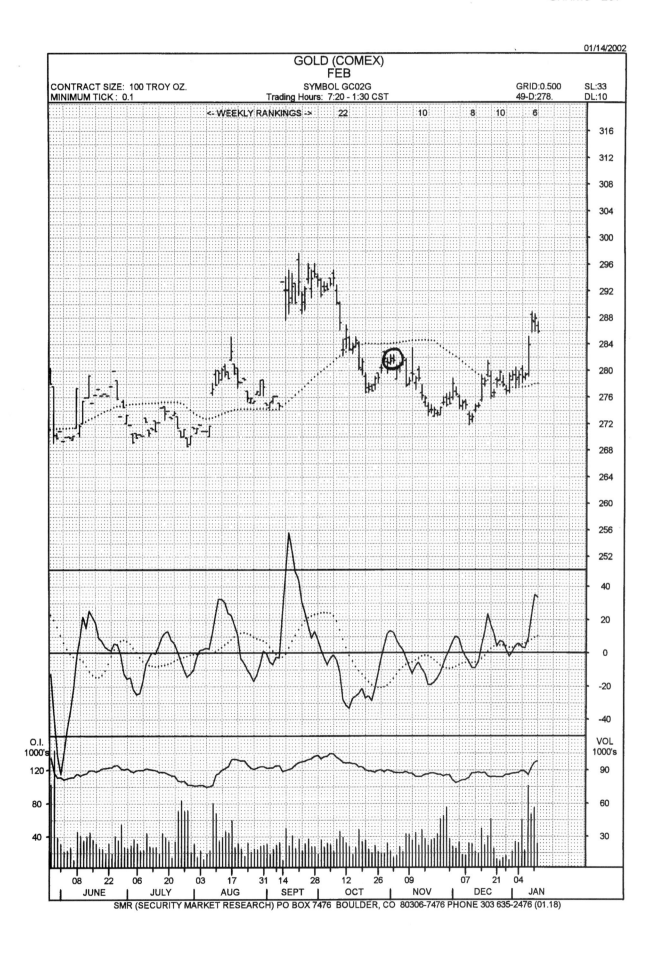

01/14/2002

GOLD (COMEX)
FEB

CONTRACT SIZE:  100 TROY OZ.
MINIMUM TICK :  0.1

SYMBOL GC02G
Trading Hours:  7:20 - 1:30 CST

GRID:0.500
49-D:278.

SL:33
DL:10

<- WEEKLY RANKINGS ->       22          10          8      10      6

O.I.
1000's

VOL
1000's

SMR (SECURITY MARKET RESEARCH) PO BOX 7476  BOULDER, CO  80306-7476 PHONE 303 635-2476 (01.18)

# Feb 2002 Gold (Jan 15)

## REAL-TIME COMMENTARY

**1/15 (Tuesday):** Feb Gold - Status - Bullish (to Neutral). Trend up and ML slightly up and so market still in concurrent mode to upside. Action slightly negative but closed closer to highs of day and this always at least a minor positive. Have now had two-day dip within an overall positive pattern and can always make some argument to initiate new longs when this the case. When in positive pattern and market "good" for upside, any more than couple days down is usually a sign upside not solid; therefore, now important for upside chances that move up tomorrow. So tough call here since lines still fully justify being (and going, since on two-day dip) long here, but this market has such long history of failing on every rally, and the other two in group (Silver and Platinum) are quite mixed at moment, so it's hard to get too enthusiastic about longs. Bottom line: Lines say can be long with stops in 280.00 to 281.00 area, but can make case for sidelines also and for moment prefer sidelines.

....................

## AFTER-ACTION CRITIQUE

I let my past experiences with this particular market overcome what was still basically a clearly positive technical picture and one which fully justified being, and going, long. Furthermore, this was true regardless of what happened next. In the long run virtually all traders will do better if they just "surrender" to any clear line patterns rather than trying to outguess them. What I mean by this is that if you are going to trade based on natural laws, and I believe this is your best and only chance for ultimate success, then it is important to actually do so every day—day in, day out.

A good way to keep yourself on the "straight and narrow" (meaning keep following natural laws and pricing tendencies) is to step back occasionally and ask yourself what would you do if coming across this situation "cold." What would you do if you had been on vacation and came back to find the current technical situation. You are a trader; therefore, you are looking for situations where the natural laws of pricing and trading indicate that one direction or the other has a meaningfully higher probability over the next few days. Walking in on this situation "cold" you would have seen the picture fairly clearly to have been one that fully justified being and/or going long.

First, the price was clearly higher now than it had been for all of the past ten weeks (with the slight exception of the past three days), so the trend was definitely up. Second, the ML was up, and since the SL two to three weeks ago was in the 0 to +5 range and was currently at +25, this meant the odds were good that the ML would keep pushing higher (unless price sold off fairly sharply over next few days). Therefore, since both trend and ML were clearly up, and most likely would stay up for immediate future, this meant this market would remain in concurrent mode to upside for next few days (at least). Third, while SL was pointing down it remained in a solidly positive pattern since it was still on a long series of higher lows and highs. Fourth, the spike rule, which had indicated a continuation up spike from several days earlier, remained in effect (price was holding above spike day's close). And finally, all this market had had in way of negative action was a routine two-day dip, with the price on the second day down closing near high's of day. Therefore, the revised and "better" bottom line here would have been: Looking at this situation objectively—and this always best way to look—can and should be, or go, long here with stops as high as 282.00 or at most down at 280.00.

(**NOTE:** *Turn the page to see what this market did over the next month.*

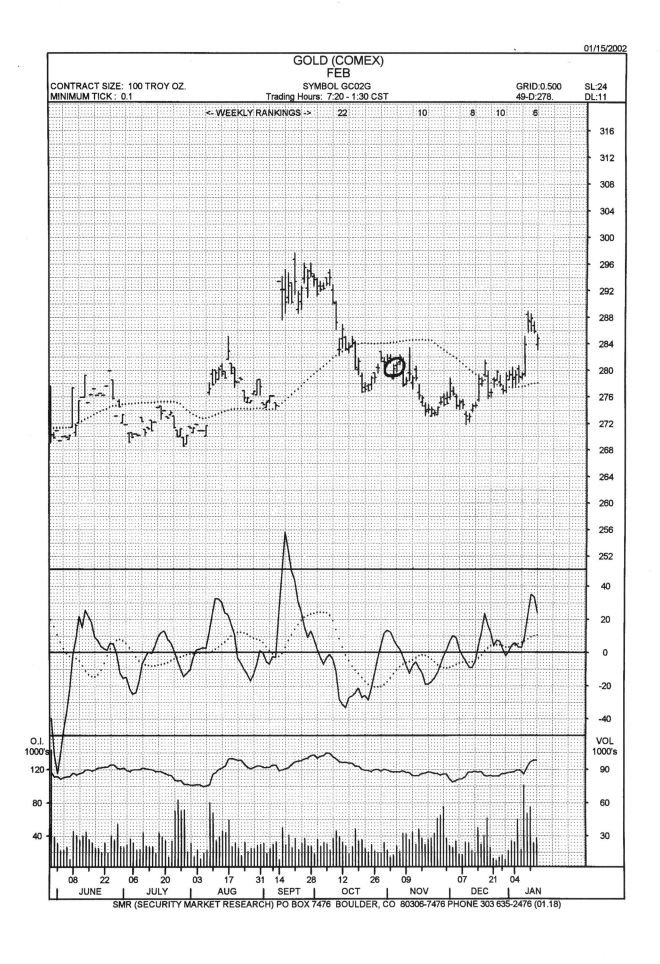

01/15/2002

GOLD (COMEX)
FEB

CONTRACT SIZE: 100 TROY OZ.  
MINIMUM TICK : 0.1  
SYMBOL GC02G  
Trading Hours: 7:20 - 1:30 CST  
GRID:0.500  
49-D:278.  
SL:24  
DL:11

<- WEEKLY RANKINGS -> 22 10 8 10 6

SMR (SECURITY MARKET RESEARCH) PO BOX 7476 BOULDER, CO 80306-7476 PHONE 303 635-2476 (01.18)

# Feb 2002 Gold (Feb 15)

**2/15:** This was a somewhat strange period in this market since had had a clear upside spike, which should have produced some good continuation, but it did not. Then, once price had given back all it had made on the spike day, plus next day—the two day move on 1/9 and 1/10 from 280.00 to 288.00—it chopped around in the 280.00 area until it started back up again. Normally, when a continuation spike fails like this one did, the price will then push lower. In addition, when a market has a clear upside breakout (as this one did on 1/9) and then the price subsequently moves back to pre-breakout levels, this is considered a "false" breakout and these usually produce sustained moves in the opposite direction of the breakout (down in this case). However, neither of these normally negative technical signs turned out to be accurate in this case since the price once again broke out to upside on the small up spike day at the end of January (move from just under 280.00 to just above 282.00). In trading we always have to keep an open mind. The various trading rules (spike rule, false breakout rule) simply reflect tendencies based on past patterns; they are not absolutes. Price always rules in end, and if the price moves clearly against what a normally reliable trading rule says it should do, then we have to believe the price, not the rule.

Unfortunately, I was a little stubborn in believing in the upside again after having been burned some on the move of couple of weeks earlier; therefore, I did not suggest going long until Gold had its second good up day on 2/1 (the move from 283.00 up to 287.00). In that day's letter I wrote: "…Hard to buy here, but lines clearly positive now and so can justify doing so….Bottom line: Can go long with stops 282.00 for now." This was a good example of the "mistake rule." Once, it becomes obvious (basis price action and lines) you have made a mistake in your analysis of the situation, then invariably the best action is to quickly get in line with the line pattern (i.e., the Status). Even getting in a couple days late in this situation, the price still moved more than enough to produce a 100 percent of margin profit (needed about a $14 move since margin was in the $1350 area). Furthermore, if a trader had entered the market when the lines first went to Bullish again (the close at 283.00 on 1/29), he would have had over a 150 percent of margin a couple of times; although the trader would have had to overrule a solid concurrent mode in each case to actually take these big profits.

I believe in the long run the best approach/method is to trade multiple contracts and then regardless of the line pattern take some profits in the 100 to 150 percent of margin profit level. While sometimes doing this will leave some profit on the table, more often it will end up making a bigger profit than if you wait for the lines to turn back to neutral. The only way you can end up making money in this game is by taking profits; there is just no other way. A 100 percent of margin profit is very good in all but the most solid of situations (i.e., when both trend and ML are very solid in same direction). Furthermore, even in these unusual cases you have to be alert to any signs the line pattern is deteriorating (as this one was on verge of doing at this point on chart since the SL was close to coming down a little too far). The problem is that when we happen to get into a trade that is working well, our eyes begin to get a little wider as we contemplate the prospect of possibly being in the middle of a "big" move. Remember, going for the really giant profits is the enemy of taking consistent good profits. Therefore, at this time in this market, if long, should have put these on "probation"—meaning been ready to get out on any negative action near term.

02/15/2002

GOLD (COMEX)
APR

CONTRACT SIZE: 100 TROY OZ.
MINIMUM TICK : 0.1

SYMBOL GC02J
Trading Hours: 7:20 - 1:30 CST

GRID:0.500   SL:2
49-D:284.3   DL:22

<- WEEKLY RANKINGS ->    7        6        6    4    38

SMR (SECURITY MARKET RESEARCH) PO BOX 7476  BOULDER, CO  80306-7476  PHONE 303 635-2476 (01.18)

# March 2002 Soybeans (Jan 2)

## REAL-TIME COMMENTARY

**1/2 (Wednesday):**  Mar Beans - Status - Bearish. Trend and ML both remain moderately down so market still in concurrent mode to downside. Action today a continuation of past few days as market just grinding slowly lower with very little in way of intra-day upside energy. With both price and SL on recent lows, this market a little oversold, but recent sell-off has now been so persistent doubt any rally can go far or last long, plus can override low SL and price when in good concurrent mode to downside, and this case here. Today the sixth day in a row down and this also indicates minor upside action due soon. So can be short, but probably best not to initiate any new shorts here. Bottom line: Can be short with stops just above 4.30.

......................

## AFTER-ACTION CRITIQUE

Status was Bearish here because the trend was down (-1 point), ML was below zero (-1/2 point) and pointing down (another -1/2), and SL was also down (-1), therefore had minus three points. Market was also in concurrent mode to downside because both trend and ML were down. Market was working on a sell signal, which came four days earlier when the SL turned down. The entry price of this sell signal was 4.28; therefore, currently had a ten-cent profit (not quite 50 percent of margin profit; margin was around $1300 so would have needed 13 cents down to reach the 50 percent of margin profit level). The only "positive" here was the fact both price and SL were at recent lows and markets always have some upside vulnerability when this is the case (because short-term momentum a little overextended). However, this can be, and usually should be, overridden when both trend and ML are solidly down. At this moment the trend was solidly down but ML was only moderately down (due to the fact would have been "taking off" a long period of low SL numbers over next few days, which meant it would not have taken much to turn the ML up fairly soon). Therefore, it was a fifty-fifty decision whether to take some profits here or just stay short. Trading is decision making, and this was just another trading decision.

If you look back on chart to around October 12, you will notice a big gap lower day. This was a good example of a news-related, with-the-trend down spike. A monthly crop report was released that indicated a bigger supply of beans than expected and this produced both a big gap lower and subsequent sharply lower close. It is easy to see how that down day would have clearly stood out on the charts and thus qualified as a "spike." Since this one-day spike was with the trend, this meant it was classified as a "continuation" spike by the spike rule. However, it was sparked by a specific news event, which meant it needed to be treated with some suspicion. I have found many, if not most, news-related, with-the-trend spikes tend to act very similarly to this one. This type of spike tends to continue for about a week or so, which seems to be long enough to at least temporarily exhaust the with-the-trend energy, and then the price tends to reverse. If the move is down, it seems that the publicity generated by this news event tends to bring in all those wanting to sell and force out all weak longs, and this fairly quickly (within a week or two) leaves the market ripe for a counter move. With-the-trend, news-caused spikes tend to create, within a week or two, an environment that makes the market quite vulnerable for some against-the-trend price movement. Look back at the Bond chart and you will see this is what happened on the bullish news event that occurred there a week or so before its major top. The same appeared to happen in stocks at end of September, a week or so after the big spike down caused by 9/11.

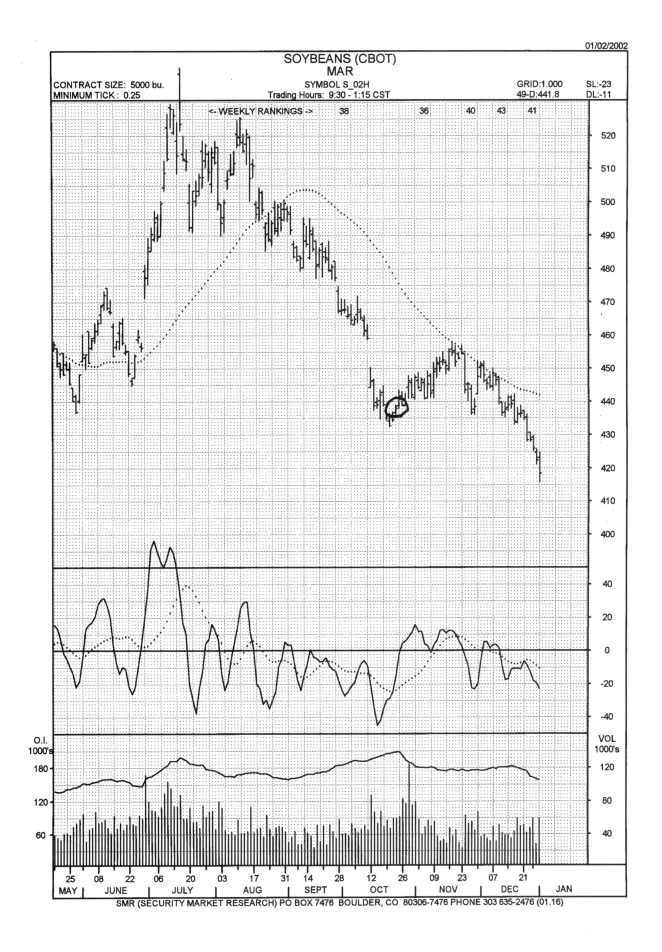

SOYBEANS (CBOT)
MAR

# March 2002 Soybeans (Jan 3)

**REAL-TIME COMMENTARY**

**1/3 (Thursday):** Mar Beans - Status - Bearish. Trend and ML remain slightly down so market still in concurrent mode to downside. Action slightly positive on decent up day but was overdue for some upside, and one day up does not change overall negative picture. However, main question for short side here remains how much downside potential have from these low price levels. COT is a background positive here since commercials at net position where rallies have started from in past. As have mentioned in past, these type of slow, grinding down moves are always difficult to trade since can go down for many days only to then go up for just a couple days and put price right back where started. And this could be case here. Bottom line: Can be short with stops just above 4.30 (preferably on close basis).

..................

**AFTER-ACTION CRITIQUE**

"COT" above refers to the Commitment of Traders report. The real problem for short side here was how easy it would have been to turn the ML up and thus turn Status from Bearish to Neutral. In a market like this one (i.e., a market that had been in a long-lasting downtrend and price had been grinding slowly, but steadily lower for past six days), it probably would have been best to lean toward taking at least some partial profits when both price and SL reached recent extreme lows (as they did day earlier here). However, as mentioned in previous days commentary, this would have been simply a trading decision. The previous two times the SL reached this general area (minus twenty) the price had rallied some or at least paused for several days; therefore, there was nothing wrong with going to sidelines during this period when we were unlikely to see much to downside (meaning probably would not have missed much even if price did push lower).

If look back on chart for previous six months or so will see that this market was fairly reliable in terms of intermediate-term price cycles tending to occur simultaneously with the cycles of ML (not precisely of course, but fairly well). Once the trend turned clearly down, then the only time a short would have had problems was when the ML was moving up decisively. Almost all the rest of time (times when ML was either sideways or down) the price energy flow was clearly to the downside.

Therefore, the current situation was still clearly negative enough to be short; however, a trader not short already would probably have been wise to wait at least another day before initiating any new shorts. So far had only had one up day and the overall pattern was not negative enough to prompt shorting after just a one-day rally.

I was sticking with the 4.30 stop level due to the fact that a move up to that level would have put the price just above both the entry level of the current trade as well as above more than a week of prices, and really should not have seen that much strength if the downside still was "good." The placement of stops is somewhat of an art; however, essentially I try to select stop points in areas where a market "should" not go if the trade is a good one—meaning would "not go" if the trade acts normally.

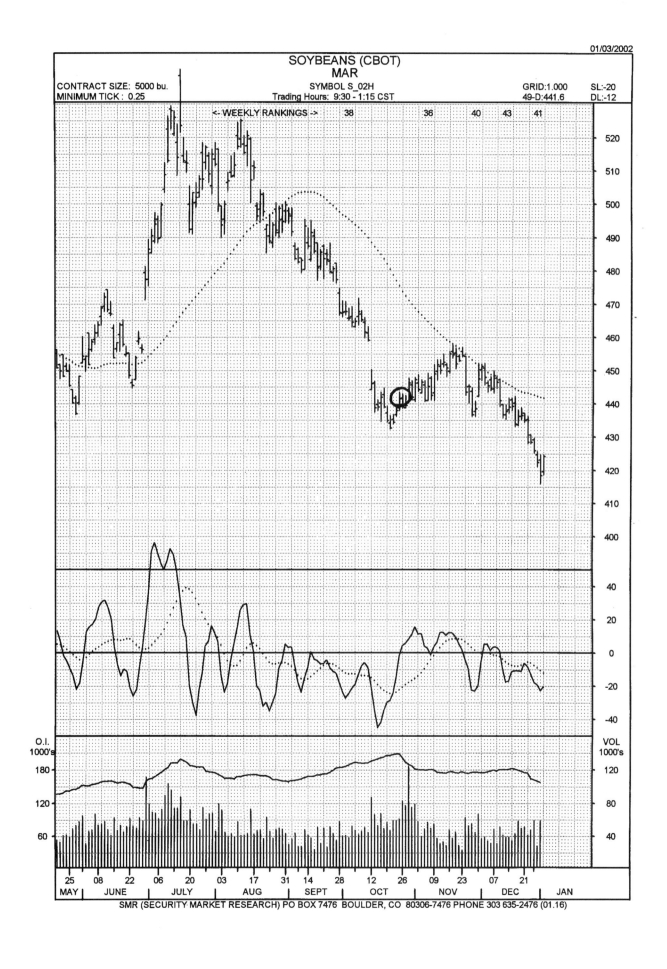

01/03/2002

SOYBEANS (CBOT)
MAR

CONTRACT SIZE:  5000 bu.
MINIMUM TICK :  0.25

SYMBOL S_02H
Trading Hours: 9:30 - 1:15 CST

GRID:1.000
49-D:441.6

SL:-20
DL:-12

<- WEEKLY RANKINGS ->     38          36      40      43      41

O.I.
1000's

VOL
1000's

MAY   JUNE   JULY   AUG   SEPT   OCT   NOV   DEC   JAN

SMR (SECURITY MARKET RESEARCH) PO BOX 7476 BOULDER, CO 80306-7476 PHONE 303 635-2476 (01.16)

# March 2002 Soybeans (Jan 4)

### REAL-TIME COMMENTARY

**1/4 (Friday):** Mar Beans - Status - Bearish (to Neutral). Trend and ML still slightly down so market remains in concurrent mode to downside. SL still on series of lower lows/highs, but this will change if up decently Monday. Action neutral on minor up day. Market now has had two minor up days within an overall negative pattern and so can make case to initiate new shorts here. So pattern at minor pivot point since if pushes higher Monday will turn pattern too neutral to stick with shorts any longer. COT in area where sustained up moves have started from in past but do not have "timing" buy signal yet. However, would be unusual if current line and chart pattern ended up marking meaningful lows so continue to see odds favoring lower in spite of positive action of past two days. Bottom line: Can be and go short with stops just above 4.30 (stops preferably not entered until after an hour or so).

.....................

### AFTER-ACTION CRITIQUE

You should be able to see why I considered this market to be at a key pivot point. At this moment the pattern was still definitely negative, but the ML was now very close to being within the margin-of-error to call up. On chart here had almost three full weeks of low SL numbers and so would have only taken one more up day to put the SL above where it had been three weeks earlier and thus turned the ML cycle up, and if ML turned up then the Status would have gone back to Neutral.

There was one other problem with shorts here at this time. After the four and a half week, shallow counter-trend rally from early October to mid-November, there had been three clear sell signals (when SL and ML turned down in mid-November, when SL turned down twice in early December, and the one several days before this point). Although the price had definitely worked lower over the time period of these sell signals, it had done so in a somewhat erratic manner. The result was the first two sell signals produced little, if any, sustained down moves before the line patterns moved back to Neutral. Therefore, at this time this market had had three clear sell signals over a six-week period in a solidly downtrending market, but none of them had produced much in way of profits. I have found that when a market gives a series of with-the-trend signals, but none of them produce much in way of profits, then this tends to be a warning sign that a particular directional move may be about played out.

However, until proven otherwise, it is usually best to stick with clear patterns, and no question the line pattern was still negative enough here to fully justify being (and going) short. This was especially so since the stop points were fairly close (only five cents or two hundred and fifty dollars a contract away).

In the daily commentary I suggested not entering stops until after the market had traded for about an hour. The reason for this is that, as a rule, against-the-trend moves occurring very early in the trading day are more often than not reversed. I have found that the longer a good early-in-the-day counter-trend move holds or keeps going, the better the odds it will continue to move against trend. Therefore, I prefer not to get stopped out in first half hour to hour when the line pattern is still clearly with the trend (as was case here). Regardless, in situation like this one, where the stop point is so close, the next day usually tells the tale for the near term.

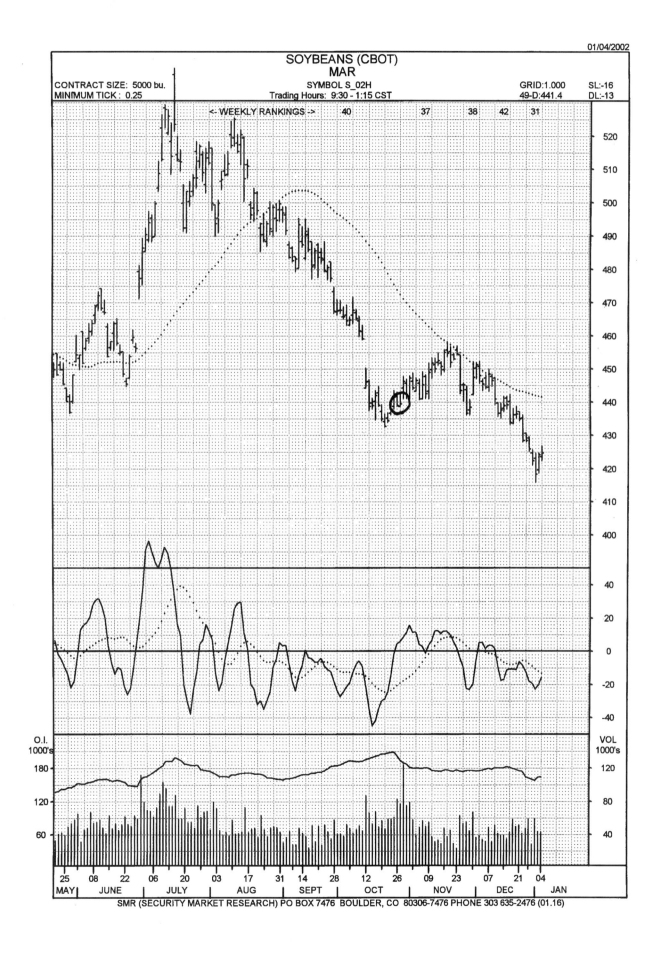

# March 2002 Soybeans (Jan 7)

## REAL-TIME COMMENTARY

**1/7 (Monday):** Mar Beans - Status - Neutral. Trend slightly down but ML now on up cycle so market now in crosscurrent mode. Good up move today supposedly prompted by hot, dry weather in South America; however, market did not hold most of gains as closed near day's lows. Pattern now neutral and so no longer justifies shorts; however, would be surprised if have seen end of downside pressure as usually need at least one bullish divergence before make any kind of meaningful bottom, and have not had that yet. As far as upside goes would need a close above 4.40 to start making legitimate case trend up. So basis lines sidelines now best, but unless see continued upside pressure tomorrow, would expect to see another downside thrust before make serious bottom. Bottom line: Lines say sidelines and agree (and if still short any Beans, would put on strict probation, meaning would cover on any upside pressure tomorrow).

......................

## AFTER-ACTION CRITIQUE

While this had some look of an against-the-trend up spike, the fact that the price closed almost on the lows of the day tended to negate this. Regardless, the line pattern (i.e., Status) was now solidly Neutral and would have not been able to turn back to negative until/unless SL turned back down (and this would have required a sharp sell-off next few days). Therefore, sidelines were clearly indicated by the lines, and could not argue with that at the time nor would I do so now.

With the up day here, this marked the third seemingly good sell signal that failed to produce much in way of profits by time the Status turned back to Neutral. In each case the sell signals had some interim profits, but none of them reached even the 50 percent of margin level before the Status switched back to Neutral. As mentioned earlier, when a series of good line pattern signals fail to work, it is usually a sign that particular direction does not have much left in it.

If look back six months on chart to the end of June, you will see another obvious, with-the-trend up spike (on the day where price gapped sharply higher). This up move was news related, so the normal expectations were that it would not last more than a week or so. As it turned out, that up move lasted slightly more than two weeks before experiencing a sharp sell off.

The soybean market is one of those markets that can make extreme, sudden moves during its growing season. This period begins in May (planting of the crop), but the key growing period is from the first of July to the third week or so of August. Should the Midwest (primarily Iowa and Illinois) run into a spell of hot, dry weather during this period (or this pattern even be forecast), then prices can react dramatically to the upside. Once in a hot, dry stretch, then should any meaningful rain fall, or even be forecast, the price can react to downside just as rapidly and significantly (or even more so). Therefore, when trading beans in the growing season you need to trade somewhat smaller positions (i.e., number of contracts) since risk per contract increases significantly. As an individual trader you always need to consider risk first, potential profit second.

01/07/2002

SOYBEANS (CBOT)
MAR

CONTRACT SIZE:  5000 bu.
MINIMUM TICK : 0.25

SYMBOL S_02H
Trading Hours: 9:30 - 1:15 CST

GRID:1.000
49-D:441.3

SL:-2
DL:-13

<- WEEKLY RANKINGS ->   40      37      38    42    31

SMR (SECURITY MARKET RESEARCH) PO BOX 7476  BOULDER, CO  80306-7476  PHONE 303 635-2476 (01.16)

# March 2002 Soybeans (Jan 8)

## REAL-TIME COMMENTARY

**1/8 (Tuesday):** Mar Beans - Status - Neutral (to Bullish). Trend marginally down but ML solidly up now so market in crosscurrent mode. Action quite positive since if recent rally was just a brief bear-market rally, then price would most likely have turned back down today. With move, and especially close, back at 4.35 level can make case the past week or so of action below this level was a final downside "washout" and this could signal a major bottom. COT is in condition where sustained up moves have started in past, and when this the case and get some bullish technicals, then can start to make decent case for "anticipation" (of an imminent trend change) long positions. Really need a close above 4.40 to legitimately justify going long since at moment trend still technically down; however, a close above 4.40 would turn trend sideways to marginally up, although action, chart and line pattern are all now positive enough to justify going long, rather than wait for "official" trend change. However, if do go long, have to be prepared for another dip before pattern turns solidly positive. Bottom line: Lines say sidelines but prefer going long in "anticipation" with stop at least under 4.25 on a close basis for now.

......................

## AFTER-ACTION CRITIQUE

In hindsight I am a little surprised I turned as bullish as did here. It was most likely due to the bullish situation in the COT report, because on a straight-line pattern basis the picture was not really positive enough to justify longs yet. However, as a general rule, if both the price action and SL are solidly positive at the moment, and neither is overextended to the upside, there is nothing too wrong with going with them. This is especially so when, and if, the trend is only marginally against your position and the ML solidly in favor, as was the case here. Therefore, while going long here was a little aggressive, there is nothing overly wrong with doing so.

I failed to mention in previous day's critique that the approach of waiting for an hour or so before entering stops would have cost extra in that particular case. However, it was not that much extra loss, and the many times doing so (i.e., waiting an hour or so to enter stops) will keep you in a good trade will be more numerous. This is just another trading decision.

The reason I mentioned in the commentary above (back in January) that would have to be prepared for another dip before pattern turned solidly positive was that almost always need to put in at least one higher low on the SL before can make a sustained up move. Most sustained price moves are accompanied by a series of higher lows/highs (if moving up) or lower lows/highs (if moving down) in the SL. Therefore, when a series of lower lows/highs in the SL is finally broken, as was the case here on this up move, then usually will not get a sustained up move until the SL makes at least one higher low.

Therefore, on a strict line pattern interpretation, sidelines was probably the more correct (i.e., intelligent, professional) position here at this time. However, I cannot fault the suggestion for "anticipation" longs too much since there was no question the price energy flow had switched to the upside. However, this definitely was not the type of line pattern I would want to go too heavily long on; it was more the type of situation where "token" or light longs would have been more prudent.

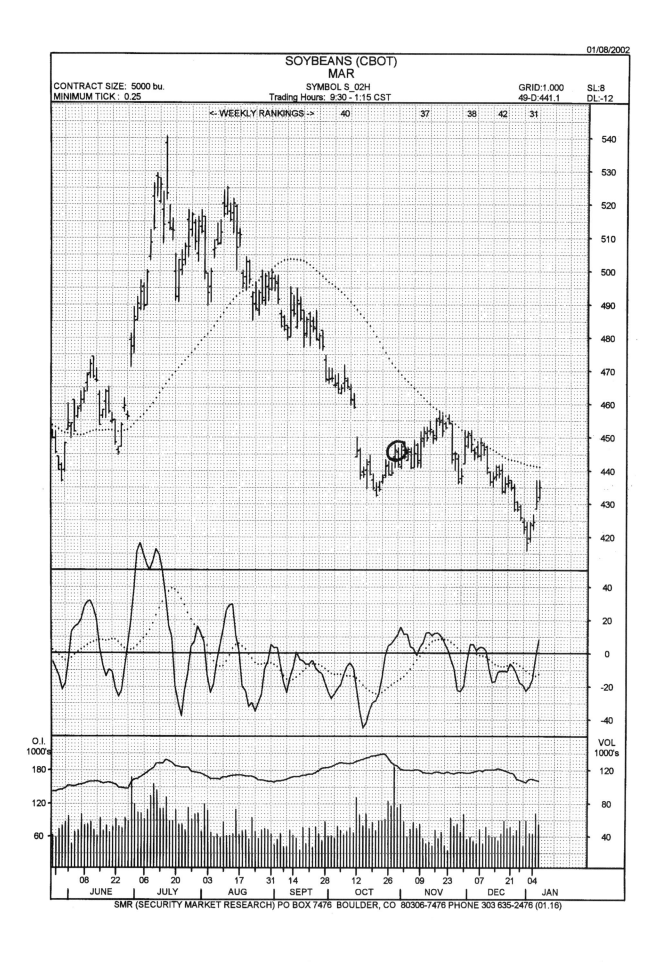

# March 2002 Soybeans (Jan 9)

## REAL-TIME COMMENTARY

**1/9 (Wednesday):** Mar Beans - Status - Neutral (to Bullish). Trend sideways but ML solidly up so market technical background indecisive at moment, but get any more to upside and will be able to call it concurrent to upside. Action on positive side as pushed a little higher with very little in way of downside pressure. Trend indecisive but momentum line pattern now fairly positive and so see odds as quite good that have at least stopped down move and probably in process of turning major trend up. Need a clear close above 4.40 to turn trend "officially" up. So picture not solidly positive yet but still see it as close enough to justify "anticipation" longs here. Have report Friday a.m., but these are usually not that important this time of year; however, there have been exceptions. So see no reason not to hold any "anticipation" longs into report. Bottom line: Lines say sidelines but continue to prefer "anticipation" longs with stops just under 4.25.

......................

## AFTER-ACTION CRITIQUE

With current price exactly the same place as it was ten weeks earlier (see circle), and price also close to being right in the middle of the past ten week's range, the trend at this time was as solidly sideways as could get. However, there was no question the momentum line pattern (pattern of SL and ML) was much more positive than negative at this time since the ML was now on a very solid (i.e., sustainable) up cycle and the SL had made a sharply higher new high (as well as gone higher than any point in previous five months). However, on the short-term negative side, now had both price and SL at recent highs, and as have mentioned, always have some near term downside vulnerability when this is the case. Also, as have mentioned, almost always need to have SL turn down or sideways at least briefly in this type of situation before will see any kind of sustained up move.

Therefore, in a situation like this one it is probably best to not get too excited about upside prospects until get some kind of down (or at least sideways) in the SL, although there are always exceptions to every rule in this game. (When dealing with an eternally unknown and constantly unfolding future, it could not be otherwise.) All we can do when trading is go on most likely future outcomes based on past patterns; we will never have certainty.

This potential for some short-term downside vulnerability is why I chose to keep the stop level in the 4.25 area, which was a fair distance down. I wanted to allow for some minor, or even moderate, temporary short-term weakness; however, I was reluctant to be out of the market entirely with both the price and SL moving up so solidly.

Again, there were undoubtedly better situations available in other markets, however I review many different markets in my daily letter and give my best read of each one as an independent entity. Additionally, I continue to see nothing really wrong with suggesting some light longs at this time in anticipation of the line pattern turning more clearly positive. When a market comes off a major bottom, as I felt this one was doing at this time, it is perfectly OK to give it more leeway in terms of what you require for a position. At major turning points it is not unusual for a market to move in the direction of new trend for some time before "correcting" back some; therefore, if you are going to be in this type of situation, then have to jump the gun a little on trend change.

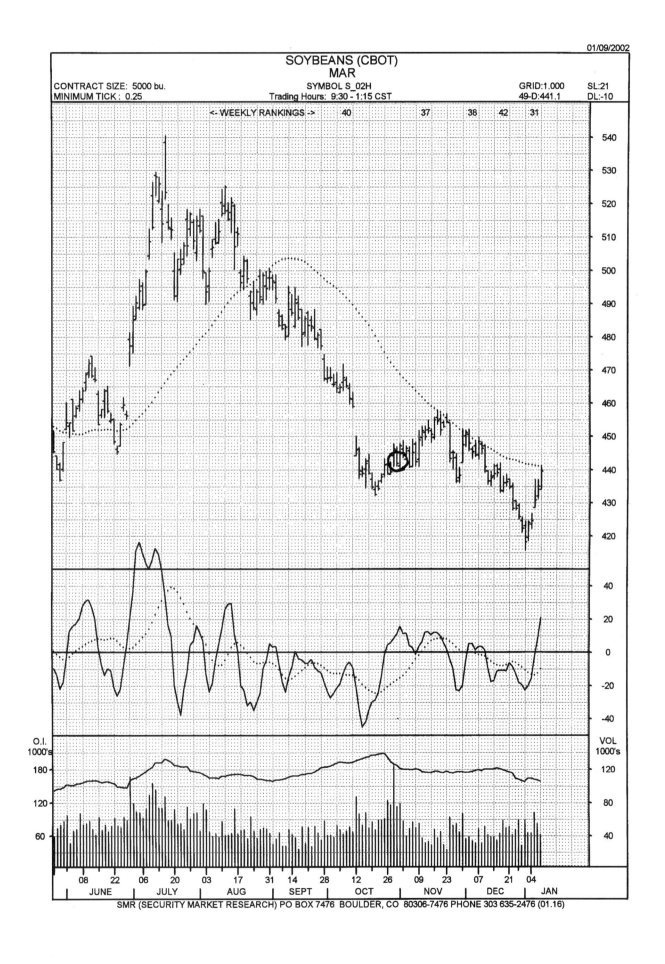

01/09/2002

SOYBEANS (CBOT)
MAR

CONTRACT SIZE: 5000 bu.
MINIMUM TICK : 0.25

SYMBOL S_02H
Trading Hours: 9:30 - 1:15 CST

GRID:1.000
49-D:441.1

SL:21
DL:-10

<- WEEKLY RANKINGS ->   40        37      38      42      31

SMR (SECURITY MARKET RESEARCH) PO BOX 7476  BOULDER, CO  80306-7476 PHONE 303 635-2476 (01.16)

# March 2002 Soybeans (Jan 10)

## REAL-TIME COMMENTARY

**1/10 (Thursday):** Mar Beans - Status - Neutral. Trend sideways to slightly down, ML solidly up, so market still has indecisive technical background. Action negative on gap lower and decent down day, but was due for a down day so nothing significant. Have crop production tomorrow a.m. and today's dip could have been some selling in advance of this. Midwinter crop reports rarely produce much in way of news or moves; however, have had some exceptions. Trend still too indecisive to make legitimate case to be/go long here but continue to view upside as having decent potential (based on quite positive momentum line pattern and bullish COT situation—commercials at net position where sustained rallies have started from in past). However, with trend technically marginally down, if the SL turns down tomorrow, will actually get a minor "line pattern" sell signal. So still like light against-trend longs here, but whenever go against trend, do have lesser odds. Bottom line: Lines say sidelines, but still prefer light "anticipation" longs with stops just below 4.25 (would not enter stops until at least hour or so after open due to report).

......................

## AFTER-ACTION CRITIQUE

The down day here was disappointing for the longs. As mentioned earlier, it is rare for a market to make a sustained up move in a situation like this without first putting in at least some kind of higher low in SL. Therefore, with SL having turned sideways here, the overall line pattern actually had a slightly more positive picture.

Once again I suggested not entering stops until after the first hour or so of trading. The reason in this case was to avoid any very short-term, aberrant-type down move as a result of a negatively interpreted crop report. Grain crop reports are currently released in the mornings two hours before the opening. Occasionally a report will produce a brief move in one direction only to quickly reverse and then move the other way. This chart pattern was one that could have easily resulted in that type of action if the report came out slightly bearish. However, as mentioned in daily commentary, grain crop reports released out of the growing season rarely produce much in way of surprises since the supply numbers rarely change much.

Therefore, I was definitely pushing it some to be long here, but in this game can take some extra risk (vis-à-vis the odds) when and if the short-term picture is fairly solid, and that was still the case here for the upside. However, any longs here would have had to have been light (i.e., small) in nature. Furthermore, if you only had sufficient equity to only trade a maximum of one contract, then in this case should probably have passed on being positioned since the odds were just not good enough.

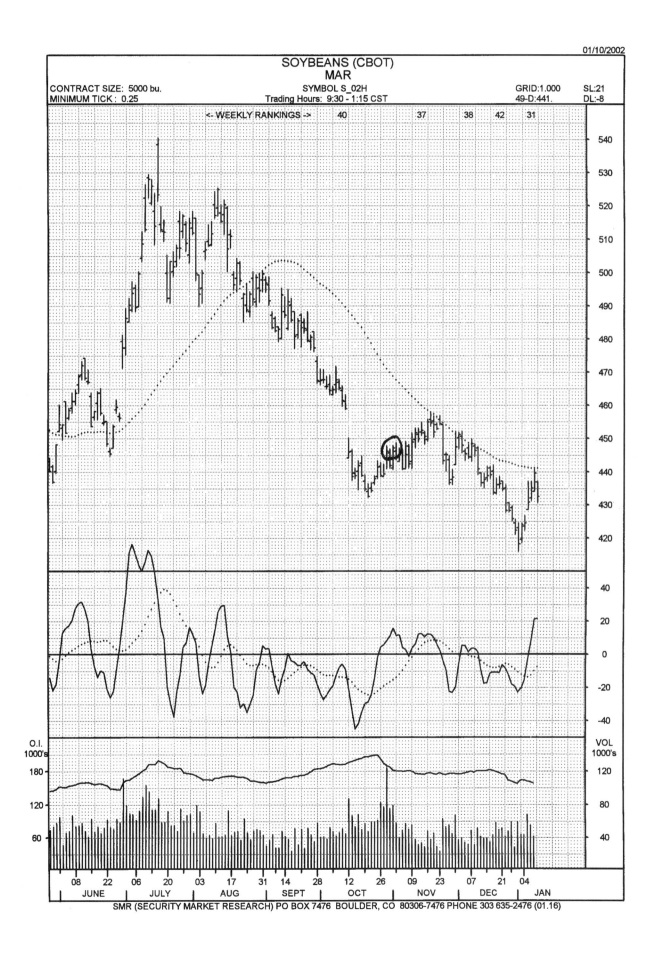

# March 2002 Soybeans (Jan 11)

## REAL-TIME COMMENTARY

**1/11 (Friday):** Mar Beans - Status - Bullish (to Neutral). Trend now sideways to marginally up and so with ML solidly up, market now legitimately in concurrent mode to upside. Action quite positive on good gap higher and close on day's highs. Report was moderately bullish, but action was better than report indicated should be and this always a good sign. So all signs now positive and so can fully justify being and going long here. Even though today's up spike was news related, fact that it was enough to change trend to upside indicates that it should be a continuation spike and not an aberration. SL now a little on high side and so could always pause briefly here, but short-term momentum strong now so see little downside risk for near term. Bottom line: Can be/go long with stops now 4.32 on close basis.

...................

## AFTER-ACTION CRITIQUE

Obviously the crop report was interpreted positively as the market gapped higher and continued up to eventually close on highs of day. This good up move finally turned trend "officially" up since now the price was slightly higher than it was ten weeks earlier (see circle).

Therefore, other than the uptrend still being marginal, the only negative here was that once again had both price and SL at recent highs. The basic rule is you can always make some case to take profits when both price and SL are at a recent extreme, unless BOTH trend and ML are solidly up; while ML was solidly up here, the trend was still a long way from being solidly up (actually trend was up here only by the most marginal amount). I believe that in the long run a trader would do better if he or she consistently took profits when in a situation like this one (price and SL at or nearing recent highs, and either trend or ML not solidly up), rather than always hang on in hopes of catching a big move. In trading it is good to have a greater fear of losing profits than fear of missing out on really big profits. On the other hand, at potential major trend changes there will always be a somewhat better case to be made for holding on instead of taking profits. As I have said, trading is decision making and whether to start looking for place to take some small to moderate profits (if long at 4.35 would need 4.49 to achieve 50 percent of margin profit) or to hold on in hopes of making a big profit (100 percent or more of margin) was simply a trading decision.

When it comes to money management—which is what the decision whether to stay in or take profits was here—following the rule "it is better to be less rich than poor" is usually a good idea. In other words, unless the background technical condition (the current strength of trend and ML) is solid, whenever price and SL approach or reach recent extreme levels, you should choose to take small to moderate profits rather than continue to hold in hopes of really big profits. Nonetheless, it is clear from reading my commentary that I was not in any way considering taking profits; however, I have a tendency to usually be more afraid of missing a move than losing some profits, and this is a personal failing. Over the years I have always had better results when I focused more on taking profits than staying in, meaning looking more for reasons to take profits than for reasons to justify staying in longer.

# March 2002 Soybeans (Jan 14)

## REAL-TIME COMMENTARY

**1/14 (Monday):** Mar Beans - Status - Neutral (to Bullish). Trend marginally up and with ML still solidly up market remains in mild concurrent mode to upside. Action mixed since up on day but closed on lows. As "general rule" can always make case to take profits when SL high, with the primary exception being when both trend and ML solidly up—and at moment only the ML solidly up since trend is just marginally up. Have had forty-cent up move in eight days and this quite a bit, so market may be a little overextended to upside (temporarily?). Tough call here now as can still fully justify longs but may need a minor dip/brief pause before ready to move up much more. With commodities in general suddenly weak again, it is hard to argue with taking profits here and then waiting for SL to come back closer to zero before going long again. However, all signs continue to point to a major bottom having been made and the major trend now being up; therefore, would not expect any dip from here to go very far or last very long. Should be good support in 4.35 to 4.40 area and this not too far from current levels. Bottom line: Lines say can still be long with stops just under 4.35 (but can make some case to take profits and wait for a moderate dip before going long again; this is simply a trading decision).

......................

## AFTER-ACTION CRITIQUE

I can see from my commentary that the minor intra-day reversal to downside which produced a close on the lows of the day started me thinking about taking profits. However, it would have been smarter to have started thinking about doing that on the previous day's close. Had I done so I would have been more psychologically prepared to sell if given some unusually good prices on this day, and definitely were given just that. There is only one way to walk away a winner in this game and that is to take profits; there is simply no other way. Therefore, it is a good idea to measure what both the 50 and 100 percent of margin profit levels would be every time you initiate a trade.

One thing that makes trading so difficult is the need to be constantly prepared for almost any possibility. To maximize results you need to prepare the night before. Before each market opens you should have a very clear view of just what type of line pattern each market is currently showing: solidly positive or negative, marginally positive or negative, clearly neutral, on the verge of going solidly positive or negative, and so on. Additionally, you should force yourself to be prepared for virtually any price action: sharply higher, sharply lower, and so on.

Most traders let emotions monopolize their thoughts—their minds are full of fears and hopes of what might happen next. The better approach is to occupy your mind with preparations for various next day scenarios. There is an old saying that is particularly true about trading: "Chance favors the prepared mind." Do not fear or hope; prepare.

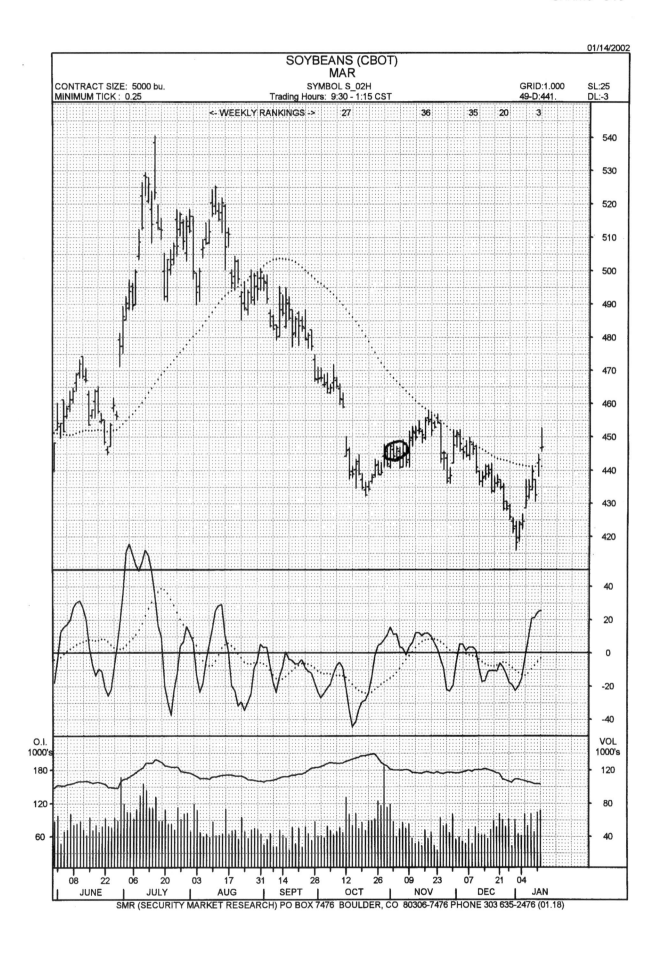

# March 2002 Soybeans (Jan 15)

## REAL-TIME COMMENTARY

**1/15 (Tuesday):** Mar Beans - Status - Bullish (to Neutral). Trend slightly up and ML solidly up so market remains in mild concurrent mode to upside. Action slightly negative as failed to produce much in way of upside action and closed near day's lows again. As a general rule, when SL on recent highs and long can always make case to sell unless BOTH trend and ML solidly up, and at moment, while ML solidly up, the trend is only marginally up. Pattern still positive enough to be long here but could have some short-term vulnerability because both price and SL are on recent highs and the uptrend still a little questionable. So prefer sidelines here temporarily since risk/reward and odds both a little shaky for longs at moment; however, on both intermediate- and longer-term basis, odds and risk/reward still clearly favor upside. If long on longer-term basis, can use stops just under 4.35. Bottom line: Lines say can be long with stops just under 4.35 but prefer sidelines temporarily.

...................

## AFTER-ACTION CRITIQUE

I was lucky here since the market gave me a second chance to take decent (50 percent of margin) profits. Frequently the market will not be so generous. An argument could still have been made to continue holding longs here since Status remained Bullish and market was still in concurrent mode to upside. However, I firmly believe in the long run a trader will do better consistently taking profits in this type of situation rather than holding on for something bigger. If this truly were one of those relatively rare situations where a major turn around in trend was occurring, there would almost certainly be a number of good entry points to reposition on long side later on. The SL and price both would almost certainly have some kind of two-, three-day dips at some point over the nest week or so; and if this happened to come from a much higher price level, then so be it. In reality, if this market had pushed sharply higher from these levels (say twenty cents or more) the next few days, then the next dip would have been an even better bet for buying, since the trend would then have been solidly up instead of so marginal.

As a trader it is vitally important to keep foremost in your mind that there will always be good opportunities down the road. This I can guarantee. Therefore, it is just not necessary to be unduly afraid of leaving potential profits on the table; there will be plenty more where those came from (if you follow the natural laws of trading).

I firmly believe, based on thirty years experience, that consistently taking profits in this type of marginal trend situation will produce much better results than trying to make sure you are positioned for that rare time the price just keeps pushing in direction of the new trend. However, ultimately in situations like this one where one of the background lines (trend and ML) is marginal and the other is clear, it will always be just a trading decision whether to take moderate profits or go for more. As a trader you just have to weigh the odds and risk/reward and make your best decision. Just remember, if the monetary result is important to you, then you have to treat trading as a business and take the businesslike action, which is to lean toward taking profits whenever they are "good" and the situation is "marginal." (Turn the page to see what happened over the next month.)

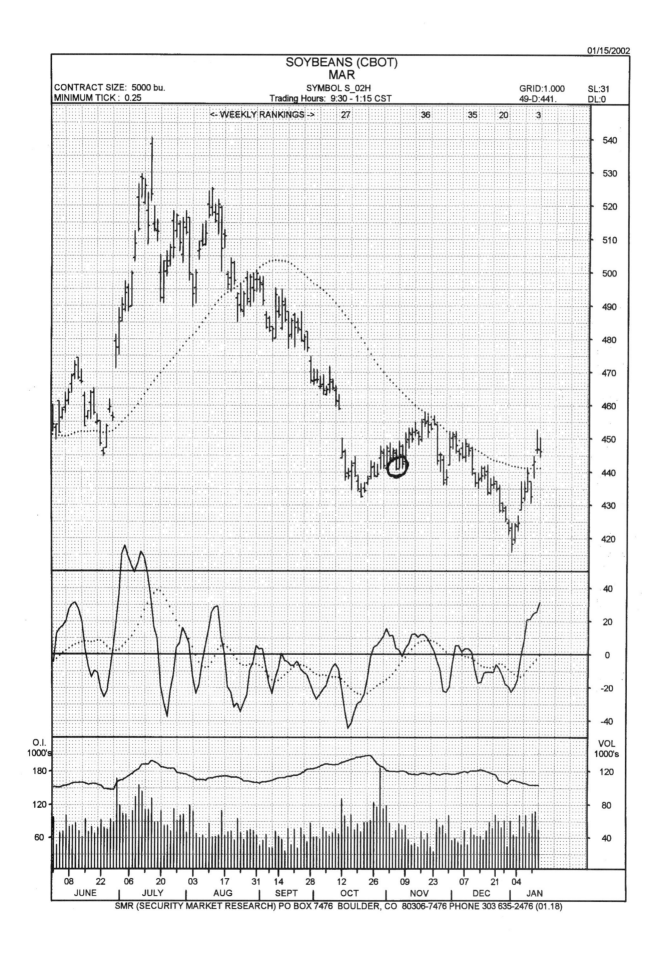

01/15/2002

SOYBEANS (CBOT)
MAR

CONTRACT SIZE: 5000 bu.
MINIMUM TICK : 0.25

SYMBOL S_02H
Trading Hours: 9:30 - 1:15 CST

GRID:1.000
49-D:441.

SL:31
DL:0

<- WEEKLY RANKINGS ->   27      36    35    20    3

O.I.
1000's

VOL
1000's

SMR (SECURITY MARKET RESEARCH) PO BOX 7476  BOULDER, CO  80306-7476  PHONE 303 635-2476 (01.18)

# March 2002 Soybeans (Feb 15)

**2/15:** This market tried the upside one more time on 1/16; however, while it closed looking quite positive that day, this strength did not last since it turned down the next day and just kept going. Once the price closed back under 4.40 again, then the trend became too indecisive to maintain long positions. Unfortunately, in the daily letter I suggested giving longs a little more time and/or using stop just under 4.35, a price that was hit the next day.

Subsequent to this mediocre trade, the market maintained a marginally negative pattern until the ML turned back up around 2/10. The lines indicated could have been short for a couple of weeks, but the price did not go anywhere. Depending precisely where any shorts were initiated and then covered, would have either made or lost a fairly small amount. However, in the daily letter during this time period, I repeatedly suggested passing on any shorts due to the quite bullish COT situation as well as the "low" price and the indecisive trend. I just did not see enough downside potential in this situation to justify the risk of being short.

As a rule, commodity markets tend to make broad bottoms and spike tops. This is due to the fact that at bottoms have, by definition, an oversupply of the commodity, and it invariably takes a long time to work this excess off. Whereas at tops, again by definition, supply is tight and price is rising in an attempt to reduce demand sufficiently to make sure supplies are never exhausted. In a free market the price will ensure we never run out of a commodity. Price will simply push up enough to make sure enough demand is eliminated so as to not completely run out of that commodity.

The newly "high" prices will encourage future increases in production (supply), and this additional supply will help bring the price back down. Therefore, if a government wants to ensure plentiful supplies at the lowest prices over the greatest period of time, then it needs to allow the free movement of price (i.e., no price controls) and be willing to tolerate the inevitable periods of unusually high prices. Short-term pain becomes long-term gain when prices are free. Short-term gain turns to long-term pain when governments control prices.

A long-term trader trading this market would have switched from longs to shorts around the first of September (in the 4.85 area), and then would have stuck with these shorts until prices finally moved above 50-day moving average in early January, thus turning the trend sideways. If using the ML (crosscurrent mode) to temporarily go to sidelines on either some or all of position, the long-term trader would have covered shorts in late October in 4.40-4.45 area and then reinstated these a month later at about the same prices. These shorts would have had some profits for a while; however, if the long-term trader had covered when the ML turned back to an up cycle in early January, then these profits would have disappeared. As mentioned earlier, if you can break even when a market is in a choppy, sideways period, then you can and should consider this a fairly successful result. Sometimes in this game, and especially in a choppy market, simply not losing is a victory.

02/15/2002

**SOYBEANS (CBOT)**
**MAR**

CONTRACT SIZE: 5000 bu.                         SYMBOL S_02H                          GRID:1.000        SL:12
MINIMUM TICK : 0.25                      Trading Hours: 9:30 - 1:15 CST                  49-D:435.3        DL:-6

<- WEEKLY RANKINGS ->        31            21        25      16        6

SMR (SECURITY MARKET RESEARCH) PO BOX 7476  BOULDER, CO  80306-7476  PHONE 303 635-2476 (01.18)

# March 2002 Wheat (Jan 2)

## REAL-TIME COMMENTARY

**1/2 (Wednesday):** Mar Wheat - Status - Bullish (to Neutral). Trend sideways to marginally up and ML marginally up so market remains in mild concurrent mode to upside. Action today slightly positive since closed back on recent highs and once again on verge of making upside-type breakout on price chart. Therefore, picture still on indecisive side but it remains positive enough to justify at least light long positions. Close above 2.96 should produce some kind of sustained upside move but have been having a hard time getting this done. Bottom line: Can be long with stops now just under 2.88.

. . . . . . . . . . . . . . . . . . . .

## AFTER-ACTION CRITIQUE

In looking at this chart picture two months after the fact I am somewhat surprised I was this bullish because the situation here is closer to neutral than positive. However, it is important to note that markets do not operate in a vacuum. There were other markets moving at the same time, and some of these markets were very similar to wheat—corn, soybeans, soybean meal, and oats. At the time, these other markets were acting firmly. Therefore, the group as a whole was showing clear signs of strength, and this group strength prompted me to look at the situation in wheat with an upside bias.

In addition, the Commitment of Traders report was showing that commercials had built their net long position up to levels where sustained rallies had started from in the past. While it is always dangerous to let the COT affect your vision, it was difficult not to do so here since it has been reliable in the past in this market. Plus, the COT report was showing commercials in corn, and beans were also at net levels where sustained rallies had commenced in the past.

If you look at this chart through those bullish "lenses," you can more easily see why I was tilting this essentially neutral picture over to one that was positive enough to justify at least light long positions here. However, I was aware the pattern was tenuous and so chose a fairly close stop—just under 2.88. A price under this level, and especially on the close, would have given this chart a clear downside tilt (since trend would then have been more down than up, SL would have turned down from lower high as well as putting in a bearish divergence with price, ML would have been within the margin-of-error to turn down, and the price would have been on the verge of a downside breakout on chart).

Therefore, the picture here was just marginally positive from a technical perspective, but since the COT was quite bullish and the other markets in the group were acting positively, I could justify long positions. Due to the situation being so marginally positive, I decided to use a fairly close stop. When odds are not so good, better not to risk as much.

Prudent placement of stops—"tight" or "generous"—is a part of money management. When the technical picture is solid, give the trade maximum chance to work by using a generous stop. When the technical picture is marginal, give the trade little chance to fail badly by using a tight stop. The more solid the line pattern, the more generous your stop; the more iffy the pattern, the tighter the stop.

# March 2002 Wheat (Jan 3)

**REAL-TIME COMMENTARY**

**1/3 (Thursday):** Mar Wheat - Status - Bullish. Trend and ML both up so market remains in concurrent mode to upside. Action very positive on potentially decisive upside breakout-type day. Can make decent case today a with-trend, non-news-related up spike, and rule is these tend to continue. This market remains clearly the most positive/strongest of group and so remains best of group for any longs. COT remains a background positive as commercials have been in area of net position where sustained up moves have started from in past (plus have "Morss" confirmation rule now in effect also since commercials starting to reverse this net-bullish position). So all signs positive here at moment, which means longs fully justified. Bottom line: Can be long with stops now 2.92.

......................

**AFTER-ACTION CRITIQUE**

Market had a big spike-type day to upside and this turned a marginally positive technical picture to one that was clearly bullish, and enough so to now fully justify longs. The trend was up (+1 point), the ML was up (+1/2) as well as above zero (for another +1/2), and the SL was up (+1) producing a total of plus three points and a Bullish Status. In addition, both trend and ML were up so the market was in concurrent mode to upside.

This big up day clearly stands out on the chart and so fully qualifies as an up spike. Since the move came without any news to explain it and was with the trend, then the spike rule fully indicated (both no news and with trend) it was more likely a continuation move than an aberration. While these types of spikes do not always continue (a similar spike day to downside five weeks earlier had not continued much lower), most of the time they do.

If throw in the continuing quite bullish COT situation and the general strength in the rest of group, all this meant that now had a solidly positive situation in this market. Therefore, even if a trader had not bought this market in the preceding few days (i.e., in anticipation of picture turning more clearly positive), there was plenty of reason to go long here.

I raised the stop from 2.88 to 2.92 since this was the starting point of the up-spike day. One part of spike rule is to consider any move back to starting point of spike as sufficient evidence to conclude the spike was an aberration. Therefore, a move back down to that level would have been too negative to stick with longs, regardless of what the existing line pattern happened to be. If the price had moved back down to 2.92 the next day, in this situation the lines would still have been bullish but the action would have been too negative to stay long. A one-day breakout to the upside followed by an immediate reversal the next day would be very unusual; however, a trader should be prepared for almost any possible price action. Placing stops in the market is one good way to be prepared for the worst.

Regardless, the overall picture here fully justified longs. Therefore, I saw no reason not to be long, and if were not already long, then should have been getting long very quickly. The "train" here was obviously leaving the station in a hurry. If wanted to be on board, then had to jump on quickly.

01/03/2002

WHEAT (CBOT)
MAR

CONTRACT SIZE: 5000 bu.
MINIMUM TICK : 0.25

SYMBOL W_02H
Trading Hours: 9:30 - 1:15 CST

GRID:0.500
49-D:290.8

SL:18
DL:6

<- WEEKLY RANKINGS ->    14         27      32    16    21

SMR (SECURITY MARKET RESEARCH) PO BOX 7476  BOULDER, CO  80306-7476  PHONE 303 635-2476  (01.16)

# March 2002 Wheat (Jan 4)

## REAL-TIME COMMENTARY

**1/4 (Friday):** Mar Wheat - Status - Bullish. Trend and ML both up so market remains in concurrent mode to upside. Action positive as kept pushing higher with little in way of downside pressure. ML usually the most reliable line for this market and this line still solidly up. This one remains best of group and so still best bet for any existing and new longs. This market usually does not make straight up (or down) moves, but no question pressure very powerful to upside at moment. If figure "official" buy signal came in the 2.90 area, then already have 100 percent of margin profit; however, since are in solid concurrent mode to upside, would override this and stick with any longs (but never argue too strongly against taking some partial profits when reach these levels). Bottom line: Can be long with stops still 2.92 for now.

......................

## AFTER-ACTION CRITIQUE

If a trader had wanted to buy on this day, he should have tried the evening market first, and if unable to do so at a reasonable (anywhere close to unchanged) price there, then he should have bought very early the next morning. Again, this train was leaving the station in a hurry here and so if you wanted to ride you had to jump aboard quickly. This meant not being too choosy about the price you paid (i.e., not waiting for a dip).

If you look at this chart you will see that the intermediate price swings in this market coincided very well with the cycles of the ML (or intermediate-term momentum indicator). Most of the traditional commodity markets tend to do this. It is a natural tendency for ML to coincide with intermediate-term price swings when dealing with a market where the supply is essentially known and the main variable is the demand. Since commodities are normally held in at least some form of inventory, this means demand can be somewhat (on a several week basis) adjusted up or down, forward and back. Therefore, there is a natural tendency for demand to lessen somewhat as price rises, and increase as price dips. This intermediate-term flexibility of demand is what produces the fairly rhythmic intermediate-term price cycles in storable commodities. However, what varies in each situation is the length and intensity of each of these intermediate-term cycles. The beauty of SMR's intermediate-term momentum indicator is its effectiveness in identifying these intermediate-term price cycles.

Therefore, in a pure commodity market like wheat (and others such as sugar, cocoa, cotton, beans, etc.) you should never be positioned against a solidly cycling ML for more than a few days, and then only if the trend is solidly in your favor. Conversely, any time the ML is solid in one of these commodities, you can make a case to be positioned with it, and especially if the trend and SL pattern concur with the cycle of the ML. Now, this does not mean you should stay with the ML cycle until it ends. It just means you can be positioned with it just about anytime it is making a solid move; although this is obviously more true when concurrent with trend than when at crosscurrents.

01/04/2002

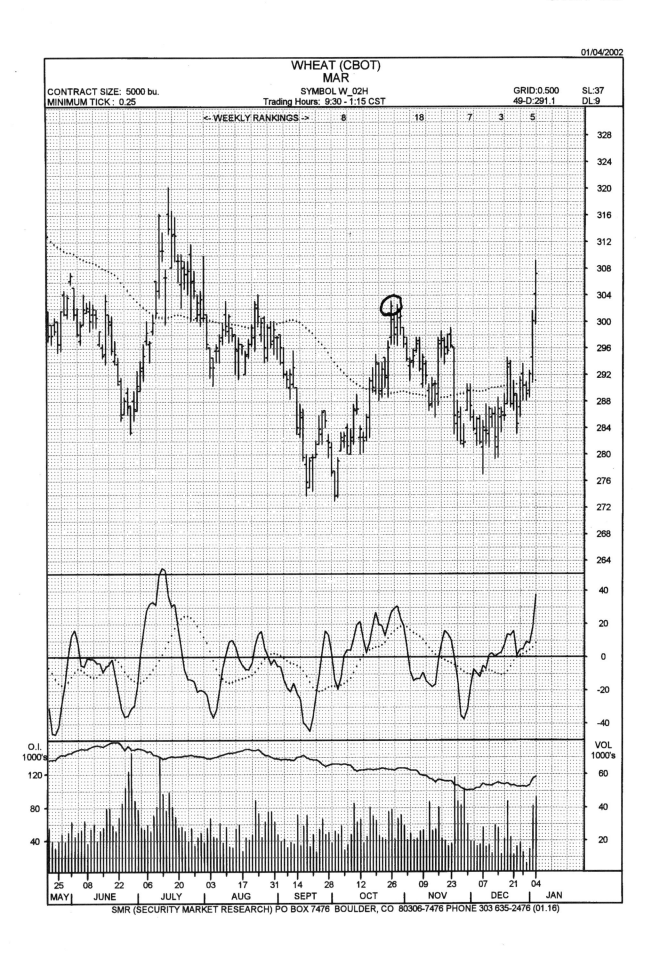

WHEAT (CBOT)
MAR

CONTRACT SIZE: 5000 bu.
MINIMUM TICK : 0.25

SYMBOL W_02H
Trading Hours: 9:30 - 1:15 CST

GRID:0.500
49-D:291.1

SL:37
DL:9

<- WEEKLY RANKINGS ->    8         18       7      3     5

SMR (SECURITY MARKET RESEARCH) PO BOX 7476  BOULDER, CO  80306-7476 PHONE 303 635-2476 (01.16)

# March 2002 Wheat (Jan 7/8/9/10)

(**NOTE:** *Have consolidated four days of commentaries onto one chart since price moved sideways during this time period. Keep in mind the difference in time to review these four days and to actually live through them. Your thoughts can produce lots of fear and hope in four days and so not as easy as it looks to just sit calmly long with stops in place.*)

**REAL-TIME COMMENTARY**

**1/7 (Monday):** Mar Wheat - Status - Bullish. Trend moderately up and ML solidly up so market remains in concurrent mode to upside. Action slightly negative on minor down day but see this as positive since this market has tendency to give back good moves quickly and so when does not it is a positive sign. Wheat is a strange market on fundamental basis in that rarely get a true shortage, but if ever get even close to one, then price can move up substantially. Really do not have good substitute for wheat (whole world needs bread), and so any threat of shortage tends to produce major upside moves, and this appears to be case at moment (i.e., have chance of shortage). However, more importantly, on technical basis all signs remain positive and continue to fully justify being long (and going long on any additional dip). Bottom line: Can be long with stops still in 2.92-2.94 area.

**REAL-TIME COMMENTARY**

**1/8 (Tuesday):** Mar Wheat - Status - Bullish. Trend and ML both still clearly up so market remains in solid concurrent mode to upside. Action neutral to slightly positive since came back late from minor early dip. Always a positive sign when any dips within solid upside concurrent mode are limited in both time and distance, and so far this has been case here past two days. With group as whole showing solid signs of putting in major bottoms and this one still being best of group, see no reason to take any profits yet (in spite of having 100 percent of margin profit), and can even still make case to be buyer at these levels. Bottom line: Can be long with stops still in low 2.90 area.

**REAL-TIME COMMENTARY**

**1/9 (Wednesday):** Mar Wheat - Status - Bullish. Trend and ML up so market still in concurrent mode to upside. Action slightly negative on minor downside reversal and third day of downside pressure; however, price remains well within bullish parameters. Past three days of slightly lower has look of bull flag which would expect to eventually break to upside. Always better if, when long, the price does not dip, but this rarely happens. Dip here has been well within acceptable levels, both in terms of price and distance. Price is on a moderate dip so could justify initiating new longs here. Group as whole showing some strength and this is positive for wheat. Bottom line: Can be (and go) long with stops still 2.94.

**REAL-TIME COMMENTARY**

**1/10 (Thursday):** Mar Wheat - Status - Bullish (to Neutral). Trend and ML up so market remains in concurrent mode to upside. Action neutral on slight up day but sell-off in final couple of minutes negated what otherwise would have been a quite positive day. Have crop production report here tomorrow, but "should" not be a major event since in middle of winter. Overall pattern remains clearly positive and indicates should see higher prices ahead. Past week of sideways to slightly lower has look of bull flag, which should eventually lead to an upside breakout. This one remains strongest/most positive of group and so still best bet for any longs. Bottom line: Can be (and go) long with stops still 2.94.

# March 2002 Wheat (Jan 11)

## REAL-TIME COMMENTARY

**1/11 (Friday):** Mar Wheat - Status - Bullish (to Neutral). Trend and ML still up so market remains in concurrent mode to upside. Action quite positive on good upside reversal and close at new recent highs. Market now poised for clear upside breakout from past week's bull flag. Therefore, all signs remain clearly positive and continue to fully justify being long. However, any failure to be up on Monday would have to be viewed as negative. Bottom line: Can be long with stops now in 3.02 to 3.04 area on close-only basis.

. . . . . . . . . . . . . . . . . . . .

## AFTER-ACTION CRITIQUE

Now the chart and line picture here was solidly positive and poised to become more so. The down move in the SL slowed perceptibly and so it was now on the verge of turning up from another higher low. The price was edging out of its recent sideways trading range to the upside, and doing this on a closing basis was even more positive. Therefore, expectations here would be for further up move the next day.

When I consider daily price action I look for both the pure up or down movement as well as how the price acts in relation to how it "should" have acted based on the line pattern. Therefore, in a case like this one I would expect no worse than a small up day next trading day, and actually consider anything less than four cents up (amount it was up on current day) to be somewhat negative. In a situation like this, if the upside was still solid, and all signs point to it being so, I would want to see the price pick up speed to the upside, and this would mean being up more on the second up day.

If use a margin of somewhere around $1000 (or a little less), and use 2.90 as the official entry level, this means that in 3.10 area would have reached the 100 percent of margin profit point. However, in this situation this could be overridden at this time since both the trend and ML were still clearly up.

Once again, whether to take profits in a situation like this one is strictly a trading decision. There is no absolute right or wrong answer, it is simply a decision. When making this type of trading decision, sometimes will be right, other times wrong. That is what trading is all about; simply cannot get away from decision making.

If you are in a position to trade multiple (more than one) numbers of contracts, then in a situation like this one I believe it is wise to take profits on at least a partial quantity of the contracts. How "partial" these profits should be is again simply a decision. However, if in a position to do so (i.e., if trading multiple contracts), I am quite certain that consistently taking partial profits as they move above 50 and 100 percent of margin levels will produce far better bottom line results than the opposite (i.e., consistently holding all contracts for the chance at the really big profit).

Therefore, all signs were solidly positive at this time; however, also had reached a 100 percent of margin profit and this always qualifies as a "good" profit.

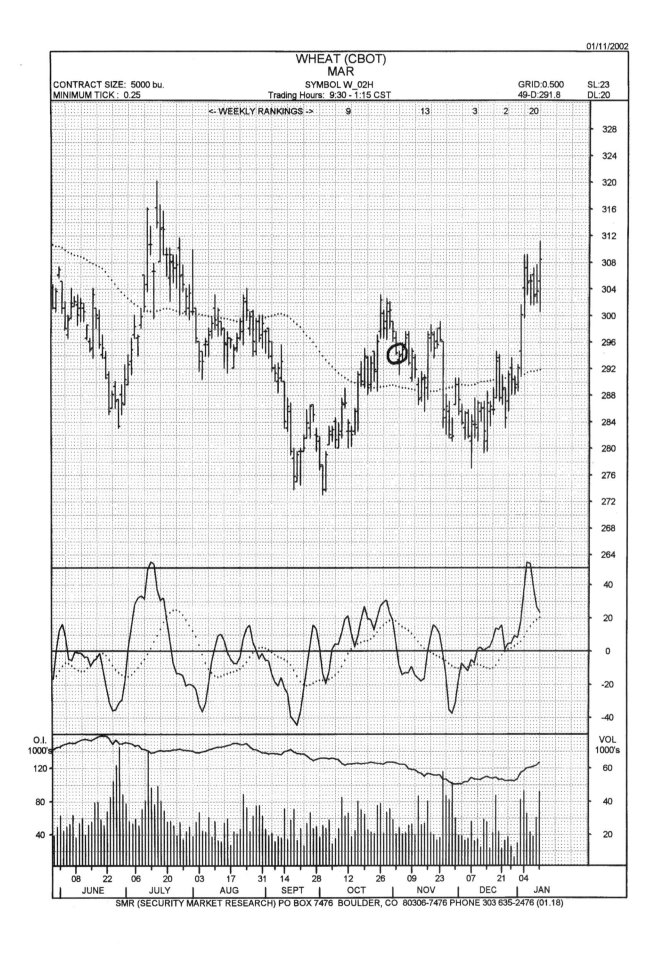

01/11/2002

WHEAT (CBOT)
MAR

CONTRACT SIZE: 5000 bu.
MINIMUM TICK : 0.25

SYMBOL W_02H
Trading Hours: 9:30 - 1:15 CST

GRID:0.500
49-D:291.8

SL:23
DL:20

<- WEEKLY RANKINGS ->    9    13    3    2    20

SMR (SECURITY MARKET RESEARCH) PO BOX 7476 BOULDER, CO 80306-7476 PHONE 303 635-2476 (01.18)

# March 2002 Wheat (Jan 14)

## REAL-TIME COMMENTARY

**1/14 (Monday):** Mar Wheat - Status - Bullish (to Neutral). Trend and ML still both up but ML now only marginally up so concurrent mode weakening. Action today quite negative on reversal day to downside. Mentioned Friday that any failure to be up today would be quite negative sign and that's what had today. So lines still say longs OK here, but now getting quite shaky and another down day tomorrow would turn picture too negative to stick with longs. "Official" entry level on current buy signal was in 2.90 area and so market has made a little more than 100 percent of margin profit and this may turn out to be all that get here. So close call here as lines and chart still say longs justified, but would not argue with taking profits and going to sidelines, or at least using fairly tight stop. Bottom line: Lines say can still be long with stops just under 3.04 (entered after first thirty minutes or so), but hard to argue with sidelines now.

...................

## AFTER-ACTION CRITIQUE

No question this action was disappointing for anyone coming into day with longs since all signs had been so positive expectations would have been quite high. However, while this was a negative day, it was not necessarily a fatally negative day. The SL only moved down slightly, so the overall line pattern remained essentially the same as the preceding day, meaning it was still solidly positive. In addition, the price did not close low enough to change the overall quite positive price chart since it closed right at the previous top of the bull flag. Therefore, it was a disappointing day but not a decisive one.

If holding multiple positions here, the most professional, businesslike action would have been to take some more profits (sell some more) while still maintaining a small long position. Again, the size of this small long position would be is just another trading decision. However, I was clearly leaning toward taking profits here rather than sticking around. There were two reasons for this: First, I found the downside reversal day to be very negative; and second, the 100 percent of margin profit level had been reached.

If you decide to be a short-term trader, then I believe it is best to be pickier getting in, sloppier getting out. Therefore, whenever you see some price action completely opposite to what the lines suggest you should be seeing (more so on an end-of-day basis, since you have to be careful about reading too much into intra-day moves), then I see nothing wrong with taking profits and going to sidelines. As an individual trader it is wise to be somewhat of a coward when holding good profits. Unless the background technicals (i.e., the trend and ML) are BOTH solidly positive, you can always make a legitimate case to take profits when they reach the 100 percent (or slightly more) of margin level.

Lines still said longs were OK here, but for the first time since the up spike day a week and a half earlier, I was no longer comfortable being long. I had moved stop level up sharply a day earlier and maintained those. Since this stop level was only three cents under the current close I saw little reason to put the trade on strict probation, which I otherwise probably would have done.

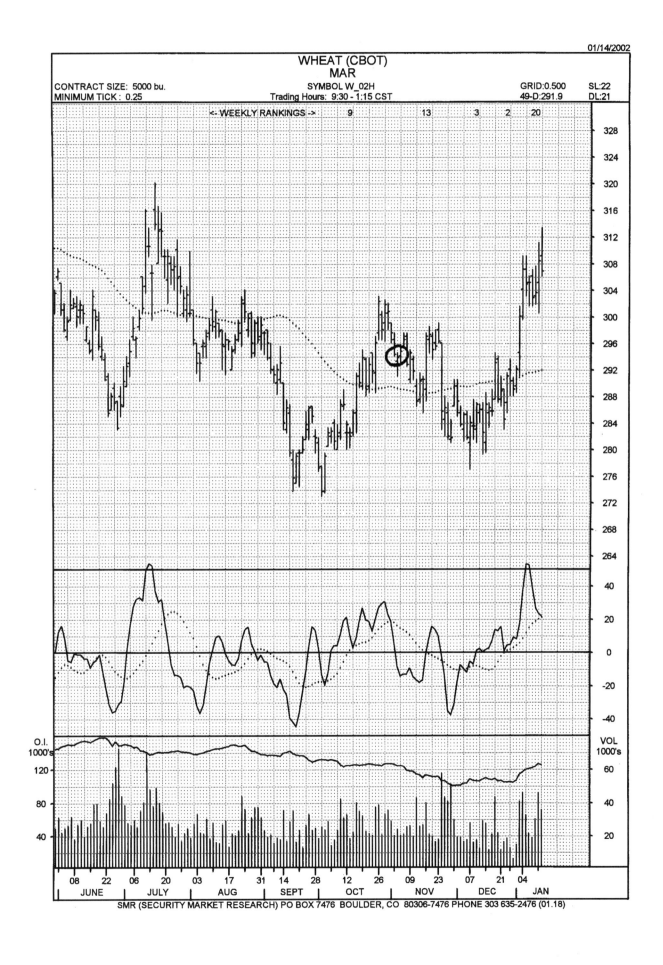

01/14/2002

WHEAT (CBOT)
MAR

CONTRACT SIZE:  5000 bu.
MINIMUM TICK :  0.25

SYMBOL W_02H
Trading Hours:  9:30 - 1:15 CST

GRID:0.500
49-D:291.9

SL:22
DL:21

<- WEEKLY RANKINGS ->        9              13              3       2       20

SMR (SECURITY MARKET RESEARCH) PO BOX 7476  BOULDER, CO  80306-7476  PHONE 303 635-2476 (01.18)

# March 2002 Wheat (Jan 15)

## REAL-TIME COMMENTARY

**1/15 (Tuesday):** Mar Wheat - Status - Bullish (to Neutral). Trend up but ML now only slightly up, so market still in concurrent mode to upside but weakening. Action slightly negative as market under light but persistent downside pressure all day and closed near low of day. Odds still favor upside as trend up and rest of picture slightly positive, but unless up sharply tomorrow, pattern will go to neutral. So tough call if still long since due for some upside action since on twelve-cent dip in day and a half within a positive pattern, but picture turning increasingly too neutral (or negative) to fully justify longs. Do not see picture as type that would lead to sustained down move, so if sold yesterday in 3.08 or higher area (easy to have done so), could make case to put limit orders for light longs in 2.98 area looking for six- to eight-cent bounce, but other than that see sidelines as best. Bottom line: Lines say can still be long, but very shaky now so prefer sidelines.

......................

## AFTER-ACTION CRITIQUE

Now, for first time since the up spike day of week and a half earlier, this chart was showing some clear downside warning signs. The main negative here now was fact the SL could not turn up and instead was picking up speed to the downside.

In a case like this I will consider the "near upturn" in the SL over the previous two days here as the same as if it had actually turned up. What you are trying to read in the three trend/momentum lines are indications of price energy flows. You should neither look for, nor expect to see, perfectly rhythmic line patterns. We are dealing with constantly unfolding unknown futures. These unknown futures are being directed by the independent trading decisions of thousands of separate individuals. While certain natural laws of trading and pricing will tend to govern the results of these aggregate decisions, these laws will produce only generally conforming results, not mathematically perfect ones. Therefore, treat near turns in the SL the same as actual turns.

By suggesting the placement of buy orders in the 2.98 area, I was simply concluding that the dip had gone too far to make liquidating any remaining longs worthwhile because I expected a resumption of the rally fairly soon. This expectation was due to the fact the overall picture was still reasonably positive here. Both the price chart and the line pattern, as well as the COT situation, remained quite bullish.

This is the main problem with the Commitment of Traders data; it is difficult to keep it in its place. It can be very helpful at the beginning of a sustained move, but once this move has gone on for both some time and distance, then the COT bias tends to become more of a hindrance than a help. It makes taking profits more difficult when they reach the natural objectives (i.e., 50, 100, 150 percent of margin profit) because it is only natural to be reluctant to get out of a move where the commercials remain at high (bullish in this case) net levels. What we need to keep in mind is that the COT data should only be used as a deep background indicator, and even then only as an extra positive or negative that might push us into otherwise marginal or not quite yet solid trades. When taking profits, ignoring the COT tends to work best. (Turn the page to see next month's action.)

01/15/2002

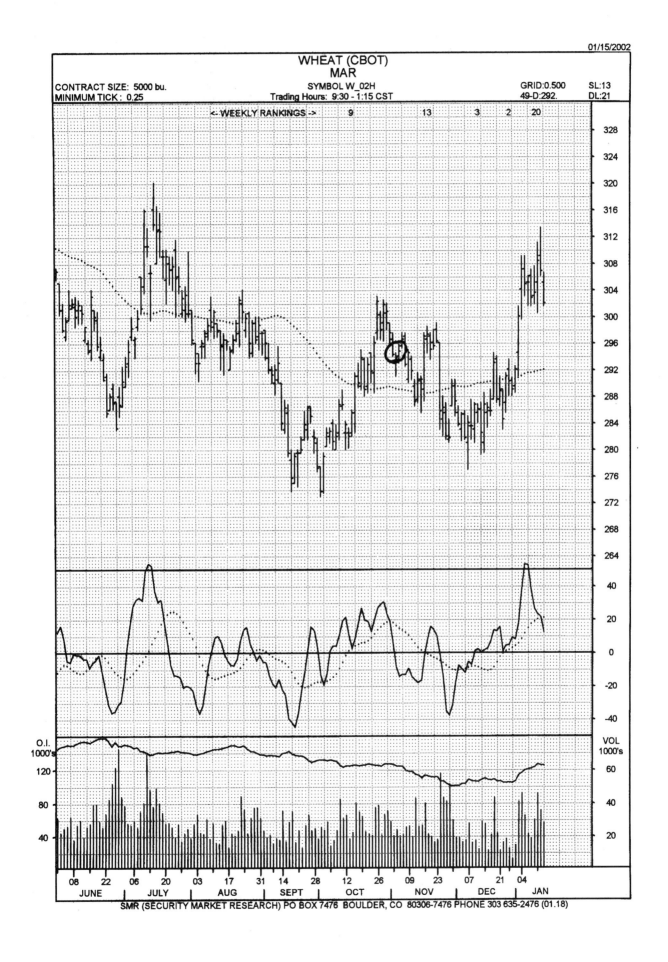

WHEAT (CBOT)
MAR

CONTRACT SIZE:  5000 bu.
MINIMUM TICK :  0.25

SYMBOL W_02H
Trading Hours: 9:30 - 1:15 CST

GRID:0.500      SL:13
49-D:292.      DL:21

<- WEEKLY RANKINGS ->        9          13       3    2   20

SMR (SECURITY MARKET RESEARCH) PO BOX 7476  BOULDER, CO  80306-7476 PHONE 303 635-2476 (01.18)

# March 2002 Wheat (Feb 15)

**2/15:** Somewhat surprisingly this market just kept pushing lower for the month after January 15; therefore, getting out early (before lines turned clearly neutral) in this case was the best approach. Once again, it turned out that simply taking profits at the 100 percent of margin level was the most profitable approach.

On 1/24 the SL turned up again (price closed at 2.98 1/2), and since the trend was still slightly up and ML was still above zero, this produced a mild crosscurrent buy signal; however, I was skeptical and wrote the following in the daily letter: "…could always surprise on upside since trend up and SL and price both moving up from recent lows, so nothing wrong with light longs here but prefer to stick to sidelines as a little too mixed. COT in Wheat now bearish and in position to support sustained down move." This skepticism proved wise since the price immediately turned down again and fairly quickly turned pattern back to Neutral. Crosscurrent signals will always have lesser odds for success, and the weaker the underlying trend, the lower the odds (in this case the uptrend had become very marginal by 1/24).

Then on 1/28 (two markets days later since 1/25 was a Friday, therefore 1/28 a Monday) the price closed at 2.92, just under the ten-week moving average, and I wrote the following: "With close back at 2.92, past three weeks of action above this level now has look of false upside breakout and an 'island,' so charts now quite negative also. COT also clearly on negative side (commercials in area of extreme net short position) and so this an added negative. If downside good for time being, and all signs indicate is, then price should not go back up to Friday's close, so could use stops on any shorts in that area. Bottom line: Lines say sidelines due to indecisive trend, but rest of picture negative enough so that now can make decent case for shorts with stops just above 2.98 for now."

The price subsequently moved slowly but steadily lower for another two weeks before first the SL turned up and then the ML followed and thus turned Status back to Neutral. If shorts had been covered at that time (with price in 2.81 area), the trade would have produced slightly more than a 50 percent of margin profit (short at 2.92, covered at 2.81 for eleven-cent profit; at the time needed about an eighteen-cent profit for 100 percent of margin profit).

Therefore, over a month and a half time period, by following the natural laws of trading and the specific rules laid out in this book, a trader could have made 100 percent profit on the upside, followed by a 50 percent profit on the down side.

Once again, notice how well intermediate-term price moves coincided with ML cycles.

(**NOTE:** *COT positions here changed quickly and significantly in only a month and a half.*)

02/15/2002

WHEAT (CBOT)
MAR

CONTRACT SIZE: 5000 bu.
MINIMUM TICK : 0.25

SYMBOL W_02H
Trading Hours: 9:30 - 1:15 CST

GRID:0.500
49-D:290.7

SL:-6
DL:-20

<- WEEKLY RANKINGS ->   39   40   42   43   40

SMR (SECURITY MARKET RESEARCH) PO BOX 7476 BOULDER, CO 80306-7476 PHONE 303 635-2476 (01.18)

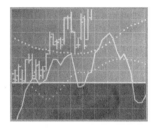

# CONCLUSION ON CHART EXAMPLES

THE FUTURE IS UNKNOWN; however, as you should have seen on the preceding pages of chart examples, there is no question prices give off many good clues as to what this unknown future *most likely* will be. Prices do not move randomly, rather prices *generally* follow natural laws. While these laws of trading/pricing do not have the mechanical precision or reliability of natural physical laws, they clearly have similar tendencies.

There is also no question that SMR's trend/momentum indicators fully qualify as reasonably reliable indicators of short-, intermediate-, and long-term price energy flows. It is also clear that when the majority of these three reasonably reliable indicators of price energy flows are pointing in the same direction, the odds will favor the price moving in that direction over the immediate future. Therefore, the three SMR trend/momentum lines, as represented by their Status and mode, are a sound starting point for any and all trading decisions.

Keep in mind I could have gone and cherry-picked "perfect" examples of the various trading rules; however, this approach would have been dishonest as well as not particularly helpful. I felt the most honest and revealing approach was to pick a two-week period ***in advance***, since this approach would present a more accurate, real-life example of the validity of the methodology laid out in this book. I chose the first two weeks of the year simply because this was a logical starting point. Based on many years of experience, I am certain I could have chosen any two-week time period and the results would have been about the same. However, do not take my word for this; test the approach and method laid out herein for yourself. If you do so, you should be able to see that markets do tend to follow the natural laws of trading.

## BOTTOM LINE

If you use some reasonably reliable indicators of trend and momentum (and SMR's lines are *at least* reasonably reliable), and then follow a few basic, natural law-based trading and money management rules, you will instantly become a competitive player (trader) in a game where most individuals have essentially no chance of competing successfully. Develop a little "art" of reading the charts and acting on what you see and you can do extremely well. Put it all together and you will have become one of the few individual traders able to win at this game on a year-in, year-out basis.

# STOCK CHARTS

I HAVE NEVER TRADED STOCKS. While many years ago I bought and sold stocks, I have never really traded them; therefore, I am somewhat reluctant to offer much in the way of advice and suggestions for doing so. However, within a month or so of my writing this we will see the advent of single stock futures trading, and as a result I am sure I probably will be doing some trading in stocks sometime in the not too distant future. How successful the single stock futures market will become is hard to guess, but it does have the potential to become a very big market.

I have always found the stock market, as well as the entire stock market business, to be somewhat strange. One important difference between stocks and commodity markets is that the stock market is primarily—almost exclusively—a one-sided market, while the commodity markets are always two-sided. By this I mean that in every commodity there are always powerful forces on both sides of the market, the long and short side; however, in the stock market virtually all the powerful forces are on the long side. This is true both on the macro and micro level.

Regardless of the commodity, there are always powerful forces among suppliers of the commodity and powerful forces among users. In addition, in the commodity futures markets there will always be a long for every short. However, in the stock market all the powerful forces are on the buyer/long side. Furthermore, in stocks there is not a short for every long, as virtually all are long. Therefore, the only people who want the prices of stocks to go down are the very small minority who happen to be short.

In discussing stock trading with stock traders who use SMR's trend/momentum lines, I have come to the conclusion that the same basic laws and rules apply. Therefore, I am quite confident that a stock trader, be it of individual stocks or single stock futures, could use the same approach/method laid out in this book with the same degree of success.

On the following three pages are the charts of WorldCom, Tyco, and Wells Fargo. WorldCom has since gone bankrupt, causing tremendous financial loss; however, anyone familiar with the natural laws of pricing would have liquidated any holdings of this stock long before it reached (essentially) zero, as it eventually did. Even at this point on the chart, several months before it hit zero, it clearly shows that the odds favored lower prices ahead. Tyco did not fare much better, as subsequent to the time period on this chart its price dropped to the twelve-dollar level. Again, anyone familiar with the natural laws of pricing would have seen the many danger signs on this chart and removed this stock from their portfolio. I have also included a chart of Wells Fargo in order to show that trends work in both directions, up as well as down. Notice how this stock adhered to its trend, first on the downside and then to the upside. In addition, please note how whenever any of these three stocks were in a clear concurrent mode (either to the upside or downside), then their price movement was fairly easy and effortless in that direction. In other words, whether it is a commodity future, a financial future, a single stock future, or just a plain individual stock, the natural laws of pricing/trading continue to apply.

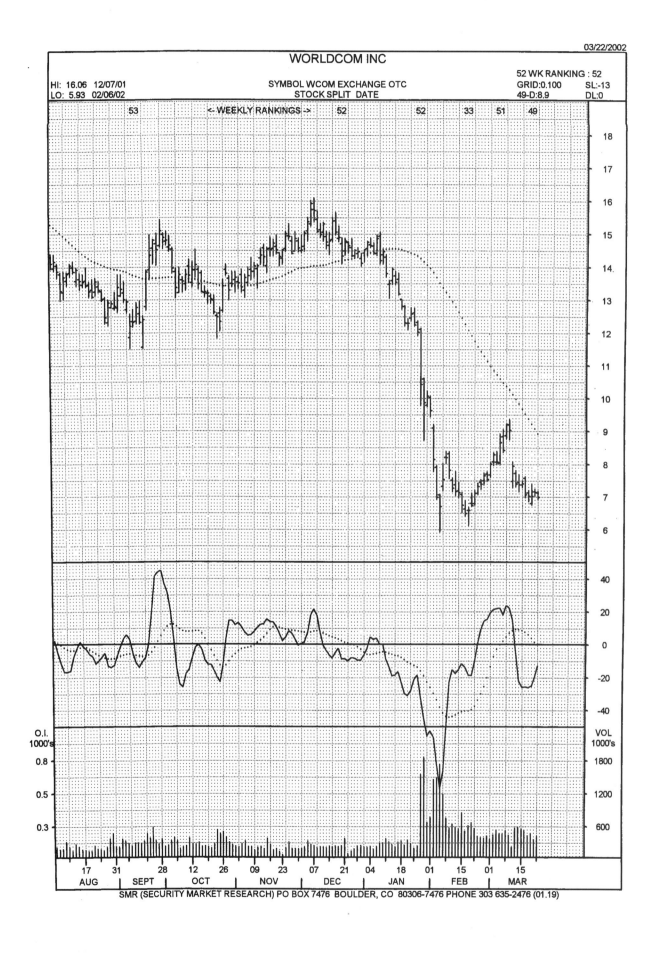

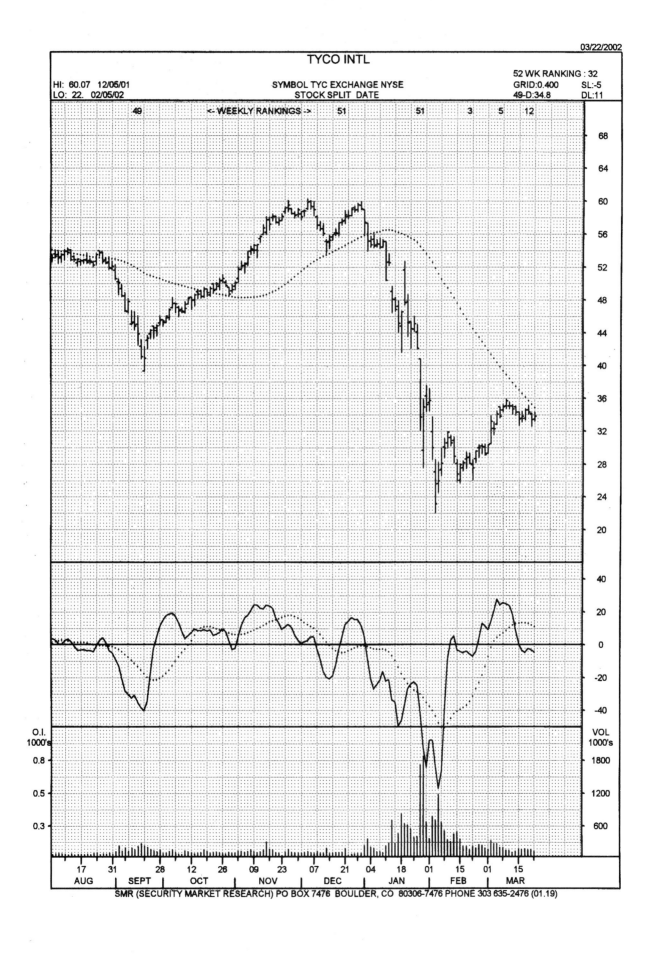

03/22/2002

TYCO INTL

HI: 60.07  12/05/01
LO: 22.  02/05/02

SYMBOL TYC EXCHANGE NYSE
STOCK SPLIT  DATE

52 WK RANKING : 32
GRID:0.400     SL:-5
49-D:34.8      DL:11

<- WEEKLY RANKINGS ->

49          51          51      3      5     12

68
64
60
56
52
48
44
40
36
32
28
24
20

40
20
0
-20
-40

O.I.
1000's

0.8
0.5
0.3

VOL
1000's

1800
1200
600

17    31    28    12    26    09    23    07    21    04    18    01    15    01    15
AUG      SEPT      OCT       NOV       DEC       JAN       FEB       MAR

SMR (SECURITY MARKET RESEARCH) PO BOX 7476  BOULDER, CO  80306-7476  PHONE 303 635-2476 (01.19)

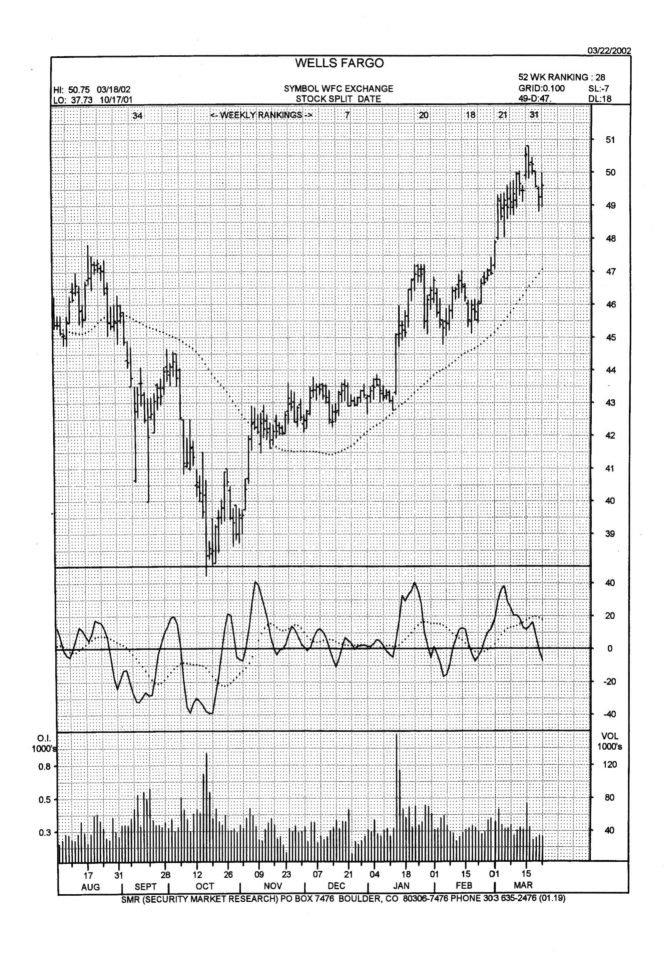

# PUTTING IT ALL TOGETHER

TRADING IS SIMPLE, BUT NOT EASY. However, if an individual has a clear understanding of the natural laws and truths that govern price movement and trading, then that individual has a good chance of succeeding.

Start with acknowledging you cannot compete in the game/business of trading on the basis of information and knowledge (of supply/demand). To believe otherwise is an enormous conceit, a conceit bordering on clinical delusion. Yet, every day tens of thousands of otherwise fairly intelligent people foolishly try to play the trading game by relying on information and knowledge (of supply/demand). They constantly search for the latest information on the markets they are trading. They spend hours studying the fundamental supply/demand situation of these different markets. They waste thousands of dollars on ever more complex, computerized trading software and systems. They search endlessly for that final, but ever so elusive, price "indicator" that will lead them from trading mediocrity to consistent success. Unfortunately, these are all fools' errands.

In order to be competitive, the individual trader—be he or she ordinary or even extraordinary—must approach trading in such a way as to instantly and permanently level the competitive playing field. The way to do this is to treat trading as a simple up or down money game—nothing more, nothing less. In real life you and I cannot compete with the best professional athletes in the world; however, change the playing "field" to "computer" golf, tennis, football, baseball, etc. and we can compete.

Approach trading purely as an up or down money game and you will instantly change the playing field to one where the ordinary individual and the large institution are on essentially equal footing. A number moving up and down is exactly the same to you and me as it is to the biggest corporations and best professional traders. So, the first step is to approach the problem of trading correctly by seeing it for what it really is: a simple up or down money game where the objective is to sell higher than you buy and buy lower than you sell.

The next step is to build your trading methodology upon natural laws. There are three natural laws of trading. The first states *the future is unknown*. This simply means not to waste time and energy on trying to see into the future. The simple truth is there is nothing to be seen when trying to peer into the future because the future is an unformed, black void. The future is always yet to be made, and what is not yet made cannot be known. This first law of trading/pricing is the "bad news" law.

Fortunately, there is a "good news" law of trading; it is the second law. This law states *continuation is more likely than change.* The second law of trading (and pricing) is merely the physical law of bodies in motion applied to prices in motion. To make your best estimate of where a body in motion will go next, you do not look in front of it, you look behind it—where it has come from. A physical body moving in a clearly defined direction is more likely to continue moving in that direction than change direction. Therefore, since prices are, in essence, bodies in motion, they will act similarly. Accordingly, the best way to anticipate a price's most likely future direction is to "see" its existing past to present price energy flow, and then extrapolate that flow forward.

In order to intelligently extrapolate a price's most likely future movement, it is necessary to have some reasonably reliable measurements of its current trend and momentum. Since we have accepted that we cannot compete in terms of complexity, it is only logical to keep our measurements of price energy flows limited to short term, intermediate term, and long term.

While there are undoubtedly many reasonably reliable indicators of price energy flow, I have found those provided by SMR to be, at least, sufficiently accurate. Of course, any reasonably reliable indicators of price energy flow can be substituted for SMR's, just so long as they are reasonably reliable. The same natural laws of motion apply regardless of the type of instruments used to measure them. I am comfortable with, and so prefer, SMR's trend/momentum indicators. The point is whether you measure speed in miles per hour or kilometers per hour, the actual speed will be the same.

The basic idea is to trade on what you "see" in the price movement rather than where you "think" the price should go. Unfortunately, we are human and so tend to see through the distorting lens of personal bias. This bias comes from our past experiences and our incidental knowledge as well as our hopes and fears about the unknown future. To help us penetrate the distortions caused by these biases, we need a mathematically objective way to measure current price energy flows. The three-point system I have laid out herein does this very well. While this point system is far from perfect, it is more than adequate.

The approach and method as laid out in this book shows you, the individual trader, how to intelligently play the trading game. However, in the end (unless you do not care about the financial results) trading is a business and needs to be treated as such. This is where the third law of trading is applied: *prices fluctuate.* This law means, to survive you must control your losses, to succeed you must take profits.

There is no other way to make money in trading than by taking profits. On the surface this is obvious, in practice it is not. Since margin is the amount you must put forward to put on a position, using margin to measure success on each trade is a sound, businesslike practice. Making 50 or 100 percent or more on a trade is an excellent return for any business. Therefore, when 50 percent of margin profit on a trade has been reached, it only makes business sense to look to see whether there is a reason to take this profit. Furthermore, should 100 percent, or more, of margin profit be achieved, it only makes business sense to take this good profit unless there are clear and sound reasons not to do so. The "clear and sound" reasons used to decide whether or not to take profits when they are good are the current price energy flows. Therefore, when holding a trade with good profits, use the three SMR trend/momentum indicators to tell you whether there are any serious signs of deterioration in the current price energy flows. And if there are, take profits; if not, hold for potentially bigger profits.

The primary reason not to take profits when they are "good" is if both the trend and the intermediate-term momentum are moving decisively in the same direction, i.e., they are moving *concurrently*. This is only logical; the longer the time period used for measuring price energy flow, the slower that indicator will be in changing its direction and the more reliable its current indications will be for the intermediate term. Therefore, long-term and intermediate-term price energy flows, once clearly established, will have a clear tendency to continue, regardless of short-term conditions.

While it is naturally sound business practice to take good profits when you have them, when and if the long-term and intermediate-term price energy flows are *concurrently* strong, there is nothing wrong—in fact it is frequently correct—to hold onto that position for a while longer, regardless of how much profit it has at the moment.

Being positioned in markets when the Status (my mathematically objective measurement of price energy flow) is Bullish or Bearish should increase your odds of success beyond a simple fifty-fifty random chance. Being positioned in markets where the Status is Bullish (or Bearish) and the "mode" is solidly concurrent to the upside (or downside) should increase your odds of success even further. However, keep in mind, in each case the proposition still will be less than 100 percent. While the odds may be above 50 percent random chance levels in these cases (Bullish/Bearish Status, concurrent mode), they always will be less than a 100 percent certainty; there will always be risk.

The businesslike approach to a situation where you are faced with a continuing series of bets/trades where the odds are in your favor on each, but never absolute on any, is to make multiple bets/trades. The way to do this is to divide your trading account (your trading capital) so as to never commit (in terms of margin) more than one quarter of the account's margin to any one market or group of similar markets. The point is, if you are placing only those trades where the odds are above 50 percent (Bullish/Bearish Status and/or concurrent mode trades), spreading your risk over many different markets will increase your odds of surviving and prospering in this difficult game. Therefore, it only makes sense to diversify.

Trade as many different markets and groups of similar markets as you can handle well. Spreading your exposure to both risk and opportunity will automatically ensure each individual trade you place will only risk a small amount of your capital. In other words, *trade small*. Trading "small" allows you to approach trading as a game you "play" rather than a potentially life or death financial situation on one trade. Trading small ensures that no one trade is overly important or significant, and thus will keep fear and greed under control.

In other words, if you have a method that enables you to consistently make trades where the odds are in your favor, then the best approach is to simply let the odds work for you by spreading out your bets. Every trader has his or her limits on how many different markets he or she can follow and trade at one time. However, once you become comfortable with this basic approach and method, you should be able to follow anywhere from six to twenty (or even more) different markets on a daily basis and then be positioned in at least three (with clearly positive or negative patterns) at the same time. Over time, as a trader becomes more familiar with this method, and more confident, he or she should be able to be positioned in as many as eight, or even more, markets at the same time—treating each market completely independently, according to its particular technical situation.

## ACTION AND ACTING

Over 99 percent of the time a trader devotes to the game/business of trading is spent on preparing to make trades. Less than one percent of a trader's time is spent on actually making the trades. Yet, 100 percent of the results of trading comes from the actual, final *act* of entering the trades. This means that 100 percent of our trading results comes from that part of the process we spend the least amount of time doing (the actual act of trading).

Knowing how to approach and play the game of trading well will only take you part way to ultimate success. Knowing "how" to trade only makes you *potentially* competitive. All that knowing "how" to do any activity does is give you a chance. It is always the actual *acting* that produces the results, not the *knowing* how to act. Knowing is not acting. Thinking is not acting. Planning is not acting. Wanting to act is not acting. Only acting is acting.

It is not enough to see, understand, and know the correct approach/method for trading. To succeed you must be able to act freely and decisively, you must be able to "pull the trigger." One of the primary reasons individual traders fail is an inability to act freely and decisively. Freedom in action comes about when fear has been minimized. Trading small and diversifying neutralizes fear.

Decisiveness in action comes from clarity. Clarity is achieved through an understanding of natural laws and the resulting probabilities.

First, of course, an individual must use the correct approach and a good method. Sadly, many (most?) traders possess neither correct approach nor good method, and as a result they have essentially no chance. They are doomed to ultimate failure, and usually sooner rather than later. Without the proper approach and method, a traders' only chance is to be lucky. However, over any extended period of time luck will never be able to overcome the wrong approach and/or a poor method. The correct approach and a good method are prerequisites to success; however, these are by no means guarantors of success. Ultimate success or failure is determined by daily action.

A good way to produce sufficiently free and decisive action is to simply surrender to the lines and price action. Surrender to the visible price energy flows. Do not think about what is going to happen, instead simply look at the price energy flows (as depicted by the lines, the current and projected Status and mode, and the action of the price in relation to the line patterns), then call your broker and place orders (at the market or fairly close limits) to position with this flow.

When profits become "good" (100 percent to 150 percent of margin), take some unless there are obvious price energy flow reasons not to do so. If a trade is showing a loss, most of the time the lines (i.e., the price energy flow) will give enough warning signs to liquidate the trade before these losses become too big. However, on those rare occasions when the loss begins to get too big (over 50 percent of margin) without any "line pattern" warning signs, then simply step aside (take the loss) until the picture clarifies.

You cannot trade without making constant decisions. Therefore, just surrender to this fact and simply act when the lines tell you to, or when you can legitimately make the case they are about to do so. If subsequent events prove your decision wrong, then simply correct this by acting again. Let your eyes see, then act on what they have seen.

I can point out a sound approach. I can show you a good method. I can demonstrate how to be businesslike. However, I cannot act for you. Only you can act, and the only way to act is to simply act.

See reality as it is, not as you wish it were. Your desires, wishes, and hopes have absolutely nothing to do with reality as it is. Once you see reality as it is, then, based on natural law, act on what you have seen. Surrender to the price energy flows by placing positions with these flows. If the lines are clear, or you can make an intelligent case they are about to become clear, just make the trade. Then continue to watch the price energy flows on a day-by-day basis and either take the profit or loss when you can make a reasonable case it is time to do so. You will rarely get in and out perfectly; just accept this. Trading is not a game for the perfectionist. Fortunately, when you use a sound approach and method, perfection is not required for success. In fact, it is possible to be quite "sloppy" on the specifics of getting in and out and still do well—if you use the correct approach and a good method.

If your account is big enough for multiple positions, take advantage of this by scaling in your orders over time (spread out getting in or out, whether over one day or several days—depending on the situation). If holding multiple positions and profits become big enough, then take some profits on the same type of scale basis. Using this approach is like the difference between using a shotgun or a rifle to hit a moving target; it is easier to hit a moving target when using a shotgun than a rifle.

In trading it is only wise to avoid all-or-nothing decisions. Diversify, scale in, scale out. Spread out your decisions (make many trades; as the lines dictate, of course) and your decision making should naturally improve. Play the odds. Let the probabilities work for you. When the odds, according to the natural laws of trading and the price energy flows, are clearly in your favor, just make the trade. When the probabilities (as indicated by the lines) materially lessen, liquidate the trade. Do not make a big deal, intellectually or financially, over any one trade. When the line pattern of a market indicates, or looks like it is about to indicate, that the odds clearly favor the upside or downside, just make the trade (at the market). Do this one trade at a time, one day at a time, trade by trade, day by day.

Trust the natural laws. Surrender to the lines and the price action. Constantly push yourself to act freely, decisively, intelligently—day by day, every day. Doing this is no guarantee of ultimate success. However, in the end, it is the best we can do.

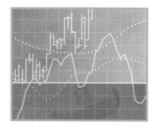

# COMMON TRADER PITFALLS

OVER MY THIRTY-PLUS YEARS OF TRADING I have seen a number of trading "pitfalls" recur fairly consistently, both in myself and others. I suggest you take pains to recognize, and then avoid, any of the following:

## TRADING AGAINST THE TREND

Excessive trading against the trend is probably the number one reason most individual traders end up losing. The trend is like the current of a river; over time it will always be easier and more profitable to go with the current than against it.

Trading with clear price energy flows has a higher probability than trading against them. The trend is the primary price energy flow. Therefore, you should make the overwhelming majority of your trades with the trend. See the wisdom of not fighting the primary price energy flow (i.e., the trend) and then simply do not do so, unless there are very good reasons.

If and when a legitimate case can be made the trend may be about ready to turn and virtually all other indicators are pointing opposite the current trend, then there is nothing wrong with going against the trend. (However remember, the price will always look "low" in down-trending markets and "high" in uptrending ones, so do not give relative price levels much weight when considering against-the-trend trades.)

Should you be one of those who insist on repeatedly trading against clear trends, then, on behalf of all with-the-trend traders, I would like to take this opportunity to thank you. Your generosity has been, and will continue to be, greatly appreciated.

## TOO MANY CONTRACTS ON ONE TRADE

This is probably the number two reason most individual traders end up losing; they trade too aggressively by putting on too many contracts (basis size of account). A key to consistent success in trading is to keep position size **SMALL**! This is so important I wish I could slam this book down in front of you and shout **TRADE SMALL!!!**

All solidly concurrent mode and/or solidly Bullish/Bearish Status trades should have a consistently better than 50 percent probability of success; however, none of these trades will ever be 100 percent certain. Therefore, no matter how good a particular trade might look, do not put on too many contracts; do not go above your personal trading limits for each market or group of markets.

Do not try to make it "all" on one trade. Instead keep position size small and allow the natural laws of trading and your reasonably reliable trend/momentum indicators maximum opportunity to work for you.

## INABILITY TO ACT FREELY AND DECISIVELY

Most individual traders have a difficult time acting freely and decisively. Once the natural laws are understood and a minimum ability to read price energy flows is acquired, then the primary reason for an inability to act freely and decisively is the fear of making mistakes.

Too many traders act as if their trading decisions are in some way permanent, thus they do not make a trade unless—or until—a situation looks perfect. Unfortunately, perfect trade setups rarely come along, and even when they do, the truth is, "perfect" does not work that much better than "good."

In order to profit from seeing the truth of the natural laws of trading, in order to make money from an ability to read price energy flows, you must be able to act freely and decisively. Your overriding daily objective is to be consistently and persistently positioned with current and projected price energy flows. Once you are able to identify these flows, there is only one way to position with them and that is by acting. Therefore, as soon as trend and momentum become reasonably clear, act!

Do not fall into the habit of waiting for a line-pattern signal to work (i.e., prove itself) before acting. To be successful you must be able to act when the lines initially begin to become clear, even if the trade still "looks" a little fuzzy and "feels" somewhat doubtful. Trade on what you see, not what you feel, even if what you see is not totally, absolutely clear.

Trading is not a game for the perfectionist or the overly timid. When positioning with clear, or presumably about to be clear, price energy flows, being "about right" in terms of your specific entry and exit points is good enough. Perfection is not necessary for successful trading; if you are trading with the price energy flows, "about" right is close enough and usually good enough.

Any excessive timidity should begin to disappear once you demand of yourself that you will correct any and all trading mistakes quickly. It is much easier to try to anticipate shifts in trend/momentum if you are *confident* you will act quickly if what has been anticipated does not come about. In other words, once you *know* (because you have demanded it of yourself) that you will not tolerate holding positions not in compliance with the natural laws and rules of trading, then it will become much easier to act freely and decisively.

When your eyes (in seeing the lines and price charts) tell you to act, then act! Your job as the manager of your trading business is to act on what your eyes see. So, when what you see tells you to act, simply call your broker and put the trade on or take the trade off—at the market! (Try *realistic* limits briefly, if you must; however, when a situation is reasonably clear, just act!)

The essence of trading is decision making, acting. If you are overly afraid of making trading decisions, then you should not trade. To be a successful trader you absolutely must be able to act freely and decisively (based on what your see).

Trading decisions rarely—indeed virtually never—feel sure and certain at the time they are made. Believe me, this is true of all traders, no matter how long they have been trading or how successful they have been. Many, if not most, of my best trading decisions were made while feeling some doubt and trepidation. However, I forced myself to act in these cases despite these doubts because I knew my decisions were based on natural laws and sound trading rules, not hunches, hopes or guesses.

Look at the charts with complete openness. Do not try to impose your hopes and desires on the reality they reflect; instead look purely, without bias, so as to see what is actually there. Then once you have seen reality as it is (pleasant or unpleasant), then act (or do not act, if so indicated) with absolute decisiveness. Look with complete humility, act with total arrogance.

## TOO MUCH OPINION

Sorry, but no one really cares where you think a market is going. Your, my, everyone's opinions about the future are just guesses. While some guesses may be more sound than others, ultimately the future is unknown. The fact is your opinions are not reliable enough to use for trading decisions. Therefore, even you should not care about your opinions on market direction and destination. Even if these opinions are endlessly fascinating, they will still have absolutely nothing to do with successful trading. In fact, strongly held opinions about market direction and destination are invariably detrimental, even occasionally lethal, for your trading.

Trade on what you see, not what you think. Remember the first law of trading: The future is unknown. Do not fool yourself; you do not know the future and you never will. The times your opinions are right will be more coincidence than expertise, the times you are wrong more chance than incompetence.

Allow the trend to determine, even dictate, your opinion about the future direction and destination of a market. The stronger the trend, the stronger your belief should be that that particular direction will continue. Let the strength of trend (or lack of a strong trend) establish the bias through which you see and trade each market.

If the trend is solidly up, then trade that market from the long side, regardless of your opinion. If the trend is solidly down, then trade that market from the short side, regardless of your opinion. If the trend is indecisive, then also act accordingly—meaning be more demanding on whether to make a trade.

Let the strength or weakness of price energy flows dictate your actions, not your thoughts and opinions.

## INSUFFICIENT PSYCHOLOGICAL RESILIENCE

Trading is a very difficult business; psychologically, it is a very tough game. Situations can turn from good to bad in minutes. The best laid plans can go completely wrong and can do so quickly and with no warning. Trading can be, and frequently is, a psychological roller coaster.

To be successful, a trader must have a great deal of psychological resilience. As a trader you need to be mentally tough. You must be able to regroup after losses; you need to be able to come back strong and levelheaded after reverses. On the other hand, it is important to avoid becoming too full of yourself when trading goes well. You need to maintain a minimum level of psychological stability.

Of course it is impossible to eliminate emotions completely when trading; however, it is possible to eliminate the effect emotions have on your trading. A trader's emotions are like the cheers and jeers of the crowd at a sporting event; their only influence is that which the participant allows. Successful traders feel their emotions, but they block them out when it is time to look at reality and then act on what they see.

Understand what emotions are, then put them in their proper place. Emotions are natural and so should not be too suppressed; however, put your emotions aside when it comes time to actually look and then act. Vent your anger at failure, enjoy the pleasure of success—if you like or need; however, when it is time to perform, put these emotions aside and focus on the job at hand, which is seeing clearly and acting decisively. Emotions have absolutely no worthwhile role to play in the actual seeing and acting of trading, so work at keeping them out of the decision-making process.

Go ahead: moan, suffer, cheer, exult. Let it all out if you must. However, when it is time to actually conduct the business of trading, simply take a deep breath, let your shoulders slump in the resignation that reality rules—not desires, fears, hope or emotions—and then humbly sit down in front of your charts and look for reality. Once you have seen the current reality, as well as the most likely future reality, then act on what you have seen. After all, if you want to succeed, this is the best you can do.

## INSUFFICIENT SELF-KNOWLEDGE

In my first book, *Intelligent Futures Trading*, I spoke of the need for a trader to discover his or her best "time style" for trading. What I meant by this was that each of us is better suited for a particular time period of trading. Some of us are better suited for long-term trading, some for intermediate-term trading and others for short-term trading.

This is the first bit of self-knowledge every trader needs to possess. I am most comfortable, and I believe best suited, for fairly active short-term trading (anywhere from several days to several weeks per trade). However, to do this type of trading well, a trader has to be willing and able to make many separate trading decisions on a daily basis.

It is important you discover your best time style of trading and then adjust the emphasis you place on each of the trend/momentum indicators accordingly. Long-term traders need to place most emphasis on the trend line. Very short-term traders need to place most emphasis on the short-term momentum line (SL). Intermediate-term traders, like me, need to balance the three lines.

When choosing your time style of trading you must be honest with yourself. Over the years I have encountered many traders who said they wanted to be short- and intermediate-term traders, yet the fact was they could not make the necessary number of decisions to do this type of trading successfully. They usually would not have much difficulty putting trades on (although they would often be too slow to get in), but invariably they would have problems taking them off. Once in a trade either the loss would be too big or the profit not big enough and so they would just sit with the trade, almost regardless of what the price and indicators did.

To be a successful short- or intermediate-term trader you must be able to make many decisions on a daily basis (of course, sometimes these decisions are to do nothing). Therefore, short- and intermediate-term traders need a high tolerance for making mistakes. The more decisions you make, the more mistakes (small and large) you will make.

Know yourself. Know what you can and cannot do, and then adjust your trading time style accordingly. There is no one "right" time style of trading; there is only the right time style for you, so it is important you find out what it is.

## NOT FLEXIBLE ENOUGH

To be a successful trader you need to be "flexible." You cannot be rigid in your thinking about direction and destination (of a market's price). If the reality of a market's trend and momentum change, then you need to be able to change your approach to that market.

Trading is like a voyage down an unexplored river. If you were paddling down that river, you would never rigidly set in your mind what your actions were going to be around the next bend. You would not say, "I will turn north just round the next bend." Instead you would learn as much as you could about where the river had been, you would pay close attention to where the river was headed at the moment as well as how fast it was moving, and then you would make your decisions accordingly.

Trading is the same. A directional path that might look clear and set one day can look completely different the next day. If and when your reasonably reliable indicators of price energy flow change or show clear signs of being on the verge of changing, then you must have the psychological flexibility to change with them—regardless of whether you want to or not.

To be a good trader you need to be a follower, not a leader. Work at seeing the price energy flow clearly, then follow it.

## INSUFFICIENT RESTRAINT

While I have emphasized the need to be able to act clearly and decisively, there is also the action of "non-acting." The need for restraint comes when a pattern is really *not* clear, even though you may wish it were (because you want to make a trade or hold onto a position). Wishful thinking is extremely dangerous in trading. It is very easy in this game to look at a chart and project your desires and hopes onto it. A trader always needs to practice some restraint when making trading decisions. A trader needs to constantly ask himself or herself: What are the lines really saying? How is the price action, really? Do not fool yourself when you look at the trend/momentum indicators; there is no point, you would only be harming yourself.

It is also very important to practice restraint during sharp price surges. It is only natural to feel an urge to buy when a price is moving up sharply or sell when it is collapsing (whether these buys/sells would be initiating new positions or getting out of existing positions).

Price always feels strong on recent highs and weak on recent lows. It is common to feel the urge to make impulse-type trades on intra-day, or several day, big price surges. Therefore, it is important to train yourself to always exercise some restraint before you make a trade.

Before acting, particularly on unplanned intra-day decisions, first pause and take a humble, pure look at the charts. Take a deep breath, try to relax, and before you act look at the chart and ask yourself whether this trade you may feel almost compelled to make is really warranted by the natural laws, the trading rules and the trend/momentum indicators. Ask yourself if a price surge has gone far enough to materially change the trend/momentum picture, or is the move merely unusually loud "noise."

## FEAR AND "GREED"

Traders commonly refer to the push/pull of fear and greed. I believe this is incorrect. The truth is more like fear and fear—the fear of losing and the fear of missing out on good profits.

Fear of losing is overcome through an insistence to rely on your trading intelligence rather than your hunches and guesses, and then keeping your positions "small."

The "fear" of missing out on big profits, the fear of missing a "big" move, is more complex. The only way to combat this "fear" (of missing big moves) is through exercising restraint. An individual trader should always consider the risk side of a trade first. Once realistic risk is factored in, only then should profit potential become part of the equation.

When holding a large profit on a trade, it is important that your fear of giving up a big portion, or all, of this profit be greater than your fear (i.e., greed) of leaving some "money on the table" by getting out too soon.

One of the best trader comments I have come across came from a floor trader quoted in *Futures* magazine. He said something to the effect that he would like to be able to have back every trade he had "left his feet" to make. What he meant by this was that any time he was so eager to make a trade that he involuntarily jumped up and down when executing it, then these trades tended to turn out poorly.

I also have found this to be true. The trades I felt no fear placing, the ones I could not wait to initiate, the ones I was so sure of I just kept adding more and more contracts, these trades have often failed, or only produced mediocre results. However, when placing many trades that ended up resulting in unusually good profits, I have almost always felt at least some fear, some uncertainty, some doubt. So, a little bit of fear about the outcome of a trade is usually a good sign, and too much eagerness is usually a warning sign.

## BEING OVERLY PRECISE ON ORDER EXECUTION

The basic problem with limit orders is they limit the potential on a trade while leaving the risk unlimited (whether getting in or out).

I once watched a wealthy, but inexperienced, trader put a sell-limit order for a very large, long position just slightly above where the price was trading. The order did not fill and for a couple of days the price hovered just below, but never quite reached, his limit; however, he stubbornly held out for his price. Unfortunately, after a few days the market suddenly sold off sharply and within a couple of weeks was significantly below his limit order. Sadly, he stuck with his original limit order all the way down until finally he was forced to sell rather than take delivery.

The difference in dollars between the price he would have received had he simply sold at the market when he entered his limit order and the price he was forced to accept several weeks later amounted to more than five-hundred thousand dollars! As soon as he placed that limit order he dramatically shifted the risk/reward on the trade. His risk on the trade became half a million dollars (or more), while his additional profit potential was limited to only a few thousand dollars. This was a horrible risk/reward ratio. The basic liability of limit orders is they instantly shift the risk/reward ratio against you, sometimes only slightly, but other times significantly.

Trading is not a precision game. Trading is not like accounting or engineering where precision is not only necessary but required. In trading all you can do is get entry and exit price levels *approximately* correct; therefore, do not try to be too precise. While there is nothing wrong with trying limit orders for a *while*, never be too stubborn about getting your limit.

On those rare occasions I do enter limit orders, I jokingly refer to them as "MIC" orders, or market-if-close orders. Naturally, there is no such order; however, the point is use a limit order if you like, but if the price comes close and you do not fill fairly quickly, then just cancel it and go at the market. Had the trader above used an "MIC" order approach rather than stubbornly sticking with his limit order, he would have taken a nice profit rather than a big loss.

Entering only on limit orders ensures you get in on all bad trades while presenting the possibility of missing some very good ones. When exiting a trade, limit orders cap your upside potential while leaving your downside risk unlimited.

An additional problem with using limit orders is the expenditure of psychic energy. Spending time and energy on precisely where to place your limit orders or repeatedly chasing a market by moving these limit orders uses up a lot of energy. This energy could—and should—be better used identifying current and projected price energy flows, and then acting to position with these flows.

Over the years I have seen far too many traders waste way too much time and energy trying to be too precise on their entry and exit points, while at the same time spending too little time and energy on seeing price energy flows and acting upon this seeing.

Strive for precision in identifying clear price energy flows, but allow some sloppiness on the specifics of entry and exit. Consistently position with the prevailing price energy flow and you should find that close enough will usually be good enough.

## THINKING "MORE" IS "MORE" WHEN USING TECHNICAL INDICATORS

With contemporary trading software, a trader has all sorts of technical indicators at his fingertips. My experience with traders who use trading software is that they have so many indicators they tend to suffer from "analysis paralysis." Since all the different types of indicators on charting software will never point in the same direction at the same time (it is mathematically impossible), there will always be some conflict, and conflict creates doubt. The greater the doubt, the less likely you will act decisively, and decisive action is one of the prerequisites for successful trading.

Remember, you must accept that you, as an individual trader, simply cannot compete in this game in terms of complex, technological expertise; therefore, it is best not to try.

Price movement is two dimensional: up or down. If an object can move only north or south, you do not need fifty indicators to tell you the direction it is moving. Since price can only move up or down, you only need a few indicators to point out its direction and momentum.

The only way an individual trader can compete in this game is to keep it simple. The more complex your analysis, the more indicators of trend and momentum you use, the more the playing field will begin to tilt away from you. When it comes to clearly identifying price energy flows, less is usually more.

## MISDIRECTED FOCUS IN SELECTING TRADES

Over the years I have seen many traders (myself included) spend too much time and effort trying to catch the beginning of major moves. These traders acted like it was always "too late" to trade any market that had already made a good move. Therefore, they would not trade any market already in a clear, solid trend (i.e., markets significantly off their recent lows or highs). Instead they would always trade markets whose trends were indecisive (in the hope they were about to start a good trending move).

Remember the second law of pricing: Continuation is more likely than change. Just as markets in clear trends are likely to continue in these trends, so too markets in sideways trends are more likely to continue to move sideways. The best odds will be in those markets already in a solid uptrend or downtrend; therefore, it only makes sense to focus your attention and effort primarily on these markets. Only trade in sideways-trending markets when the momentum line pattern indicates a good chance for a near-term move big enough to change the trend to clearly up or down.

Focus on those markets where the price energy flows are solid, or you can make a legitimate case they are about to become solid. Do not waste time, energy, and margin on indecisive situations solely in the hope of being in right at the beginning. Not only is it always unlikely you will be able to get in right at the beginning of a big trending move, more importantly it is not necessary for success.

## TRADING ON "HOPE"

The final pitfall I want to point out is the sometimes terminal mistake of trading solely on "hope." Virtually every time a trader takes an unusually big loss it is because he or she stuck with the trade long after the trend/momentum indicators turned against it.

The trader I mentioned earlier who ran ten thousand up to over three and a half million and then back to essentially zero was a classic example of this. The positions that made him the money were initiated because he could see their price energy flows were pushing clearly in one direction. However, once these price energy flows had obviously changed direction, he did not get out. Instead he held on in the "hope" this change of price energy flow would be short-lived; unfortunately for him they were not.

The future is unknown; this is the bad news about futures trading. However, the good news is continuation is more likely than change. If the price energy flow of a market is clear, then the odds will favor that market continuing to move in the existing direction. To stick with a trade after the price energy flow has obviously changed is to flout the natural laws of pricing. When hope and natural law conflict, natural law will invariably prevail. If all you have going for you on a trade is hope, you have essentially no hope.

# FINAL THOUGHTS ON TRADING

THAT IS ALL. I know no more about trading worth passing on to you.

Virtually everything I have pointed out in this book I learned the hard way: through the painful process of trial and error. Be advised though. Following everything in this book is no guarantee of eventual success; however, follow the approach and method laid out herein and you *will* become instantly competitive. Use this approach and method, follow these trading rules and you will be a competitive player in this simple—but oh so difficult—game. Nonetheless, in the final analysis, trading is as much an art as a science. You need the fundamental science of trading and pricing (i.e., the natural laws and sound trading rules) for a foundation, but in the end it is your artistic-trading talent, your decision-making talent, that will determine your eventual success or failure. You have to be able to act in a fairly accurate and timely manner, and this is not easy to do in this game, even if you know what you are supposed to do and when you are supposed to do it.

Trading is very much like professional sports, an individual sport like golf or tennis. When it comes time to play the trading game, you are essentially alone on the field of competition. I—and others—can suggest, advise, and coach, but you alone make the decisions. You make the trade. You get the profit. You take the loss. You get the credit. You take the blame. You are completely responsible for your ultimate success or failure. Luck plays a role but will not make the difference. In the final result it is you alone, and your day-by-day actions, that will make the difference.

Any art takes time and effort to get the hang of it. Even the greatest athletes, musicians, and artists (*and* traders) have needed time and effort to master their craft sufficiently to produce consistent success. In trading, as in sports, it takes time and effort to train the mind and body to work together well. As an individual trader you need to be multifaceted, you need to play different roles in the trading process. It takes time to get each of these roles working in sync. So, do not expect to follow this approach and method and instantly produce good profits. You have to work at it; and even if you do, there is still no guarantee of success. Trading is an art, and proficiency at any particular art is not accessible to all.

I could work at singing or playing the piano every day for the next twenty years and I would still not become proficient enough to play Carnegie Hall. I just do not have the intrinsic talent for either. Trading is no different. Some of us are simply not suited to trade and thus never become proficient enough to succeed, regardless of time and effort. Look at art, music, and professional sports; many try to become successful professionals, but only a few make it. Each of us has our particular talents; it is possible trading is not one of yours.

However, the trading game is unique because it is potentially open to virtually all of us, while careers in art, music, and sports are not. Regardless of time and effort, I could never succeed at any professional sport. In addition, I could practice the piano, violin, or singing forever and still would never become proficient enough to be a successful professional. However, I can compete—and have a decent chance to do so successfully—in the "sport" and "art" of trading, but it takes effort, paying attention, and the ability to act in at least a somewhat decisive and timely manner. In other words, trading is one big-time endeavor where the average man or woman does have a realistic chance to compete successfully.

Just as in sports, every day in trading is different. Yesterday and today's success is no guarantee of tomorrow's success. Whoever you are, whatever your reputation, whatever your past success, you have to produce every day, day after day, day by day.

Look at great athletes; they work at their sport endlessly. Nothing is given them based on reputation. They have to go out on the field and produce every time just as if it were the first time. They have to—and do—work hard at their craft. They never coast. They never relax. They constantly try to improve. They always strive to compete at their maximum personal level. You and I need to approach trading the same way; be assured, most of our competition will. Work, study, strive, compete, pay attention, be tough, act.

This is a very difficult game to win at on any kind of consistent basis. Almost all individual traders end up losing. Therefore, to be one of the few winners, you must, by definition, act differently in at least some way. Remember, futures trading is a zero-sum game. There are thousands of very bright, very talented, very knowledgeable, very aggressive people out there who want to take your money—and not just some of it, all of it! They do not care if taking your money hurts you and your family badly. They do not care if you lose your children's college fund, your retirement money, your house, indeed everything you own and even all you can borrow. They do not care if your losses destroy you completely. They do not care about you in any way whatsoever. "They" are the "market." The market never rests. The market is always well prepared, always ready to play hard, ever ready and eager to take your money. So, when you are in the market, you had better be just as ready and prepared.

The opposition will not give you any breaks whatsoever, so never expect one. When trading you must always be ready to make the hard decisions, you must always be prepared to act decisively and intelligently. You must always be ready and able to do what is required to survive and prosper, whether you want to or not, whether you feel like it or not.

Never underestimate this business, always maintain tremendous respect for it, never lose sight of the fact it can be brutal—and sometimes suddenly and unexpectedly so. However, follow the approach and method laid out in this book, maintain the discipline to make the hard decisions, and you will have a fairly decent chance to beat it. But be clear on this; to do so you will have to work at it, every day, day by day.

## BOTTOM LINE

We trade the **PRICE!** We do not trade the lines. We do not trade trend and momentum indicators. We do not trade the Commitment of Traders report. We do not trade sentiment. We do not trade supply/demand. We do not trade news. We trade **<u>PRICE!!!</u>** We do not get paid for being right about anything but the price. We use the lines (our reasonably reliable trend/momentum indicators) to help us trade the price; however, never lose sight of the fact we trade only the price, nothing else.

When you drive a car you look at the speedometer and other indicators on the instrument panel. You watch the white and yellow lines on the road. You pay attention to the speed limit, other highway signs and the actions of other drivers. Then you put all these indicators together and drive the best you can, the safest you can, as intelligently as you can. If the highway is icy, there is thick fog or the traffic is heavy, you do not simply plow ahead at the speed limit regardless. What you do is use your intelligence to process all these indicators together, see reality as it is, and then make your best decision how to drive on that particular highway at that particular time.

Trading is the same. Do not fall into the trap of following the lines blindly, oblivious to the price action. Use the lines to point out the best markets to trade, the direction to trade these markets, and *approximately* when and where to execute your trades. In other words, use some common sense; every situation is a little different. We use the lines to point out opportunities where the odds favor being able to sell higher than we buy and buy lower than we sell. The lines rarely tell us exact tops and bottoms or precise entry and exit points. They will simply gives us fairly reliable opportunities and probabilities for the next few days—with emphasis on next few days (i.e., not forever).

Trading is a never-ending process. Trading is not searching for that one great trade that will produce total, final victory. Trading is a constant process done on a day-by-day basis. If you cannot accept this fact, if you do not have the energy for this type of day-by-day working process, then you should not trade. If you are not capable of making almost constant decisions (including decisions to do nothing), with most of these decisions being far from obvious, then you should not trade.

Mistakes are inevitable in trading. Just accept this. For an active trader, going more than a few days without making a mistake would be very unusual. Therefore, when you recognize you have made a mistake—and you will make many—simply correct it. What you are trying to do in this game is make more correct decisions than incorrect ones.

Like a professional athlete, you simply do your best to perform at the highest level you can in each situation and then hope in the end that this is enough to result in success. If it is not, then you somehow just have to do better next time or else look for another game to play, another job to pay the bills.

All you can do when trading is make each decision as intelligently (meaning in accordance with natural laws and proven rules) as you know how. That is all. You cannot predict the future, but you can consistently identify and position with clear price energy flows. Do this consistently and persistently and you will have a good chance of succeeding, as long as you remember to accept profits when they are good and take losses before they become too bad.

# MY STORY,
### plus how Hillary Clinton "really" turned $1,000
### into $100,000 in nine months

BORN IN MIAMI IN 1944; father a pilot for Pan American Airways (PAA at the time, later Pan Am). Soon after, my father was transferred to Guatemala City, Guatemala, where we lived for three years. There I learned Spanish (before English) and picked up my nickname—Chiquito became Chiqui, which in turn became Chick. Guatemala was followed by two years in Houston, after which my family (by now with two sisters and a brother) moved to Rio de Janeiro, Brazil. My Spanish turned into Portuguese. I spent first through sixth grades at the American school in Rio (Escola Americana). Wonderful, innocent, blissful times. However, when PAA closed its pilot base in Rio (planes were getting bigger, which meant progressively less need for far-flung pilot bases), my father transferred to London, England. We spent one year there. I attended a traditional English boys boarding school; interesting experience but would not want to repeat it. Language was essentially the same but culture could not have been more different. As a sixth/seventh grader I studied Latin, French and algebra, along with the usual subjects. Played cricket and rugby. For breakfast beans on toast took the place of pancakes, fried kippers replaced eggs and bacon, although I did grow to like Yorkshire pudding as well as a few other assorted English "delicacies."

My father was transferred again, this time to the States; me by now with a strong English accent (which disappeared quickly). Spent three years in northwestern New Jersey (Sparta/Lake Mohawk). The switch from English boarding school to American junior high was another major cultural shift.

After three years in New Jersey, my father took what turned out to be a permanent leave of absence from Pan Am and we headed back to Brazil, São Paulo this time, where he opened a branch office for a New York Stock Exchange firm, Fahnestock & Co. I spent junior and senior years of high school attending the American school in São Paulo (Escola Graduada de São Paulo). More wonderful times, among the best of my life. Brazil is a great place; Brazilians are warm, friendly and happy. At that time violence was unheard of in Brazil; unfortunately, in this regard, they have since caught up with the rest of the world.

After high school I went on to Colgate University in upstate New York and experienced another major cultural shift. Good education, good experience, but cold and an all-men's college; I considered neither a positive. Graduated in 1966.

Upon graduation was commissioned a Second Lieutenant, United States Marine Corps, followed by five months of officer training in Quantico, Virginia. And then it was on to Viet Nam. Spent a total of nineteen months in Viet Nam, first fourteen months assigned to Headquarters

Company, Third Marine Regiment, in Dong Ha, a few miles south of the DMZ. Final five months were spent at headquarters in Danang as a briefing officer. Was fortunate all my assignments were headquarters, "desk"-type jobs. However, I did go through over a hundred different artillery and rocket attacks—they all missed. The lieutenant who relieved me in Dong Ha was hit (minor wound) the day after I left. In war, as in trading, timing is critical and luck always plays a role. Left Viet Nam at the end of 1968. Final six months of my military "career" were spent with the Fifth Engineer Battalion, Camp Pendleton, Oceanside, California.

My first trade was in stocks. Our last two summers in New Jersey I worked as a caddy at the Lake Mohawk Golf Club (played during the week, caddied on weekends). Carried "double" for three dollars a bag, plus tip. Tips ranged from fifty cents to a dollar per bag. A great "loop" was eight dollars—two four-dollar bags; however, most loops were seven dollars and a few only six. Took most of the money earned and bought five shares of Pfizer for seventy-five dollars a share. Few months later it was one hundred and twenty-five dollars. I could do the math. Five shares times fifty-dollars profit on each equaled two hundred and fifty dollars net in my pocket. Even assuming all eight-dollar loops, that turned out to be the equivalent of thirty days of lugging two heavy golf bags around five miles of rolling meadows. A somewhat lazy teenage boy notices facts like these.

Having always been fairly good at math as well as board games, I managed to win the chess championship at boarding school in England, a major event and a big upset. My younger brother and I were the only Americans in the school (out of ninety students, ranging in age from six to thirteen), and neither of us knew any Latin, French or algebra when we enrolled. Therefore, in those subjects we were placed in classes with the much younger kids. The natural conclusion was that Americans must not be very bright and thus just could not be any good at a complex game like chess.

Anyway, a numbers-type game like the markets had a natural attraction to me. I bought and sold some stocks during my time in the Marine Corps, but not very successfully. My timing was not very good as was unfortunate to get back to the States in early December of 1968 just as the big bull market of the sixties ended. Therefore, since my stock trades done with war savings were disappointing, I soon quit trading stocks.

I had made my first futures trade while on the special thirty-day leave awarded to those who extended their Viet Nam tours by six months. Timed my special leave to coincide with my brother's graduation from Illinois Institute of Technology in Chicago. The family had come up from Brazil for this and so I met them in Chicago. My father took my brother and me in to visit the Chicago Mercantile Exchange. Fahnestock's floor broker ("Wally") arranged floor passes for us and after a brief tour my father asked him if anything looked good. Wally said he liked a pork belly spread (August/February, do not remember which way). He said it was four hundred dollar margin. I was feeling somewhat flush with cash after fourteen months of earning combat pay and having almost zero expenses. Since I was also feeling reasonably lucky after successfully dodging all sorts of "incoming" south of the DMZ, I decided to go for one spread. I watched as Wally went into the pit and had the order executed. Two weeks later I closed out the trade with a net profit of four hundred dollars (which incidentally was 100 percent of margin). Again I did the math: one month as Marine Corps first lieutenant in Viet Nam paid about five hundred dollars; two weeks of occasionally interrupting golf, beach, and assorted other pleasant activities to check on a couple of numbers going up and down had returned four hundred dollars. It did not take too much in the way of brain power to note the differences in effort and return, as well as the extreme differences in comparable risk/reward. I did not realize it at the time but I was hooked.

After discharge from the Marine Corps in June of 1969 I headed up to Aspen to decompress. This was another extreme cultural shift: Marine Corps officer to ski resort "bum." Did construction labor for a few months; earned three dollars an hour with time and a half for overtime. Then when snow started to fall, came up with the idea of starting a business delivering hot meals from restaurants to tourists in their condos. I called it the "Moveable Feast." Did not make me much, but paid food and rent and left the days free for skiing.

My stock trades had not worked very well ever since the market had turned persistently weak. However, since my return from Viet Nam I had been watching the movement of those pork belly spreads. I did not know anything about pork bellies other than it was slab bacon; nonetheless, I noticed these spreads appeared to move within fairly well-defined upper and lower limits. So I started trying to trade these spreads using these apparent ranges. When a spread would near, or reach, its recent high or low area I would trade it to go to the other end of its presumed range. This worked amazingly well and produced a steady stream of good winners.

After a while a friend did a few of these trades as well. Her father, hearing of her interest and success, sent her an ad from *The Wall Street Journal* for a small futures brokerage house in Chicago (MS Commodities). I answered the ad and talked to one of the "brokers," or more accurately, one of the salesman/account executives. He was slick. A fast-talker full of information and knowledge and with what seemed like direct connections to the trading floor. Being just a couple of rubes up in the Rockies, we were impressed.

In April the snow melted and the ski season ended. I decided to put my career in construction labor on hold (now that is *real* work) and try to get a summer job on the floor of "Merc" (i.e., the Chicago Mercantile Exchange). I contacted MS Commodities and told them I was looking for a job. Flew up to Chicago for an interview. I thought I was applying for a summer job on the floor—clerk, runner, whatever. The principal of MS, Maurie Schneider, thought I wanted to become an account executive/broker and offered me that job. I said sure, why not? Fortunately, one great policy this firm had was for all new brokers to spend their first few weeks in the business working on the floor, first as a "runner" (running orders into pits) and then as an order clerk. I thought then, and still do, that this was an excellent idea. Even a few weeks on the floor of any futures exchange is an invaluable experience for any trader.

After a few weeks on the floor I moved upstairs to become a "broker." Filled out a four-page form, paid five dollars to a notary to verify my signature, and in a day or so I was an "official" futures broker. Today the same process includes a lengthy cxam and lots more paperwork.

All of this took place at what I call the "old, old" Merc at 110 North Franklin. That Merc was a small and friendly place compared to today's behemoth. It was easy to get on the floor so I would go downstairs frequently; our office was one floor above the exchange. I would try to listen to anyone and everyone, especially floor brokers. This experience proved very valuable throughout my brokerage and trading career. Primarily it taught me that, for the most part, those on the floor are no different, no smarter, no better at trading than anyone else; they just pay much lower commissions—plus they have a few other "special" advantages I will get into later.

Other than the time working on the floor, my "training" to become a futures broker was to listen to our firm's top salesman make a few telephone sales pitches. The brokerage business is first and foremost a commission business, meaning the emphasis is on sales, i.e., bringing in new money. After this "training" I was assigned a desk and given a small stack of leads generated from advertisements like the one I had answered.

I started making sales calls. Telephone sales is essentially a numbers game. Even for the best sales-people most calls are unsuccessful; however, if the sales pitch is at least minimally persuasive and if enough calls are made, then eventually an account executive will start to bring some money in for trading.

Naturally, hanging around the exchange every day with its many "experts," it did not take long before I completely discarded my simple, but very effective, method of trading belly spreads. I was quickly and completely immersed in all sorts of much more "sophisticated" knowledge and information: daily hog and cattle slaughter numbers, the weights of hogs and cattle coming to market, weekly out-of-town belly storage, monthly cold storage, quarterly pig-crop reports, and so on. Unfortunately, my trading results seemed to move in inverse relation to my market sophistication. The better I became at sales and the more expertly I could spout "inside" information, the worse my trading results became. I soon knew virtually everything there was to know about hogs, cattle, and bellies, except the part about where their prices were most likely going.

The problem for the investing/trading public is that insider-type "expertise" about markets "sells" far better than simplistic notions of repeating price patterns, regardless of their relative effectiveness. However, I was no different from the poor prospects I was pitching. I felt my lack of success was primarily due to a lack of the "right" information and knowledge; therefore, I always kept my eyes and ears open for more information and knowledge, especially when on the floor.

Once the markets closed each day—at that time the big markets at the Merc were the bellies, cattle, and hogs—the trading floor would empty like a theater after the end of a movie. Clerks, runners, exchange workers, and floor brokers (i.e., members) would pile into big elevators and head up to their offices. On one such day I had been on the floor at the close and so joined the crowd in one of the elevators. Ira Brill, a floor broker associated with Heinold Commodities (a semi-legendary futures firm that had their offices right next to ours), piled in behind me.

The bellies had been strong that day and Ira started talking about how bullish he was and why, and as we walked down the hall he continued to "pitch" the upside of the bellies. Being a novice, naturally I was easily impressed by a strong opinion held by a professional, especially a floor broker. So I went directly to my phone, started calling clients and giving them the same bullish-belly pitch. I emphasized that this information came directly from a floor trader, true insider stuff, and thus always impressive.

The next day I started buying bellies on the open and quickly built up a full position. Unfortunately, the market opened about unchanged and then headed south for the rest of the day. By the close it was down sharply and all my early buys were deep in the hole. Concerned, I headed down to the floor to check with Ira. I caught up with him just as he was getting in the elevator to head up to his office. Before I could say a word he started talking about how *bearish* he was on the bellies and giving numerous reasons why. On the walk down the hall I asked what happened to his very strong bullish outlook of the day before. He looked at me a little quizzically, said something like, "oh, that was yesterday, they looked different today," and walked away.

I learned two important lessons from this. First, never rely solely on another for trading decisions. If you cannot see the *intelligence* of a trade for yourself, then you should not make it. Naturally, there is nothing wrong with listening to others point out what they see happening in a market. However, the ultimate decision maker on your trades has to be you, and you alone. Never follow another blindly, regardless of that person's record or reputation. Second, good traders trade the *price*, not the "story," even if they might talk primarily about the story. Many traders will use a "story" (i.e., some fundamental, "logical" argument) to help generate the confidence to act decisively. However, in reality they are simply following the price. Then, when and if the price action changes, they go with these changes and simply modify the background story to support their new position.

After about a year in Chicago my business had grown to where I was earning a modest living, but it was a continuous struggle. Like every other broker in our office, and our firm, all my clients slowly but steadily lost money and eventually had insufficient funds left for trading. This meant I had to work constantly at bringing in new money.

MS had a branch office in Salt Lake City. Unfortunately for MS, the manager of that office suddenly skipped the country and as a result left the office in need of some new personnel. He turned out to have been an embezzler at his previous firm and in a desperate attempt to get out of a big financial hole had made huge bets on an old-crop/new-crop bean spread, both for himself and his clients. The spring planting intentions report came out "wrong" and the spreads moved sharply against him. He and his clients were essentially wiped out and rather than face this he just took off, leaving many unsecured debits behind. Feeling like a very small fish in a big pond in Chicago, I volunteered to go to Salt Lake and help keep that office going. I thought that there, with my Chicago experience, I might be able to come across as an "expert." Fortunately this turned out to be true, although more from the standpoint of bolstering my personal confidence. Feeling and acting like an expert produced better results, both in bringing in new money and trading. Humility is essential when looking at a chart, but what is needed when acting is confidence, even some arrogance.

However, even though my trading improved, this only meant that my clients were losing money more slowly. The bottom line was they were still losing. I had had over eighty clients in my first two years in the futures trading business and every one of them ended up a net loser. This sad result was also true for every other broker at that firm, a total of more than thirty brokers. As I have said, all of us knew almost everything about the markets except where the prices were most likely headed. We knew everything but how to trade profitably.

A year after arriving in Salt Lake I left MS Commodities and joined a New York Stock Exchange firm, duPont, Glore, Forgan. Finally, after two years of great effort but consistent failure, my clients started making money. The new firm was not the difference as they did not provide any meaningful help in trading; rather it was simply just a case of eventually beginning to be able to "read" price moves a little better. Within six months of joining duPont I was the number one broker in the office, the fourth biggest producing broker in the firm and, more importantly, virtually all of my clients were making steady profits.

I probably would have stayed with duPont, Glore, Forgan for many years but the firm was in deep financial trouble and was on its way to disappearing. Together with Walston & Co.—another firm in financial trouble—they decided to merge. At that time (the early seventies) Wall Street in general was experiencing severe back-office problems. Volume was outstripping the ability of firms to keep track of it. The brokerage business was not fully computerized yet and too much of the trade processing was done the old way: manually. To the "rescue" came Ross Perot. He took over the merged firm of duPont, Glore, Forgan and Walston and attempted to apply to the brokerage business the computerized expertise of his successful software firm EDS. He was going to save Wall Street by showing it how to computerize. Unfortunately, Mr. Perot's attempt to save Wall Street ended almost as quickly as his abortive run for the presidency in 1992; in less than a year the merged firm went out of business.

When the two companies merged into one they closed a few of their branch offices, and Salt Lake was one of these. I quickly found a new home at E. F. Hutton. Business continued to improve as my clients prospered. Salt Lake City is a great place to live, especially if you like skiing and other outdoor sports. However, after a while I decided Salt Lake just was not the place for me. So, I pulled out Hutton's list of branch offices and looked for someplace new. Heeding the long ago but still sound advice of Horace Greeley, I looked only west. On the list was a place called La Jolla. It had a good sound to it, so my girl friend and I flew down to check it out. One month later we were happily settled in a nice house a couple of blocks from the beach. That was early 1973 and I have been in the San Diego area since, almost thirty years now. For someone who had never stayed in one place longer than a few years, that is a good endorsement of this area.

My clients and brokerage business continued to do well. I was the top producer (of commissions) in the La Jolla office every year, and several years was the top producer in Hutton's Southern California region. In addition, I was consistently among the top fifteen producers in the firm (out of several thousand brokers). Since I also consistently ranked at the bottom in terms of opening new accounts, my success was primarily due to the fact my clients made money. While I had a few clients (two in particular) who traded their own accounts, the bulk of my business came from about twenty moderately-sized accounts I managed. These managed accounts consistently made about a 100 percent a year in profits. However, the work was a grind, with constant pressure. I have always found it much more pressure and strain to trade for other people than for myself. In trading, many of the best trades turn out to be ones that are at least somewhat counterintuitive. These trades can be more difficult to make if you feel you might have to explain why you did them should they happen to go wrong. It is much easier, and usually more profitable, to trade when no explanations of action are required.

Finally, in the spring of 1979 I had had enough of trading for others and quit/retired from the brokerage business. Other than a brief—and ill advised—return to Hutton a few years later, I have been on my own since. During the twenty-some years since I left the brokerage business I have traded (almost) exclusively for my own account. For about fifteen years this trading went quite well. I had some tremendous years and many good ones. Then in the early nineties my trading started to go badly. I am still not sure why, but all of a sudden I started losing consistently and could not turn it around. Before long I had completely lost my confidence as well as most of my trading equity. A trader without confidence will almost always lose.

I had always done my trading mostly by feel and intuition. By this I mean that I had never laid out in writing a clear approach and method. Therefore, once I lost my confidence I had nothing concrete to fall back on. I had also always operated independently, so I did not have anyone to help me when I got into trouble with my trading. When you are an individual trader, if you lose your trading capital, you are out of the game. For over twenty years, whenever I ran into a losing streak I had always been able to pull it together and come back from the brink of disaster. This time I could not. Finally, in desperation, I rented out my house (by now I was living in a terrific house in the hills above La Jolla) and headed up to a family cabin in northern Minnesota to try to recapture what I had lost: my ability to read markets and my confidence. I started to put down in writing what worked in trading and what did not. Over a period of time this writing turned into my first book, *Intelligent Futures Trading*.

It was around this time that news of Hillary Rodham Clinton's extraordinary success in trading cattle futures came out. She had opened a futures trading account in 1978 with $1000, and within nine months it had become almost exactly $100,000. Friends asked me what I thought about this. Was it possible? Likely? Legitimate? Did I believe it? My answer was the same to all who asked: It was definitely possible, but I would need to see how it was done in order to know whether it was legitimate or not.

By that time in my career there had been numerous times when I had taken small amounts up to very large amounts in fairly short periods of time, both for clients and myself. Here are just a few examples: $1000 to $20,000 in less than a year (for a client); $3000 to $150,000 in about six months (for me); $5000 to $100,000 in less than six months (for a client); and $50,000 to $1.5 million in less than a year and a half (for me). Then, of course, there was the client I mentioned earlier who ran $10,000 up to almost $4 million in less than seven months (and then back to zero over the following two months). Therefore, I knew that Hillary Clinton could have legitimately run $1000 up to $100,000 in less than a year. The question was whether it had been done honestly.

I watched Mrs. Clinton's famous White House press conference where she claimed the account and the profits generated in it were completely legitimate. Unfortunately, she did not give any details, so I still could not make an informed judgment. When doubts about her story persisted, the Chairman Emeritus of the Chicago Mercantile Exchange, Mr. Leo Melamed, was asked to travel to Washington to review the trading records of her account and then provide an expert assessment of its legitimacy. After examining these records, Mr. Melamed told the press, and through them the people of the United States, that his opinion was Mrs. Clinton "[…] did nothing wrong" and that "Hillary Clinton did not *herself* violate Chicago Mercantile Exchange rules." And further, that "[…] at times Mrs. Clinton's account had been *thinly* margined […]" (all quotes from *Escape to the Futures*, Leo Melamed, John Wiley & Sons, 1996). However, he pointed out, this margin problem was not a customer violation and thus was primarily an issue between her and her broker. Around the same time, Mr. Jack Sandner, the Chairman of the Chicago Mercantile Exchange, told reporters that "it is very possible [to make $100,000 on a $1000 cash investment] if you are lucky enough to be in a market that has a precipitous *trending* move. And 1978 and 1979 was the biggest *bull* market in the history of the cattle market" (*Washington Post*, 3/30/94). In other words, he maintained that since Mrs. Clinton was trading a very strong, uptrending market, her tremendous profits were not overly unusual.

Shortly thereafter I came across a newspaper article (*Los Angeles Times*, 5 April 1994) where my former acquaintance, Ira Brill, was quoted as saying he had been the floor broker who had filled Hillary Clinton's cattle orders. He stated that at that time he had been buying and selling cattle in six-hundred-contract lots for Hillary's broker (the Springdale, Arkansas, office of Refco & Co.). He further stated that these trades were not assigned to specific accounts until after the market closed. Upon reading Ira's words I recognized some clear warning signs and instantly became very suspicious about Mrs. Clinton's explanation, as well as the legitimacy of her profits.

However, the press had stopped covering the story and I did not give it much more thought until I happened upon an issue of *National Review* with Hillary Clinton on the cover (*National Review*, 20 February 1995). Inside was a story by Caroline Baum and Victor Niederhoffer that provided extensive details about Hillary Clinton's commodity-trading profits. Unfortunately for Mrs. Clinton, these details were extremely damning.

The *National Review* story confirmed Ira Brill's comments by stating:"One of Refco's Springdale brokers at the time has admitted under oath that the firm was buying and selling blocks of contracts and allocating them to customers after the market closed."

Reading this reminded me of an incident my very first day at the Merc in the spring of 1970 when I observed one of our firm's order clerks come up from the floor and drop a big stack of orders on the desk of the firm's top producer. I then watched as "D.C." decided (after the day's results were known) which trades would go into which accounts.

The fact that Mrs. Clinton's broker was routinely waiting until after the day's results were known before assigning trades to specific accounts is only part of the evidence her profits may have been achieved illegitimately. Even more incriminating is the pattern of trading in her account. As mentioned, Mr. Sandner implied her success was not exceptional since anyone trading with that particular strong uptrend in Cattle could have started with a little and made a lot,and many had. The problem with this argument is that (again quoting from the *National Review* article): "[…] *most* of her [Hillary Clinton's] trades, including her first two, her last two, and her single most profitable trade, were initiated from the *short* side […]"

Mrs. Clinton's story is she opened her Refco futures account to capitalize on an expected big up move in cattle prices (apparently doing so on the suggestion of Mr. James Blair, the general counsel of Tyson Foods, one of the major corporations in Arkansas at the time). Strangely, though, the very first trade in her account was to go *short* ten contracts of live cattle (a trade that produced about $5300 profits in one day). In fact, the account's trading records evidently show that a large part of Mrs. Clinton's cattle profits came from trading *against* her stated purpose in opening the account (as well as Mr. Sandner's supposedly relatively easy, big-money uptrend).

According to the *National Review* article, thirty-three trades were made in the account.The vast majority were for small quantities of contracts in various markets. These trades evidently either lost or made only fairly small amounts. However, the trades that were for very large quantities of contracts "just happened" to turn out to be quite profitable, and instantly so. In other words, there were numerous small trades with a success ratio of around fifty percent, and then there were occasional huge (relative to the size of the account) trades with a success ratio of essentially one hundred percent. These exceptionally large-sized trades produced all, or virtually all, of the account's profits.

Connect this pattern of trading (i.e., all the profits coming from occasional huge trades that showed instant big profits) to her broker's practice of delayed assignment of trades and any knowledgeable observer instantly would have a good "read" of what really happened in her account: Large trades that ended the day with big profits and were originally intended for another account were being placed in Hillary Clinton's account instead.

Based on my experience, what happened here was that someone else trading with Mrs. Clinton's broker periodically would tell him something like the following: "Take fifty of those cattle we sold near the high's of the day and put them in Hillary's account instead of mine." Since the trades the office was doing were not assigned to specific accounts until after the close, this switch would have been easy to do. Then, within a few days, these big profit trades would be closed out. The net result of these trade manipulations: Without any real risk or effort, Hillary (and Bill) Clinton ended up a hundred thousand dollars richer. The records show that as soon as the total profits generated by this simple, but effective, trade manipulation reached just under $100,000, the account was closed.

In his book *Escape to the Futures*, Mr. Melamed vigorously defends Mrs. Clinton in this affair. Part of this defense is, since overnight trades have intrinsic risk, and virtually all of her cattle trades were held overnight, this means profitable outcomes could not have been prearranged. Technically this is true, but it is really only a half-truth. The fact is, the big contract cattle trades in Mrs. Clinton's account had substantial profits at the close of their first day. In other words, the evidence indicates they came with large profits already built in; therefore, true risk was minimal. This was like someone being given an eighty or ninety yard head start in a hundred yard race and then claiming the race was an equal competition simply because there was some risk of losing. While technically true, in a case like this, the "risk" would be too minimal to prove the race a genuine contest.

Hillary Clinton's cattle trades were no different. Plus, in Mrs. Clinton's case the big "head-start" cattle trades appear to have been put into her account repeatedly and so the net risk was, in reality, nonexistent. Every trader in the world would gladly take on this kind of so-called "risk."

This little "trick" of moving trades from one account to another after the results are known is a familiar one to many people in the business. It is a very simple and effective way for an *unethical* broker to manipulate trading results among the accounts he is trading and controlling. Few members of the general public or news media realize how easy it is for an *unethical* member/broker controlling and directing the trades in multiple accounts to tamper with the allocation of trades among these accounts, and in so doing, manipulate the results. My thirty years of experience in the futures business has exposed me to a number of such incidents involving various different brokers. I have the strong impression this practice (manipulating results by moving trades from one account to another) is not that uncommon in certain parts of the business.

A little story will illustrate this. I heard the following "true" story thirdhand so I cannot use the principals' names, but it has a definite ring of truth to me as I am also personally acquainted with some of the "players." Apparently "L" had been brought before his exchange's disciplinary committee for various rules infractions, including manipulating results by delayed assignment of account numbers. While being lectured to about his actions, "L" became a little exasperated and blurted out something like "look, every single one of you,"—and one by one he pointed to each member of the committee—"has done the exact same things I did, so quit reading me the riot act and give me a break here!" Unfortunately for "L," committee chairman "B" simply leaned forward and calmly replied, "But 'L,' the difference is you got caught."

Following are a few positions the *National Review* article stated Mrs. Clinton's account held during the nine months it was open, along with the equity in the account at each time. If you are an experienced trader, I ask you to judge for yourself how likely it is positions like these would be *legitimately* held by a trader with an annual income and net worth of about $50,000 (as was the case with Mrs. Clinton and her husband at the time).

The excesses started with the very first trade in the account when it held ten contracts of Live Cattle with an equity of only $1000. A few of the other more ridiculous positions were 62 contracts of Cattle with an equity of only $13,000; 90 contracts with only $6000; and the most extreme of all, 115 contracts of Live Cattle with a *debit* equity of $18,000.

The margin for one Live Cattle contract at that time was around $1200. On Mrs. Clinton's first trade the margin requirement was $12,000, so since the account had only $1000, she would have had an $11,000 margin insufficiency (or margin call). On the 62 contract trade, the margin requirement was $74,400: margin shortage $61,400. On the 90 contract position, the requirement was $108,000: margin insufficiency $102,000! Or to put it another way, on this trade Mrs. Clinton's margin call alone would have been twice her and her husband's annual salaries (and net worth). These margin deficiencies were not "thin"; they were grossly extreme.

At the time, Cattle was moving as much as $400—or even $600—a day per contract. Do the math here and ask yourself how realistic it would be for a trader with so little income and net worth to be holding positions this big. On both the 90 and 115 contract trades, Mrs. Clinton's account was risking—and therefore could have easily lost—as much as $50,000 a day, or even more. Therefore, to believe Mrs. Clinton's story is to believe the wife of the Attorney General/Governor-elect of Arkansas repeatedly bet a year or two of her and her husband's combined salaries (and net worth) on the next day or two move in Cattle futures!

Keep in mind that in futures trading the broker is responsible for any losses a customer cannot cover. The blunt fact is Hillary Clinton could not have come close to covering the potential losses on these large position cattle trades. Had the trades actually been legitimate (i.e., had true risk) and gone badly, Hillary Clinton might have had to declare bankruptcy during Bill Clinton's first month or so as governor. The more important point, though, is that when a customer is holding big positions, but only has a small amount of equity in his or her account, the net result is that the broker is taking virtually all the risk while the customer gets to keep any profits. No sane broker does this and no business-minded brokerage house allows one of its brokers to do this (particularly not for clients unable to cover any losses). Unrecoverable losses, or unsecured debits as they are called, are detested by brokers and principals of brokerage houses because they come right out of the broker's or principal's pocket, i.e., his bottom line. However, the evidence in this case indicates there never was any real risk of loss since Mrs. Clinton's broker apparently was willing and able to periodically transfer big-profit trades originally intended for one or more other accounts into her account instead.

Let me put Mrs. Clinton's story of her trading profits in terms anyone can understand. Say a politician (a non runner) claimed to have run a world class time in a past New York marathon. While extremely unlikely, it would be theoretically possible. Then it is revealed the politician supposedly ran the first hundred yards in ten seconds, put in about half a dozen sub-four-minute miles periodically throughout the middle of the race, and then finished up by doing the final two miles at a world-record pace of under eight minutes. Judging this story based on these details, anyone—whether a witness or not—could categorically and accurately state the entire story was completely false.

Therefore, based on the information provided by Ira Brill, the sworn testimony of a broker in the Refco Springdale office, the substantial, detailed evidence contained in the aforementioned *National Review* article, and my thirty years of experience in this business, it is my strong professional opinion that the near $100,000 in profits generated in Hillary Rodham Clinton's Refco trading account were achieved through fraud. What this means to me is that virtually every word Mrs. Clinton has spoken about this affair has been a lie.

In his book *Escape to the Futures*, published in 1996, Mr. Melamed states: "Is there more behind Hillary Rodham Clinton's cattle trades than the records reveal, as some suggest? I could find nothing." Not only do I find this statement difficult to believe, I also find it very puzzling. First, it is simply inconceivable to me that Mr. Melamed (as well as any other Merc official who examined her trading records) did not fairly quickly recognize that the cattle profits generated in this account were a fraud. For me this case is not a close call; this fraud was obvious. And second, Mr. Melamed himself has stated (in an interview with Charles R. Babcock of the Washington Post, 27 May 1994) that: "The new records also raise the possibility that some of her (i.e., Mrs. Clinton's) profits—as much as $40,000—came from **larger trades ordered by someone else and then shifted to her account.**"

This is a stunning admission by Mr. Melamed. The point here is the evidence that Hillary Clinton's cattle profits were produced through trade manipulation is so convincing that, in a moment of spontaneous candor, even her primary Merc defender could not suppress the obvious. Mr. Melamed quickly attempted to modify this incriminating statement by nonsensically claiming, "Even allocated trades would not necessarily have benefited Clinton." (Same interview, *Washington Post*, 27 May 1994.) However, it was too late; the lethal damage to Hillary Clinton's case had been done. Mr. Melamed then quickly got back on message in that interview by repeating what has been his mantra on this affair, "[…] Mrs. Clinton violated no rules […]" Of course, whether or not she broke some arcane procedural rules of the Merc is not, nor has it ever been, the point.

Many members of futures exchanges solicit individuals to entrust them with money to trade on a discretionary basis. Then some of these brokers trade both their own accounts and these discretionary accounts at the same time (both on the floor and off). What few of these clients or the general public know is how easy it is for these members to unethically give losing, or less profitable, trades to certain clients while keeping the better ones for more favored accounts and/or themselves. Full disclosure of the trade manipulation in Hillary Clinton's account would have received broad media coverage and thus would have exposed, to both former and current clients, how easy it is for members of a futures exchange to use the same, or similar, tricks. Naturally, national exposure of this type of trade manipulation would have been (and no doubt still is) a very unattractive prospect to many in the futures industry.

Most of the trading public believe that when an order is placed on a futures exchange it is in some way irreversibly "marked," from start to finish, for the individual placing it. This is not true. In essence, all trades on futures exchanges are done "nominally" in the name of the member firm; then the member firm sub allocates these trades to their individual customer accounts.

Due to the high leverage in futures trading, it is possible for a customer to lose more than he or she has in his or her account. Therefore, the only way to ensure there are always funds available to pay all winners is to make the member firms responsible for their client's losses, and then leave it up to them to collect from the client. The chain of financial responsibility goes from client to client's account executive to branch office to brokerage house to clearing firm to the exchange's clearing corporation. Eventually someone must come up with the cash to pay the winners. A high-leverage, zero-sum game has to be structured in this manner. So, from the exchange's viewpoint, financially it is the brokerage firm making the trades and holding the positions, not the individual client. This is why trades are done in member firms' names. While the nature of futures trading requires this, it also makes it extremely easy for members of futures exchanges to cheat their discretionary clients. The only way to ensure that cheating by members of these exchanges is rare, rather than commonplace, is to depend on the honesty and personal integrity of the exchange's individual members and senior officials.

After all this you might be wondering if the futures exchanges are honest enough for your business. In spite of the above, I believe the answer is an unequivocal yes—as long as you do not open a discretionary account with a member of a futures exchange. Any trade you or I put on as retail customers of a brokerage house will be treated legitimately from start to finish. It is extremely difficult to manipulate trades on true customer directed orders. No brokerage firm or floor broker messes with account numbers on customer-directed orders. First, it is too difficult. Second, there is just no point in doing so—potential gain is small, risk very large. Serious corruption will only occur with discretionary accounts, or accounts treated as if they are discretionary accounts (such as Mrs. Clinton's unquestionably was). I believe many members of futures exchanges treat their discretionary customers honestly; however, it is important to be fully aware of how easy it is to manipulate the results. This means that anyone opening a discretionary account with a member of a futures exchange should take great care to ensure this individual is honest.

As far as order execution, while on rare occasions a customer might be "nicked" a little by a possibly "intentional" bad fill, I believe these instances are few and far between. Filling brokers are usually way too busy to even think about cheating. Most filling brokers do an amazingly good job, considering the volume and speed of today's markets. The bottom line: For individual retail customers who make their own trading decisions, the game is honest. Your orders remain your orders from start to finish. With only the rarest of exceptions, customer orders are executed honestly and on a best-effort basis.

Throughout all the controversy and commentary about her commodity trading profits, Hillary Clinton has been uncharacteristically fairly quiet; however, the story she has told, as well as the multiple changes in this story, speaks loudly and revealingly. According to the *National Review* article, first she said she did her own research and placed all the trades herself. Then she said Tyson Foods attorney James Blair advised her, but she made the decisions *about contract size* and placed the orders herself. Finally, at her news conference she said, "Jim would call me on a regular basis and I would make a decision whether or not I would trade, and then the trade would be placed. Often he placed it for me" (Claudia Rosset, *The Wall Street Journal*, 26 October 2000). Mrs. Clinton made one more extremely revealing comment at that news conference. When asked about what she would have done had some of her big trades lost large amounts, she responded, "I didn't think it was *that big a risk* [...]" (*Washington Post*, 23 April 1994).

Officials at the White House presenting themselves as speaking for Hillary Clinton also made some intriguing and conflicting comments, such as: "[...] the White House portrayal of Mrs. Clinton as an exceptionally canny and attentive commodities trader [...]" (*LA Times*, 5 April 1994). Then a few days later the White House story had become "[...] she was not a passionate trader who kept up with every move of the market" (*Washington Post*, 10 April 1994). And then there was this interesting statement from the White House about the actual trade executions: "[...] she made her own decisions, often after reading *The Wall Street Journal*, and personally ordered her trades. She was trading with Mr. Bone, she talked to Mr. Bone" (*Washington Post*, 31 March 1994). However, Robert "Red" Bone, the manager of the Refco office and her broker, one day earlier had been quoted as saying, "I can't recall ever dealing with the Clintons" (*New York Times*, 30 March 1994). Additionally, while Mrs. Clinton and those professing to speak for her have stated she had a non-discretionary account, Mr. Blair (the Tyson attorney who advised her) has said that "[...] Bone sometimes made trades on behalf of his clients even if they had not authorized them" (*LA Times*, 5 April 1994).

History has shown that truth is the bedrock of every good society. Nothing is more revealing of a society than its baseline level of honesty. Good societies have always had a high baseline level of honesty, bad societies a low one. Therefore, everyone operating at the highest levels of our society has a profound responsibility to maintain a high, baseline level of personal honesty. I strongly believe those involved in this case failed to do so.

All lies are not the same. They range in seriousness from inconsequential to violations of the law (i.e., perjury). However, at the apex of dishonesty there is the most serious lie of all, and that is the personal "word of honor" lie.

At any one time the United States of America awards only one individual, and his immediate family, the privilege, honor, and responsibility of residing in the people's house, the White House. We are not entitled to have a president (and family) we like, nor are we entitled to have one whose beliefs and actions we agree with; however, we are absolutely entitled to a certain minimum level of personal honesty from our president (and his spouse).

When press reports of possible financial corruption by Hillary Clinton surfaced (i.e., her almost $100,000 in commodity profits), she was under no requirement to call a nationally televised press conference to respond, yet she did. However, once having done so she had an obligation to the American people to be honest in her statements and answers (both actual and implied). While she was not under oath during that press conference, she was speaking under a much higher law: the personal "word of honor" of an occupant of the White House. Therefore, she had an absolute moral obligation to ensure that what she said and implied during that press conference was honest and true. Unfortunately, for both Mrs. Clinton and America, she failed to meet this obligation.

The evidence is overwhelmingly persuasive that Hillary Rodham Clinton called that infamous press conference for the sole and explicit purpose of intentionally deceiving the American people. There is absolutely no doubt that she looked the American people in the eye and repeatedly and blatantly lied about her actions in this affair. In so doing she not only disgraced herself but also diminished the office of the Presidency, as well as caused harm to the very soul of America.

I believe such an extreme level of personal dishonesty is a political "capital" offense and should automatically disqualify the perpetrator from any future political office. If Hillary Clinton had gone into private life after leaving the White House, I would not have included any of this in this book; however, since Mrs. Clinton has subsequently pursued a political career and reportedly may one day seek the presidency itself, I feel it is important that somewhere, someplace, there be a true and accurate, permanent report of her dishonesty in this affair. Since I am somewhat uniquely positioned to expose this fraud, I feel it my duty to do so. (No member of a futures exchange, and especially not the Chicago Mercantile Exchange, could write what I have written here, i.e., the truth. If they did, they would find themselves "ostracized.")

As for us individual traders, while I can neither prove it nor even argue it well, I have no doubt that in the end it is better to fail honestly than succeed dishonestly (although it definitely does not feel like it at the time). Of course, better yet is honest success, an outcome which cheating precludes. Therefore, we should consider ourselves fortunate Hillary Clinton's foolproof "method" for producing trading profits is not available to us, and be thankful honest success is. The most likely path to this honest success is to follow the natural laws of trading and comply with reliable trading rules.

When I rented out my house in the hills above La Jolla and headed to our family's cabin in the north woods of Minnesota, I did so in a desperate attempt to regain a lost ability to read and trade the futures markets well. I sought to clear my mind and take a fresh look at what does and does not work in trading. I needed to find some fundamental truths and reliable rules; I needed a solid foundation to build upon. I believe I did this and I have done my best to convey all of this to you.

What I came up with that very cold, but surprisingly wonderful, winter of isolation became *Intelligent Futures Trading*. After it was published I started putting out a daily market letter applying the principles laid out in that book (info available at www.chickgoslin.com). What I subsequently discovered and developed while applying these truths and rules in my daily market letter has now become this book, *Trading Day by Day*. I plan on continuing to write the daily letter for at least a "while" after publishing this second book. I believe the best way to show the effectiveness and worth of any approach and method is to do so on a day-by-day, real-time basis. I am confident the approach and method laid out in these two books can withstand any real-time test.

# NOW, ONE MORE TIME

WHAT WE ARE TRYING TO DO HERE IS MAKE MONEY BETTING ON THE FUTURE. The problem is, the future is unknown. Fortunately, the past reveals that continuation is more likely than change. However, this continuation is not a straight line; it is irregular. Therefore, the intelligent approach is to trade only in the direction of the primary price energy flow, using secondary price energy ebbs and flows to time these trades.

There is no "one" correct way to trade successfully. What I have done here is point out some pricing and trading truths, some natural laws. I have shown you a reasonably reliable method for timing trades as well as sizing positions on those trades. I have given you some pricing and trading "rules" that work well. Now it is up to you to take what fits you, discard what does not, add in anything of value you have found elsewhere, and then structure the best approach and method for you.

Following the approach, method, and trading rules laid out in this book will instantly make you competitive in this high risk/high potential game. However, it will not guarantee your success. In the end you need to match approach and method to your personality and trading equity. You need to keep your emotions under control and consistently and persistently act intelligently. In the end you need to make trading work for you; no one else can do this for you. I have given you some very good tools to help you do this, but only you can use them correctly and well.

This is a tough game, always respect it. Take it slowly. Play the probabilities. Go with the price energy flows, not against them. Take some profits when they are good; take losses before they become too big.

Finally, I wish you a little bit of luck. A little luck from time to time always helps.